The Doomed Horse Soldiers of Bataan

The Doomed Horse Soldiers of Bataan

The Incredible Stand of the 26th Cavalry

Raymond G. Woolfe Jr.

ROWMAN & LITTLEFIELD
Lanham • Boulder • New York • London

Published by Rowman & Littlefield
A wholly owned subsidiary of The Rowman & Littlefield Publishing Group, Inc.
4501 Forbes Boulevard, Suite 200, Lanham, Maryland 20706
www.rowman.com

Unit A, Whitacre Mews, 26–34 Stannary Street, London SE11 4AB

Distributed by NATIONAL BOOK NETWORK

British Library Cataloguing in Publication Information Available

Library of Congress Cataloging-in-Publication Data
Names: Woolfe, Raymond G., Jr., author.
Title: The doomed horse soldiers of Bataan : the incredible stand of the 26th Cavalry / by Raymond G. Woolfe Jr.
Description: Lanham : Rowman & Littlefield, 2016. | Includes bibliographical references.
Identifiers: LCCN 2015039187| ISBN 9781442245341 (cloth : alk. paper) | ISBN 9781442245358 (electronic)
Subjects: LCSH: United States. Army. Cavalry Regiment, 26th. | World War, 1939–1945—Campaigns—Philippines—Luzon. | World War, 1939–1945—Cavalry operations.
Classification: LCC D769.325 26th W66 2016 | DDC 940.54/25991—dc23 LC record available at http://lccn.loc.gov/2015039187

∞ ™The paper used in this publication meets the minimum requirements of American National Standard for Information Sciences—Permanence of Paper for Printed Library Materials, ANSI/NISO Z39.48-1992.
Printed in the United States of America

Contents

Introduction

Colonel Edwin Price Ramsey
Former U.S. Army Mounted Cavalry—26th Regiment
(Philippine Scouts)

I am pleased to introduce Raymond G. Woolfe's fine and only all-inclusive, accurate account of the valiant but ill-fated 26th Cavalry (Philippine Scouts). This was the last and final horse-mounted cavalry regiment in the United States Army to ever go into combat in an intact, unified fighting force. Mr. Woolfe is a powerful writer with an exceptional feel for descriptive narrative. His accounts of the 26th Cavalry's opening battled were so real and chilling in detail of the telling that they gave me nightmares of recall.

The vivid accounts of the regiment's violent delaying actions, such as Lingayen Gulf, Damortis, Rosario, The Bued, Binalonan, Culis and the long ordeal on Bataan literally left me in shock and made me feel like crying while reading and remembering the horrors of it all. As for his account of the U.S. Cavalry's last horse-mounted charge at Moron on Bataan, Mr. Woolfe is on the money. I suppose I ought to know; I led it. Mr. Woolfe accompanied me, physically walking the Moron battleground on foot, as well as a great number of the other fighting places of the 26th. His research was as physical and meticulous as he could make it and this book reflects that dedication to detail.

Throughout the book Mr. Woolfe drew strongly on his knowledge and love of horses from a life of professional steeple chase riding and love of playing polo for his descriptions of life in the regiment. His compassion for the courage, loyalty, and terrible fate of the beloved 26th Cavalry horses (and mules, too) shines through his narrative.

Today's mechanized cavalrymen may have been deprived of horses, but they are strongly imbued with the traditions and hard-charging spirit of the soldiers in boots and spurs who went before them. I know that I shall carry that spirit always until I am given my place at The Old Canteen at Fiddlers' Green.

This is a book well written of men well remembered.

—Edwin Price Ramsey

Fiddlers' Green
(The Cavalrymen's Poem)

Halfway down the trail to Hell
In a shady meadow green
Are the souls of all dead troopers camped
Near a good old-time canteen,
And this eternal resting place
Is known as Fiddlers' Green

Marching past, straight through to Hell,
The Infantry are seen,
Accompanied by the Engineers,
Artillery and Marine,
For none but the shades of Cavalrymen
Dismount at Fiddlers' Green.

Though some go curving down the trail
To seek a warmer scene,
No trooper ever gets to Hell
Ere he's emptied his canteen.
And so rides back to drink again
With friends at Fiddlers' Green.

And so when man and horse go down
Beneath a saber keen,
Or in a roaring charge of fierce mêlée
You stop a bullet clean,
And the hostiles come to get your scalp,
Just empty your canteen,
And put your pistol to your head
And go to Fiddlers' Green.

1

Twilight of Empire's Paradise to the Dawn of Hell

SUNDAY, 7 DECEMBER 1941, MANILA TIME

FORT STOTSENBURG, NORTHERN LUZON, some fifty miles north of Manila and adjacent to Clark Field Air Force Base

It was the eve before Hell in Lotus Land.

On that clear, pleasant afternoon, Maj. Gen. Jonathan M. Wainwright, riding his favorite field mount, Little Boy, was refereeing a polo game being played by officers of the prized regiment of his Northern Luzon command, the 26th Cavalry Philippine Scouts. In the Fort Stotsenburg team's first season game versus the Manila Polo Club, cavalry dash failed to win the day over the older, experienced club players, but spirits were not dampened. The 26th, with which Wainwright had served, was the last fully operational horse-mounted combat unit in the regular U.S. Army. The regiment, composed of American officers and Filipino ranks and noncommissioned officers, was under the direct command of a shortish, bulldog-like colonel from Brooklyn named Clinton Pierce, a first-rate professional soldier.

Born in June 1894, Clint Pierce was a consummate "horse soldier." He believed in horse cavalry as much as Phil Sheridan or George Patton had, even though his name is not that well known. A sad note of history is that a man so devoted to the horse cavalry would also soon be forced to sound taps for it. As a boy he grew to only five feet six, but he was built like a fighter and, though always outgoing, he could often be pugnacious. His demeanor served him well in his long years of soldiering. First attending Brooklyn's Polytechnic Institute, he went on to the University of Illinois in

1

1914 as an engineering major. A member of the Illinois National Guard's 1st Artillery, he went into full service as a corporal, serving in the Mexican border dispute and punitive expedition under "Black Jack" Pershing against Pancho Villa in 1916. In March 1917 he received a temporary commission as a second lieutenant and was assigned to the 12th Cavalry in Columbus, New Mexico. Never returning to engineering school, Pierce remained as a career cavalryman, moving from one regiment to another. In the course of his service, he was for a time an able instructor in the Fort Riley, Kansas, cavalry school. A man of intense nervous energy, Pierce was a popular officer at both Fort Riley and Fort Bliss, where he proved outstanding in a wide range of post activities, including polo, horse shows, steeplechase racing, and even amateur dramatics. In February 1940, accompanied by his wife, Margaret, daughter, Jean, and mother, Mrs. H. C. Pierce, the now Lieutenant Colonel Pierce was transferred to the Philippines and assigned to the 26th Cavalry PS at Stotsenburg. In October 1941 he was made full colonel and took over command of the regiment.

Polo was considered as much a training and toughening up activity as it was recreation for the horse soldiers, the game's origins going back some 250 years to conditioning programs of Afghani Pathan light cavalry preparing for their various wars and celebrating victories by using the vanquished's heads for playing balls. Picked up on the hard way by the English, polo became a traditional activity to toughen and sharpen the edge of fighting spirit among officers of their armies around the world. Old hands of the American horse cavalry soon followed suit, subscribing to polo's benefits with open enthusiasm, which included junior officers routinely going into deep hock for tailored breeches and a coveted pair of status-marking boots from Peal & Co. bootmakers in London.

Although a good crowd had come up from Manila for the game, there was a touch of loneliness about this day's event being played on the broad expanse of the parade ground bordered by rows of acacia-shaded officers' houses on the north side and stables, workshops, and barracks on the opposite side. While a good crowd of Filipino enlisted troopers cheered and gambled wildly on the sidelines, missing were the customary gathering of gaily dressed wives and ladies and elegantly dressed spectators visiting with high-goal guest teams, although the girls who had come up from Manila put real life into the annual officers' postgame party, which lasted well into the morning. For months, clouds of war between the United States and Japan had been gathering ominously. As a heartbreaking precaution, the U.S. personnel had been shipping home military wives and dependents from the outlying Pacific Islands. In the various regiments and other army, air force, and naval units, sentimental farewells and sadness were quickly countered by rigorous increases in training. The halcyon pleasures of coveted duty in the Philippines were now fast taking a back seat to apprehension and an accent on military proficiency. The 26th was not found lacking.

At this point the 26th was split, with several troops serving on detached duty. B Troop of the 1st Squadron was assigned to patrol duty northeast of Cabanatuan in the Baler Bay area, difficult terrain on the Pacific side of Luzon. F Troop, under command of Maj. Thomas J. H. Trapnell, had been on station at Nichols Field on the outskirts of Manila. F Troop had, in a sense, served as Gen. Douglas MacArthur's "palace guard," performing all manner of ceremonial duties while being a showpiece of the "Fil-American" units at various formal celebrations, honor guards, parades, and the like. One of their most noted crowd pleasers with the public and special guests was their impressive mounted acrobatics team (referred to as "monkey drill" by the troopers), who performed all manner of gravity-defying feats such as "Roman riding" (the rider controlling up to four horses at a gallop and riding over jumps while standing bareback on his mounts) and "pyramids" (up to ten troopers stacking themselves on each other while the "base" stood bareback on the galloping horses). It was one thing that made these troopers elite among their own people.

Before the departure of dependents, by far the most elegant activity for all were the polo games at the softly beautiful Manila Polo Club, where officers of the 26th were often matched in games with visiting high-goal teams from the states. Even the aloof General MacArthur loved and had played the game. On such occasions, the sharp *thwack* of a mallet head on a soft, pliable willow wood ball was the loudest sound to be heard in the green expanse surrounded and perfumed by a lush explosion of manicured tropical vegetation—bougainvillea, orchids, broad hibiscus, shady acacia, whispering firs, tall, swaying palms, and ancient, twisted amlang trees—all complementing the pristine, mirror-shined, dark native woodwork of the main clubhouse.

On one such Sunday, Tom "Trap" Trapnell squeezed his polished-booted legs hard against his pony's sides, racing boot to boot, spurs and buckles clicking, with the opposing player beside him, eyes riveted on the small white ball now flying in the direction of the goal posts at one end of the field. Both men leaned hard toward one another, bringing the racing ponies' bodies into an ongoing collision, pushing hard, each trying to ride his opponent off the line of the ball to maneuver for fair shooting position.

Trapnell, lean and roughhewn, with a West Point football and boxing veteran's strength, gained position and leaned into a full swinging forehand, whipping the flexible cane mallet shaft with its hardwood striking head at the still-bouncing target. The satisfying jolt of a cleanly hit ball traced up his arm, and his eyes coursed over his pony's straining neck, watching with an inner thrill as the white ball arched in dead-eye trajectory between the white- and red-halved uprights.

"Hot damn!" he cried with glee as he pumped his mallet arm up and down and checked his mount out of the dead run.

"Nice play, Trap," said his civilian opponent Peter Perkins, touching the brim of his white pith helmet in brief salute. Peter was an eight-goal, top American amateur polo player. "That's one helluva nice pony you've got there."

"Thanks, Peter," answered Trap as they turned to walk their horses back to center field where the rest of the players were lining up for the referee to throw the ball back in play. "He just got shipped in a couple of weeks ago from the remount in Front Royal, Virginia. He acclimated to the humidity here and takes to everything like an old hand. I really like him. He's made to be regular army, the kind of horse you can count on to take care of you in a pinch. He'll do."

Seated at shaded tables along the sidelines, men in crisp, dress-white tropical uniforms and linen suits sat with ladies and young women resplendent in loose, filmy afternoon dresses and ribboned, wide-brimmed sun hats in defense from the ordinarily enervating climate of the Philippines. Glasses with rum punches and lime fizzes were raised in salute as enthusiastic applause floated out across the field to the players of choice. It was the kind of afternoon that made all glad to be alive and many of the men even gladder to be professional cavalrymen with a choice duty station in the Philippine Islands. The sweet, pungent smells of fresh-mown grass, saddle leather, sweating horses, and tropical flora were a heady mixture to those who were enjoying the best that peacetime duty in the South Pacific could offer.

For Trap and his fellow officers of the 26th Cavalry, this was the stuff of dreams for every young man who ever yearned for life in the horse cavalry, complete with adventure, pomp and ceremony, rugged military dash, and manly relaxations. Who could not envy to some degree the lot of these horse soldiers, in their prime and among the last of their elite breed in a military being forced by the demands of modern warfare to grudgingly change with the times? This was the twilight that came between a bygone era of fluttering flags, bugles, and gleaming sabers and replacement by colder, efficient, metallic, machine-dealt death.

But for this day at least, such things were not on the minds of those present for this Sunday's polo match. Players and spectators alike looked forward to postgame cocktails, a refreshing tub, and fresh change into evening dress. That particular evening, they would go on to watch a few innings of the regimental enlisted men's baseball game against Nichols Field airmen, before returning to the cool, elegant country club house for a splendid dinner dance, where the officers and their ladies would join members of the American business and diplomatic community and selected friends from the Philippine elite. The rigors of off-duty social schedules often put demands on young officers to maintain a level of soldierly activities to match the pace. On other days and evenings there were such pleasantries as golf at Fort McKinley or Manila's lovely Wack Wack course, dinner and gambling at the fashionable Jai Lai Club, and the chance to keep company with lovely women, many being the pretty army nurses from Sternberg General Hospital.

It was a gentle, splendid time, a splendid life, typical of both the high point and the closing days of America's only and last fling at empire inherited from Theodore Roosevelt's "bully" little war against the Spanish.

As the 7 December afternoon game at Fort Stotsenburg was playing out its final chukker, Staff Sgt. Ramon Ramirez was making his cursory Sunday afternoon inspection tour through the regimental stables, seeing to it that the on-duty privates and corporals had completed all the basic daily necessities. In the quiet of late afternoon the only sounds were horses munching on grain or hay, the stomp of a hoof here, a snort there, the occasional buzzing of a fly intruding the air space of the spotless stables. Here, too, was the sweetly pungent smell of horse cavalry in the tropics. The clean smell of fresh hay and soft, saddle-soaped leather mixed with the faint smell of ammonia and the horses themselves, still again offset by the perfume of the lush tropic vegetation that ringed the area. Peace and orderliness reigned undisturbed with ample time to let one's mind dwell in anticipation of that evening's regimental bowling championship with winners' kegs of good San Miguel beer.

Ramirez crossed the stable area to the edge of the parade ground where 1st Lt. John Zachary Wheeler, that evening's duty officer, waited for his sergeants to report. Johnny Wheeler was a mild-mannered, gentlemanly young officer from St. Paul, Minnesota, where he had grown up with a passion for the outdoors. He admired the gentle-natured but tough little Filipinos put under his command to make into fighters. He also stood in awe of the natural beauty of their homeland. An avid reader and serious student since early boyhood, his favorite reading was of King Arthur. In the coming months, no man would live truer to the tenets of the Round Table than this soft-spoken cavalryman.

Ramirez approached Wheeler and came to an abrupt and flawless position of attention, saluting sharply. His classic, flat-brimmed campaign hat, adorned with an insignia that read "Our Strength Is in Loyalty," was tipped smartly and rakishly forward until it almost touched the bridge of his nose, forcing his head and neck into a stiff, bulldog-like posture in order to see out from under the brim, the chin strap tightly in place. On his collars, his brass unit insignia pins gleamed. The spotless, starched khaki of his uniform was accentuated with razor-sharp military creases in their prescribed positions and was adorned with a webbed canvas duty belt from which hung a mirror-polished leather pistol holster and ammunition pouch. His legs were encased in laced leather leggings, which topped ankle-high laced, duty riding shoes, all polished to a state suitable for use by any discriminating lady as a makeup mirror. There was not merely military pride and regulation reflected in this man's uniform and demeanor but social station as well.

Typical of the transformation of ordinary, country Filipinos that took place in the scouts would be the case of Pfc. Juan Beduna, a corporal at the outset of war. He had joined the 26th Cavalry when it was organized in the early twenties. He'd been a mule-skinner, farrier, orderly, and general all-around trooper. He'd had little education to speak of, attending grade 1 in a little nipa school in his home barrio. Once in the scouts, he managed to acquire a limited command of what was commonly known amongst them as "Quartermaster English," or army lingo. He always surprised himself by answering, "Yes, sir/right away, sir/and very well, sir," even when he didn't actually understand what his superiors were saying. Beduna's one weakness was that the words "No, sir" were not in his vocabulary. In spite of his linguistic shortcomings, he was an excellent soldier, swordsman, and rifleman and an expert in both mounted and dismounted pistol firing. He was always selected as the commanding general's orderly whenever he went on post guard because he dressed immaculately in spotless, expertly tailored khaki breeches and blouse, brass buttons, mirror-shined riding boots, and gleaming spurs.

One afternoon, as his immediate commander was practicing with some remounts for polo, Beduna was called to the sideboards to bring up a horse. It was a young roan, half-thoroughbred, about sixteen hands tall, ornery and mean. Beduna was having difficulty putting a snaffle and curb-bit into the horse's mouth. It reared and raised its head beyond Beduna's reach. "Hurry up, Beduna," the lieutenant called out. Beduna, in his characteristic fractured lingo, replied "Yes sir, but it is very hard to put the bridle in my mouth, sir!"

The 26th Cavalry Regiment was an elite unit among an elite segment of the U.S. Army in the Philippines, the Philippine Scouts. They were first organized as a native counterinsurgency constabulary in 1901 under Gen. Douglas MacArthur's father, Arthur, during his time as army commanding general. After proving their mettle as a crack fighting force, they were subsequently integrated as regulars in the U.S. Army in 1913, becoming part of what was then known as the Philippine Garrison, a regular U.S. Army establishment commanded by American officers and including a permanent contingent of regular army enlisted ranks. The Philippine constabulary remained as a separate Filipino law enforcement unit.

The vast and coveted Philippine archipelago consists of 7,100 islands and islets, of which only 460 have an area greater than one square mile, and only 11 can boast areas greater than a thousand square miles. In 1898

America became the latest of a series of conquerors and foreign rulers including Chinese, Muslim Malays, Spaniards, the English, and Spaniards again until 1 May 1898, when Commodore George Dewey and the American Navy defeated the Spanish in Manila Bay and title to the islands was granted by the Treaty of Paris in December of that year. The Filipinos had initiated their first important encounter against the heavily, well-armed Spanish at the barrio of Balintawak in 1896 led by a warehouse laborer from Tondo named Andres Bonifacio. (In one instance of particular irony it was learned that the well-entrenched Japanese 5th column in the Philippines maintained one of its most concentrated centers of operations in the large Balintawak Brewery prior to the 8 December 1941 attacks.) The desperate revolt went on to be led by Emilio Aguinaldo, a resourceful Filipino military commander who delivered a see-saw series of defeats and counter-defeats, the last of which involved a brilliantly constructed system of trenches around Manila and Cavite designed by Lt. Gen. Edilberto Evangelista. The trench style of warfare, combined with malaria riddling the Spanish ranks, delivered the telling blow. Heads of the Spanish military and occupation were sent home in disgrace. The Spanish suffered their final debacle eighteen months later at the hands of the American Navy and ground troops, who went ashore to consolidate the American assault. Possession of the Philippines made America truly an Asiatic power with full responsibility for maintaining peace in its sphere of influence. America had fallen into the role of imperialist without premeditated intent. At first the Filipino insurgents hesitantly joined forces with the Yanquis, suspicious of the new force but glad to be rid of the Spanish. Yet an inflammatory air of bad faith in the international agreements led Aguinaldo's chief advisor, Apolinario Mabini, to rethink the situation. A chance encounter between a trigger-happy American sentry and a four-man Filipino patrol on the evening of 4 February 1899 ignited the Philippine-American war, developing into the bloodiest conflict fought in the Filipinos' long struggle for independence, which lasted until 1902. The U.S. High Command, led by Maj. Gen. Elwell S. Otis and division commander Brig. Gen. Arthur MacArthur, had in truth been waiting for such an incident to undertake an offensive that would entail conquest of the entire Philippines. A large number of American commanders were Civil War veterans. Col. Frederick Funston, who led the force that captured Aguinaldo in Northern Luzon, won the Medal of Honor and was promoted to brigadier general. On the Filipino side, the long, costly conflict brought a number of notable national heroes to the fore, including scholar and poet Dr. Jose Rizal, Gen. Antonio Luna, Col. Francisco Paco Roman, Generals Mariano Noriel and Pio del Pilar, and Lt. Col. Antero Reyes, who led his force to inflict a humiliating setback on American general Loyd Wheaton at Luzon in San Pedro Makati. The Filipino insurgents drew principally on Spanish and German armaments and ordnance abandoned by the Spanish, including artillery, Maxim machine guns, and Mauser rifles (the infamous "Spanish Hornet"), from which the Filipinos frequently made the fatal mistake of removing the rear sights, thinking them a hindrance and causing their aim to be almost invariably too high. The ever-present, razor-sharp barongs and bolos were a constant and costly menace to American troops, as was the deadly curved kris, a short sword favored by the fanatic Moros of the southern islands.

On the other hand, the Americans were physically bigger by a foot than the average Filipino, and they were well equipped; they went on to develop a new generation of combat weapons during the insurrection, including Hotchkiss revolving cannons, improved .30- and .45-caliber Springfield rifles, and machine guns. One particular piece, nicknamed "the Moro stopper" because of its impact, was conceived by Gen. Arthur MacArthur himself, the prototype of the Colt M1911A1 .45-caliber semiautomatic pistol. It became the standard sidearm of U.S. military services and remains principally so to this day.

The southernmost islands persisted as the most hostile resistance to the Americans. Moro natives in the Visayas, Mindinao, and other southern provinces—mostly Muslims of ancestry from the Indian subcontinent, Malaya, and Java—frequently worked themselves into a frenzy and ran amok, at times in a combined state of religious fervor and half mad with pain induced either by binding themselves tightly in bamboo or winding an elastic vine around their genitals.

Many an American found himself being overrun by a crazed, bullet-ridden Moro whose momentum simply did not allow the latter to know he was already dead on his feet.[1] The .45 was the American reply.

The Philippine insurrection developed into both a costly and controversial war, which drew increasingly strident criticism from Washington. American troops, besides inordinately high battle casualties, were losing thousands of personnel from malaria, other native diseases, snake bite, and other tropical hazards. Pressure grew to find avenues to peace with the Philippine populace and establish some form of order. When the first civil governor of the Philippines, William H. Taft, adopted a policy of naming prominent Filipinos to civil posts in the organization of his administration, Filipinos showed the first signs of turning their attention away from war and gradually back to focus on a future Republic of the Philippines. Martin Delgado was appointed governor of his province on Luzon, and other prominent Filipinos were named to important posts in the Supreme Court and various important bureaucratic offices such as boards of health, provincial government offices, and public schools, things unheard of under Spanish rule. Slowly but gradually this prudent policy began to smother the flames of insurrection and led an increasing part of the general population to warm toward American protectorate rule. Pockets of resistance remained, most frequently in the Muslim provinces, Samar, and some of the most remote areas of the mountainous extreme north of Luzon. Ambushes by independent guerrilla groups who worked fields by day and stalked Americans by night persisted. Most casualties were inflicted by soldiers being hacked to death by bolos instead of more merciful gunshot wounds. American losses almost doubled in the face of this infinitely more dangerous type of warfare, at which the Filipinos proved expert.

A campaign by Americans was led to press civilians and captured rebels into labor to clean up and restore filthy barrios and improve agriculture. It was a long and bloody process, which entailed countless ambushes and reciprocal, sometimes atrocious violence by the Americans, but gradually the resistance narrowed down to a final stronghold on Samar. In a violent final sortie, marines led by Gen. "Howling Jake" Smith scattered the stubborn holdout forces led by Gen. Vincente Lucban, who was finally captured in February 1902. His counterpart in the Luzon province of Batangas, Gen. Miguel Malvar, surrendered on 16 April, thus putting a de facto end to the war against the United States.

The last vestiges of rebellion still remained with the Moros, led by Sultan Jamalul Kiram II. Maj. Gen. Leonard Wood, who had been named governor of the Muslim provinces, came to Jolo in August 1903. In his determination to solidify American control over the Mindanao Muslims, Wood brought in Capt. John J. "Black Jack" Pershing, a forty-two-year-old West Pointer and veteran of Apache and Sioux Indian campaigns who, as a first lieutenant, led his famed, all-black 10th Cavalry (the "Buffalo Soldiers") up San Juan Hill next to Theodore Roosevelt and his Rough Riders against the Spaniards in Cuba. Pershing, a commonsense and diplomatic officer, studied Muslims' dialects, customs, and religion and treated them, if not as equals, at least certainly as human beings. He spent hours each day receiving delegations and hearing petitions and complaints. He also mingled with them socially. Once, on 4 July 1902, he invited seven hundred of his Moro neighbors for the occasion and encouraged his officers and men to mix and show common humanity toward their guests. Observing Muslim tenets, no liquor or pork was served, but a half dozen calves were roasted in open pits, and vegetables, fruits, and rice cakes were served generously. This benevolent attitude, unfortunately, was interpreted by the Moro leaders as weakness, and attacks against Americans renewed. Pershing wasted no time in taking punitive actions, making use of the newly formed Philippine Scouts extensively, which ultimately ended in a successful campaign to end Moro resistance. Before complete pacification was achieved, Pershing was transferred back to the United States for reasons of ill health. The first recognized hero since Dewey, Pershing was promoted in 1906 to brigadier general by the now President Theodore Roosevelt.

In the course of that tragic and costly conflict, the United States had sent

126,468 troops across the Pacific and had spent over $300 million to conduct the war. In 2,811 recorded clashes with the Filipinos, the Americans lost 4,234 men and 2,818 were wounded. The Filipinos lost 16,000 soldiers in battle while an appalling 200,000 civilians died due to war, famine, or disease. Tens of millions of pesos worth of property was destroyed. The Filipinos had lost more against the Americans than against the hated Spaniards in deaths and property lost, but for two more generations, their struggle for full independence would continue. Notably, leaders of the Philippine Catholic Church exhibited strong desire to free Filipinos from the control of foreign Catholic friars in their country. From this developed the Philippine Independent Church. At first, the church was in full sympathy with the insurrection because Americans, being largely of Protestant faith, represented "heretics" to be resisted. Bishop Gregario Aglipay, a priest from Batac, Ilocos Norte, was foremost in supporting the resistance against the Americans. His revolt included continuation of the presence of Jesuit friars in his country, but, in reality, it was more a desire to be free from dictatorship by foreigners. His struggle with the Philippine courts would continue for years.

The Moros, especially in Sulu, still stubbornly refused to capitulate, fighting not only as enemies but as religious fanatics. In October 1905, the Philippine Scouts, now integrated into the regular American army's table of organization, first acquitted themselves in one of the bloodiest battles ever fought against the Moros. A company of American infantrymen were aided by the scouts, a special unit composed of American officers and Filipino soldiers, created in 1899 when a Filipino segment of society in Luzon known as Macabebes formed its nucleus. In a surprise attack on the holdout Datu Ali at his hideout on the Malala River near Simpetan in the present-day district of Kidapawan, they gained complete victory, killing Ali and several hundred of his followers. Although the clashes in the southern provinces dragged on for some time, the back of the resistance was finally broken in 1906 in a battle around the volcanic mountain Tumatangis, the tallest peak on Sulu located just southwest of the town of Jolo. In a battle remembered as the "Battle of the Clouds," Americans combined with scouts and constabulary overwhelmed the hard-core rebels, killing some six hundred of them. American casualties totaled twenty-one killed and seventy-three wounded. A number of these included Philippine Scouts.

General Pershing returned to the Philippines in 1909, and, principally employing columns of Philippine Scouts, virtually annihilated Moro resistance at the battle of Bud Bagsak, the last large-scale action fought by Americans in Mindinao and Sulu until their final withdrawal from the Philippines years later. Pershing exposed himself constantly with his front-line troops and was recommended by his subordinate officers for the Congressional Medal of Honor. He refused, however, saying, "I went to that part of the line because my presence there was necessary."

As for the Philippine Scouts, they continued to play a vital part in the reconstruction of life in the Philippines. Integrated into the U.S. regular army in 1913, not only were they now an important constabulary arm, but their units became highly visible through ceremonial duties and other public exposures, contributing greatly to Filipino pride in the reputation of the scouts, their own people, as a crack segment of the American forces in the Philippines. By 1940, Philippine Scout units were up to a strength of some six thousand effectives. The rifle marksmanship of these troops was exceptional, and with understandable good reason. Considerable extra time was spent by these men on the army's rifle ranges, fine tuning their marksmanship to an almost astounding degree. Their motive was clear cut. Higher degrees of marksmanship merited extra pay, a significant factor considering that Filipino troops serving in the U.S. Army and performing equal duties and more than American regulars were paid in pesos rather than dollars, about a third less compensation than enjoyed by their American peers. The Filipino reaction to such inequity was sheer, characteristic determination. When the Americans' new Garand M-1 semiautomatic rifles were first introduced for use in the Philippines, scout units were the first troops to be issued the new weapons. It would later prove a wise and prudent move far beyond the imagination of U.S. Army decision makers and a curse to Japanese invaders in 1941 when jolted by a new level of firepower from ground troops.

In the years following the Philippine insurrection, American influence and material efforts brought Filipino living, educational, and legislative standards to levels unheard of before by the citizens of that vast archipelago. Beginning with Pres. William McKinley's successor, Theodore Roosevelt, benevolent social changes were put in place. Contrary to the energetic, often bombastic Roosevelt's much publicized "speak quietly but carry a big stick" philosophy, Filipinos gradually came to find Americans a positive force in long-neglected social reform. There is no denying that a pervading air of superiority and bigotry amongst Americans toward "their little brown brothers" continued to exist, but on the whole, American and Filipino relations evolved into one of general friendship. In 1913 the Philippines were granted free-trade status with the United States, and three years later, by the Jones Act, they were granted a limited autonomy. A steady succession of American politicians encouraged a friendly relationship between the two countries, and a steadily increasing sentiment for Philippine independence flourished in the U.S. Congress. In January 1933, a bill for Philippine independence passed Congress over Pres. Herbert Hoover's veto but was vetoed in turn by the Philippine legislature. On 24 March 1934, the bill, with some changes, was passed again as the Tydings-McDuffie Act and this time approved by the Philippine legislature. The act did leave open for question the status of naval reservations, but it authorized the president to negotiate with the Philippine government for American bases in the islands. The closing date for such negotiations was set at two years following recognition of independence. A year after passage of the act, the Filipinos adopted a liberal constitution based on America's model and established an interim government termed a commonwealth.

Elections were held, and Manuel Quezon was chosen as president. Before the end of 1935, the Philippine National Assembly met to draft plans for defense of their country. On 23 March 1935 the Constitution of the Philippine Commonwealth was signed by Presidents Franklin D. Roosevelt and Manuel Quezon and witnessed by key members of both governments. The die was finally cast for true Philippine independence. The Philippines would remain a U.S. commonwealth with full independence scheduled to be granted in 1946.

In the years between 1935 and the Pacific outbreak of World War II in December 1941, American and Filipino cooperation flourished, putting in place much-needed public works and utilities, health services, and an effective public school system. The University of the Philippines was founded through both the efforts of Philippine hierarchy and generous grants from government and private business sources in America. The university was to form the foundation for developing a progressive Philippine intelligentsia, including medical professionals, future government and municipal leaders, and the fine arts. Americans in substantial numbers took up residence in the Philippines, engaging in a wide range of commerce. Extensive mining, timber, sugar production, construction, and salvage operations flourished in the rich, natural endowments of the islands. However, the Philippines continued to lag badly in the areas of good roads, rail transportation, civil power and communications systems, and adequate commercial sea transport facilities. Yet the Philippines steadily developed into one of the richest producers of sugar and rice in Asia, and its far-ranging mountain areas are a coveted source of gold, silver, and more important base metals such as iron, chrome, manganese, copper, and lead. Over time, Cavite on Manila Bay became one of the most important merchant shipping and military naval harbors in the Pacific. A second American naval base at Subic Bay was also intended to harbor significant U.S. naval strength. Clark and Nichols air bases were the two largest air force facilities, with smaller fields scattered throughout Luzon, on Bataan Peninsula, and the island fortress of Corregidor guarding the entrance to Manila Bay.

There did exist, in truth, a subtle kink in the interrelationship between Americans, both civilian and military, and Filipinos. American servicemen, despite surface friendliness and camaraderie, tended to harbor an ingrained bigotry toward Filipinos, thinking of them as in some way innately inferior to Caucasians. While Americans readily associated and socialized with Manila's social elite and openly courted gorgeously beautiful senoritas, there existed an underlying line of distinction. Even the liberal Army-Navy Club, an elite social center for Americans on Manila's prestigious Dewey Boulevard, prevented Filipinos from the membership roster. Such social barriers were destined to come down years later in the face of war clouds. Old-time American residents, referred to as "sunshiners" and "sunshine Americans," went to great lengths to sponsor parties that, on the surface, crumbled such social barriers. Officers and even the U.S. High Commissioner sanctioned opportunities for Americans to meet and socialize with beautiful Filipina "*quaparitas.*" On the other hand, American enlisted men tended, in large part, to consider the Filipinos as a lesser race to be used and enjoyed in a servile manner in general. The one sector of the U.S. Army that engendered genuine respect and comradeship bordering on brotherhood between Americans and Filipinos was in the ranks of the Philippine Scouts.

Ironically, energetic entrepreneurs, artisans, and laborers from another country, Japan, came to the Philippines in substantial numbers. They proved resourceful and instrumental in the country's high-grade hemp production, fishing, agriculture, and other businesses. At the time, there was an air of cordial relations between the Asiatic Filipinos and Japanese residents in their country. By 1941 there were almost thirty thousand Japanese nationals in the islands, more than two-thirds concentrated around Davao, chief port of Mindanao. What went unnoticed, however, was that many Japanese specially picked for the purpose had positioned themselves throughout the islands to study the terrain, looking for strategic obstacles and the potential for possible conquest of the Philippines and its vast natural resources, sorely needed by Japan.

In 1941 the populace of the Philippines, mostly of Malayan ancestry, numbered some 17 million. The rest included some 117,000 Chinese, the Japanese contingent, and almost 9,000 American civilians. Over sixty-five dialects were spoken in the islands. When the Americans first took over, very few inhabitants spoke Spanish. After some forty years, about 27 percent were speaking English and 3 percent spoke Spanish. In 1937, Tagalog, the language of the most wealthy and influential residents of central Luzon, was chosen as the basis for a national language, although almost twice as many people spoke the Visayan dialect.

Militarily, the Philippine Islands represent a planner's worst dreams. For the most part, the far-flung archipelago is largely mountainous with elevations as high as ten thousand feet. Narrow coastal plains are scattered throughout the islands, which are crisscrossed with many short, swift-running streams, some very deep. Large plain areas and navigable rivers are few. While all the islands have sand beaches, open lowlands inland suitable for military maneuver are rare. Luzon, with one-tenth of its area comprising a large plain and another five thousand square miles forming a vast river valley, is virtually the only Philippine island whose terrain and infrastructure could permit large-scale military operations.

"EL SUPREMO": DOUGLAS MACARTHUR BEGINS HIS REIGN IN THE PHILIPPINES

Prior to establishment of the commonwealth government in 1935, there had been no effort to prepare any form of Philippine defense force. Up until that time, the United States had taken on the full load of military security for the islands and maintained a garrison for that purpose that numbered only ten thousand men, half of whom were Philippine Scouts. The national police force consisted of the quasi-military Philippine Constabulary organized in 1901. Except for the latter force, the Filipinos had no military tradition on which to found a national defense force. Since 1913, the Philippine garrison was called the Philippine Department and was commanded by a regular American general officer. Organizing a proper defense force for the islands was a primary priority for President-elect Quezon, but there was no likely Filipino with the proven military and executive ability to lead such an organization. Quezon sought help from the United States, and in the summer of 1935, his pleas were answered by an old friend and military veteran of Philippine campaigns, Gen. Douglas MacArthur, at that time chief of staff of the U.S. Army. Quezon requested that MacArthur be freed to become chief military advisor to his new government in the organization of a Philippine national army. Pres. Franklin D. Roosevelt readily consented, and arrangements for MacArthur's new posting were made posthaste. The general's title in his new role was designated Military Advisor to the Commonwealth Government. He was given broad authority for his mission to "aid in the establishment and development of a system of Philippine National Defense." MacArthur was authorized almost unlimited discretion in his decisions for implementing his task, and, although no official connection existed between the Philippine Department and the regular U.S. Army command in the country, Washington informed the U.S. commander in the Philippines, Maj. Gen. Lucius R. Holbrook, that "assistance to General MacArthur would be the most important peacetime mission of your command."

In a sense, for Douglas MacArthur, the assignment was a grand homecoming of sorts. His father, Gen. Arthur MacArthur, who had served so prominently militarily and as general-governor in the development of the Philippines at the turn of the century, had made the name MacArthur a prominent one in that country. Douglas, who had been in the islands both as a boy and as a serving young officer, knew the islands well and had many intimate friends there, including two young lawyers who were to be future Philippine presidents, Manuel Quezon and Sergio Osmena. At West Point, where he had served with distinction, both scholastically and athletically, MacArthur had chosen the Engineer Corps, considered elite. His first assignment as a fresh new lieutenant was to the Philippines, where his routine required him to tour Luzon extensively. Ironically, one of his routine tasks was to help survey the Bataan Peninsula. It was there that the young officer was first blooded—ambushed by two guerrillas, MacArthur, a pistol expert, dropped them both. After almost a year recovering from malaria in San Francisco, in 1905 MacArthur was given a choice assignment, aide to his father as an official observer of the Russo-Japanese War. There he was impressed by the grim, iron determination of Japanese officers and of the bold, unquestioning courage of the common Japanese soldier. At that point, after extensive Japanese conquests, MacArthur made prescient note that "it was evident that they would eventually strike out for control of the Pacific and domination of the Far East." This thinking was in strange contrast to his dangerous miscalculation and underestimation in 1940–1941 of Japanese capabilities and resolve to achieve their ends by any means they judged expedient.

In the years after service in Japan with his father, MacArthur steadily climbed the often difficult rise that a military career involves, marked by outstanding high points. In his family life, however, there were setbacks and difficult times. In 1910 his mother, to whom he was closely endeared, was struck ill with an unexplained malady from which she never recovered, despite exhaustive research. In 1912, his father and mentor passed away, placing on Douglas a burden that led him to request duty in Washington, where he would be provided with quarters sufficient for the family. Washington, however, became the launching place that would ultimately lead him to the most senior post in the army, chief of staff. He, and his illustrious background, caught the attention of then Chief of Staff Maj. Gen. Leonard Wood, who appointed him to the General Staff, regarded as the central brain of the army. This prestigious position placed MacArthur within the innermost sanctum of Washington's power and social brokers. Responsibilities given to him included being a key part of planning for mobilization contingencies and presenting these plans to Congress. His horizons for advancement were now almost limitless, and his reputation as a staff officer who was sometimes outspoken but honest and straightforward in defense of his beliefs put him in good stead with those who made the wheels turn in both government and military matters. In the following years, circumstances in the world took his military career on a varied and noteworthy course, including Veracruz, Mexico, where his courageous and militarily adroit exploits earned him commendation for the Medal of Honor by General Wood in 1914—not only was this an honor, but it was tradition, as his father had won it before he was born. The War Department turned it down, and though MacArthur was incensed and asked for a review of the matter, the medal was still denied him.

In July 1914 the world burst into the flames of World War I. MacArthur, now a major, worked directly with the chief of staff and secretary of war, Newton Baker, laying the groundwork for imminent mobilization of U.S. armed forces. The United States finally, after numerous provocations, declared war on Germany in April 1917. Like all his peers, Douglas MacArthur champed at the bit to go with the troops to France. His wait was not long, and, newly promoted to full colonel, he was made chief of staff of the newly formed 42nd "Rainbow Division" under Gen. William A. Mann, soon to retire. MacArthur was the dominant figure in the division, and after two and a half months of intensive preparation, twenty-seven thousand men of the Rainbow shipped out to become the leading edge of Gen. John J. Pershing's American Expeditionary Force (AEF). In the following months MacArthur became one of the best known officers in the AEF, for both his individual panache and his demonstrations of extraordinary courage and daring. The latter included voluntarily leading a particularly savage French trench-raiding party, which killed and captured over six hundred Germans. He received his first decoration, the Croix de Guerre, from the French and was awarded the Silver Star by the U.S. Army. Later in the Lorraine region, he earned the Distinguished Service Cross for valor in leading at the forefront of his troops. He was also "slightly" gassed in that action, earning him the Purple Heart. Behind the scenes, MacArthur's mother, seeking to take advantage of an old friendship with General Pershing, wrote him a letter imploring that Douglas be promoted to general rank. Although MacArthur's relationship with Pershing was somewhat strained by some of the young colonel's idiosyncrasies of dress (affecting a floppy hat, wearing colorful turtleneck sweaters, brandishing a riding crop, etc.) and other eccentricities that tended to popularize him with the common soldiers as a colorful fellow, Pershing nevertheless felt him deserving of promotion to brigadier general. At the brutal fighting around Chateau Thierry, at St.-Mihiel salient, and in the brutal campaign of the Argonne Forest, MacArthur went on to amass three more Silver Stars and a second Croix de Guerre. On 11 October 1918, during the assault on Côte de Châtillon, MacArthur was badly gassed and almost blinded. For a second time he was recommended for the Medal of Honor but instead had to settle for another Silver Star and Purple Heart. By the end of the war on 11 November, MacArthur had become one of the highest-decorated officers to come out of WWI, but to his festering disappointment, the Medal of Honor had still been denied him.

Following the war and after sobering up from the loss of lives, there was a massive outburst of antiwar and antimilitary sentiment in America. West Point Military Academy became a prime target, to the point that there was pressure in Congress to abolish it altogether. The new army chief of staff, Peyton C. March, chief artillery officer under Pershing in WWI, assigned Douglas MacArthur to one of the most daunting assignments of his career, that of superintendent in charge of West Point. He was motivated by MacArthur's liberal thinking, which he felt could be put to good use revitalizing the "hidebound and narrow curriculum" of the academy and putting an end to pointless emphasis on "hazing." "West Point is forty years behind the times," he advised MacArthur, "and I want you to revitalize and revamp the Academy."

MacArthur felt himself foremost a soldier and tried to beg off, but he was given no choice. With his now sixty-seven-year-old, seriously ill mother, he embarked on what would be a vicious political and administrative battle with the War Department, the faculty, the alumni, the Corps of Cadets, and Congress, but under his guidance West Point became a thoroughly transformed and progressive institution.

While there, his personal life took a radical turn. He fell in love with a wealthy divorcée named Louise Brooks, daughter of one Oliver E. Cromwell, a prominent New York attorney and ardent yachtsman who died when Louise was quite young. Her mother remarried to a Philadelphia millionaire banker, and Louise herself later married a successful Baltimore contractor. They had a daughter and son. Louise's family was prominent in the international set and was friends with General Pershing. In the course of events, Louise is reputed to have become infatuated with one of Pershing's aides, John G. Quekemeyer. Whatever the case, in 1919 in Paris, Louise and Brooks were divorced, and a year or so later, while acting as Pershing's official hostess when he was posted in Washington, she met MacArthur, and the two warmed to one another. There was a glitch, however. Pershing, who never really warmed to MacArthur, objected to the latter's West Point reforms. Pershing informed MacArthur that at the end of the 1922 academic year he was to be detached and posted to the Philippines. Simultaneous to the public release of this news, MacArthur and Louise Brooks announced their engagement. There was a media frenzy hinting MacArthur had been "exiled" because he had won out in a love triangle involving Pershing and Louise. Pershing tried to put the matter at rest with a public announcement that it was all "damned poppycock" and that General MacArthur was being ordered to the Philippines because he stood at the top of the list for officers needed for foreign service, and he went on to laud him as "one of the most splendid types of soldier I have ever served with."

MacArthur and Louise were married on Valentine's Day 1922 at the Stotesbury Palm Beach mansion El Mirasol, and after completion of the academic year at West Point they sailed for routine garrison in the Philippines. They were accompanied by Louise's two children. MacArthur's frail mother returned to Washington to live with her older son, Arthur. Although living was relatively Spartan after the stimulation of West Point, MacArthur felt at home in the islands. While he undertook his military duties, he took advantage of the opportunity to indulge in one of his favorite athletics, polo, at the Manila Polo Club and was generally content with the posting. However, Louise missed the fast social life of Washington and New York and grew increasingly listless and bored.

MacArthur had been in Manila for only about four months when bad news came from his brother Arthur's wife, Mary, that his mother was critically ill and not expected to live. Douglas, Louise, and the two children sailed home on emergency leave, but upon arrival, Mrs. MacArthur Sr. was much improved. Douglas returned to the Philippines shortly after, but the visit was to be the last time he ever saw his elder brother. Arthur died of appendicitis that August. In the year following, the elder Mrs. MacArthur resumed her determined entreaties to General Pershing to promote her son to major general. Finally, worn down, Pershing, in one of his last acts in office, gave in, making Douglas MacArthur the youngest major general in the army. At the time of his promotion, MacArthur was ordered back to command III Corps area with headquarters near Baltimore where Louise had a rather grand estate, Rainbow Hill. Once back in her element of frenetic social activity, Louise was again content. For MacArthur, on the other hand, it was a dismal time in his military career. Appointed a judge in the infamous court-martial of his personal good friend Gen. William "Billy" Mitchell, the long trial and its questionable outcome were an ordeal for the conservative-thinking MacArthur. The outcome of the trial was the root of animosity toward MacArthur by a significant segment of American airmen, which would have future ramifications in the war to come.

At home, MacArthur's life was anything but serene. Now thoroughly disenchanted with military life, Louise pleaded with Douglas to retire to civilian business life and seek his fortune. MacArthur turned a deaf ear to such ideas, his ambition set for chief of staff. The conflict was irreconcilable and the couple separated and ultimately divorced on 18 June 1929. Louise was granted the divorce in Reno and persisted in blaming the failed marriage on "an interfering mother-in-law." She married and divorced twice more.

In summer 1928, MacArthur was once again assigned to Manila, this time to the top military post of commander of the department of the Philippines. He recorded in his personal memoirs that "no assignment could have pleased me more." He found Manila still to his delight and soon formed a warm cadre of staunch friends, including close and lasting relationships with his old friend Manuel Quezon and the new governor general, Henry L. Stimson. In 1928 in a series of complex maneuverings with the new Republican president, Herbert Hoover, MacArthur steered his course through heavy and influential pressure to become appointed chief of engineers, knowing it would negate his hopes to become chief of staff, and positioned himself to be recommended to succeed then Chief of Staff Gen. Charles P. Summerall. Turning down the prestigious post of chief of engineers was a high-stakes poker gamble, but if he did not chance it, his ultimate goal of chief of staff would be forfeit. It paid off. On 5 August 1930, as his tour of duty in Manila was coming to a close, Douglas MacArthur received the long-awaited cable from the War Department informing him, "President has just announced your detail as Chief of Staff to succeed General Summerall." Initially thrilled, MacArthur had subsequent disturbing considerations. The United States had sunk into the terrors of the Great Depression, and pacifist sentiment was acute. His hesitations were cut short by his mother, who admonished that if he showed timidity in his new challenge, his father's spirit would writhe in shame. From then on, Douglas MacArthur didn't look back.

On 21 November 1930, MacArthur, then fifty years old, became the youngest chief of staff in U.S. Army history. Accompanied by his mother, now seventy-eight and in poor health, who had been living with Arthur's widow, he took residence in Quarters One at Fort Myer, Virginia, the spacious home of chief of staff. It was a time when the nation was in turmoil. The Depression had deepened, rumors flew that Communists were bent on fomenting revolution, and the army was a prime target for downsizing by a Hoover government determined to cut expenditures. From an authorized strength of 285,000 men and 18,000 officers, Congress cut funds with the result of reducing the service to a skeleton force of 125,000 men and 12,000 officers, making the army sixteenth in size in the world. This number, however, still included 6,000 Filipino Scouts. Even further cuts were advocated, but MacArthur proved a stubborn and effective defender of the army in these dark times, lashing out at pacifists in one typical statement, "Any nation that would keep its self-respect must be prepared to defend itself. History has proved repeatedly that nations once great which neglected their national defense are dust and ashes as a result."

Ironically, just at that time, led by the ambitious and aggressive Japanese army chief of staff, Hideki Tojo, Japan took over the weak but strategic country of Manchuria. Japan's march of aggression in the Far East had begun. In the United States MacArthur held off yet another cut in the army's officer corps by a hairline vote.

As the Great Depression spread relentlessly over America, more families went steadily under, and citizens had to focus on basic provision for their families. In 1924 an act of Congress decreed that WWI veterans would receive a bonus in 1945, but many veterans agitated for an immediate payment. In 1931 Congressman Wright Pitman introduced a bill providing for just that. It was resisted, and in May 1932 hungry, penniless veterans descended on Washington in droves. They set up shabby tent cities on the mall and agitated in support of Pitman's bill. President Hoover and General MacArthur were convinced that the mob was the work of a Communist conspiracy in the interest of overthrowing the government and igniting revolution. Pitman's bill passed the House but lost in the Senate. Hoover had declared himself prepared to veto a passage. Part of the so-called bonus army gave up the fight and left the capital, but some ten thousand remained, becoming more angry and aggressive each day. On 28 July, Washington police fired on the holdouts, killing two veterans and wounding many more. Hoover wasted no time in ordering Secretary of War Hurley to instruct MacArthur to employ troops to disperse the mob. Discretion and moderation were stressed, but the message was to get the job done.

MacArthur, in uniform complete with his rows of award ribbons and accompanied by Majors George Patton and Dwight Eisenhower, led federal troops against the rebellious veterans. Tear gas was employed, rather than small arms, but it was still an ugly and tragic scene. Many of the ragged veterans routed that day by the conspicuously beribboned general had fought at his side in France. To many, MacArthur became a traitor to his comrades-in-arms that day, never to be forgiven. In an ill-advised meeting that MacArthur had with the media, his ego took control of his better judgment, with the result that he was widely vilified in the nation and sowed the seeds of wary distrust with America's future president, Franklin D. Roosevelt. It was also the foundation for serious future rivalry between the army and navy. FDR had been head of the Navy Department when he had met MacArthur, and, while a mutual respect existed between the two men, the feeling was hardly shared by the quasi-socialistic proponents of Roosevelt's New Deal policies. This became acutely evident when huge amounts of money and effort went into forming the Civilian Conservation Corps to provide jobs and revitalize the nation while Roosevelt ordered MacArthur to cut the army's budget by a shocking 51 percent with comparable reductions for the National Guard and reserves. MacArthur, in an emotional, personal entreaty, urged the White House to reconsider, even to the point of orally resigning his post. He was so sickened by the confrontation that he literally vomited on the White House steps afterward. Roosevelt ostensibly stood by MacArthur's side, yet the War Department slashed the army's budget even further by every possible dime. The production and development of new, innovative weaponry such as tanks and new aircraft was particularly hard hit by the cuts, leading to wide, misdirected resentment toward MacArthur by tank and air corps leaders. This furor coincided with the burgeoning rise of Japanese Far East aggression and Germany's blatant rebuilding of its army and air power in defiance of post–WWI agreements.

MacArthur was due to step down in the fall of 1934 as army chief of staff according to the standard term of four years, but Roosevelt felt it prudent to extend the general for a second term, the consideration of conservative elements in the government being prominent in his thinking. After some heated debate from all sides, FDR announced on 12 December 1934 that he would reappoint MacArthur long enough for the general to oversee the 1936 War Department increase in budget by $355 million spurred by the deteriorating world situation. At the same time, there was a government move afoot to divest itself of the Philippines.

In 1934, Congress approved the Tydings-McDuffie Act, which authorized commonwealth status for the Philippine Islands in 1935 with a provision for complete independence by 4 July 1946. MacArthur and army war planners were now compelled to reassess U.S. military policy regarding the Philippines. Since the United States took possession of the Philippine Islands in 1898 following the Spanish-American War, a plan had existed to defend the island nation from outside, potential aggression, foremost in mind being Japan. The plan had been designated "Orange," essentially of naval origin, which provided that in case of an attack on Luzon, the defense garrison would fight a six-month delaying action, then fall back to the rugged Bataan Peninsula and hold the island fortress of Corregidor to block Manila Bay from invading forces. Meanwhile, the U.S. Pacific fleet would come to the rescue and destroy the invader in an all-out sea battle. The plan, while not rooted in reality, nevertheless remained firm U.S. military policy. More pragmatic analysts insisted that the U.S. fleet would have to fight its way through land-based air power based on numerous islands mandated to Japan following WWI. Now that the Tydings-McDuffie Act was law, the most prudent solution seemed to be to encourage the Philippines, with U.S. help, to gradually build up a self-sufficient military force to defend the islands until independence in 1946.

General consensus among American military planners concluded Plan Orange to be rife with weaknesses and that to send the U.S. fleet in an all-out charge to the Philippines in face of a Japanese invasion would be sheer madness. In November 1934 the War Department sent a formal recommendation to MacArthur that a gradual evacuation of all U.S. military personnel be completed by 1946. His abrupt reply was to the point: "Not approved." He declared Plan Orange a "completely useless document" and expressed his view that if hostilities with Japan occurred, two divisions should be sent to the Philippines, not with any idea of withdrawing to Bataan but with the intent of defending "every sacred inch" of the Filipino soil. His disagreement fell on deaf ears in a penny-pinching Congress. It can be said that MacArthur's view of Philippine defense was as unrealistic as he considered Plan Orange, and in the resulting debate MacArthur was left to reluctantly swallow the ambiguous Plan Orange as policy.

In summer 1935 MacArthur's tour of duty as chief of staff was nearing its end. At fifty-five he was only nine years short of accepted retirement age.

The prospect of being forced to finish out his career in a lesser duty posting was abhorrent to a man of MacArthur's deep pride. The answer to his quandary came from the changes taking place in his beloved Philippines and his old friend Manuel Quezon. In the course of a visit to Washington, Quezon, by then the preeminent statesman of his country, ardently requested MacArthur to come to the Philippines to help him upgrade his country to modern maturity and to plan its still primitive defenses. MacArthur loved the Philippines, and his family name was already legendary there. The ten years left to him before retirement literally coincided with the transition of the Philippines to independence, and he would have the notoriety of helping found a new nation. It was heady stuff to both his ego and his desire to finish out his career with significance.

President Roosevelt did not hesitate to approve the arrangement, but there was a problem of title and official status in the new position. Under the new U.S.–Philippine relationship, the office of U.S. governor generalship had been replaced by a less pretentious office of "high commissioner." MacArthur declined that office when he found that it would necessitate his resignation from active armed service and therefore be entitled to far less retirement income. An alternative was decided upon under which he would be made a "military advisor" to Quezon, remain an active U.S. Army officer, and receive a generous additional annual $33,000 salary from the Philippine government. It was initially agreed that he would retain his four-star general's rank, but as the result of a dispute with FDR over his successor as chief of staff, Roosevelt reneged on the arrangement and demoted MacArthur to the rank of a two-star major general, to which the latter responded with some rather salty language. Many opinions abound on this action on the part of Roosevelt, but it is thought by many historians that FDR's move was calculated to keep MacArthur's sometime runaway ego in check. At any rate, the demotion did not serve to raise the general's standing in the eyes of the Filipinos, who stood to gain so much from MacArthur's guidance.

MacArthur's journey back to the Philippines was a voyage of mixed emotions. He was accompanied by his ailing mother, now eighty-three years old; his widowed sister-in-law, Mary; an army physician, Dr. Howard J. Hunter, to help Mary care for his mother; and Maj. Dwight D. Eisenhower, forty-five, who had been MacArthur's aide in Washington for over two years and who would now be his chief of staff in the Philippines. Also with them was a Spanish-speaking former academy classmate, Maj. James B. Ord, whom Eisenhower had recruited for his linguistic and other special qualifications. The party was rounded out by MacArthur's personal aide, Capt. Thomas J. Davis, and several clerks.

During a shipboard cocktail party, MacArthur met a young woman named Jean Marie Faircloth. She was bound for Shanghai but soon became an intimate regular of MacArthur's entourage. There were all the appearances of love at first sight.

The otherwise pleasant voyage was marred, however, by a severe decline in the health of the general's mother. When they arrived in Manila, MacArthur's intended triumphant return was darkened by the realization that his mother was dying. Auspicious social and political engagements had to be canceled, and on 3 December 1935 Mrs. MacArthur died of cerebral thrombosis. MacArthur felt more than the loss of a mother—she had been his closest and most loyal comrade through the years.

His loss was softened somewhat by his increasingly close relationship with Jean Faircloth. Then thirty-seven and unmarried, she was a petite (barely five feet tall), dark-haired, vivacious lady with flawless social graces. A southerner from Nashville, Tennessee, Jean was the daughter of a wealthy, aristocratic mill owner and was descended from a prerevolutionary family. MacArthur confided in his memoirs that she had retained fully the feisty but preferable side of a Southern rebel background. By sheer coincidence her grandfather, Confederate Captain Richard Beard, fought opposite MacArthur's father at Gettysburg's Missionary Ridge. Beard became prominent in Tennessee politics and, in addition, four of Jean's great uncles also served in the Confederate Army. She had been raised on tales of the Civil War and was fascinated by all things military. Her father died in 1929 and left her a wealthy woman. She became well traveled and was knowledgeable, bright, and witty. Her closeness to MacArthur grew quickly, and she canceled her trip to Shanghai. She was constantly at his side and a comfort to him through the loss of his mother; all of Manila could see that the couple had become inseparable. A quiet courtship ran its pleasant course.

In the meantime, MacArthur had been struggling to whip the Philippine defense force into some kind of operational consistency. On 15 November 1935 Manuel Quezon was inaugurated president of the Philippine Commonwealth. Almost immediately afterward, MacArthur, with the assistance of Dwight Eisenhower, Major Ord, and other personnel from the army in Manila, set about activating the plans begun in Washington and labored on during the voyage to Manila for building a Filipino military establishment literally from scratch. The plan was loosely formed along the lines of the Swiss military of the time. The foundation of the army would be composed of a core cadre of trained, professional soldiers to be drawn chiefly from the in-place constabulary. Beginning with this embryo, the goal was to train some forty thousand citizen-soldiers annually at a planned one hundred camps throughout the archipelago. To provide officers, a national military academy modeled on West Point would be instituted.

The end goal was to have a fully trained forty divisions—some four hundred thousand troops—by 1946. This army was to be augmented by a proposed air force of 250 planes—fighters, light to medium bombers, and

reconnaissance planes. A navy was planned in the form of fifty motor torpedo boats (PT boats) of British design and construction. Their specifica-
tions called for a sixty-five-foot-long, thirteen-foot-wide beamed craft of
lightweight (primarily plywood) construction, powered by three twelve-
cylinder engines with a top speed of around forty-one knots (about 60
mph). It would carry a crew of twelve and armament would consist of two
torpedo tubes, depth charges, and twin light antiaircraft (or .50-caliber)
machine guns. The Filipinos had managed to purchase only two PT boats.
The Philippine government was to bear the estimated $8 million annual
cost of this combined defense force. The long-term tentative agreement provided that the United States would supplement this force with additional,
necessary military equipment and supplies at cost or on long-term loan.
The objective was an ambitious one, and until the Philippines could prove
militarily self-sufficient, Plan Orange was to remain in effect.

In a lofty public statement, MacArthur swore that "by 1946 I will make
these islands a Pacific Switzerland which would cost any invader a half million men, three years and five billion dollars to conquer. I am here by the
Grace of God to defend the Filipino People. This is my sacred destiny."

The plan looked conceivable on paper. Making it a reality was another
matter. Skeptics began to rear their heads. The Filipinos were taken aback
by the financial cost. Some politicians complained that there was a potential that a militarized Philippines would antagonize the already aggressive
Japanese. Others recalled the high price of Philippine insurrection and
feared that arming the Filipinos was tempting renewed troubles. The U.S.
War Department felt operating a military on a shoestring was a setup for
disaster. The result was that U.S. aid came in a mere trickle, mostly in the
form of obsolete materiel. The beginnings of the Filipinos' effort to arm
themselves could only be called piecemeal at best and primitive at worst.
However, the Filipinos themselves were not lacking. They were, as they had
already proven, capable of being fine troops with intelligent individuals for
a capable officer corps. But there was the problem of many different language dialogues to cope within a unified force. They were being equipped
at a snail's pace, mostly with outdated, inefficient equipment. It was a
bumpy start at best, and Filipino leaders were not happy about it.

At the same time, MacArthur had serious problems in the realm. Manuel
Quezon had high ambitions of his own, which included agitating in Washington for full independence for the Philippines by 1938. His persistence
managed to antagonize Franklin Roosevelt and his New Deal government,
who stalled on any arms assistance to the Philippine government. In early
1937 MacArthur accompanied Quezon on a trip to Washington to plead
the case for the Philippine plans. FDR refused an audience with Quezon
but received MacArthur. After some heated discussion, FDR finally agreed
to see Quezon, who simply complicated matters further with his insistence

on immediate independence. In doing so, he completely frustrated Mac-Arthur's requests for military materiel assistance from the War Department for the fledgling Filipino armed forces.

While in America, MacArthur had the occasion to tend to some personal matters. He and his family, accompanied by Jean, went to Arlington National Cemetery, where he had pledged to inter his mother beside his father. He and Jean then traveled to New York City, where on 30 April 1937 they wed in a quiet civil ceremony in the New York City Municipal Building. Shortly thereafter, MacArthur, Jean, and their entourage returned to Manila. The MacArthurs would not set foot on U.S. soil again until 1951.

In Manila, MacArthur and his bride took up residence in what were to become almost legendary quarters in a spacious penthouse over a modern new wing of the beautiful Manila Hotel with spectacular views of Manila Bay. On 21 February 1938, a son was born to them. He was named Arthur.

Following the stormy visit to Washington, it seemed that plans were afoot by powers unknown, but with FDR's apparent approval, that Mac-Arthur be removed from his Philippine command. A letter from Chief of Staff Craig was received informing the general that upon completion in 1937 of two years' tour of duty, he was ordered to return to the United States for "other duty." MacArthur was stunned and disillusioned. Quezon, who was also dismayed, promptly obtained approval to offer MacArthur the position of military advisor to the Philippine government, bestowing on him the rank of field marshal of what was still a nonexistent Philippine army. MacArthur promptly accepted, and on 31 December 1937 he officially retired from the U.S. Army credited with thirty-eight years of honorable service. The retirement, however, and cessation of any official status with the U.S. War Department, swept all promises for U.S. military assistance in the form of aid and materiel to the Philippines off the table.

Although the literal dismissal outraged many of his allies and admirers in the United States, MacArthur gave aid and comfort to his detractors by appearing for a public military review in a field marshal's uniform of his own design, which would have better suited the gaudy Hollywood parody of a small-time potentate. It was essentially a white, military-cut sharkskin suit with red piping on the lapels and topped off with a general's four stars. A gold baton was carried as a final accent. He was made cruel fun of by liberal political foes and the press alike, who branded him with spiteful labels such as "The Napoleon of Luzon" and "Manila's Caesar." The genuine heroism and accomplishments of his military career were buried in the shuffle. There was both embarrassment among more conservative Filipinos and noticeable grumbling among Philippine politicians about his $16,500 salary augmented by defraying the expense of his penthouse, all paid by hard-pressed Filipino taxpayers. Perhaps MacArthur's ego had brought this upon him, but perhaps also it was his way of demonstrating that he was not prepared to bend to or for anyone whom he perceived as stepping in the way of what he felt sincerely was his appointed destiny.

In the long run, it was to be the Japanese who stalled the anti-MacArthur steamroller. From 1937 through 1939 the Japanese war machine swallowed Manchuria and invaded mainland China in the most brutal fashion imaginable. With Hitler's seemingly invincible Germany running rampant in Europe, by 1940 the Japanese sensed opportunity in Southeast Asia. The Germans had successfully distracted much of the attention and power of colonial powers with interests in Asia such as Britain, France, Belgium, and the Netherlands, and when France surrendered, the Nazi-controlled Vichy government allowed the Japanese to move into French Indochina unopposed. In September 1940, the Japanese, in a move that Hitler saw as freeing his juggernaut to devote all its attention on Europe, entered the treacherous Tripartite Pact with Germany and Italy. The following April, Japan signed a neutrality pact with Russia, thus freeing the Japanese to extend their empire southward without interference. In July 1940, the United States cancelled its 1911 commercial treaty with Japan and generally clamped down on commerce and the export of all strategic materials to the Japanese. At the same time, America extended generous loans to China and Chiang Kai-shek's Nationalist government, now at war with Japan. Japan was being painted into a strategic and material needs corner from which only further Asian conquest could extricate her.

It was a sobering time, and real fear began to rise in the Pacific. The U.S. Congress suddenly saw an urgency to fund serious defense of American interests and bases in the Pacific, including Alaska and Panama, the loss of which would directly pose a threat to the continental United States. Army Chief of Staff Gen. George C. Marshall saw the country in a serious quandary. He observed that "adequate reinforcements for the Philippines at this time would leave the United States in great peril should there be a break in the defense of Great Britain." What the United States needed now more than anything else was time, and Japan's occupation of the strategic bases in southern Indochina was dire warning that time was in short supply. The Philippines were now almost entirely surrounded, and measures to strengthen their defense could be put off no longer. America's situation in the Far East was now truly precarious.

The Filipinos now felt truly threatened, yet under the circumstances, their military plans were still barely stumbling. The National Assembly begrudged MacArthur a mere half of what he needed to build an effective force. He was unable to attain his target of training forty thousand men per year, but by sheer determination, he neared his goal. Toward the end of 1940, roughly thirty-five thousand men had completed a mandatory six-month army training period. The embryo air force had only forty obsolete planes and about one hundred qualified pilots. The "navy" still had only its two PT boats, based at Cavite amidst the American fleet present.

Meanwhile Quezon vacillated, secretly trying to bargain a nonaggression pact with Japan. His relationship with MacArthur became tense. To add to their differences, Quezon, disillusioned with the progress of the military program, pushed through an added cut in MacArthur's already strained budget and, to add insult to injury, publicly stated that "the Philippines cannot be defended even if every last Filipino citizen were to be armed with modern weapons." It was the worst kind of defeatism being voiced from the very top.

MacArthur did have one particularly valuable asset in his position in the person of his amiable and able chief of staff, Dwight D. Eisenhower. For six years the younger officer, still attached to the U.S. regular army, had labored steadfastly and persistently to help MacArthur achieve his objectives for the Philippine defense force. It was overall a thankless job, and in later years when Eisenhower had risen to the position of powerful leadership in Europe and relations became strained between the two men due to politics, "Ike" commented that he had benefited from "four years of studying dramatics under MacArthur." However, in 1939 when Eisenhower was transferred back to stateside duty, the two men parted on friendly terms and Eisenhower recorded that working with MacArthur had "brought an additional dimension to my experience." He was replaced by an officer of a far different cut, Lt. Col. Richard K. Sutherland. A Yale graduate, he had entered the army as a private in 1916 and served in France with the AEF. By the end of WWI, Sutherland rose through the ranks to captain. He remained in the army and went on to attend the Infantry School, Command and Staff School, École Supérieure de Guerre, and the Army War College. He was considered a brilliant, hardworking career officer, and in 1938 after a tour in Shanghai he was chosen to be MacArthur's new chief of staff. Gen. George C. Kenny, who had served with Sutherland for several years, conceded his outstanding organizational and executive abilities but frowned on the latter's strong traits of egotism and arrogance. Sutherland, a man of handsome bearing, was brittle and aloof but an untiring worker. Picked by MacArthur from his post as senior officer in the U.S. military mission, Sutherland would go on to the rank of brigadier general in August 1941 and would remain MacArthur's chief of staff until 1946. MacArthur was not well served by one of Sutherland's failings: he had an obsession for shielding the general, even to the point of arbitrarily assuming responsibilities and making decisions that should have been left to MacArthur himself. The unfortunate consequence of these traits was a significant factor in driving a wedge between MacArthur and many of his most important subordinates, not to mention creating an atmosphere of isolation, which rankled the common soldiers and sailors under MacArthur's USAFFE (U.S. Army Forces

Far East) command. Getting past Sutherland and his immediate staff to address MacArthur directly about military contingencies became increasingly difficult and was cause for a number of serious emergencies later on.

On 26 July 1941, Douglas MacArthur was recalled to active duty with the U.S. Army. He was restored to his permanent rank of major general, which he held before his retirement in 1937. General Marshall had made his move to put a finger in the dike. Effective on 27 July, approval came down that promoted MacArthur to the rank of temporary lieutenant general, and he was put in charge of the organization of USAFFE. Establishing headquarters at No. 1 Calle Victoria in Manila's walled city, MacArthur faced three immediate, urgent tasks. First was to establish and organize his U.S. regular army command on an efficient basis. He put Sutherland in charge. With the exception of a small coastal defense force, naval forces, however, would remain under separate U.S. command of the newly formed Asiatic fleet under Adm. Thomas C. Hart and would be based at Cavite on Manila Bay's south shore and Subic Bay northwest of Bataan. By October, Hart's principal strike force was a flotilla of six WWI-vintage S boats and twenty-three fleet boats, the largest concentration anywhere of U.S. submarines. The subs were armed with new, secretly developed torpedoes actuated by magnetic exploders. In support were four maintenance tenders. The second challenge was to activate and train the Philippine army. Third, MacArthur had to secure necessary and adequate materiel and reinforcements to put his entire Philippine command on an immediate war footing. This would be easier said than done, and time was running out.

Washington finally was compelled to reassess the military situation in the Philippines and pay attention to what MacArthur had been insisting for years. The forces there were woefully inadequate to implement the vaunted Plan Orange. Dramatic, if not frantic, steps were taken to expand the Philippine defense forces. Orders came down to mobilize the Filipino army (twelve infantry regiments on paper but far less in reality) and merge it with the regular American garrison. By December 1941, USAFFE's Philippine Department could in reality field 22,532 men, 11,972 of whom were Philippine Scouts. Of the 1,340 officers, 775 were reservists on active duty. The largest contingent of men was assigned to the infantry. The Coast Artillery Corps was second, with 4,967. Almost the entire command was stationed on Luzon.

The largest single U.S. Army force in the Philippines was the Philippine Division commanded by Maj. Gen. Jonathan M. Wainwright. Except for the troops in the 31st Infantry Division (Army United States; AUS), with an authorized strength of 2,100 men, and a small number of military police and headquarters personnel, the bulk of regular U.S. Army troops were Philippine Scout regiments—these were the 45th and 57th Infantry, the 86th (388 men) and 88th (518 men) field artillery regiments, and the 26th

Cavalry Regiment, consisting of two squadrons of three troops each plus headquarters. The Philippine Army's combined infantry and artillery units could field ten divisions, or roughly 100,000 men.

Materiel supply reinforcement had been magnanimously promised by Washington in the form of a considerable number of up-to-date fighter and bomber aircraft, modern artillery, and the newest small arms, including semiautomatic M-1 rifles, new machine guns, and ample stocks of current munitions. Very little materialized, and the Philippine defenders were left largely with WWI-vintage small arms, machine guns and artillery, outdated, defective ammunition, and a motley collection of largely obsolete aircraft. Of all the fighting units, the Philippine Scouts, who drew constant field duty, were considered elite and, as such, were the best equipped. They were the only units issued entirely with the limited supply of Garand M-1 rifles. Bolt-action 1900 Enfields and 1903 Springfields were the standard small arms of the other units.

The state of the Philippine Army bordered on the tragic. Many officers and noncoms were untrained and unqualified for their assignments. Many first sergeants and headquarters personnel could neither read nor write. Training facilities and equipment bordered on nonexistent. There were so few improvised target ranges that many Filipino troops went into battle without ever having fired a shot. Uniforms, usually consisting of blue denim fatigues, were piecemeal, old, and often unserviceable for wear. Shoes were thinly rubber soled and wore out quickly. Personal equipment —such as blankets, mosquito bars, mess kits, shelter halves, and the like— was in serious short supply. The supply of Enfield and Springfield rifles was sufficient, but the supply of ammunition, bayonets, entrenching tools, packs, gas masks, and helmets was not. To augment the short supply of steel helmets, makeshift headgear made of coconut shell was often issued. The average Filipino soldier was as willing and courageous as any man in the world—he had proven that over the years in the insurrections—but he was being horribly short-changed in preparedness for a large-scale modern war.

In December, the 26th Cavalry had a strength of 784 Filipino enlisted men and 54 American officers. Their home station was Fort Stotsenburg. Troop F was stationed on detached duty at Nichols Field south of Manila. In addition to being horse mounted, each squadron had an armored scout car platoon equipped with field communications equipment. Pride in their regiment and morale were high. They would earn the everlasting gratitude of Gen. Jonathan Wainwright as his mainstay in the awful days to come.

Most of the South Pacific's twentieth-century equivalent of "Lotus Land" inhabitants were sleeping peacefully on the night before Monday, 8 December 1941, Manila time, totally unaware of and unprepared for the violent whirlwind that was already gathering to descend on them with stunning fury in a mere few hours. In the stables at Stotsenburg, here was peace and only an occasional snort of a horse to clear its nostrils or a stomp to rid one of an annoying fly. It was a quiet night in the home realm of the 26th Cavalry.

NOTE

1. Refer to Carlos Quirino, *Filipinos at War* (Philippines: Vera-Reyes, Inc., 1981).

2

Hell Comes for Breakfast

Fort Stotsenburg, Northern Luzon, some fifty miles north of Manila and adjacent to Clark Field Air Force Base

Hell came calling uninvited for breakfast.

In the wee hours of the morning in the Philippines, 7 December quietly crossed the international dateline. It was now Monday, 8 December in the islands. At 3 a.m. Lt. Johnny Wheeler, the duty OD (officer of the day), was awakened in shock by the night duty sergeant shouting the horrifying news that the Japanese had bombed Pearl Harbor. Bedlam in Wainwright's HQ building followed. Everywhere the alarm was shouted: "The Japs have bombed Pearl Harbor. This is no drill! Repeat! No drill! No shit, people! It's a damned war!" shouted an almost hysterical duty NCO on the loud-speaker intercom.

All American and Filipino installations were roused and put on immediate full alert. Upon being awakened, General MacArthur's air force commander, Gen. Lewis Brereton, put all air force commands on full alert. At the time, Brereton's command possessed more aircraft than the entire Hawaiian department had. These included some 35 late-model Boeing B-17D bombers (the largest contingent assigned to any U.S. Army force) and a fighter force that included over 107 efficient, heavily armored Curtiss P-40E interceptors plus an additional 135 older-model aircraft of all types, including obsolete Martin B-10B and Douglas B-18A twin-engine bombers and a sad array of outdated fighters, including Seversky P-35s and old-fashioned Boeing P-26As, most of which were assigned to Philippine air forces scattered at the smaller fields. Although the air corps was making training and expansion facilities a priority, construction funds were slow in coming. Brereton's air command was still at a disadvantage, having only three first-line fields—Clark, Nichols, and Del Monte—capable of handling bombardment squadrons, which meant a serious inability to disperse the units of larger planes. The fighter squadrons on Luzon could use Nichols, Clark, Del Carmen, and Iba. There were numerous other smaller fields, mostly used by the Philippine Army Air Corps due to their low-speed, outdated planes.

By 5 a.m. Brereton was at the door of MacArthur's headquarters office in Manila at No. 1 Calle Victoria, an address deep in the narrow streets and massive stone walls of the "old city" and known as "House on the Wall" (a series of unattractive, interconnected structures built literally on top of one of the ancient walls). He had come in desperation to make an immediate request seeking permission to mount a B-17 bomber strike on Japanese airfields on Formosa. General MacArthur's brittle, protective chief of the "palace guard," the autocratic Gen. Richard K. Sutherland, refused Brereton an audience with "El Supremo." The general was too busy. At 7:15 Brereton went to MacArthur's office to again request permission to attack Formosa. Again he was told to "stand by for orders." At this time, he received a transoceanic telephone call from U.S. Air Force Chief Gen. "Hap" Arnold telling him the extent of what happened at Pearl Harbor. By now, reports of enemy air activity were coming in fast at air force headquarters, so at 8 a.m. Brereton ordered all operational craft into the air so they wouldn't be caught like sitting ducks as had their comrades at Hawaiian fields. In the rush, bombers were ordered aloft to patrol without bombs. At 10 a.m., by now in utter despair, Brereton renewed his plea to be able to carry out some form of preemptive raid on Formosa. He pleaded by telephone to Sutherland that if Clark Field were to be attacked successfully, "we would be unable to respond effectively with our bombers." Sutherland grudgingly told him to proceed with preparations but to await clearance from MacArthur before initiating any offensive operations. On hanging up, Brereton ordered his adjutant, Lt. Col. Eugene Eubank, back to Clark Field with orders to initiate photographic reconnaissance missions immediately to southern Formosa for clearer situation intelligence. MacArthur had finally, but far too belatedly, reached the conclusion that Formosa must be bombed.[1] In the meantime, the main of Brereton's aircraft were still flying in circles to avoid being caught on the ground by Japanese attack, and they were now fast running short of fuel.

For some time, the Japanese had been intently watching the rapid buildup of American airpower in the Pacific with increasing concern and designated it as a priority target. Japanese air commanders of 11th Air Fleet HQ at Takao Harbor Naval Airfield on Formosa, and others on the seaborne carriers, were becoming alarmed and frustrated by delays caused by fog and foul weather robbing them of the element of surprise. Every passing hour increased the threat of American air attack by Clark-based heavy B-17 bombers on their bases. Japanese pilots meanwhile performed preflight personal preparations in line with Bushido traditions. Small locks of hair, fingernail clippings, letters, and other personal effects were put in small packages to send to their families for use in memorial shrines; last prayers and homages to the emperor had been performed; traditional ceremonial cups of sake and small rice cakes had been taken as their final meal; and most wore "thousand-stitch belts" (belly bands worn as good-luck charms put together collectively by mothers, wives, sisters, and friends until each belt had one thousand stitches). Last donned were *hachimaki*, white head-bands adorned with the red ball national symbol and patriotic words signi-fying the young warrior's readiness to die for his emperor and Japan.

Finally, in the early hours of 8 December, the weather lifted, and the Jap-anese 11th Air Fleet finally went into action. The initial flight of two twenty-seven-plane flights of twin-engine Japanese army bombers (Mitsubishi Type 97 KI-21, code-named "Nells" by the Allies) and dive bombers (Aichi Type 99 D3A, "Vals"), escorted by eighty-four A6M Reisen Zero-sen ("Zeke" or "Zero") fighters, was scrambled and began its 270-mile flight to the Philip-pines. At twenty thousand feet over the South China Sea they rendezvoused with two more flights of Mitsubishi Type 1 G4M "Betty" twin-engine bomb-ers from Tainan Field and additional fighter support of 34 more Zeros. Their attacks, coordinated with carrier-based Japanese aircraft bound for northern Luzon targets, would strike their preselected targets fast and hard according to plan. Shortly before 9 a.m. enemy bombers were reported by the aircraft warning service on Luzon to be headed south over Lingayen Gulf toward Manila. It was this report that was largely responsible for Clark Field's B-17s to be sent up without bombs. The 20th Pursuit Squadron made up of P-40s scrambled to head off the attack while the 17th Pursuit Squadron took off from Nichols Field to cover the base at Clark. However, the Japanese army planes had been limited to targets north of the 16th lati-tude. They turned east and split into two groups as they approached Lin-gayen. At 8 a.m. the first group struck the northern Luzon mountain city of Baguio, the Philippine "summer capital," where Quezon was staying at the time. It was here, too, that the first 26th Cavalrymen came under fire. A small number of them were in Baguio having come off routine, detached patrol duties in the Cagayan Valley region. The main strikes were concen-trated on military barracks and installations in and around the city. The accuracy of this attention could be largely attributed to the thorough prewar work of Japanese fifth column "tourists," "businessmen," and "field labor-ers." This first wave of Japanese army bombers returned to base unscathed without any contact with American aircraft. On the heels of the initial attack on Baguio, the Japanese next struck the strategic Tuguegarao air base to the northeast on Luzon at 9 a.m., wreaking havoc on Philippine air defenses on northern Luzon.

At 10:15, the fog had cleared sufficiently enough for a formidable force of 11th Air Fleet planes of the navy's Koku Sentais to take off. Three groups totaling 108 twin-engine bombers—accompanied by Aichi D3A Val dive bombers and escorted by 84 first-line naval Shi Zero Mitsubishi A6M2s equipped with drop tanks to increase range—began their run to attack Clark, Iba, and Nichols. The Japanese had picked only their most able and experienced pilots for this mission. The Zero was at that time by far the most feared fighter in the Pacific and Far East skies. Its only disadvantage was that its designers had sacrificed much crucial armor plating as the price for superior speed, range, and maneuverability. The Zero's chief adversary in 1941 was the Curtiss P40, which, though slower, could outdive Zeros and absorb much more punishment because of its significantly armored construction. American pilots had learned much from Gen. Claire Chennault's legendary AVG (American Volunteer Group) "Flying Tiger" airmen, who had developed tactics against Zeros in China. Their principal strategy was to gain superior altitude, make a diving attack on the Zero, and keep on diving to low altitude where the powerful Curtiss engine's torque could deliver speeds up to some 500 mph at rice paddy levels. Dive, hit, and run for the nearest clouds or get as close to the deck as possible was the order of the day for pilots who knew better than to try to turn with a Zero. Had Chennault's advice been heeded more seriously in Washington, it would have saved the lives of many American pilots in the Philippines who were facing the A6M2 Zeros for the first time and were stunned by the encounter with a high-performance fighter they had no idea the Japanese even had the capability of putting in the air.

At approximately 11:30 a.m. all American aircraft were ordered to land at their home fields for refueling, arming with one-hundred- and three-hundred-pound bombs and new orders. At Clark, while ground crews worked feverishly in hangars and on runways to ready planes for return to the air, the air crews rushed to mess halls to grab what might be their last meal for some time. It was there that they would greet the stunning arrival of war in the Philippines. To this day, military historians debate the details of the sequence of events that fateful morning, but there can be no denial of the end results. The USAFFE in the Philippines was largely caught flatfooted on the ground and flattened as an effective fighting force.

Japan's leading Zero ace, Saburo Sakai, flew in one of the large formations assigned to strike Luzon. The fighters and bombers were airborne by 10:45, and Sakai recalled what it was like that fateful morning. "The fighters broke up into two groups, one staying with the bombers as escorts, while the other flew ahead to tackle the expected interceptors, which we felt certain, after the long delays in our attack would be awaiting us in great strength. This would be no Pearl Harbor. I flew in the first wave, and our formation moved up to 19,000 feet. . . . And then the Philippine Islands hove into view, a deep green against the rich blue of the ocean. The coastline slipped beneath us, beautiful and peaceful, without another aircraft in the air! Then we were back over the China Sea.

"At 11:35 p.m. we flashed in from the China Sea and headed for Clark Field. The sight which met us was unbelievable! Instead of encountering a swarm of American fighters diving at us in attack, we looked down and saw some sixty enemy bombers and fighters neatly parked along the airfield runways. They squatted there like sitting ducks! The Americans had made no attempt to disperse the planes and increase their safety on the ground. We failed utterly to comprehend the enemy's attitude. Pearl Harbor had been hit more than five hours before; surely they had received word of that attack and expected another one against these critical fields!"

At 11:45 a.m., Monday 8 December, what is often called the "Second Pearl Harbor" began as did the first. Japanese "V" formations made up of twenty-seven bombers each approached Clark Field from the northeast appearing over the four-thousand-foot-high peak of Mt. Arayat with the midmorning sun gleaming silvery on their wings. Once again Japanese airmen were to be joystruck at the sight of yet another mass of helpless American armed might neatly parked on runways before hangars with brightly checker-painted roofs presenting a perfect target for Dai Nippon's sword to fall. The defenders' antiaircraft attention was largely turned northwest as they had been expecting a strike from the west using the approach cover of the Zambales Mountains and the high peak of the dormant volcano Mt. Pinatubo. On the ground, American airmen were crowded in the mess halls wolfing down a late breakfast while their planes were being refueled for another takeoff. Their food was hardly cooled before chaos rained down on them. The horror and disaster of Pearl Harbor repeated itself at Clark Field, Iba, Nichols, Manila, Cavite naval facilities, and Subic Bay, making the one-sided opening of hostilities in the Philippines a military disaster beyond comprehension for American armed forces.

Before it was singled out for destruction by Japanese bombers on 10 December, Cavite Naval Base had come in for some special preparatory attention from Japanese fifth columnists, who had widely sabotaged naval fuel supplies by doping gas and diesel with melted wax so engines would stall at critical times. Motor Torpedo Boat Squadron Three (consisting of six Packard engine powered PT boats under U.S. Navy command) was especially hard hit by such treatment with some frightening results in subsequent combat situations. The Cavite raids created havoc with the submarine facilities and caused abandonment of the submarine war plan. In addition to obliteration of their repair facilities, 233 key, new, superscript magnetic torpedoes were lost. Adm. Thomas Hart quickly ordered the three surviving submarine tenders—USS *Holland, Otus,* and the oldest ship, *Canopus*—transferred to naval facilities at Subic Bay. All fled south except *Canopus,* ordered to stay put to service surviving subs. The newest fleet submarine, *Sealion,* was damaged beyond repair, but her sister ship *Seadragon,* with repairs from *Canopus,* fled south.

The Japanese planes came over at altitudes of 22,000–25,000 feet, bombing at will with little fear of American antiaircraft guns, whose inadequate shells were exploding a good 2,000–4,000 feet short of their intended targets. In the words of one observer, "The Japs flew in neat formations" like a flock of well-trained buzzards "at altitudes simply too high for our guns to get at them." After fifteen minutes of bombing and following the second formation, thirty-four Zeros swooped in with merciless, low-level strafing attacks on both the grounded American planes now fully replenished with gas and ammunition and all of Clark's remaining facilities and installations. It was a devastating mix of firepower lasting for over an hour, which afforded little or no chance for the hapless defenders to react with anything but pathetically frantic and sporadic gunfire. Some of the low-flying Zeros seemed to almost scrape the ground as they buzzed the infuriated, terrified men on the field. Defenders could literally see the faces of the Japanese pilots and screamed tearful curses of rage at the men flying the red "meatball" or "flaming asshole" circle insignia emblazoned on the tormenting aircraft wings and fuselages.

At the first wailing of air raid sirens, men streamed from the mess halls and hangars only to look up and see gleaming bombs fishtailing downward toward them. Then the whole world began to reverberate and shake with the force of violent explosions splitting eardrums and rending men's bodies into grisly fragments. There were desperate attempts to fight back. Men dashed to sandbagged heavy machine gun positions and others tried to man the guns of grounded planes. Gunners, mostly of the 200th Coast Artillery (anti-aircraft) worked frantically to return fire. A large percentage of the antiaircraft ammunition misfired due to corroded fuses in shells manufactured most recently in 1932. One gunner observed later that only about one in every six shells fired even exploded.

American pilots who had survived the first onslaught raced to any planes still intact only to make suicidal attempts to get airborne from an airfield that was fast becoming nothing more than a mass of bomb craters. Amidst the terrifying avalanche of fire, three P-40s of the 20th Pursuit Squadron somehow struggled into the air, but five others were blasted by bombs as they attempted to taxi for takeoff. Five more met their fate under the savage strafing attack of Zeros. The pilots of the three rugged P-40s who did manage to get airborne at least got the small but sweet satisfaction of downing four of the enemy fighters.

Saburo Sakai made particular note of them in his recollections. "We still could not believe that the Americans did not have fighters in the air waiting for us. Finally, after several minutes of circling over the fields, I discovered five American fighters at about 15,000 feet, some 7,000 feet below our own altitude. At once we jettisoned our external drop fuel tanks, and all pilots armed their guns and cannon. The enemy planes, however, refused to attack and maintained their own altitude. It was a ridiculous affair, the American fighters flying around at 15,000 feet while we circled above them. Our orders precluded us from attacking, however, until the main bomber force arrived on the scene. At about noon, the twenty-seven bombers with their Zero escorts approached from the north and moved directly into their bombing runs. The attack was perfect. Long strings of bombs tumbled from the bays and dropped toward the targets the bombardiers had studied so long in reconnaissance photographs. Their accuracy was phenomenal! It was, in fact most accurate bombing I ever witnessed by our own planes throughout the war. The entire base seemed to be rising into the air with the explosions. Pieces of aircraft, hangars and other ground installations scattered wildly. Great fires erupted and smoke boiled upward.

"Their missions accomplished, the bombers wheeled homeward. We remained as escort for another ten minutes, then returned to Clark Field. The American base was a shambles, flaming and smoking. We circled down to 13,000 feet and, still with no enemy opposition, received orders to carry out strafing attacks.

"With my two wingmen tied to me as if by invisible lines, I pushed the stick forward and dived at a steep angle for the ground. I selected two undamaged B17s on the runway for our targets, and all three planes poured a fusillade of bullets into the big bombers. We flashed low over the ground and climbed steeply on the pullout. Five fighters jumped us. They were the first American planes I had ever encountered. [These were a flight of fighters of the 17th Pursuit Squadron up from Nichols led by Lt. John Posten.] I jerked the stick, slammed rudder and spiraled sharply to the left, then yanked back the stick for a sudden climb. The maneuver threw the enemy attack off, and all five P-40s abruptly rolled back and scattered. Four of the planes arced up and over into the thick columns of black smoke boiling up over the field and were gone. The fifth plane spiraled to the left—a mistake. Had he remained with his own group he could have escaped within the thick smoke. Immediately I swung up and approached the P-40 from below; the American half rolled and began a high loop. At 200 yards the plane's belly moved into my sights. I rammed the throttle forward and closed the distance to fifty yards as the P-40 tried desperately to turn away. He was as good as finished, and a short burst of my guns and cannon walked into the cockpit, blowing the canopy off the plane. The fighter seemed to stagger in the air, then fell off and dived into the ground. That was my third kill—the first American plane to be shot down in the Philippines.

"I saw no other fighters after that, but other Zero pilots caught a group of planes in the air. Later that night back in Tainan, our claims were for nine planes shot down, four probably destroyed in the air and thirty-five destroyed on the ground."

Raw, spontaneous courage and selfless acts of bravery were more than commonplace among those on the ground at the receiving end of the awful aerial assault. They literally became the order of the day. At the first stunning impact of the huge explosions erupting in their midst, men were first stupefied and disbelieving, then leaping into action amidst the scene of destruction and horror. In the mess halls, supply buildings, and hangars, huge shards of glass became flying razors inflicting unbelievable wounds. Airman Harold Feiner recalled that a man working next to him arming machine gun ammunition into the wing of a P-40 was literally decapitated by a huge fragment of glass from one of the big hangar door windows, covering him and others around them in blood. In a melee of frenzied reaction, men were running, stumbling, and tripping in their rush to get to battle stations and man every weapon that would shoot. Some even climbed into wrecked bombers and frantically worked the retractor handles of .30- and .50-caliber machine guns, which could still be aimed upward and fired. Others dashed to assist fallen wounded in an effort to get them to medical help. Fire and dense dark smoke was everywhere, roaring and crackling like some live wild beast, spreading to anything that would burn—rubber, trees, the tall cogon grass around the edges of the fields and runways and buildings. It was a scene out of hell and there was no letup as the strafing and bombing Zeros swooped in again and again to complete what the high-level bombers had begun. The deadly thoroughness and methodical precision of these strafing attacks were borne out in painful detail by American ground crews later surveying the damage. The angles and patterns of the bullet holes and shell damage indicated clearly that the Japanese had almost surgically directed their runs in evident crisscross and checker pattern attacks to achieve maximum impact saturation. Little was left that would be of any use to the defenders, including especially the taxi and takeoff runway strips. This careful precision was not reserved just for Clark Field but was repeated again and again at all of USAFFE's air bases, regardless of how small. For all practical purposes, American and Philippine airpower had been methodically and thoroughly blasted out of existence, and official Allied reports made no effort to belittle the accuracy and effectiveness of the Japanese air assaults, differing only on air-to-air combat.

Official Japanese records show that five Zeros were missing after the operations. One was reported shot down by ground fire and four others crashed from battle damage while returning to base. Sakai insisted that no Zero was shot down by American fighters, but the American side of the story disagrees, claiming at least two Zeros were shot down in air combat over Clark by a P-40 piloted by Lt. Randall Keator. At Clark Field, over which Sakai and his group attacked, four P-40B Tomahawks got into the air to intercept the attackers. This report contradicts Japanese claims that American fighters circled at fifteen thousand feet without engaging, and the conflicting versions have never been reconciled.

American reports differed from those of the enemy. At Iba Field a group of P-40E Kittyhawks (a P-40 version with more engine power and six .50-caliber machine guns, which was a major improvement over the older P-40B Tomahawks) of the 3rd Pursuit Squadron were just swinging into their landing patterns when the first Japanese struck. The American pilots were low on fuel, angry and frustrated that they had been unable to close with the Japanese. At that moment Japanese attention focused on Iba, and the American fighters were caught in a maelstrom of explosions. The P-40E pilots reacted instantly, slamming open their throttles and climbing in desperation to turn into the attackers, but before they could gain sufficient speed or altitude the Zeros swarmed all over them. Lt. Jack Donaldson surprised the Japanese pilots by swinging about sharply and driving all out after two Zeros, damaging both heavily. Japanese reports indicated this was the sum of retaliation. Before the one-sided fight ended, with Donaldson's aggressive reaction providing the only real resistance, five P-40Es were shot out of the sky and three other Kittyhawks were forced to crash land.

At Del Carmen, its old P-35 fighters scrambled and gained height advantage just in time before drawing attention from the attacking Zeros. The dauntless pilots dived their pitifully old fighters into the midst of a large Zero formation. With "ridiculous ease" the Zeros turned and with blinding speed scattered the P-35s. To the consternation of the Japanese pilots the old P-35s recovered and snarled back into the fight. What the Americans lacked in performance from their outmoded planes, they made up in killer instinct. Their furious reaction disrupted what had been the smooth rhythm of the attack by confident Japanese pilots. The attackers recovered quickly though and set about shooting the P-35s to ribbons, but by some charmed miracle, none of the Seversky fighters were shot out of the sky, although several landed as "flying wrecks." Their valiant resistance, however, resulted in much reduced devastation of their home base, Del Carmen.

Nevertheless, Japanese radio reports flooded message centers with accounts of Japanese successes. One Japanese staff communicator, Masatake Okumiya, recorded ecstatically that "our exuberance rose steadily as an unending stream of messages described courageous and amazing victories won by our naval air units. My apprehension faded with the increasing number of reported victories. Incredibly, the first five hours of war were totally in our favor." And so they were, and continued to be, with the Japanese using the Zero with devastating effectiveness. Pilots of the few remaining, intercepting P-40s did everything humanly possible to penetrate Japanese bomber formations only to have Zeros sweep in and frustrate their attempts with a virtual wall of cover for their bombers. By the evening of 10 December, the American fighter defense of the Philippines was decimated to near impotence. The interceptor command could count on a total of twenty-two P-40 and eight P-35 fighters for the entire Philippines, many of these barely fit to fly. Reaction at MacArthur's Manila headquarters was to order all fighter combat to cease immediately. The few remaining fighters would be used for reconnaissance only unless attacked.

One bright spark did emerge from those next days of desperate air combat in the person of Lt. Boyd "Buzz" Wagner, Del Carmen Field's CO now at Clark. In the week following 13 December, he was attacked while flying his P-40 on recon and a daring one-man ground attack mission far north on Luzon at Aparri, which the Japanese were now using as a forward base. Wagner shot down five Zeros to become the first American ace of the Second World War. Otherwise, however, the opening days of the Pacific war were a dismally one-sided show in favor of the Japanese. By 12 December, the Japanese enjoyed complete air supremacy over the Philippines.

The collateral damage to towns, villages, and barrios adjacent to the Allied military bases also took a heavy and particularly poignant toll among civilians, shopkeepers, and civilian service workers employed at the bases and by individual military personnel. American military quarters, long considered the most plush deal in American services around the world, suddenly became deprived of trustworthy and efficient housekeepers, *lavenderas* (laundresses and cleaning boys), and *amahs* (child nurses), who for pennies made American military life in the Philippines the envy of their comrades-in-arms everywhere. The work and purchasing power of the American servicemen also meant critical work and income for Filipinos on the lower end of the country's economic ladder. Around Clark were the bigger commercial towns of Dau (known well for its bars, many run by retired servicemen—the "sunshine Americans"—who had decided to settle in the Philippines with Filipino wives or mistresses, cheap hotels, and clip joints catering to the pursuit of a "good time" by enlisted men) and Angeles (where men could get good, cheap laundering and repairs of clothes and uniforms as well as various souvenirs and gifts for home).

The barrio of Sapangbhato (known to most Americans as "Sloppy Bottom"), like Angeles, was home to many families of Filipino troopers from Stotsenburg and wives and mistresses of American enlisted men. There was great concern among 26th Cavalry troopers about their families, many of whom had lived in the area for generations, when the attacks came. Stuck at Stots when the general alert was activated, they desperately sought news of their loved ones once the attacks started. Many lost relatives or had relatives hurt in the bombings, and these losses hit the regiment as hard as casualties in its ranks. Because of the closeness of the 26th members (many of its personnel were the sons and grandsons of 26th Cavalrymen dating back to the origins of the regiment), many borderline authorization exceptions were made so troopers could check on their nearby families. The effect on morale was a critical factor in keeping the 26th together at peak efficiency for the difficult times ahead.

The initial reaction from Washington to the disaster at Clark and the other bases, including the great, strategic naval yard of Cavite, was delayed in coming but explosive. Even though MacArthur had radioed that the tremendous losses had been "due to overwhelming superiority of enemy forces," Air Commander in Chief "Hap" Arnold felt some failure of command had taken place in the air forces under his jurisdiction and decided to put Brereton on the carpet, contacting him by transoceanic telephone. A shaken Brereton had just returned from his survey of the devastation at Clark only to receive a call from a furious General Arnold demanding an explanation why an experienced airman like himself could have been caught flatfooted with his planes on the ground. Afterward, Brereton, feeling that he had not given Arnold a sufficient explanation, promptly reported the conversation to MacArthur, asking his support in presenting his case to Arnold. As recorded in his diary, a shaken Brereton turned to his aides and told them that an irate MacArthur had chewed him out and told him "to go back and fight the war and not to worry about things beyond his station." His subsequent request to Sutherland to get Chief of Staff Gen. George Marshall on the phone was apparently fruitless, and no record of the conversation exists.

The fact remained, regardless of who was at fault, that the Japanese had successfully eliminated America's airpower in the Southern Pacific. Their main invasion of Luzon would now be virtually free of any interference from the skies.

NOTE

1. Debate among historians still continues over circumstances surrounding the failure to bomb Formosa in time. Some of these have literally stated in their arguments that the stubborn failure of MacArthur and his staff to heed Brereton's warnings and pleas to bomb Formosa would, in similar cases, be sufficient for calls for court-martial and/or dismissal.

3

The 26th Goes to War

6 DECEMBER 1941, PHILIPPINES TIME

Gen. Jonathan M. "Skinny" Wainwright had just returned from Clark Field, "sort of a continuation of Stotsenburg,"[1] where, on orders from MacArthur, he had met for several days with U.S. Air Force CO Maj. Gen. L. H. Brereton and Air Force Colonels Eubank and Emmett "Rosie" O'Donnell to assess precautions against sabotage and determine where the 26th Cavalry and other units at Stots would prove most useful in the event of attack. Wainwright, a seasoned veteran of the horse cavalry, had been assigned on 28 November by MacArthur as commander of all Northern Luzon forces, taking over from Brig. Gen. Edward P. King Jr. MacArthur, however, withheld some critical authority, keeping it under his direct command from Manila headquarters, not the least important aspect of this being the control of the U.S. Army's armored reserves in the Philippines, a factor that would later prove critically important, as well as frustrating, to Wainwright.

War appeared imminent, and tension was thick enough to be cut by a knife. However, MacArthur firmly believed that any war with the Japanese would not begin until April or May 1942, and he was very optimistic about the overall readiness of the forces at his command. What General Wainwright found in the course of his inspection tours painted a far different picture.

Wainwright had been scheduled to do a more extensive inspection of four scattered Philippine divisions in Northern Luzon under the command of Gen. Clifford Bluemel. These forces were badly undermanned, undertrained, and short of all types of ammunition and any means of communication. The men did not even have helmets aside from those made of coconuts. They had no antitank battalions whatsoever, and what artillery they did have (mostly British 75mm guns and 2.95-inch mountain howitzers) were obsolete and short of any means of transportation. To top it all off, the men were not only barely trained and undisciplined, they were led by extremely inexperienced Filipino officers. Wainwright would later remark that "the Philippine army units with the North Luzon force were doomed before they started to fight. That they lasted as long as they did is a stirring and touching tribute to their gallantry and fortitude. They never had a chance to win."

He readily concluded that the U.S. Army's Philippine Scout (PS) units were by far the best trained and prepared units at hand, especially the 26th Cavalry. Even so, he drew up rough plans to do the impossible—defend some six hundred miles of open coastline with untrained troops and understrength units.

The brightest spot in this dismal picture was the 26th Cavalry, which had been tirelessly training as though they were already at war. The regiment never moved without full packs, equipment, and wartime ammunition loads. Since an invasion was expected to come after dark, the 26th's night field problems were stiff and exacting. Training was first perfected in classrooms and then moved to the field where platoons competed vigorously against one another. Each exercise was followed by blistering critiques that spared no one, including the regimental commander, Colonel Pierce. Exercises were repeated to correct revealed weaknesses. Blank ammunition of all calibers helped accustom both men and horses to gunfire. Special attention was given to conditioning horses and mules to combat emergency movement. Horses were repeatedly loaded on and off trucks to accustom them to rapid mobile travel.

"I had been riding around on automobile cushions for about a week or so," recalled Wainwright, "and itched to get back in the saddle on my thoroughbred Little Boy. [Colonels] Eubank and O'Donnell had only recently arrived in the P.I. and leading a flight of thirty-five B-17s. We talked extensively about what a perilous flight it was in those days and difficulties of rapid reinforcement. But then, I had nothing to do with the air forces. They were commanded by Gen. Brereton who was directly responsible to MacArthur."

The 26th Cavalry Regiment PS was at that time somewhat scattered around Luzon. All were regular U.S. Army troops, being part of the twelve-thousand-man Philippine Scouts authorized by U.S. Congress in 1922 and composed of Filipino enlisted men led by American officers. The 26th's regular makeup consisted of two squadrons of three troops each, with a headquarters and headquarters service troop and a machine gun troop. All told, the regiment's nominal strength at the outbreak of World War II was 54 officers and 789 enlisted men, a grand total of 843 men. Most of the regiment was stationed at Fort Stotsenburg, with various units detached to other locations for various duties with other parts of U.S. and Philippine

military forces. Fort Stotsenburg itself was first established as a bivouac for
U.S. cavalry units chasing Filipino revolutionaries during the insurrection
in 1901. Stotsenburg was located mainly in the province of Pampanga on
the mountainous island of Luzon and was situated along the eastern foothills of the Zambales Mountains, a chain of peaks ranging from six thousand to ten thousand feet, running some 150 miles from its beginnings and
rising from the area of Lingayen Gulf and continuing in a southeasterly
direction to Mariveles on the Bataan Peninsula, where it ends in Manila
Bay. The military reservation roughly forms the western boundary of
Luzon's central plain and divides the narrow coastal province of Zambales,
shoring on the China Sea, from the central provinces of Tarlac, Pangasinan,
Pampanga, and the northernmost part of the Bataan Peninsula. Over
156,000 acres in area, the reservation juts northward deep into the province of Tarlac and east some fifteen miles to the village of Dao near the
large town of Angeles, Pampanga. In 1941 the layout of Stotsenburg's main
compound (which stayed nearly the same until the eruption of Mt. Pinatubo on 2 April 1991 and has subsequently been lovingly restored) was
roughly a simple rectangle built around the main parade ground (or quad),
which doubled as the polo field for the cavalry. The HQ building for the
regiments stationed there was located at one end a few hundred yards
across the quadrangle from the officers' club midway along a road bordering the south side of the quad. The west half of the quad, with the flagstaff
in front of post headquarters, was used for ceremonies and parades, while
the east half was used as a training ground and the polo field. All along the
south side, facing the polo field, were the barracks and orderly rooms, each
with its own tack rooms, stables, and blacksmith shops about two hundred
yards in the rear. All along the north border of the quad was a long row of
houses and bungalows comfortably shaded under big acacia trees, amlangs,
and mimosas. These were the quarters for officers, bachelors as well as
those who were married, and their families. In 1937 the United States
began to construct its major air bases in the Philippines. The largest of
these, Clark Field, was finished in 1938, sited as a relatively smaller but
critical appendage on the eastern edge of the big main installation. The
other major bases were Nichols (just south of Manila), Iba on the west
coast, Nielson (Brereton's HQ at the outset of war), Del Monte (on Mindanao), and Del Carmen (a fighter base near Clark). Other smaller auxiliary
fields were scattered around the islands for emergency purposes.

"On the afternoon of December 6, I held an inspection of the Stotsenburg contingent of the 26th Cavalry, A Battery of the 23rd Field Artillery
Philippine Scouts, and one pack train on the thousand-yard long parade
ground at Stotsenburg," recalled Wainwright in his biographical papers.
"They were the extent of my available units at the fort. Other units, including National Guard tanks were still under direct control of MacArthur's HQ

in Manila. I turned in about eleven o'clock that Saturday night and later on had many occasions to remember that I got a good night's sleep. It was the last decent sleep I was to have for three years and eight months."

On Sunday, Wainwright worked on plans to finish his inspections and that afternoon refereed a regimental polo game. Edwin Ramsey, from Wichita, Kansas, twenty-four years old and then a lieutenant in G Troop who played on his favorite horse, Bryn Awryn, would recall, "That day we were to play the first game of the season against Manila Polo Club on our grounds. The Fort Stotsenburg team was made up of two of us from the 26th and two from the tank battalions who had formerly been National Guard horse cavalrymen and were experienced players. To make it short, we got our tails beat off by the team from Manila who had been playing together for a long time. Regimental commander Col. Clint Pierce threw a big party anyway, cocktails and a cookout at his quarters and General Wainwright who had umpired partied as hard as any of us."

During the course of the dinner, the main topic of conversation leaned toward talk of the old cavalry days. In one particularly ironic exchange, they made joking fun about a local paper's latest weekly movie review. It was about a new Errol Flynn film about Custer's Last Stand entitled *They Died with Their Boots On.*

After leaving the party Wainwright and Pierce on horseback made a final inspection of some 26th elements and its pack train. Wainwright then went to bed at about 11 p.m., only to be awakened with a severe headache at 4:35 a.m. the following day, Monday, 8 December, by the phone in the next room. It was then only 7:35 a.m. Sunday, 7 December, in Pearl Harbor. He instantly sensed it was bad news. The caller was Col. Pete Irwin, MacArthur's assistant chief of staff for operations.

"Admiral Hart [whose Asiatic Fleet lay in Manila Bay] just received a radio message from Admiral Kimmel at Pearl Harbor informing him that Japan has initiated hostilities!"

Starting to dress with one hand and jiggling the phone with his other, Wainwright called his aide Johnny Pugh. "Johnny!"

"Hello," a sleepy voice replied. "Yes, General?"

"The cat has jumped."

FIRST BLOODING OF THE 26TH

As soon as Wainwright heard that Hickam Field in Hawaii had been bombed, he called Clark Field, but they had already been informed. At about dawn Pugh arrived at Wainwright's quarters and was given an urgent list of desperately needed ammunition and equipment and told to rush it to Manila HQ. He was also ordered, "While you're down there find Tom

Dooley [another able officer from the 26th who was Wainwright's junior aide] and send him back here at once." Dooley was in Manila saying good-bye to a pretty English girl who was sailing for Australia.

Shortly after 9 a.m. MacArthur's HQ communicated that Baguio, ninety-five miles above Stots, had been bombed. Now, MacArthur's HQ warned Wainwright to take every precaution against a possible Japanese paratroop landing at Clark and the surrounding area. Wainwright immediately deployed Col. Clinton Pierce's 26th Cavalry to the north and east of the field. Having no infantry available, he put his little pack artillery battery at the west end of the fort's parade ground and instructed the gunners to set their fuses to zero and load with shrapnel so they would be able to rake the area if necessary. After using the public phone system to issue necessary orders to his field commanders, he left his office and went over to his quarters to direct boxing and storing of some personal effects and start packing his field equipment. By 12:30 he walked out on his porch headed for his headquarters.

Suddenly the roar of a flight of approaching planes drummed in his ears. He ran down on the lawn just as the attackers thundered over the backdrop of the Zambales Mountains, about eighty of them, including mainly bomb-ers but accompanied by dive bombers and fighters. The ground shook as they swept over Stotsenburg on their way to loose hell on Clark Field. The very air rattled with the awful concussion of the explosions. Wainwright's Filipino house boy, Felemon San Pedro, terrified, ran wide-eyed from the house. In his frenzy, he had jammed on Wainwright's helmet.

"Mother of God, General, what shall I do?" he shouted.

"Well, don't just stand there, man! Go get me a bottle of beer," Wain-wright yelled irritably. ("I seemed to bring the boy out of shock," Wain-wright recalled, "and it seemed to help him. Anyway, I damn sure know the beer helped me!")

Finishing his beer, the general strode over to his headquarters, which was quite close to the No. 1 gun of the battery protecting the parade grounds. He went over and stood near it, watching the futile black bursts of their hastily makeshift antiaircraft fire trying to follow the Jap bombers. Sud-denly he heard the moist impact of metal against flesh and bone, and turn-ing, he saw one of the gun crew falling near him. His face was a bloody pulp. A bomb splinter had streaked all the way over from Clark, about twelve hundred yards away, and hit him in the lower forehead just below his helmet. Capt. Alva Fitch, the pack battery commander, and Wainwright immediately leaned over the young Filipino trooper and saw that his face was severely lacerated. "Get this man to a doctor," ordered Wainwright.

Fitch and another trooper put their hands under the boy's head, but he stirred, opened his eyes, and wiped a dirty hand across his face. "No!" he said sharply. "Have to stay by my gun . . . stay by my gun!"

Just then, Tom Dooley drove up with brakes screeching from the direction of Clark and jumped out of the car. "Tom," demanded Wainwright angrily, "you damned fool, did you drive through Clark in this bombing? If I didn't need you, I'd bust you to private."

"Yes, sir," Dooley answered, "you sent me orders to report to you as fast as I could, and I was a damned sight worse afraid of you than Jap bombs!"

Wainwright stalked inside his HQ with Dooley on his heels and promptly wrote out orders that gave Dooley and the young gunner Silver Stars, most probably the first decorations awarded in the Pacific war, knowing all the time that his people were in a war for which they were no more prepared to fight than a child against a seasoned, professional pugilist, short on everything but raw courage.

As for the expected enemy paratroops, the only parachutists captured by 26th troopers that day were a half dozen American airmen who had bailed out of a disabled B-17. Twenty-sixth Cavalrymen who crashed through thickets in a valley east of Clark efficiently rounded them up at some considerable risk to the frightened, bewildered fliers.

Confusion and chaos reigned at Stotsenburg for the better part of two days as unhindered Japanese Zeros returned again and again to inflict deadly strafing attacks and low-level bombing. Amazingly, the long row of officers' houses under the spreading shade of big acacia trees facing the big, open parade ground was virtually untouched. On the opposite side of the field, the troop and stable areas were less fortunate, and during these initial assaults, the 26th Cavalry suffered its first casualties.

At 9 a.m. on 8 December, A Troop was in bivouac fifteen miles north of Stots, having arrived soon after daylight. On arrival, horses had been groomed and equipment cleaned at a leisurely pace. After breakfast all but picket-line guards were resting. Lt. Arthur K. Whitehead was dozing off when a car drove up and skidded to a stop. There was some sudden rushing around and a babble of excited voices.

The troop commander and a newly arrived officer from regiment were talking excitedly out of hearing to most present. Then the troop was assembled. Capt. Jack Kramer made the announcement that the United States had declared a state of war with Japan, and went on to give the news of Pearl Harbor. The news was no real surprise. It had been expected for months, but the reality of it was hard to accept. The general orders were that the regiment was to join up in the Bamban River Valley after dark, or before if enemy planes were not overhead. The rest of the 26th had left Stotsenburg at dawn.

Guns were loaded, WWI-style steel helmets covered with mud, and air scouts were posted. All tents and vehicles were camouflaged and horses were dispersed in ground depressions. Light machine guns were set up on the hilltops surrounding the troop position with riflemen surrounding them as air scouts.

Japanese planes were observed flying overhead toward Clark, and the heavy *whump* of exploding bombs and the rattle of heavy machine gun fire told the story of the debacle that was taking place. Clouds of black smoke were rising over Clark, and the realization that this was war began to take hold. Knowledge that Americans and Filipinos, some who were friends, even relatives, were dying down there in that violent maelstrom hit hard with the men of the 26th watching it from vantage points where they were dispersed in the hills. When the bombers passed over on their return home, the men looked up to see smaller dots doing what appeared to be wild acrobatics above the pall of smoke. Three of these became more visible as they maneuvered north toward the troop areas. The lead plane was of a different silhouette than those following. Shortly it could be discerned that the fighter in front was a P-40 and its followers were Zeros. Suddenly the P-40 stopped its evasive movements and seemed to go dead in the air, trailing smoke. The unrelenting Zeros kept machine-gunning the American plane until it crashed into a nearby hill. Warnings came repeatedly from observation posts as low-flying Zeros were sighted flying north over the area causing a scramble for cover by troopers and their horses. Yet the horses behaved with admirable calm in the terrible din while they and the troopers huddled in mango groves as shrapnel from bombs and antiaircraft fire rattled through the tree branches and to the ground all around them.

At about 3 p.m. word came down the line to saddle up. The commanding officers wanted to get on the march back to Stotsenburg before dark. The route took them by way of the highway from Tarlac to Mabalakat, a paved road bordered by dirt shoulders. Beyond the shoulders were deep ditches or barbed-wire fences, literally impossible to get a horse out of once in, so dispersion along the road was a necessity. Air alerts en route slowed the pace repeatedly, and being so exposed was nerve wracking. It was certain that they were seen by the enemy, but that day, however, horses were apparently not on the Zero pilots' menu, and the column got to the Bamban River crossing safely. Horses were then widely dispersed along the stream and watered. At dusk they turned off the highway at Mabalakat and took the back road leading to Stotsenburg. Along the sides of the road groups of heavy-ordnance personnel and their equipment were dispersed under cover of thick tree growth. They looked frightened and bewildered, many of them fresh from the States.

Farther along the troopers passed 90mm antiaircraft guns in sandbagged dugouts. Seeing these troops in helmets, carrying gas masks and fully armed with live ammunition was a change. Their vehicles were camouflaged and newly dug foxholes pitted the area. There were none of the usual wisecracks about horse cavalry, who were routinely dressed ready for combat and used to it. Now there were only looks of worry and concern. The shock of the Clark raids was getting to everyone. The cavalrymen, comfortable now back in the saddle, were in far better spirits.

As the horsemen neared the fort, they veered off the road to the north and passed down into the Bamban Valley and up the river past the bivouac area they had first been ordered into that morning. At around 8 p.m. they filtered on to the Bamban sector of the Stotsenburg grounds. The horses were simply unsaddled and fed a bag of oats. Most of the men fell asleep in their ponchos and raincoats before getting supper. The more vulnerable kitchen trucks had delayed coming in until after dark.

The Bamban River Valley on the north side of Stots was a broad, deep gulch, as much as three miles wide in places with high banks. The rocky bottom was covered largely by thick, low scrub brush and broad patches of tall, old-growth tropical trees of varied kinds, all offering good concealment.

The next morning a large number of men from the 26th ventured back onto Stotsenburg proper to check on the stable areas and gather up bits of equipment that might be useful later on. They weren't entirely clear on the best protective procedures in the event of such an attack of deadly strafing, but from what they heard from miserable, disheveled survivors of the Clark raid, many who had come over to take refuge at Stots, the potency of the Jap air force had earned a high degree of respect and apprehension from all who had been on the receiving end of its savagery. Stots had been bombed and strafed the previous day, but the damage was nothing compared to that described at Clark. The precision had been amazing, even to the extent that decoy dummy aircraft and vehicles had been ignored, indicating some very efficient intelligence work by the Japanese.

By afternoon, the general consensus was that all precautions possible had been taken against surprise air attacks. Positioned in the valley made the regiment vulnerable to being caught unawares, so orders were to remain motionless any time enemy planes were overhead. Horses were watered and men were fed at the mess trucks and then returned to their positions of cover. Responsibility lay heavy on squad leaders to know the exact whereabouts of their men and platoon sergeants around the clock. The regiment was still minus two troops. Capt. Johnny Fowler's G Troop—with junior officers Cliff Hardwicke, Lt. Carol Calhoon, and Lt. Ed Ramsey—was still in northeast Luzon on the coast at Baler and Dingalen Bay areas. They had been assigned by 2nd Squadron CO Capt. Jim Blanning to be sent by truck and scout car on reconnaissance and possible combat patrols against fast, southward-advancing Japanese spearheads. The Japanese were encountering little resistance from the pathetically unprepared Philippine army units in their path after coordinated initial landings on North Luzon at Aparri and Gonzaga by the Tanaka detachment on 10 December under air cover by planes flying from a newly captured airfield (which had been taken 8 December on the little island of Batan).

Trapnell's F Troop had still not rejoined the regiment from its largely ceremonial "palace guard" duty in Manila, but they were on the way to do so by grueling, forced march since they were released and ordered on 10 December, almost immediately after hostilities had begun. At noon that same day, the huge naval facilities at Cavite were bombed by a formation of fifty-four heavy bombers. One submarine was destroyed at the docks, and destruction of docking facilities, ammunition dumps, rearming facilities, and harbor channels rendered Cavite almost useless as a base of naval operations. Nine bombers turned from the formation and took a heading over the heart of the city of Manila flying in the direction of the main port area and the inner harbor. They had evidently spotted the big transport *Mareschal Joffre* anchored there, which, from its peculiar superstructure, resembled a carrier or large warship. The bombing missed the French ship but sunk several other smaller vessels anchored nearby. The planes then rejoined the main formation to continue the attack on Cavite and then move on to bomb and strafe Nielson Field. That day, Maj. Gen. Lewis C. Brereton had moved the USAFFE headquarters south to Del Monte on the island of Mindanao to relative safety.

On that morning of 10 December, shaken and exhausted air corps personnel from Clark were eating at the 26th Cavalry mess. Many had not had a meal since the 8th and most had no idea where their units were. Staff was obsessed with the threat of paratroop landings, and these stragglers were armed with rifles and dispersed around Clark to meet any such attack. The Philippine division (Philippine Army) was ordered that day to move to the vicinity of Mt. Arayat to counter a reported enemy paratroop landing and to reduce all hostile activity in that area. They were then to occupy at once a position in the general vicinity of Layac Junction, from which it would cover withdrawal of troops to the Bataan Peninsula. This was the first overt order indicating staff's long-range plans to put into effect the War Plan Orange strategy calling for an overall concentration of all forces for a delaying defense on Bataan until expected reinforcements from the United States and Australia would arrive to alleviate the situation. The Philippine division was also to resist any hostile landings in the vicinity of Subic Bay with its big, vital naval installations and to prevent enemy advance from that direction, including extending beach defenses from Bagac to Aglaloma Bay. The 26th was ordered into positions in the hills northeast of Clark and along the north edges of the runways to break up any such attacking formations. They were supported by the regiment's machine gun troops, most already in good, prepared positions. By dark, no paratroopers had shown, but the men had a good chance to observe the destruction at Clark. Pretty

much everything had been burned to charred rubble, and anything standing was so shot up it looked like a sieve.

Just before dark, the 26th 1st Squadron, reinforced with some of the
newly arrived 75mm guns mounted on half-tracks, did a thorough search
east of Stots and Clark, again looking for any signs of paratroops. Again
none were found. The same was the case that night on patrol through the
town of Dau. By now the conclusion had been reached that any suspect
parachutists seen in the past two days were not paratroops but Allied airmen bailing out of crippled planes. Going through Dau, the patrols passed
some big 155mm "Long Toms" on their way out to various defensive desti-
nations from where they had been stationed at Stots. The next morning the
Japanese were at it again, their bombers passing over at 10,000–15,000 feet,
safely out of range of American antiaircraft. With next to no defending aircraft left to fly, the enemy pretty much had it his way and could pick targets
at will. However, low-flying, strafing Zeros were receiving fire from machine
gun positions, and rounds could be seen ricocheting off their sides. The
Japanese also appeared to be taking aerial photographs of new defensive
positions, but their air superiority, though a constant concern, was something the defenders were learning to cope with out of necessity. In the afternoon of 11 December, the 26th left Bamban, moving to new positions in
the woods near Taconda Hill about a mile and a half south of Stots. Here
the men dug slit trenches and foxholes, many of which had sides reinforced
with the trunks of banana trees, whose pithy nature had a welcome ability
to slow a bullet or shrapnel. Air alert and noise discipline was a permanent
state now, and troopers kept a constant awareness of where all the protective holes were. The only protection from strafing was to scramble as fast as
possible into the nearest deep hole or depression. The only protection for
the horses was to have them well disbursed and tied in a river bed or some
other depression well covered with foliage from above. It was the dry season, so sleeping on the ground was fairly comfortable.

White mosquito netting bars were routinely dipped in coffee to make
them less conspicuous when spread over bed rolls and men. There were
regular forays back to Fort Stotsenburg's main center to get necessities from
barracks, officers' quarters (most of which were untouched), and the
crowded post exchange, which was still operating for men needing odds
and ends and wanting to get radiograms out to families.

On the morning of the 12th, there was an officers' call held in the headquarters building at the west end of the parade ground. The appearance of
the post was considerably altered. Foxholes and slit trenches had been dug
everywhere, and machine guns with scouts manning them were in advantageous locations for antiaircraft fire. Near the post HQ a battery of mortars
was in position. Two Jap pilots shot down in the first days were brought in
that morning. They were tough-looking characters with bristly, black mus-

taches and close-cropped hair. Rumors were abundant. It was said a German pilot had been downed and taken in a nearby barrio, and it was rumored that the tough (and often bloodthirsty) little *negritos* of King Tomas's tribe (none of whom could speak any language but Tagalog, the primary dialect of the Philippines) had taken two more Jap pilots up in the Zambales Mountains and their heads presented to the post commander stuck on spears. Confirmation of these events was elusive, but the reputation of the ferocity of the *negritos,* all sympathetic to the Americans, was well-established fact.

Also on 12 December enemy transports with naval escort offshore in the vicinity of Legaspi, Bicol Peninsula, started landing operations with a force estimated as a reinforced brigade. At 6 a.m. Nichols Field was bombed heavily. Fort Wint, near Subic Bay, and the city of Olongapo were also bombed.

By midmorning, officers of the 1st Squadron were assembled on the porch of the HQ building of the 26th. The meeting had no sooner started when the *crump!* of explosions could be heard from the direction of Clark. The sound of approaching heavy motors grew louder, and there was little doubt now that Jap bombers were headed for Stots. The meeting ended abruptly and men headed for cover. The bombers came in slowly and low enough that bombs could still be seen in the open racks, then being released and fishtailing toward the men on the ground. Clark Field had had another thorough working over, and now Stotsenburg was the center of attention. This time, the impact was not to be light, and the 26th stables and barracks were prime target areas. A stick of bombs landed in the regimental HQ area, taking out an antiaircraft emplacement and blowing its crew to shreds. HQ and its motor pool were hit hard this time, and some jeeps were hit squarely and obliterated along with the rear of the building. Two of the barracks and two stables were torn apart. Horses of the regiment that had remained on post were mostly gathered in the hard-hit machine gun troop stables, where a single bomb killed twelve of them outright. Arthur Whitehead was brokenhearted to find out that the beautiful little chestnut thoroughbred mare he had picked out on arrival in the Philippines and developed into a first-class mount was one of the casualties, along with twelve others. Whitehead's personal car, parked behind the stable, was also destroyed. The wounded horses were a heartrending sight. One with part of his lungs exposed by shrapnel was standing, legs spread wide apart, wild eyed and gasping for breath. Next to him stood a dazed gelding hit in the flank, intestines exposed and a hind leg broken.

The stable sergeant, with tears in his eyes, seemed paralyzed by the pitiful sight of the first horses he had ever seen wounded. He had his .45 out and was shakily preparing to put the animals out of their misery when the sympathetic regimental veterinarian came upon the scene. "Here, let me do that," he said, looking sadly at the pair. "You have other things to tend to, Sergeant." Hatred for the Japanese and their sudden butchery welled up in him as he carried out the grim, pathetic task.

About this time, the 26th HQ got word to detach some of the regiment's scout cars to relieve an overwhelmed Philippine army division fighting in the Cagayan Valley region in Northern Luzon, seriously weakening the regimental strength even further. On the afternoon of 12 December the regiment was ordered to a forest midway between Fort Stotsenburg and Angeles to the north. This necessitated crossing a considerable stretch of open ground, and all indications now pointed to unwelcome attention being given the cavalry by Japanese air reconnaissance. The open area was several miles long and was to be crossed one troop at a time. Speed, dispersion, and knowledge would be crucial now—once a Zero began its dive to make a strafing pass, a man on horseback had to keep alert enough to gallop clear of the strike area. Moving fast and well spread out, the troops made the crossing without loss even though several strafing passes had been made by single Zeros. Had they attacked in pairs, the outcome might have been different. The regiment then stayed in the woods between Stotsenburg and Angeles for a couple of days. Fire discipline became a real concern. Rifles and pistols had been routinely carried locked and loaded for days, and occasionally a trooper would accidentally discharge a weapon. Awareness of loaded weapons had to be constantly cautioned by officers and noncoms to the now severely fatigued troopers.

Just before leaving Stotsenburg's Target Hill area (where most of the rifle and machine gun ranges were located) 1st Lt. William Liesenring was sent to HQ Northern Luzon Forces (NLF) to relieve Capt. Paul Jones, who resumed duties with the regiment as communications officer. When Jones rejoined the regiment in Pampanga, he brought news that the Japanese had made another landing in the north, this time at Vigan, and in strength. He also informed Colonel Pierce that Wainwright was moving his HQ to Bamban, a small sugar refining town several miles north of Fort Stotsenburg on the main Manila road north. He added the welcome information that Capt. Alva R. Fitch was to be attached the next day to the 26th Regiment with his Battery A, 23rd Field Artillery, a pack artillery unit, horse and mule drawn, of 75mm field guns. This was a welcome boost to the regiment's commanders, whose heaviest weapons consisted of .50-caliber machine guns and grenades.

The constant bombing and strafing were being accepted relatively, if not stoically tolerated, as unwelcome routine by most, but there was an overwhelming urge to fire back at planes. This impulse was sternly squelched by officers and noncoms, who, frequently with a swift kick to the hindquarters, reminded troopers that such duck shooting activity would have little effect other than dangerous revealing by muzzle flashes of the regiment's concealed position. Gradually, trigger fingers relaxed as men got used to living around the clock with fully loaded weapons that fire discipline prevented them from discharging. For the first time in five days nervous jitters began to gradually give in to fatigue, and one by one troopers dozed fitfully in the darkening shadows of the thick canopy of trees. All were either in or near a hole or slit trench. It had become reflex.

Older Filipino troopers—like 2d Squadron Sgt. Maj. Eliseo Mallari, Cpl. Pedro Abad (the oldest corporal in the regiment; his minor infractions seemed to be an addiction, which kept his stripes down to two), 1st Sgt. Justin Bulawan, and others—turned their thoughts in emotional concern to their families still in the villages and barrios near the areas most targeted by the Japanese bombings. Tomorrow would be Sunday, and most of the troopers, almost all deeply religious and devout Catholics, crossed themselves with such worried thoughts in their poor, tired, and battered minds.

The regiment remained in the forest until the evening of Sunday, 14 December. Fortunately, the skies had clouded up again, and there was some respite from the ceaseless threat of Japanese aircraft. Even though the men were on alert the entire time, saddles were stripped and horses' backs and legs were lovingly sponge bathed and rubbed, hooves were checked and feet picked and cleaned. Animal and man meant life to one another.

The men ate field rations from saddlebags, and horses were fed from the grain bags carried on every trooper's saddle. There were some edible grasses in the area, but in general, forage was pitifully scarce.

On that Sunday afternoon, welcome orders had crackled in on the duty HQ scout car radio from Wainwright's new location. The 26th was now to move up to Bamban and go into bivouac there as force reserve. The word was quickly passed to pack gear and saddle up. At dusk, under the cover of darkness, the regiment fell into column and began the move north toward Angeles. As they moved out of the forest toward the main road, the scout cars led off, their engines growling in low gear as if attempting to whisper. As they gained distance, all became silence except for the swish of tall, rough cogon grass brushing on the men's legs and along horses' sides and the muffled crunch of hooves breaking grass and hard dirt underfoot. This was punctuated occasionally by a hoof striking a stone in the dirt and the faint jingle of bridles' curb chains and soft clinking of gear. Even this was swallowed in the perpetual hum of cicadas and other night insects. The night sounds seemed to whisper reassuringly to the horsemen that the dogs of war were sleeping. Then the sounds of hooves clopping on solid surface indicated that they had reached the macadam highway that led north from Manila. As the column approached the town of Angeles on the outskirts of Clark Field, they were joined by Alva Fitch and his battery of pack artillery. Led by officers and noncoms on horses, the artillery column was chiefly made up of heavily laden mules led by scout artillery men on foot. Each 75mm cannon was broken down into three main groupings—the wheels and carriage, the block and trails of the gun, and the breech and recoil mechanisms. Ammunition was packed separately. Each of these loads was carried by one mule rigged with a special oversized version of the Phillips cargo pack used routinely by cavalry supply animals. At best, it was a cumbersome load for the mules, and their rate of march was much slower than the main 26th column. The slowing down of the march by Fitch's heavily loaded unit was perceptible to all in the regiment and largely worrisome to troopers used to the relatively free swinging movement of light horse cavalry.

They reached the buildings on the northern edge of Angeles, usually a bustling and boisterous town this time of night. But this night Angeles loomed dark and quiet before them. It seemed as if war had transformed it into a ghost town. Only the clattering of horses' hooves echoing through the empty streets marked their passing, and many a 26th trooper's mind dwelled on the whereabouts and condition of his family and friends nearby and in the barrio Sapangbhato. Sad little Christmas lanterns glimmered forlornly in some of the windows of the houses. After all, the holiest and happiest of seasons was beginning.

Once out of town, the column picked up the pace, and the 26th broke into a trot. The change in rhythm helped break the depressing reverie and homesick musings. Minds turned once again to the business at hand. Now just monotony and fatigue began to settle in to saddle-weary bodies. The column now turned north on Highway 3 toward the town of Bamban, another twenty-five miles away.

The weary, drowsy column of cavalry and artillery men finally arrived at Bamban at about 1 a.m. on Monday, 15 December. There they set up encampment and picket lines for the horses west of town several hundred yards north of the Sugar Central refinery, where General Wainwright had set up his new NLF headquarters. The troopers riding point for the column found a regimental staff headquarters motorcycle parked by the road with Cpl. Eulalio Arzaga nearby motioning them toward the assigned regimental bivouac area with a handkerchief-covered flashlight. Colonel Pierce and his executive major, Lee Vance, stood by the communications scout car and supervised the dispersal of the regiment. The area was composed mostly of bamboo groves interspersed with cogon grass, scrub thickets, and occasional acacias and amlang trees with their huge spreading surface roots. While the troop commanders reported to regimental HQ, the junior officers and noncoms supervised as horses were stripped of gear and rubbed down and picket lines were set up. That done, the weary men immediately broke out entrenching tools and began burrowing into their new positions, and exhausted, unlucky sentries were posted. Men still had to hike back and forth to the nearest wells in the area with collapsible canvas buckets and water each horse individually. They then gave each a small amount of grain. It was almost 3 a.m. before the tired regiment was able to close out their long day. While the cavalry was getting settled in, the sounds of more horses and mules came from the direction of the road. Fitch's trailing, exhausted pack artillery unit had finally caught up and were greeted by Pierce and Vance, who directed them to their positions. Pierce told Fitch, "When you get your people settled in, we'll go over and check in with Skinny." The artillery men were already unlimbering guns and caissons and unharnessing horses and mules. Pierce was thinking what welcome company Fitch's guns would be when things got serious on the ground in the days to come.

There in Bamban the 26th and the supporting units went into bivouac and remained for several days. It was a welcome break from the constant movement. Regimental headquarters were set up in a nipa shack at the edge of the highway. The troopers and horses were bivouacked farther to the rear in a coconut grove. Most of the residents of the barrio had taken to the hills, but often during the day they came down to visit and sell food and produce. There was a barber among them who stayed busy giving many troopers their last haircut for a long time—for some, their last. Some radios were available, and many listened to Manila reporting on air raids and various enemy landings in northern and southern Luzon. The reaction was in large part an eagerness to meet the Japanese head on and confidence that help from the United States would soon be on the way to relieve the situation.

General Wainwright's new headquarters was established with sparse accommodations nearby in the buildings of the Bamban Sugar Central Company. When MacArthur, almost as soon as War Plan Orange was put into effect, had bestowed the dubious distinction on the fifty-two-year-old veteran cavalryman Wainwright to become the acting commander in chief of operations on Northern Luzon with the daunting assignment to oversee a delaying action southward to protect MacArthur's main withdrawal of his forces on to the peninsula of Bataan, he had done the old soldier no favor. It was a crushing order.

The Philippine Scouts, principally the 26th Cavalry, were to be Wainwright's anchor for his holding action. The Philippine army divisions were crumbling and little else was available. Wainwright was ordered to put together a counterattack using the now seriously understrength 26th as his spearhead with a hodgepodge of undermanned and underequipped support. It was a formidable assignment that now hung Skinny Wainwright out on a thin limb.

About a half mile from where the 26th was setting up its bivouac that night, Wainwright and his red-eyed staff were agonizing over their maps, such as they were. The maps of Northern Luzon were woefully inadequate, of low quality, and often inaccurate. They were even supplemented by Texaco oil company road maps, frequently the only maps that many commanders on company, troop, and lower front-line unit levels were equipped with. It was an oversight that made an already difficult job border on the impossible. However, even with these poor maps, a frightening picture was emerging clearly. Literally unhindered, the Japanese were consolidating their grip on the northern end of Wainwright's turf. Col. William Brougher's understrength, inadequately trained 11th Division, Philippine army, whose responsibility was to defend all of Luzon north of Lingayen Gulf, was spread paper thin. In their defense area lay the vital Cagayan Valley, a fifty-mile slash of coastal plain along the Cagayan River cutting through the rugged, strategically impossible mountains on both sides—the Cordillera Central Mountains on the west and the Sierra Madres to the east—and running from the north coast to a point at which the two mountain chains join. The strategic Central Plain, farther south, runs from the Gulf of Lingayen on the west coast to Manila itself. MacArthur had long ago divined that the main Japanese invasion assault would strike at Lingayen. The preliminary northern landings on the 8th by the Tanaka detachment at Aparri and Gonzaga some twenty miles to the east and the Kanno detachment farther south on the west coast at Vigan on the 10th were now obviously strikes to divert Fil-American defenses north and tee up Lingayen for the main blow. MacArthur ordered immediate air strikes at the landings, his G-3 concluding (correctly) that the Japanese "most assuredly" were attempting to seize airfields, including the vitally strategic base at Tuguegarao in northeast Luzon, providing advance bases from which their fighters could support Formosa-based bombers ravaging Luzon. When Wainwright first heard of the landings, he believed them to be a feint to draw his main forces, the 11th and 21st Divisions, away from Lingayen Gulf and weaken his already weak defense forces in that area. He thus decided not to offer opposition to Tanaka since the only practical route south was down the Cagayan Valley. He also believed that a battalion at Balete Pass in its path could stop "a fairly considerable force." He concentrated the main of his forces at Lingayen, but he did take the precaution of sending several scout cars of the 26th Cavalry to the Cagayan Valley to provide communications with 11th Division troops in that area. MacArthur concurred, and Manila HQ issued orders to destroy bridges in the valley and block Balete Pass.

On 10 December, a company of the 3rd Battalion, 12th Infantry, located at Aparri was commanded by a young reserve officer, Lt. Alvin C. Hadley. When the two companies of the Tanaka detachment came ashore at dawn, Hadley reported the landing to battalion HQ at Tuguegarao and was ordered to attack immediately and drive the Japanese into the sea. Estimating the size of the landing force as considerably larger than it was, he chose to withdraw south along Route 5, apparently without firing a shot.

American air force reaction was another thing. As part of the Tanaka detachment was debarking at Gonzaga, two B-17s appeared overhead. They were from Clark Field with orders to attack and sink any and all Japanese naval vessels and transports. The first bomber, carrying eight six-hundred-pound bombs, attacked the transports, hitting one before being driven off by Zeros. The second B-17 was piloted by the now legendary Colin P. Kelly Jr., the first American war hero and recipient of the Distinguished Service Cross. Kelly had orders to attack a Japanese carrier supposedly near Aparri. He had taken off hurriedly during an air raid on Clark and subsequently had only three six-hundred-pound bombs aboard. Unable to locate the reported carrier, he decided to attack what he thought was a large battleship, later presumed to be the *Haruna*. Two of his bombs missed. The third was a direct hit, and on withdrawing, the ship was seen to be dead in the water amidst dense black smoke. On returning to base, Kelly's plane was jumped by two Zeros and shot down. All of the crew bailed out safely except Kelly, whose body was later recovered in the wreckage. In actuality, Kelly's plane had not hit a battleship but possibly one of the two Japanese heavy cruisers covering the landings. The battleship *Haruna* was supporting the Malayan invasion at the time. Nevertheless, Kelly had displayed exceptional courage by staying with his plane in order for his crew to escape. (However, his crashing B-17 almost hit Tom Trapnell's F troop on their way from Manila!)

On 11 December, great excitement broke out in Manila. Wild rumor spread that a huge battle had taken place up at Lingayen Gulf—that the Japanese had landed in force and had been soundly repulsed. The root of all this imaginative news was caused by overanxious gunners of a 21st Field Artillery battery who opened fire on "dark shapes" seen approaching the beaches from the gulf. They were immediately joined by salvos from 155mm coastal guns and practically everything else capable of firing a projectile, from cannons to pistols. What had set the night ablaze was simply a small Japanese reconnaissance vessel scouting out the intended landing waters. Veteran *Life* magazine photographer Carl Mydans hurriedly commandeered transportation up to the "battle site." An American major greeted him grinning. "Looking for bodies to photograph? Sorry, there ain't none."

Some weeks later when Wainwright's North Luzon Forces were fighting a desperate, phased withdrawal to protect MacArthur's WPO-3 plan, Mydans's wife, Shelley, handed him a communiqué that *Life* had sent them in Manila. It read, "ANOTHER FIRST-PERSON EYEWITNESS STORY BUT THIS WEEK WE PREFER AMERICANS ON THE OFFENSIVE."

Mydans's wife showed him her reply: "BITTERLY REGRET YOUR REQUEST UNAVAILABLE HERE."

Meanwhile, Colonel Brougher was able to field only one of his battalions, the 3rd Battalion 2nd Infantry headquartered at Tuguegarao just fifty miles south of the Japanese beachheads. Tuguegarao with its vital airfield was not only on the main southward invasion route, it was a prime target, providing the enemy with an ideal springboard for their air forces to strike deep into Luzon. Under constant bombardment from enemy aircraft already flying from other captured air strips in their first northern assaults, the 3rd Battalion abandoned the Tuguegarao defense area with little opposition and beat a hasty retreat down the Cagayan Valley.

So, by 5:30 on 12 December, the Tanaka detachment had delivered to the Japanese Army Air Force its third and most important airfield, Tuguegarao, over fifty miles into Fil-American territory. Fully armed short-range Japanese fighter planes of the 50th Fighter Regiment and light and dive bombers from the 16th Light Bombardment Regiment could now fly sorties at will to pummel Wainwright's NLF around the clock. The significance of the devastating loss of American and Filipino airpower under Bushido's first brilliant strokes would take on a frightening new dimension for Fil-American ground troops. All Wainwright's eastern sector force could hope for now would be to carry out MacArthur's plan to hold off the enemy at strategic Balete Pass at the bottom of the valley.

Skinny Wainwright writhed in professional frustration. Like a chess player cornered between two costly moves, he felt compelled to stand fast and hold the bulk of his defense force in position to meet what all had agreed would be the main assault from the China Sea against the beaches of Lingayen. Lieutenant Cunningham's 26th Cavalry communications unit of scout cars in the Cagayan Valley had painted a dark picture of a quickly disintegrating situation up there. Meanwhile, the Japanese commanders were rethinking their own strategy. The Tanaka and Kanno detachments had been ordered by Gen. Masaharu Homma to secure the northern beachhead and airfields. But now it was fast becoming evident to Homma that there would be no American counterattack, and in the face of rapidly fading resistance, he ordered his two northern assault forces to regroup as one force, leaving only defensive garrisons at the newly won airfields. The two Japanese assault groups now quickly maneuvered to link up. The Kanno detachment at Vigan now struck north and quickly seized a fourth airfield at Laoag. The Tanaka detachment broke off its push south down the Cagayan Valley and marched back north and around the northern tip of Luzon to meet the Kanno force on the west coast. The combined force now began its plunge southward down coastal Route 3 toward Lingayen to converge on the very area where Homma's main invasion force would arrive, the La Union Province on Lingayen Gulf. They had veered away from the expected Cagayan Valley route and now would throw the brunt of their force against the flanks of the waiting Lingayen defenders. MacArthur's vision of a Thermopylae at Cagayan's Balete Pass would never materialize. It was simply ignored and bypassed.

Once aware of this sudden shift in concentration, Wainwright moved frantically to meet the now double threat to Luzon's western coastal sector.

As the 26th Cavalrymen and their mounts gradually succumbed to the deceptive quiet of the early morning hours with the easy sounds of a gentle breeze whispering through the bamboo around them, the dogs of war relentlessly stalked toward them. The destiny of the horse soldiers was already being forged in the rugged mountains to the north and in the harbors of Formosa.

TUESDAY, 15 DECEMBER, BAMBAN

The day began with troop-level inspections, and the regiment gave evidence of being in good order. But what started as a fine, routine day for the refreshed 26th became, by 9 a.m., trouble.

A motorcycle slid to a stop in front of the regimental command post (CP), and a courier from General Wainwright dismounted, saluted, and handed a paper dispatch to Harry Fleeger.

"For Colonel Pierce, sir. I'll wait in case there's a reply."

Fleeger ducked into the CP overhang where Colonel Pierce was reading day reports on yesterday's field preparations.

"Something here from Skinny, Clint."

Pierce looked up and reached for the paper. "The regiment is in pretty good shape, Harry, from the looks of things." He opened the paper and read. "Damn!"

"What is it, Clint?" asked Lee Vance, bringing his camp chair upright from where he had been leaning against the scout car wall of the enclosure.

"Skinny wants Jim Blanning to replace Bill Leisenring as NLF HQ commandant. He said he needs Blanning's savvy until his HQ is more completely organized and operating efficiently."

This was a blow. Capt. James C. Blanning was an officer of unusual quality. Loss to the regiment of Blanning's ability and experience would hit hard at this critical time and would be felt all the way down to platoon level. Pierce sent word immediately to Blanning about the temporary reassignment and turned over his command of the 2nd Squadron to F Troop's Tom Trapnell, whose promotion to major had been expected while stationed in Manila.

At around noon, Lt. William P. Leisenring reported for duty from Wainwright's HQ. He was the bearer of another message from Skinny.

"Colonel Pierce, the general wants you and your staff to report to him pronto, sir. Something's up."

"OK, Lieutenant, and thanks. You check in now with Herb Wills and tell him I said to assign you one of the scout cars that needs an officer. That's where I need you most right now, and Bill . . . I'm very glad to have you along with us. I think I'm going to need all the good old hands like yourself I can muster or shanghai from Skinny or rescue from MacArthur's pencil pushers in Manila. I think we're in for one hell of a fight, and just between you and me, I think Georgie Custer might have had better odds going for him at the Big Horn."

Pierce then turned to Sgt. Maj. Apriano Masiclat. "Sergeant Major," he directed tersely, "go tell Captain Blanning to grab his gear on the double and get ready to ride over with us to General Wainwright's HQ."

Shortly, Pierce, Blanning, and the 26th staff clumped up on to the porch of the manager's office of Bamban Sugar Central. Tom Dooley, General Wainwright's junior aide, swung open the screen door and beckoned them in. As they entered, Wainwright motioned them over to a table where the general and Johnny Pugh were bent over their maps. The room was stiff with tension. Intelligence had now confirmed that the Japanese Tanaka force from the Aparri beachhead was moving swiftly to link up with the powerful beachhead of the Kanno detachment around Vigan and act as Homma's flanking force.

"Clint, we've got real trouble on the coast. The Jap landing force at Vigan is stronger than we first thought. I don't know if those green Philippine army people are going to be able to contain that beachhead for long, and here," he pointed, "the enemy force that hit Aparri and Tuguegarao are repositioning for a push south. I've got to pull the 26th out of reserve and get you up to Rosales so you can set up a defensive line and be in position to counterattack any break through to the Central Plain. I want you to take up positions here [he indicated] along the Agno River. We're stretched pretty thin to hold the line all the way from the southern end of Lingayen Gulf up to Vigan."

He paused, taking a deep breath. "Vigan worries me, but if I send everything up there to hold the dike, Lingayen is wide open for landings farther south. Intelligence still doesn't have any clear picture on Jap intentions for a main landing, but we still suspect they'll hit farther south here in the La Union area. If they land and link up with this other bunch, all hell will break loose."

Wainwright looked Clint Pierce straight in the eye. "Somebody's got to stop them."

The enormity of what was being asked of the little cavalry regiment hit like a stone in his heart, but Clint Pierce replied quietly, "When do you want us to move out, General?"

"Be ready to ride by nightfall. With the air attack situation the way it is, I don't want you on the roads by day if it can be helped. Split the trip into a two stage march. You're going to have to push fairly quickly, and you'll probably have to make some more fast marches later on when I need you to plug the holes."

Wainwright paused again, tight lipped. "Clint, for reasons of speed, I'm going to have to pull Fitch and his pack battery out of your command. They'll be transferred south where Mac has ordered us to set up main lines of resistance."

This was a painful order for Wainwright to have to give to his commanders, but it was based on practical logic. After the column had left Angeles, the 26th, with its mile-eating, alternating walk-and-trot cadence, had soon outdistanced the heavily laden artillery column. Wainwright knew it would be no different on the march north to Lingayen and recognized that in the face of need for speed to carry out his orders to get into position as a blocking force against the invaders, there was no choice open to him but to cut the artillery from the main column's march route.

Shocked by this news, Pierce and his officers felt a cold prickle of apprehension and disappointment. Loss of the artillery would weaken their delaying capabilities considerably, but they too realized the demand behind the decision. It was a clear and simple case of no choice but the one they had been handed.

Wainwright read the concern on their faces. "I know. I hate to do it to you; I realize how much you need Fitch's guns. But a pack outfit just won't be able to keep up with your bunch on the move. I can't afford to slow you down, and I can't afford to lose Fitch and his guns in a fast shuffle."

"Can you give us any heavy support at all, sir?" asked Pierce in desperate hope.

"I'm trying to get a section of 75mm SPMs [self-propelled mounted guns] attached to you in Rosales, Clint. That should give you what you need."

"That would be great, sir."

"Clint," said Wainwright solemnly, "help me keep the gate closed, will you? I have a gut feeling I'm going to have to count on a lot from you and your boys. You're cavalry, and you're regulars. The way things are shaping up, it's going to be people like you and your regiment who will have to put some backbone in this Coxy's army we've got up here and keep 'em from falling apart on me."

Wainwright smiled thinly. "Well, I guess that's about it. Good luck and godspeed to you all, gentlemen."

"Thank you, sir," replied Pierce. "We'll do our best for you, Skinny."

With that, the cavalrymen all snapped to attention and saluted the tall, grim general who stood across the table from them. He stiffly returned the formality. They were all friends in that room in the abandoned sugar mill, but they were first and always regular soldiers. The regulation farewell neither reflected nor lessened the sentiment beneath.

Major Dooley made an attempt to lighten Skinny's tense, gloomy concentration on the maps and the situation. "Excuse me, General, Clint Pierce and Alva Fitch are still out here and are probably still pretty tired and dry from that ride."

"Well then, Tom, go bring some scotch. Those fellas are probably damned dry from the ride and all this damned tension around here."

Wainwright put on his campaign hat and stepped out into the muggy night air. Pierce and Fitch both snapped to and threw him a salute, which was answered in kind.

"I'm glad you fellas are still here. Right now, I need some extra company around this place. Let's have a drink and let me get some air. War on paper can be damned tiring at times. Come on over to my quarters and let's have a drink to your safe arrival."

The men went over to the sparsely furnished manager's quarters where Wainwright was billeted and a round of scotch was poured and a toast was proposed by Skinny. "To horse soldiers. I wish I had more of you! Now, Clint, what do you say we go over to your area and let me have a look around. I seem to think better when I can smell horse sweat and leather. You know, things move at an awful fast pace with the stuff we're up against now. Horses relax me a little."

Pierce finished off his drink and climbed on the motorcycle he and Fitch had ridden over on. The other men got in Wainwright's battered Packard and followed him to the cavalry's bivouac area. They were greeted by Lee Vance and Bill Chandler. After general inquiries as to the condition of the regiment, Wainwright asked, "Where are your picket lines set up, Lee? If you don't mind, I'd like to see my horses Joseph Conrad and Little Boy." These horses, which he had brought with him from the States, were beloved by Wainwright.

"Of course, sir. Sergeant Masiclat, would you please show the general over to First Squadron's picket line. I believe Corporal Abad of A Troop is assigned to General Wainwright's horses."

"Right away, sir," replied Masiclat, a crisp-looking master sergeant standing to one side. A man with phenomenal powers of recall, he was the youngest regimental sergeant major in 26th history. Even professionally jealous peers and older noncoms conceded readily to the man's remarkable administrative and leadership qualities.

"Please, this way, sir," he said, leading Wainwright into the shadows of the thick bamboo area where the squadron's horses were picketed. The sentry on the picket line snapped to with his M-1 rifle held smartly at high port.

"Private, General Wainwright would like to see his horses, Joseph Conrad and Little Boy. Can you find them for us?"

"Most immediately, Sergeant Major," replied the young trooper in the musical, lilting mixed accent of Tagalog-tinged English. Smiling only as an eighteen-year-old Filipino soldier can to a general, he added, "It is very good to see you here, sir."

Masiclat grimaced, but Wainwright put a fatherly hand on the young soldier's shoulder and answered, "And it's good to see you here, too, son. It's been a rough week, hasn't it, lad."

"Not too bad, sir. We will do what you are needing us for at all times, sir," he replied with as grim and determined a look as he could muster. "Your horses are just down here, sir."

The two troopers stood quietly to one side as the tall, graying fifty-one-year-old cavalryman stepped up to a big bay horse, cupping its soft muzzle in his big weathered hands, leaving his cheek close to the horse's as he crooned affectionately to him and then to the other, a big chestnut. They stood there for a few moments, the cavalry chargers and their general who had more than his share of the world weighing on his thin shoulders.

"Don't forget to duck, you two," he said with mock firmness as he gently rubbed the soft, velvety noses. Then he turned away without a word and headed back toward the regimental CP. He paused for a moment and turned to the two troopers at his heels.

Addressing the young private, he spoke gently. "You take care of yourself, son, and don't ever forget to do the same for them," he said, nodding toward the horses standing along the picket line. "Remember, you count on each other."

Sergeant Masiclat thought he detected an audible catch of emotion in the crusty old soldier's voice. As he returned to his headquarters that night, General Wainwright writhed in professional frustration, every ounce of the terrible weight of responsibility pressing relentlessly down on that deceptively frail frame of a courageous and compassionate leader of men in the face of horror.

NOTE

1. *Wainwright Papers: Historical Documents of World War II in the Philippines,* out of print.

4

Interlude in Manila

MONDAY MORNING, 15 DECEMBER 1941

Lt. Henry Mark awoke to the insistent nudge of a booted foot. "Wake up, Mark!" a harsh, intruding voice growled, dissolving the dreamy image of a young, pliable, aspiring actress about to surrender to Mark's flawless seduction. "You've just had your chubby ass volunteered to go in to Manila!"

The phantom warmth of California vanished in a burst of rushing pain and the cold reality of Mark's saddle-weary body. He lay curled up almost hidden from view among the twisted roots of a big, tortured-looking amlang tree. He had collapsed there at about 3 a.m. after securing his platoon in their position after the regiment's arrival in Bamban. He lay with his head cradled on his saddle with his rain slicker tossed over his upper torso, having bothered neither to shuck his boots nor to rig his mosquito bar to ward off the voracious insects' nocturnal foraging. Sleep had been instantaneous.

The invading voice persisted.

"C'mon, Hank, wake the hell up. Colonel Pierce is sending a detail to Manila to pick up some motorcycles and you've been nominated to lead it. C'mon, WAKE UP, you lazy sonuvabitch!" shouted Capt. Joe Barker, B Troop commander, as he shook Mark violently by the shoulder.

Mark bolted upward and protested, "Why me, sir? I just went to sleep. Besides," he continued, starting to collapse again, "I've got my platoon to look after. They NEED me!"

"They'd sell their sore asses for two bits to get a rest from you for a day, Mark. Now wake up and listen. The old man got a message from the quartermaster that there is a surplus of new motorcycles sitting on the dock at Port Elliot, and we can have as many as thirteen. I just wish they were jeeps. Anyway, Major Ketchum knows you ride cycles so he volunteered you to

Pierce. Hell, you love the bright lights anyway. Manila! You should be thanking me, you Hollywood bum."

"Why do we need more motorcycles? We've got plenty already," grumbled Mark as he strained back into a sitting position. But already the germ of appeal to the idea was setting in. What the hell. He'd been in the field without a break for the whole week since the Japs hit Clark Field, and most of that time had been in the saddle. Maybe there would be time out for a few drinks and maybe even a swing by the Manila Hotel to see what might be found in the way of available ladies, preferably travelers from the states.

"Oh, we've got cycles alright," observed Barker, but we need those things for reconnaissance. Vance and Chandler reckoned that where we're headed, there's liable to be one hell of a mortality rate on vehicles."

Mark wasn't really crazy about the term "mortality" in light of current developments.

"The cycles will give us more fast transport for couriers and help the staff keep communications tight if things get as rough as I think they're going to."

"Alright, alright, I'm convinced. I volunteer."

"You don't have a choice, Mark," smiled Barker, "but I knew you'd recognize a good thing when it popped up. Bring us back some scotch if you can, that's all. You'll have plenty of room. The cycles have side cars."

Just then, Cpl. Eulalio Arzaga from headquarters troop came up at a run. "Excuse me, sir, but the truck for Manila is waiting for us."

Mark hastily grabbed up his pistol belt and campaign hat. "Joe, seriously, what about my men?" he asked as he collected himself.

"Don't worry, Hank, Major Ketchum said he'll have Sergeant Bulawan himself look after them. They couldn't be in better hands, so get a move on."

Mark crashed through the thicket following Arzaga to the clearing where the regimental CP was located. There he encountered the eternal drill field military form of Maj. Lee Vance waiting for him.

"Good morning, sir," gasped Mark as smartly as he could muster while jamming on his hat followed by a stiff salute as he pulled up short before the formidable executive officer.

"Good morning, Mr. Mark. You look a bit harried; I hope we didn't disturb you. Right. Now then, have you been filled in on the detail you're taking into Manila?"

"Yes, sir. Lieutenant Barker told me the purpose, sir, and where to go."

"Very good, then. Here are your authorization papers for the pick-up of the equipment. Chaplain Zerfas and Lieutenants Chamberlain and Hendricks will be going along with you as well as Sergeant de Mesa and some enlisted men. All of the members of the detail are experienced motorcyclists. You will report back here as soon as possible with the vehicles. If we have to move up in your absence, General Wainwright's HQ will fill you in on our whereabouts and you will join us there. Have a good trip, but stay alert and keep a sharp watch for Jap air activity. They'll be dogging that road from Manila."

"Yes, sir, and thank you, sir," replied Mark, coming to a semblance of attention. "Will there be anything else, sir?"

Vance's military armor relaxed momentarily into a grin at this likable junior officer. "Of course there will be, Mark. You can make certain you bring HQ some scotch while you're at it." With that, the veil of soldierly correctness fell back in place, instantly retrieved. "Now, on your way lieutenant."

Mark snapped a smart salute and wheeled toward the truck. "C'mon, Padre," he called out as he passed Lt. Mat Zerfas. "Let's get on the road before the shopping list gets too big to handle. I guess they figured I'd need someone like you to keep me straight on this little mission, but I warn you," he chuckled, "I'm Jewish, so you can't count on me."

"Hey, Harvard," Mark motioned to Lt. Steve Chamberlain, an affable young officer from New England. "You and Hendricks will have to get in back and ride the rods with the troops." He and Zerfas climbed into the cab of the waiting truck carrying the Manila detail. Arzaga sat waiting at the wheel.

"Let 'er rip, Corporal," cheered Mark as he slammed the door, confident that he was en route to better things if only for a day.

Just as they were about to pull away, Jim Blanning ran up with a letter.

"Mark, see if you can get this mailed for me if the Pan Am Clipper is still flying. It's to my wife with news for some of our families."

Mark noted the somber note in Blanning's voice, and a slight shiver of foreboding ran through him.

As Mark and the Manila volunteers reverberated off down the pitted macadam road, Vance shook his head, mouth pursed in a tight lipped grin. He turned, motioning Blanning to join him, and walked briskly to where the regimental CP had been set up under the thick, lacy foliage of a cluster of big acacia trees. Colonel Pierce's "office" was an overhang formed by a tent fly attached to the tree and supported by two poles jammed into the ground. Its sparse furnishings consisted of two open-trunk-style field desks propped up side by side on some folding camp stools. Everything was calculatedly set up for instant departure upon command.

Col. Clinton Pierce and Californian Maj. Bill Chandler, the regimental S-2, were bent over the field desks scrutinizing maps. Maj. Harry Fleeger, the S-1 and main liaison to HQ NLF, stood looking on. Chandler, like Pierce, was a neat, compact man of about five feet six but of a slighter build. He appeared to be tailor made for the cavalry, which liked its men to be a light load for its horses yet tough and capable on the ground. This man, with kind, intelligent eyes and a striking air of competence, would soon prove that he fit to a tee all of the cavalry's sternest ideals and standards.

Harry Fleeger, on the other hand, was a tall, solidly built redhead who looked as though he would be at home playing the part of cavalryman, tall cowhand, or a swashbuckling count for the director of some adventure film. He loved the life of the cavalry, especially anything to do with competition on horseback. Whatever he lacked in brilliance in any horse sport, he more than made up for with his ardent enthusiasm. Unless duty or lack of a mount curtailed him, Fleeger never missed one of the officers' steeplechase races back at Fort Riley, Fort Sill, or Leavenworth. His enthusiasm and gutsy courage had won more than one of the rugged cross-country races, such as the day in 1938 when he won the punishing three-mile Fort Leavenworth Hunter Chase on an aging charger named Sparker, who demolished practically every obstacle in his path in order to survive the run and win. War he was finding to be an even rougher game, but his heart was in it just as if it would be another good steeplechase.

As Vance ducked under the overhang, Pierce motioned him over.

"Lee, from what I've been told of the reports coming in from Hardwicke and others up North, the Japs have reversed their field in the Cagayan Valley and are up to something. Skinny and his people think they're moving to link up with their bunch around here at Vigan." Pierce punched the map with a powerful forefinger. "It looks like they want to try to shove down the coast rather than slug it out with us at Balete Pass. If this is the way it is, they're playing a new deck of cards and the roof is going to fall in around La Union. You'd better get Sergeant Masiclat to call in the squadron and troop commanders for a conference. I have a hunch we'd better get ready to pack up and move pretty damned soon. When the word comes, I want the 26th ready to hit leather on a moment's notice."

Throughout the day the officers and men of the 26th took the regiment apart piece by piece, including both livestock and equipment, checking, treating, cleaning, oiling, counting and recounting everything in the supply equipment and ordnance inventories.

Weapons were completely stripped and their parts laid out on blankets and canvas sheets to clean and check every piece for replacement survey if necessary. All knew there would be no latitude in the coming days for malfunctions in fighting equipment. It should be noted here that the most significant individual weapon utilized by the 26th was the .30-caliber Garand M-1 semiautomatic rifle. This rifle, which was now being issued as the standard shoulder weapon for the entire U.S. military as fast as it could be manufactured, was in limited supply in the Philippine defense forces. Upon availability, the first units issued the new weapon in full were the U.S. Army's elite Philippine Scout units. The remaining M-1s went to the army's principal infantry defense force, the 31st Division. The significantly increased rate of fire that could be put down by an individual unit with the semiautomatic M-1 would prove to be a telling equalizer for vastly outnumbered U.S. and Filipino scout troops in the days to come.

Pfc. Jacinto de La Cruz, of F Troop, machine gun platoon, was thinking of his family as he began to break down his air-cooled .30-caliber light machine gun. He was frightened for them. They had remained in the barrio of Dau near Fort Stotsenburg when he had gone with F Troop on assignment to Nichols Field, but his father had brought his mother, his sisters, and Consuela, his soon-to-be-bride, down on Sundays and fiesta days to watch him perform with the regiment's monkey drill team, an entertainment favorite of all at parades, horse shows, and fiesta displays. They would hold their breath in a mixture of apprehension and pride as the wiry little Jacinto would daringly work his way up from his horse to the shoulders of his fellow troopers to be the top-most man on the heart-stopping "pyramid" formed by galloping horses, their riders standing "Roman style" with feet straddling from one horse to the next, carrying the top man aloft. It was a real crowd pleaser, and Jacinto remembered with a warm feeling the special station his feats, including vaulting on running horses, had earned for him among his fellow troopers and with family and friends in the barrios.

A quiet, religious man, Jacinto de La Cruz, like so many of his fellow scouts, was a typical product of the agricultural provinces that had raised him. The regiment was his joy, his fulfillment as a man, his claim to station. To be the best at things within that station was the stuff of dreams for a farm boy become horse soldier. Things had happened so fast after the first bombings, and what with F Troop so constantly on the march, he had not been able to see his family or Consuela at all. Some of the men from other troops who had been able to get home briefly had told him that his people were okay but that his family's house had been hit in the bombing. It was little comfort.

"Who are these bastards who come and drop bombs on my family and kill my friends? And in the season of Christmas!" reflected this quiet man as he cleaned the death tool put in his care. He caressed the machine gun as he methodically stripped it and arranged its parts on the blanket in front of him. "Gun, you and I will meet them soon and we will show them they cannot hurt good people. Gun, we will finally be close to them instead of looking up at them in the sky. Then we will be able to watch death in their eyes and give back to them the pain they brought here."

It was a fine, beautifully kept gun, and Jacinto knew its every part intimately. Time and time again he and the gun had proven together on the ranges and on maneuvers that they were meant for each other. He knew the gun was an instrument of violent death, but he had come to feel that it was part of him, that it had a life that breathed and felt with him when he touched it. It was his private source of power, there to do his bidding at the touch of his finger. His personal angel of vengeance, the gun would feel only his anger and carry it only where he directed it. It could not be evil because he did not think of himself as evil, and the gun was as himself.

Jacinto dug some more cleaning patches out of his pack, dipped them in gun solvent, and began to bathe the weapon. He replaced a worn extractor and shortened a spring for added tension. Then he treated every part to a thin coat of oil, enjoying the sensuous feel of the purifying fluid on the cold metal. When finished, he checked the head space to be sure it was correct before he guided the barrel through the receiver. He watched the blunt nose slide smoothly through the perforated steel jacket until it locked home, the muzzle appearing now like the ready mouth of a deadly snake. He shoved the bolt into the grooves on top of the barrel extension, inserted the back plate, jammed it down, and twisted the spring head with a thumb nail until it snapped in place. Finally, he screwed on the muzzle lock and slammed shut the hatch cover. He pulled the retractor handle and smiled thinly as the bolt slammed home with a comforting, metallic *clack!* Pulling the trigger, he heard the gun tell him with a sharp click what he already knew. It was ready to perform its appointed task.[1]

He anointed the instrument with a final kiss of oil and whispered, "Soon gun." Only then did he take a piece of torn cloth and wipe the ritual residue from his hands.

In keeping with standing orders since leaving Stotsenburg, all rifles and pistols were being kept loaded and locked except while being cleaned. Fire discipline in the shadow of Wainwright's HQ was just that extra degree important. Stoicism gradually replaced fury at the Japanese aircraft that cruised the skies with maddening nonchalance, hunting at will. Accidental discharge had become a thing of the past. The 26th troopers were a step closer to becoming seasoned to war.

Lt. Clayton Michelson, DVM, assigned by the veterinary corps to the 2nd Squadron, was making his rounds. He checked in with the platoon leaders and noncoms, taking their lists of injuries, sores, and ailments among the horses and pack mules. He followed up with examinations at every picket line, administering treatments where necessary and passing out medicines and prescribed advice for the troopers assigned to his patients. The teachings and wisdom of cavalry manuals developed by veterinarians through the years were becoming increasingly clear in their purpose to Michelson as he worked. A horse or mule can perform its mission for an organization of which it is part only if it is in fit and serviceable condition. It is considered to be in that state when the body can perform without fatigue or injury the work and services required of it. Keeping the animal in that state requires perpetual attention to proper feeding, grooming, and veterinary supervision. While systematic exercise is preferable, it is not always possible under field conditions, but physical stagnation is out of the question. So it was that the 26th troopers were indoctrinated in putting daily exercise of their mounts and pack animals at the top of their priorities. Under difficult circumstances, even hand walking the animals as a minimum conditioner was somehow carried out. No one could predict when a fit horse would be the determining factor between life and death for a trooper, and no man wanted to be caught in that situation with an animal that could not meet muster.

No less important than the condition of the animals themselves was the condition of the tack and riggings used on them. New saddles and riggings had to be carefully broken in, leather softened, canvas made pliable where sharp edges would come into contact with flesh, and any adjustments made before use in the field or on a march. Every effort had to be made to ensure that saddle blankets, girths, and the mohair pads and cinches of pack rigs were kept free of dried sweat, caked mud, sand, and grit. Injuries from pack and saddle constituted the most frequent causes for disabilities among the animals, the two primary causes for such problems being friction and pressure. Friction was aggravated by the presence of sand, mud, sweat accumulation, and miscellaneous grit grinding between the animal's skin and the material of the tack and riggings. These problems also pointed up the vital importance of an animal's grooming, especially in keeping clean the areas in contact with its burden. Another target for scrutiny was the presence of screwworm egg deposits in the animals' hair and especially in any area affected by wound or abrasion, no matter how slight. The voracious appetite for live flesh of the larvae of the screwworm was an ever-present danger and, left unchecked, could cause havoc of hideous proportions. A coal tar smear was kept on hand by the vets for any such sign or incidence of infestation.

Pressure problems could be caused and aggravated by extra heavy loads and the periods of time elapsing between saddling and unsaddling or unpacking. It was not enough to labor with sponges and saddle soap to keep tack soft and pliable. When encamped, troopers made every effort to keep saddles and riggings off the ground and free of dirt, mud, and ground insects. Some were hung; some were put on improvised racks such as the branch of a tree. Others were simply put on top of other gear free from contact with the ground. Waddle blankets were washed out when possible but always brushed out at least and dried before another use. While some galls and sores from tack had to be expected—especially in the Philippines where conditions encouraged rot—skin ailments, tropical sores, insect bites, and other extreme physical invasions were kept to a surprisingly low level by high standards of stable discipline. A 26th trooper whose animals caught the eye of the vet or stable sergeant too often could count on severe personal problems until the situation improved.

While the vets made their rounds and troopers labored with brushes, curry combs, sponges, oil, and saddle soap, the farriers tramped around in their split leather aprons on the lookout for anything that called for mending in the regiment's feet. Each carried a small wooden tray box that bore nails, rasps, files, clinchers, hammers, and tongs, which were the tools of his trade. "No foot, no horse" was an old adage among horsemen. The men paid special attention to their horses' feet, because trouble there could mean life or death to a cavalryman, and no shortcuts were ever taken in the 26th on that account. All through the bivouac the small portable forges roared from continuous blasts of air as troopers cranked the bellows while smiths forged new shoes and repaired old ones. Noncoms checked with every trooper to assure that he had a complete spare set of shoes in his saddlebags. Luzon's rugged terrain would take a terrible toll on feet and shoes in the hard days to come.

As the sun dropped close to the Zambales Mountains, grain and forage from the supply trucks out of Stotsenburg were carried to the picket lines. Bales of hay were broken open along the lines, and nose bags for grain were filled and adjusted on the animals. Grain was never poured on the ground for the animals because that much of it would be lost, and the bags prevented the animal from picking up potentially dangerous matter in the dirt. The area of every picket line was checked and cleared of any presence of the dozens of varieties of plants and flora present in the Philippines that are sickening and even fatal to horses and mules. The animals were also fed a mess-kit spoonful of salt, always a necessary ingredient in their diet but especially so in the debilitating climate of the Philippines. When available, it was mixed in the grain at least three or four times a week. As for water, it was kept in front of the animals as constantly as supply and the efforts of the men could make possible. This often necessitated long, repeated treks to and from streams and wells with canvas field buckets. It was tedious, but a far lesser evil than a deprived horse.

Sup. Sgt. Juan Dalipe paced from one field kitchen unit to the next where mess men's efforts were spilling smells of cooking into the bamboo thickets. Dalipe, satisfied with their progress, turned to survey the bivouac. These were his charges, his children to feed and clothe. There were eight hundred of them, and they were hungry. It had been the best kind of soldier's day, and he had the duty to see that they were given the best kind of reward there is for a soldier in the field—a hot, cooked meal.

"Sergeant Major Masiclat," Dalipe called out as he strode over toward the HQ area. "Tell your bugler to sound mess call before it is too dark for these worthless troopers of yours to see what we have for them. And send over some orderlies to lend a hand, too. The cooks have fixed up a fine officer's mess. They may not have many chances left to show off for the old man before we truly go to war."

Master Sgt. Apriano Masiclat, at twenty-five the youngest sergeant major in the regiment's history, turned his attention from a radio operator to his supply sergeant. He straightened his husky form and clasped his arms behind his back. "It had better be good, Dalipe. Those bums have done their first real day of work since this war started, and I think they are very tired and impatient. If it's slop, your cooks will probably end up in their own pots. Our men haven't forgotten all the old Luzon ways, you know," he growled menacingly, alluding to traditions of cannibalism known to have been practiced in some remote areas of Luzon's formidable mountains. Masiclat roared with laughter at his own humor and summoned the duty bugler, Private Rom from E Troop.

"Rom, blow chow and then go get some yourself."

Shortly, the men of the 26th were sprawled cross-legged eating from mess tins heaped with steaming chicken, beans, corned beef, the staple rice they preferred over potatoes and bread, and banana and canned fruit pudding. This day—with its business-as-usual military routine finished off by a generous hot meal provided by the efficient presence of supply and mess trucks—had served to ease tensions and veil the dark threat of war waiting for them farther north.

At officers' mess the food was better than the mood. Radio reports from Hardwicke and his bunch up in the Cagayan Valley, fragmented dispatches, and rumors all painted a gloomy picture of deteriorating circumstances in the north. A contagion of apprehension hung heavy with these professionals, who had no illusions about who would be thrown into the breach if the thin lines of MacArthur's fledgling Filipino army gave way to the veteran, battle-hardened Japanese invaders. It was a time that demanded confidence in their ability and training, for those would be their only comfort. Lt. Clint Seymour, the wag of the outfit, broke the silence.

He looked up from his supper—by far, relatively, his most sumptuous meal in a week—and declared in mock solemnity, "And so the condemned ate a hearty meal before their appointed day to die." He ended with a deep, chortling laugh. The others looked up, momentarily startled. They then slowly broke into quiet, strained laughter.

Clint Pierce shook his head in a tight-lipped smile. He had made the rounds of his tough but barely tested little regiment that afternoon, and he was gratified with what he had seen. Given what little they had, his command was as ready as professional soldiers could be made for the ordeal to come.

While the 26th Cavalry was putting itself in order that day, Lt. Henry Mark and his motorcycle transport volunteers were seeing a frighteningly changed Manila. The one-time Pearl of the Orient had become a tarnished, battered ghost of her former self. She now seemed like a ragged old beggar woman reeling in pain and confusion, caught midstreet in a sudden rush and roar of uncaring traffic, clinging to her forlorn past finery and being ground up by a fury and sadness she could not comprehend.

The trip from Bamban to Manila on Route 3 was about eighty miles, normally about two and a half hours considering the towns, villages, and narrow roads. No such speedy pace was enjoyed by the cavalrymen that day. The first signs of problems came as they encountered a stream of military traffic moving north as Americans and newly formed Filipino army units moved toward Luzon's defense lines. About thirty miles from Manila the roads became a scene of increasing chaos, which offered no sign of letting up all the way to the city. It was a cross tide of human misery. Residents of the besieged city struggled to flee from the terror of the bombings in Manila to get to what they perceived to be safety in the countryside. Frightened refugees from the provinces floundered in the opposite direction to escape the invaders in the north and seek sanctuary within the city walls. It was a scene dangerously reminiscent of the tragic, fear-driven stampedes that had turned so many European roads into choked, seething charnel houses and had, to the calculated delight of marauding Germans, all but paralyzed allied military transportation.

Vehicles of every description fought for road space. There were red and yellow Pambusco buses; private automobiles, the old and battered being virtually indistinguishable in the choking gray dust from prized newer-model Fords, Buicks, and Chevrolets; and even luxury touring cars whose wealthy occupants reckoned their country retreats to be safer than their embattled town houses. The drivers all raced their engines, fumed, blew their horns, and lurched in frustration and futility in the ponderous stream. Wooden-wheeled ox carts plodded along, heaped pitifully with household possessions, children, chickens, and elders, drawn by big, lumbering, wide-horned carabao and tan, hump-backed Indian cows. All these scraped and bumped amongst old commercial delivery trucks and cars. Two-wheeled, iron-tired calesas and four-wheeled carramotas jammed with women, children, and luggage snailed along, drawn by small, straining Mongolian ponies whose thinly covered ribs heaved with the effort of pulling their loads.

Other beasts, being driven on foot, were laden to the point of staggering with pathetic heaps of furniture and possessions stuffed in big wicker baskets, sacks of grain, rice, and bundles of fruit. Most of the refugees traveled on foot. They all carried something, anything. There were knapsacks, suitcases, and shirt bundles. Some carried bizarre burdens, their last ties to normality. Here a young man carried only a prized fighting cock, gently stroking its feathers; there an old woman hugged a single family portrait; a small child clutched a pair of candlesticks; an old man carried an ancient phonograph equipped with a large, ornate horn. Others trudged along while leading or herding with sticks their goats, pigs, and family dogs. Children wailed, women crooned, old men scolded, and young men cursed as they all vied for the path to an undetermined fate. It was mindless and heartbreaking, and the cavalrymen on the truck swore silently at the scene and the enemy who had caused such suffering.

Along the way, exasperated, tough Filipino constabulary troops labored to clear some semblance of a route for military priority traffic struggling to get to where it was so desperately needed. They bullied, threatened, pushed, and even clubbed. They fired shots in the air. Somehow the mass of desperate human despair would weave almost imperceptibly to one side to allow passage, only to close again behind as would water settling in the wake of a passing boat. Mark clenched his teeth and tried to close his ears to the curses and shouts of protest, suddenly feeling that his uniform marked him as being neither friend nor foe but simply part of the war that had intruded so cruelly in the lives of these forlorn travelers.

He looked at his watch. It was almost 10 a.m.

"Corporal Arzaga, how far is it to the city now?"

"About ten miles, sir. We can get off this main road soon maybe and take side streets through the Tondo section down to the waterfront. Better time that way, sir. I am familiar with the way. I have family there."

"Arzaga, I think you're related to the whole damn island," poked Mark. "But that's great if it can get us out of this mess and to the docks sometime this week!"

When they finally reached the outskirts of the city, the air had thickened with a haze of greasy smoke. Toward Manila Bay scores of black and gray columns could be seen reaching up from the Manila Port areas and Cavite Naval Yard beyond. All of Manila appeared to be under a dark, swirling shroud. Here the war was again a tangible, visible thing.

Arzaga turned off the main road and the truck whined into the populous Tondo district. Lying on the north bank of the Pasig River, which roughly bisects Manila, this area was populated by native Tagalog who still lived in small nipa huts, palm thatch and bamboo houses raised on piles and densely packed along rough, narrow streets and on the mud flats of tidal creeks. Originally the coastal village of Tundo, it had been inhabited before the first founding of Manila directly across the Pasig, itself built on the burned-out ruins of the village of Maynilad (from a Tagalog phrase *may nilad*, meaning "where the nilad [a flower] are"). Now much of it comprised the poorest section of the city.

As Arzaga maneuvered through the teeming slum, they were hit with the rank smells of dusty streets, rancid coconut oil, and the steaming, fermenting muck around the bases of the nipa houses. To this was added the pervading reek of oily smoke from the bombing across the river. As they passed through, inhabitants stood in doorways and on the road edges watching with the passionless eyes of those who have resigned themselves to accepting whatever miserable hand fate dealt.

Mark fished a paper out of his pocket. "Okay, Corporal, we've got to get to Azcarraga Street. It's number 26. That's where the quartermaster said to report to Motor Transport. It's the Escuela something or other."

Arzaga looked mildly startled. "That's the Escuela de las Senoritas, sir. A girls' school. We are only a few blocks away now."

"Oh, perfect," chuckled Chaplain Zerfas.

"Don't worry, Padre," consoled Mark. "Those young ladies are probably long gone by now. Probably under lock and key to keep them away from the paws of those Manila garrison regulars."

They soon pulled up in front of a big old Spanish building with mossy, smooth stone walls and a lacy wrought iron gate over the front entrance where two MPs armed with tommy guns lounged in the doorway. The area was alive with soldiers and military vehicles. In addition, commercial buses and trucks of all descriptions jammed every inch of parking space. They had been hastily appropriated for military transport use.

Mark was escorted in to the office of Col. Michael A. Quinn, Chief of Motor Transport Service.

"Ah, you must be Colonel Pierce's man. Okay, Lieutenant Mark, you and your men can pick up the cycles over at the army pier in the port area. We're transferring everything over here as fast as we can to get it clear of the port. The Japs seem to have a particular taste for bombing everything in sight over there. But as far as I know, those cycles are still there for the pick-up. Better get a move on, though. The Nips have been plastering the whole port, and you don't want to get caught up in it, believe me." Quinn glanced at his watch. "Come to think of it, you and your men had better have chow here with us. We eat around eleven because the Nips have been bombing every day at noon. You can set your watch by them. This way we can get fed before we hit the shelters. You can head for the docks after the all clear sounds."

"No great guarantee there'll be anything over there to pick up, is there, Colonel?"

"Nothing is sure these days, Lieutenant, except maybe that tomorrow will probably be worse than today. The sergeant will see you out and direct you and your men to the mess area. Good luck and my regards to Colonel Pierce. I used to like watching you guys play polo."

"Thank you, sir," replied Mark. "Not much polo lately, I'm afraid. We're a little too busy. Well, thanks again for the cycles, uh . . . that is, if they're still there after lunch."

Shortly, Mark and his men were seated at the long mess tables in the school's old auditorium drinking coffee and smoking cigarettes when the Manila air raid sirens began to scream. Church bells chimed in assistance, producing a cacophony that guaranteed a sufficient air of panic to get people under shelter. The mess hall was evacuated in a thunderous rush of feet. Outside, men hurled themselves into a variety of shelters ranging from foxholes to slit trenches, shallow ditches to elaborate sandbagged dugouts. In the distance they could hear the all too familiar pulsing drone of Japanese heavy aircraft engines. The sirens subsided and the bells fell silent. A gradual sporadic ripple of distant pops and *pom-pom-pom* of antiaircraft guns joined by the staccato of machine guns grew into a steady din finally punctuated by screaming whistles punctuated by the heavy thuds of bombs hitting. The ground became alive with vibrating concussion, which now resembled the sensation of hearing and feeling the approach of an oncoming train.

"Aw, hell! They're gonna hit here in town again," somebody moaned.

Mark strained into a tight fetal position against the dugout wall, making himself as small as he possibly could. He opened his eyes long enough to venture a look over at Chaplain Zerfas, who peered back at him in tight-lipped silence. "Please pray, Padre. Christian is fine. I'm not particular, I swear!"

Zerfas smiled thinly, closed his eyes, and began to move his lips in silent supplication.

Mark muttered to himself, "God's up there in the same direction as those Nips. Please let Him get to me before they do!"

The heavy, reverberating *whuummps* of bombs got steadily louder. They didn't sound like the short, neatly abrupt slam of a gun. The noise was raucous and indistinct, like a painfully loud blast of deep static on a radio.

Suddenly it came.

First there was a down-key whistle, then a hollow, tearing sound like heavy cloth being ripped. Finally, a pronounced *whooosh* of air drowned out all other sound. It resembled a super amplification of someone having their breath knocked out. Men drove their faces into the dirt and stiffened into a frenzied convulsion of fear. The unbelievable concussion slammed into them like the muzzle blast of a cannon. There followed an astounding rush of silence, broken only by the clicking of falling dirt and stones. Stunned minds refused to allow taut muscles to release the men's bodies from the vice of their terror. They wanted to open their frozen eyes to see the light to confirm that they were still alive. They wanted to shout in dazed relief that they were not dead, but their jaws were clenched in rigid paralysis. The acrid smell of cordite burned their bleeding, concussion-rocked nostrils and penetrated deep in their throats.

Someone was screaming.

Mark gradually forced his eyelids open. "I'm still alive!" his mind howled. He focused on Chaplain Zerfas, and their eyes met in a mutual bond of gratitude.

The screaming continued, joined now by the long moan of all-clear sirens. Slowly, dazed men forced themselves to rise from their places of refuge like the resurrected. Looking skyward, they began to breathe long, deep breaths into lungs constricted by the paralysis of tension, marveling in the most elementary sensation of life, nerves uncoiling in an almost hysterical rush of relief.

The area came alive with suddenly aware people busy coping with the aftermath of the storm. There was an ugly, smoking gouge in the street not ten yards from where Mark emerged from his shelter. The man who was screaming lay writhing by a burning, shattered truck as the ragged stump of a severed leg squirted blood in a pulsing stream. He slammed his hands into the ground in shock and frenzy as others fought to get a tourniquet in place. Suddenly he sagged in the stillness of death. The shock had been fatal.

Mark looked frantically around him and was relieved to see the 26th troopers dusting themselves off and coming over to join him.

"Corporal Arzaga," Mark quavered, "let's get the hell out of here."

The detail loaded up and set out toward the smoke-shrouded port area, passing through devastation on their way. The poor of Manila had been hit hard that day. Fires blazed around deep smoking craters amongst the crowded nipas. People raced frantically to beat out flames and salvage the remains of belongings from smoking wreckage. Those with nothing now had less. Others, untouched, brushed past the victims of calamity, intent on their own need to carry on for survival.

The cavalrymen crossed the Pasig River on the still intact Santa Cruz Bridge. The murky river was alive with frightened life. Little inter-island steamers making their way to the open waters of Manila Bay chugged through swarms of rafts and *cascos* (dugouts) stacked high with coconuts and bales of copra, being frantically poled and paddled to the last open markets by boys and young men who kept frightened eyes constantly turned toward the hostile sky. There Japanese fighter aircraft still roamed at will like hungry, circling hawks. The smoldering, gutted hull of a coastal steamer lay forlornly in water up to her wrecked pilot house alongside the splintered copra docks, testimony to the tenuous existence of life on the besieged river. On the muddy, debris-strewn shores, women moved back and forth under the palms to resume washing and beating wet clothes on the rocks. They too kept constant, apprehensive watch for the war birds' next pounce. Farther downstream, camouflaged barges bearing food, fuel, and munitions clustered for off-loading at docks obscured by camouflage netting and foliage. Life on and along the Pasig still went on.

On the bridge, burdened people scuttled hurriedly back and forth on their errands of everyday life amidst the carnage. The city had come alive trusting that the Japanese routine would not alter and they could move in the open until the next onslaught. The pall of smoke was even denser now, and the smell of burning wood and scorched metal permeated the air, settling deep into noses and searing throats.

The truck swung west past the ancient moss-covered walls of Intramuros, the old, walled Spanish city within Manila where MacArthur's headquarters were located and where Filipino cadets and conscripts had once drilled on the green with wooden rifles. They crossed over the broad expanse of Dewey Boulevard and on toward the Manila South Harbor on Manila Bay. Everywhere they looked they saw a city transformed. Sandbags were piled high against stately buildings and around entrances. Store windows were crisscrossed with wide tape in the style of the London Blitz protective practice. The verdant parks and lawns were pockmarked with patches of bare earth gouged by bomb craters, foxholes, and trenches. The lacy fronds of tall, graceful palms now shielded antiaircraft guns and machine guns whose haggard gunners lounged nearby waiting for the next Japanese air attack. The streets and sidewalks were littered with broken palm fronds, shattered tree trunks, and twisted burnt-out vehicles of all kinds. The stench of death hung heavy from the strewn carcasses of dead animals, many still harnessed to the hulks that they were drawing when they died. They passed lines of trucks filled with grim, dust-covered soldiers, many of them Filipino conscripts who had been handed their first real rifle only days before.

Driving was a hair-raising process. Vehicles hurtled at high speeds in every direction, their operators, oblivious to the most rudimentary safety precautions, ignoring any and all attempts at traffic control or signals. The official cars were the worst, however. The war served as a blanket excuse to declare carte blanche behind the wheel, and the road death and injury toll soared.

The port area with its steel piers and long, corrugated iron sheds came into view. A filmy mist of oil and soot drifted down from the black smoke billowing from dozens of fires. The lovely, imposing old customs buildings were gutted and belching smoke, and the piers and wharves were a jungle of mangled steel. Still, soldiers and longshoremen could be seen laboring like ants amid the wreckage and waiting stacks of freight. Inside the huge doors spaced along the long pier sheds waited mountains of cargo and goods, much of it vital to MacArthur's soon to be beleaguered defense forces. The real wonder of it all was that so much remained intact despite the incessant enemy bombing.

Incongruous to the chaos of the docks were the graceful palms lending their eternal and enchanting greenness and delicate peace along the long shoreline walls rising out of the mud flats. On the bay beyond the Muelle, freighters and naval vessels lay caught like trapped birds on the water. In the shallows and along the rubble-strewn jetties of the military and merchant marine piers, blackened stacks and shattered superstructures of broken ships rose like tombstones. As it later turned out, however, most of the ships in Manila Bay managed to slip out through the mine fields and escaped south, thus depriving the Japanese of a golden opportunity to cripple much of the Allied Pacific merchant fleet.

At the now almost empty Motor Transport Service area, the harried officer in charge directed Mark and his detail to the waiting motorcycles, Harley-Davidsons equipped with sidecars. It was after four in the afternoon by the time they had their convoy organized. Mark called his officers together, and his suggestion to stay over in Manila until after midnight to eat, rest up, and then travel under the cover of night met with instant approval.

"I can probably get billets and mess for your enlisted men over at the HQ battalion area in the Old City, Lieutenant Mark," offered the motor officer, "and you guys can probably get taken care of at the Army-Navy Club. Somehow they're still operating, so you could have a bath and a good meal."

These arrangements were welcomed and the officer made the calls. Mark mounted one of the Harleys and shouted, "Let's saddle up and get this show on the road." He booted over the starter and the machine came to life with a satisfying, throaty roar. This was repeated by the other cavalrymen, and the cycles moved off in a din followed by the supply truck. One of the older troopers recognized the jaunty little tug boat with a brass stack that served as a ferry over to the Cavite naval yards. Intermittent booms could be heard from that direction and smoke still roiled upward from the oil tanks at Mapaju. There was an eerie false twilight over the bay. Smoke from a thousand fires filtered the sun's light to a dirty red glow as the motley little 26th Cavalry column started back toward Intramuros.

Inside the walls of the old city they passed the heavily guarded "House on the Wall" at No. 1 Calle Victoria where Gen. Douglas MacArthur had his USAFFE headquarters. It crossed every man's mind that inside that building their fates were being determined, and from the soldier-in-the-line's point of view of the awesome scope of war, the task of the men in there was formidable beyond any comprehension. At Estado Mayor, the lovely old palace of the Spanish mayors that served as quarters for HQ Battalion of the American 31st Infantry, Mark checked in with the officer of the day and made provisions for the temporary billeting of his scouts. He left Sergeant de Mesa in charge. Then he and the other officers, doubled up and utilizing the side cars, headed out toward the Ermita area behind Dewey Boulevard. Making their way through the big shopping area, they were watched by shaken and bewildered store keepers standing in the doorways of shops where little Christmas displays cried out in a pathetic effort to maintain a semblance of normalcy. But the streets had become hauntingly quiet. Missing were the herds of ragged little shoe-shine boys and the raucous, aggressive street vendors with their rice cakes, ices, and pungent peppers in brine. No slim mestiza nurse maids were to be seen with Caucasian children in the little parks. Missing were the sounds of plaintive pianos and Tagalog love songs mixed with music from juke boxes in the bars on the side streets where villainous *bugaos*, smoking harsh, stinking Filipino dobies, hustled the virtues of their mestizas with nicknames like Betty Grable, Alading, and Mabel. Gone were the beachcombers, the stranded, hopeless "bamboo Americans" who drowned out life in the oily gray swirls of "square face" gin, which smelled of shellac. Gone were the little calesas and carramotas with bells jingling on their harnesses. Gone even were the old moocher women, some of whom had probably met Admiral Dewey himself steaming into Manila Bay on his mission to rout the Spanish, begging centavos to get high on betel nuts and pass out in the streets.

Replacing them now were furtive black marketeers and roving bands of looters and hoarders, many of whom were quite capable of killing for survival rations. Bolts of cloth and broken goods dropped by the scavengers lay in the streets in front of burned-out shops and empty food stalls. The few shoppers hurried warily along the sidewalks clutching precious bundles. It was a dangerous and dismal shadow of what had been a lovely, thriving city.

Mark and his companions felt their spirits lift slightly as they swung out once more on Dewey Boulevard, Manila's tree-lined "Golden Mile" where grand residences and private enclaves looked out on the bay. They swung noisily through the lavishly landscaped gates of the imposing old Army-Navy Club and dismounted off to one side of the circular drive. Here, nestled in a cushion of huge, ancient shade acacia trees and lush tropical shrubbery and flora, there was an impression of oasis from the nightmare outside. Only the sandbags piled around the main entrance and the omnipresent odor of smoke gave lie to the illusion.

Entering the high-ceilinged front hallway, the dusty cavalrymen were scrutinized by the piercing eyes of bygone admirals and generals following them from their stations on the hallowed walls and by curious glances from servants and current military members. The pride of the cavalry carried the day. There is something about the rakish feel of wearing boots and britches and the steely flourish of spurred heels that lends extra inches in height to one's self-esteem under critical observation. Filthy or not, the horse soldiers were second to no one.

They were shown to the downstairs level where showers and a pleasant dormitory for overflow and transient guests were located. Soon, the miracle touch of hot water, soap, and fresh, borrowed razors gave them new life. Drinks were brought to them by white-coated stewards, and Filipino valets laid out fresh linens and gave their uniforms as good a cleaning as time and superficial brushing and dusting could provide. Their boots disappeared only to return freshly cleaned, oiled, and polished. It was a fine world again for the moment.

Upstairs in the main dining room blackout curtains shielded the big windows that looked out toward Manila Bay, subduing the usually lavish atmosphere of the place. At supper they learned from some embassy military attachés that there was a dinner dance going on up at the famed and luxurious Manila Hotel. Most of the remaining American community in Manila had moved or had been moved there or to the solid stone Bay View Hotel, also on Dewey Boulevard. Both places offered relative safety, and concentration of noncombatants would facilitate organization for hasty evacuation to transport still thought to be forthcoming from the States.

The idea of an opportunity for possibly a last festive occasion appealed to the cavalrymen. The prospect seemed to lift the fatigue from their weary frames, and again Mark led the way. As they pulled up to the stately building, which was (and still is) probably the most elegant hotel in the Far East, liveried and white-gloved attendants, outwardly oblivious to the rumpled appearance of the latecomer cavalrymen and presenting an almost bizarre contrast with the sandbagged ramparts protecting the entrance, stepped out to usher them in. The plaintive sound of an orchestra playing "Deep Purple" floated through the lobby from the big Fiesta Room on the terrace beyond.

Mark and his company made their first foray on the bar and then settled down to survey the scene. What they beheld was straight out of the setting of a surreal hallucination. Under splendorous, ornate Christmas decorations hanging from breathtakingly carved mahogany ceilings, well-groomed men, some in black tie and tails, others in tropical white linen jackets and suits, swayed with fashionable-looking American and European women in filmy, summery dresses flowing with their movements. There were exquisite Filipinas and mestizas in their elaborate, glittering ethnic costumes and dazzling jewels; men in ornate barong tagalogs; Indian women in intricately woven saris with diamonds worn in position in one nostril; Orientals in seductive silk—all floating by in trance-like gaiety, rippling with quiet conversation and forced laughter. Mark was surprised to find that he felt queerly uneasy. Rather than offering respite from the horrors outside, this deceptive, last gathering of the international set had more the atmosphere of a wake than a grand party. The expressions of his comrades hinted that they felt the same. He ordered another drink, a double gin, and downed it unceremoniously. The warm glow of the alcohol began to relax his tense perceptions, and he was waiting for another glass when he sensed an unbelievably soft touch on his arm. As he turned, the clinging residue of oily smoke was driven from his senses by an air of delicate, expensive perfume.

"How do you like our little party, Lieutenant? I suppose it's one of the last flings of the doomed, really, a bit like those poor souls who danced while the Titanic went down, don't you think?"

"I don't know. . . . I . . . ," Mark found himself on the edge of stammering, caught short by the beautiful young woman before him. "Um . . . uh . . . please, would you like a drink, ma'am?"

"Oh, yes, please! A gin sling would be wonderful," she replied quickly with a brittle laugh.

She was dressed in a low-cut black silk dress, stunning in its simplicity and reaching alluringly down her long legs to the floor. The only jewelry she wore were two braided gold chains at her neck, their rich yellow accented to a burnished glow by the reflection of deep auburn hair, which framed the high-cheeked oval of her face. Mark motioned to the bartender, grateful to have something to break his momentary paralysis. He ordered and turned back to the girl.

"My name is Ann," she said. "Last names don't matter much here tonight."

"I'm Hank Mark," he replied quickly, "and I feel a little embarrassed. I seem to know you from somewhere. . . . I mean, is that possible?"

"I don't think so, Lieutenant, but then maybe I just remind you of someone back home. I got caught here on the way back to the States from visiting family in Singapore. Not a good place to be these days, but then neither is this, despite all the glitter in here. I don't suppose I'll get out now."

"Oh no, I'm sure you'll be okay. The Pan Am Clipper is still making runs the last I heard. Besides, don't let yourself get caught up in that defeatist stuff, Miss . . . uh . . . Ann. Despite what it looks like now, we're going to stop them. All we've got to do is hold on until they get the fleet in here and get us reinforcements and planes to . . ."

"Stop it, Lieutenant," she snapped testily. "I know you have to believe that crap or get shot, but I don't have to delude myself. There are a lot of Japanese out there. They want this place and we're just in their way just like the English are in Singapore, and those people seem to be taking anything they want in this part of the world. . . . Oh, dammit!" She looked down, chin quivering, and fished a silver cigarette case from her small evening bag.

"Look, I'm sorry. I don't mean to be such a cynic. I'm just frightened, that's all." She looked up at Mark again, her eyes drilling into his. "Hey, soldier, got a light for a girl?"

"Sure, here," Mark replied in a strained voice, snapping open a lighter.

"Look, I'm scared, too. I don't believe all that stuff about help because I have to, well, like you said I have to. I believe it because if I don't I might just come apart myself and let both myself and my men down. The cavalry really means something to me, our regiment especially. I kind of had things fall in my lap back home, but out here I had to grow up and square away. Now for once in my life I don't want to be just another lightweight or the one to screw things up. I guess I've done enough of that in my life up until now."

"Hey, cavalry," she smiled at him. "What say we go outside for some air and sneak a look at the lights on the bay. I think this place is getting to both of us."

"The only lights out there tonight are fires, I'm afraid, but I still think it's a pretty good idea. Let's grab another gin and go."

"Hey, Mark, what is this beauty you're hogging to yourself?" interrupted Steve Chamberlain. "Aren't you going to introduce us to the lady?"

"Later, Harvard, right now we've decided we need some air."

"Then, by all means, kick on, Lieutenant! Good evening, Ma'am. Pleased to make your fleeting acquaintance," Chamberlain gushed. He bowed theatrically, lifting his glass.

"Thank you, kind sir," she curtsied in comic courtliness and, clinging to Mark's arm, drew him toward the blackout-curtained doorway to the terrace. Under an overhanging roof of scarlet bougainvillea, they bought drinks at the famed Bamboo Bar. The overhang, some five feet wide, gave protection from blowing rain in the typhoon season, eliminating the stuffiness of glass windows. Mynah birds and parakeets were settling themselves to sleep in the leaves. The willowy mestiza Filipina who served them wore a pink jasmine flower over her left ear, indicating by custom that she was available.

Outside, the peaceful rustle of the wind in the palms accompanied by the song of frogs in the marsh flats along the shore muffled the dull, intermittent thumps of explosions in the distance. They walked out past the poolside tables to a low wall overlooking the bay. There was almost no moon, but the air had cleared enough so they could see whitecaps on the water. Fires from a few still-burning ships and stricken installations over in Cavite eight miles away cast a sputtering glow on the view.

"If you can forget what they are, the fires are really beautiful over the water, aren't they?" she mused softly. "Like lanterns at one of those lovely fiesta parties in Southern California."

"Are you from there?" asked Mark hopefully.

"Yes, just outside Los Angeles. . . . And you?"

"I am too. Los Angeles, I mean. Small world, isn't it?"

"Not that small. Los Angeles is a big place, cavalry, but it is nice to be with someone from home."

She turned to him, and he felt his throat tighten at the tawny loveliness of her. He touched her hair and gently drew her to him. "I can still hear the music. Would you dance with me, Ann? I haven't danced with a real girl in a long time."

"Sure, cavalry, it wouldn't be right to waste nice music, even here."

They embraced and began to sway slowly to the soft music, which filtered out to mix with the wind in the palms. Then she leaned back and tilted her face up toward his. They kissed, long and gently. Sweetly. Mark started to speak but she placed her fingers over his mouth.

"Please, just hold me, cavalry. I need someone to do that right now. Badly."

They stood there for a long time. A frightened girl far from home and a stoutish young cavalryman who had just danced his last dance and kissed his last girl. Neither had a tomorrow.

Later, as Mark went out the front entrance portico of the hotel to rejoin his comrades at the Army-Navy Club, he was caught up short by the popping sound of gunfire beyond the green across the street.

"Probably looters, sir," said one of the doormen. "The air raid wardens and police, sir. They are shooting at anything that moves at night. They are all afraid of spies, you know. Please be careful on your return sir."

"Thanks, I'll try," replied Mark. Suddenly he stopped in midstep. Turning to the doorman and pulling some currency out of his pocket, he asked in a conspiratorial tone, "Say, can you maybe get me a few bottles of good scotch at this hour to take with me? I promised some friends in the north. They really like Dewar's if you can find some."

"I will be glad to, sir, but please, sir, keep your money. You are with 26th Cavalry Philippine Scouts, I think, yes?"

"Yes, that's right. I am."

"Okay, sir, I have a cousin in the 26th. He is named Arzaga."

"That figures," laughed Mark. "He's related to the whole damn island, I think. But you take the money, dammit. He's a friend of mine and if you're family, I know you can use it better than I can where I'm headed."

"Thank you, sir. You are very kind, and I will be sure to find you Dewar's, and God bless you and all of your comrades in this terrible time. And I wish you and all of your regiment a happy Christmas! I will have the Dewar's brought to you at the place where you are staying. Where is that, sir?"

"The Army-Navy Club on Dewey Boulevard."

"I know the head steward there, sir. You will have your scotch in a very short time. God bless you, sir, and try to kill some of those bastard devils for us who have been killing our people for no reason."

Mark didn't feel quite as dismal now and hurried back to collect his men for the trip back to the regiment. Later, as they roared north in the silent hours shortly after dawn, he looked back toward the dim, fire-lit outline of the beleaguered city.

He sensed somehow that he would never see it again.

NOTE

1. These private musings were related to the author by the trooper, who spent his last years in New Mexico.

5

The Road North and the Nature of the Enemy

TUESDAY, 16 DECEMBER 1941

Village of Bamban

The mission is defined.

While Colonel Pierce and his staff were meeting with Wainwright, the 26th Cavalry continued care of horses and mules and preparations of equipment. More troop-level inspections gave evidence of the regiment being in good order. Not knowing what was taking place at Wainwright's headquarters, the illusion of calm for the now-rested cavalrymen was not to last for long.

In the midst of the regiment's quiet day, a sudden guttural roar drowned out command problems at hand for the moment. The din announced the return of Henry Mark and his Manila motorcycle gang. Mark pulled up in front of the CP and brought his Harley-Davidson with its fully loaded sidecar to a skidding stop. He dismounted and entered the CP with serious formality. Having made his perfunctory report to Vance, he saluted, ducked out of the enclosure, and returned immediately bearing a large yellow box.

"Compliments of the Manila Hotel and Corporal Arzaga's cousin," he beamed and passed out several bottles of Dewar's to the officers and one to Sergeant Bulawan. "With your permission, Major Vance, there's a few cases of San Miguel in the truck for the troopers."

"You're impossible, Mark," scolded Vance with less than his usual military enthusiasm.

"Yessir, I know, sir."

"I hate to say it, but you may still make a soldier. Get out of here and give that beer to the troops before I figure a reason to lower the boom on you. So, how are the vehicles you picked up, Mark?"

"Well they got us back here from Manila in good order, sir, so I guess they're okay. Anything else, sir?"

"No, Lieutenant, that will be all for now. Carry on—and don't overdo the booze. I have a feeling we'll be moving out very shortly."

On return to the 26th CP from the commanders' meeting with Wainwright at Sugar Central, Pierce called an officers' conference and passed the word for the regiment to make preparations to march that night. One welcome piece of news did temper in part the grim circumstances of the day. Word came down that Skinny Wainwright had gotten a change of orders from MacArthur. No longer was he to attempt to defend all of Northern Luzon. He was to establish a new line of defense from the West Coast just north of San Fernando, La Union, to Luzon's West Coast. Everything north of the line was to be yielded and all units pulled south to the new defense area. This afforded Wainwright some needed concentration of his forces, but it still left the gnawing concern that a main enemy landing in the Lingayen Gulf area, twenty-seven miles south of his defense lines, might cut off his main force. What he did not know was that another Japanese shoe was about to drop.

Nightfall found all signs of the 26th bivouac and picket lines erased. In their place was a regiment packed and standing to in the order of march.

"Okay, Lee," Pierce ordered Vance, "give 'em the word to mount up and move out."

Vance barked the orders. "REG'MENT! STAND TO HORSE! PREPARE TO MOUNT."

The orders were echoed down the column by troop commanders and noncoms. The men of the 26th stood to with a single, audible smack of boot heels and the ring of spurs.

"MOUNT!"

The creaking of leather as several hundred men settled into their saddles in unison was followed by a roar of engines as drivers started up scout cars, trucks, and motorcycles. All then moved off to assigned column and route positions.

"FORWARD, AT A WALK, HO!"

There was an immediate creaking of leather, jingle of the metal of equipment, and the scrape of hooves.

Horsemen nudged their mounts, and the 26th Cavalry was on the move once more. Its strength, less the detached G Troop still on patrol at Baler Bay and the scout cars on watch in the Cagayen Valley, was now at a mere 699 men of the ranks and 32 officers. If ever a terrier moved forth to challenge a bear, it happened on that night.

The dark was filled with the sounds of night—the rustling of animals in the trees and underbrush, the peeps and rasps of insects, the occasional small splash of something scurrying into the water of the nearby rice paddies. The ground was becoming more hilly, and the trees seemed bigger, their huge leaves making the dark even blacker.

The regiment traveled all that night and did not halt until just before dawn. Cold camp was made under tree cover north of Capas until nightfall of 17 December , when the march was resumed. They reached Gerona, the halfway mark, before daylight of the 18th. All that day, the cavalrymen lay in a coconut grove west of the little town. The night moves had avoided enemy air attention, but Japanese planes were ever present in the daylight hours. There had been no sign of friendly aircraft for several days. The sight of a jaunty little American P-40 with its stubby, solid strength and white star with red-balled center insignia would have been a welcome one to men whose eyes constantly turned skyward only to find malice there.

17 DECEMBER 1941

Kirun, Northern Formosa

A misty rain enshrouded the still floodlit wharves of Kirun, giving a ghostly quality to the massive activity under way as several thousand men labored to fill the bellies of a score of transport ships, Japan's intrepid *marus*, whose shadowy outlines hugged the waterfront like so many huge sea creatures waiting to be fed. Mountains of supplies, military equipment, vehicles, tanks, artillery pieces, horses, pack mules, and soldiers themselves were slowly filling the great maw.

It was 5 a.m. on the morning that the Japanese main Philippine invasion force would commence its departure. Kirun, where the loading procedure had begun the previous day, was to be but one of the points of origin. Elsewhere, two other convoys were being prepared, one at Mako in the Pescadores Islands and another at Takao in Southern Formosa.

Led by a motorcycle with a machine-gun-mounted sidecar, three Nissan sedans, marked with military insignia, the top half of their headlights painted black for air raid precaution, swung onto the quay and came to a halt where a group of army and naval officers and civilian officials were directing the loading and laboring over cargo manifests and tally lists. As the procession came to a halt, soldiers, some with the red-and-white armbands of division military police and some with the insignia of the dreaded Kempei-tai military security forces, sprang from the first and last cars and took up guard positions, weapons at ready. Others sprang from the center car and opened the rear passenger doors. The presence of Kempei-tai signified extraordinary security conditions and the importance of the passengers who emerged and passed through their escort, now standing at stiff attention, to receive the greeting salutes of the officers of the loading party.

In the fore was a bullish man with the stalking gait of a heavyweight wrestler. At five feet ten inches, Lt. Gen. Masaharu Homma, commander of the Japanese 14th Army assigned to the conquest of the Philippine Islands, towered over most Japanese of that day. This imposing stature was accentuated by a muscular frame topped by a clean-shaven head thrust into his officer's forage cap like a projectile into the breach of a cannon. Beneath this formidable outward appearance, however, dwelled a peculiar combination of the quick, original, and shrewd intelligence of a warrior leader blended with the surprising sensitivity of a poet. Homma, whose favorite means of relaxation was writing poems and short plays, was utterly loyal to his emperor, his superiors, and his duties as a professional soldier, which he held sacred. Homma would prove a relentless foe but at the same time would temper duty with a sense of prudence and humanity, which were destined to be his undoing. This, then, was the face of the chief adversary to be met by the 26th Cavalrymen and their comrades-in-arms.

Masaharu Homma at the age of forty-seven had already accumulated an impressive array of credentials and experience for the task at hand. After graduating from the Japanese Military Staff College, he became a close friend and later a perennial aide-de-camp of Emperor Hirohito's brother, Prince Chichibu. Homma earned a coveted assignment as a military attaché to the Japanese embassy in London. In 1918 he saw his first combat while serving as an Allied observer with the British army in Europe, where he was awarded the Military Cross of the British Empire for his service under fire. Homma remained with the British army of occupation in Cologne, where he honed his proficiency in the English language. He returned to London in 1921 and was transferred to serve as an attaché in India from 1922 to 1925. Spending a total of eight years in close association with the British, Homma so thoroughly steeped himself in their ways that he became known to his fellow Japanese officers, many of whom thought him too pro-British for his own good, as "the linguist with the red nose." In that period and later, in the course of duties utilizing his highly valued command of English, Homma also developed a special, and ironic, admiration for the United States and Americans. It was a sentiment peculiarly shared by a surprising number of his junior officers of the Japanese military. In 1932 his linguistic abilities served to distinguish Homma with Emperor Hirohito.

British Lord Victor A. G. R. Lytton, who had visited Manchuria to scrutinize Japanese policy and war activities, wrote a damning report on Japan and the dangers of her growing expansionism and sinister policies for presentation to the League of Nations in support of demands to expel Japan as an "outlaw nation." The delicate duty of reading and translating the four-hundred-page report and condensing its main points for Hirohito's consumption went to Homma, now the newly appointed chief of the War Ministry's press relations. Time was of the essence. In a single all-night effort, Homma produced the necessary mountain of neatly hieroglyphic notes for the purpose. The result was a successful Japanese effort to remain in the League after "recognition" of the newly independent state of Manchuko, formerly Chinese Manchuria.

Later, Japan withdrew from the world organization on her own volition. Face had been preserved. Homma, as chief of the army press bureau, learned better than his fellow generals the importance of good press relations, and afterward, his entourage always included Japanese war correspondents and often foreign journalists. He went on in 1937 to become director of the Intelligence Department in the Army General Staff, a position he held during the infamous Rape of Nanking, which occurred in the wake of a costly conquest of the capital of Chiang Kai-shek's Nationalist China. His inside knowledge of responsibility for the grisly blood orgy— which included not only the wholesale rape and murder of some 20,000 women, the murder of some 100,000 other civilians, and the mass executions of more than 125,000 Chinese military captives, thousands of whom died excruciatingly as subjects for bayonet and officers' sword and target practice—was a sickening and sobering revelation to Homma of the murky paths to be navigated in the hierarchy of Japanese military and political power.

Homma's stature as a leader of the outspoken pro-British minority in army circles and his positive sympathies for the United States served to put him in poor stead with one particular politically ambitious and rising star of the inner circles of Japanese power. This was former Imperial Guards officer Lt. Col. Hideki Tojo, destined to become Japan's World War II shogun as prime minister, war minister, home minister, and chief of the organization of General Staff. Shortly after Nanking, Homma had put himself on public record as declaring that Japan was disaster bound unless peace could be achieved immediately. He viewed Tojo as a danger to Japan's welfare and voiced his fears to his closest confidant, Gen. Akira Muto, Chief of Military Affairs Bureau. Homma predicted then that Tojo would prove a poor choice for minister of war.

In a twist of irony, Homma, when assigned the mission of conquering the Philippines, came under the power of another murky figure disfavored by Tojo but one who would also earn Homma's own contempt and undying hatred. Lt. Col. Masanobu Tsuji, referred to widely as "The God of Operations," had become a factor in the fate of the Philippines when in January 1941 he was assigned to the planning staff of Japan's fateful "Strike South." Behind him lay a sinister path of accomplishments that had steered his malignant but brilliant career to influential power far out of proportion to his relatively minor rank as a mere colonel and made this Rasputin-like fanatic a feared man. Born in 1901 of "uncertain parentage," Tsuji by age twenty-nine had become a self-made and known fanatic among young army officers after graduating from Japan's Imperial Military Academy with honors. His reputation drew royal attention and in 1930 he was recruited by the emperor's cabal through the prestigious Cherry Society, which propelled him on to the staff college. While there, the young Tsuji drew the favor of Maj. Gen. Tomoyuki Yamashita, a true professional and the strategic genius and early military bane to the World War II Allied cause who would later become known as the "Tiger of Malaya" and conqueror of Singapore. As an aide-de-camp to Emperor Hirohito, Yamashita had been assigned to establish an undercover network to root out plotters in the Army's "Strike North" circles. He enlisted the colorful and puritanically devoted Tsuji as an agent and in 1934 placed him in the Military Academy as an instructor and the morals guardian for a dissident company of cadets. It was during this time that Tsuji also acted as tutor to the youngest and brightest of Hirohito's brothers, Prince Mikasa, during his term as a cadet. Their close association would prove a foundation key to Tsuji's climb to influence.

In the course of his duties counseling cadets, Tsuji uncovered a plot by a group of young reformers in the officer corps to incite cadets to join an armed coup intended to open Hirohito's eyes and to persuade him to "renovate the nation." Tsuji, in cooperation with the secret police, foiled the uprising and ingratiated himself to the emperor and the chiefs of staff in the process. He was promoted to major.

By 1936 the Japanese Army had capitulated to the willful Hirohito's personal rule. Now in imperial favor, Tsuji became an unpopular but effective missionary in the army for Hirohito's gospel of Asia for the Asiatics—with Japan as the guardian master, of course. Hirohito, no slouch in the art of ruthless power manipulation—contrary to the prevailing and resoundingly false image encouraged for postwar political expediency at the end of WWII and generally preserved to this day that Hirohito was an innocent dupe and pawn of the Japanese militarists—was resolute in his determination to fan the winds of war. In childhood his education had been entrusted to Gen. Maresuke Nogi, a distinguished patriot and trusted favorite advisor to Hirohito's grandfather Emperor Meiji. As headmaster of the famous Peers School for young nobles, Nogi took an intense interest in the quiet young prince, who responded by addressing him in forms ordinarily reserved for a father only. Nogi had himself been raised in the traditional and Spartan code of the samurai. As a child, if he complained of the cold, he was made to stand naked in the snow as his father poured buckets of icy well water over him. At sixteen he lost an eye learning fencing. At twenty-eight, while commanding troops in battle for the first time, he was surrounded during the Satsuma clan's samurai uprising of 1877. Crippled in one arm and one leg, he was disgraced in his own mind by the capture of the imperial colors under his charge. Despite his limp and ability to see the world with but one eye, Nogi became one of Meiji's fiercest and most loyal generals, sacrificing three of his own sons in battle with the Russians at Port Arthur. Narrowly avoiding defeat, he asked the emperor's permission to commit ritual suicide, hara-kiri (belly cutting). He was refused by Meiji, who told him "Not while I am alive, Nogi. That is an order."

Nogi adhered without question to the sacred samurai creed of Bushido, the way of the warrior. This bleak off-shoot of Buddhism embraces the virtues of killing with honor, "magnanimity" toward the chastened and defeated (meaning, more often than not, doing one's disgraced enemy the "kindness" of providing for him a ritual or "warrior's" death, a favor later to be extended to all too many hapless Allied victims in its perverted practice as applied to prisoners during World War II), and utter ruthlessness toward "the base and mercantile." The Japanese warrior was conditioned through the ages in the contradictory philosophy that demanded he strive to bring beauty into death and to seek true beauty only in the spirit world of death, the only reality, and it was to this purpose that the samurai was instilled with appreciation for contrived artistic refinements in life, such as poetry and painting. Thus is the real significance of the misleading poetic appeal of the samurai's elaborate display of ceremony and decorous appearance while engaging in martial arts and the crafts of actually meting out brutal death. He must seek truth in the sword, and his life must be lived such that his soul may be as pure, unblemished, and sharp as the blade. The pleasures of life, which ease the pains of the body and the agony of the mind, are considered opponents to the true samurai, for they only detract from his attention and dedication in training and preparing for death. True enlightenment must come through absolute self-control, obedience to his emperor and shogun as they represent the divine extension of Buddha's arm, and reverence for his ancestors, who, knowing the true purity and beauty of death, would recommend him to the divine being. Only in this way in the mind of the Bushido samurai could the eternal and merciful love of Buddha be realized. To be conquered into submission rather than welcome a cleansing death was unthinkable, a lesson that was to be cruelly taught to Americans and Filipinos in the dark years of WWII. Bushido was a creed filled with dark ironies counseling a life of peace through purity and strength while making a virtue of violent death and absolute, unquestioning obedience; and it was zealously prescribed by Nogi in his tutelage of the young Hirohito. The disciple prince was drilled incessantly with it and daily was subjected to the rigors of life as a samurai initiate. On one occasion Nogi ordered him to stand under a glacial waterfall until he could prove his ability to overcome shivering. Finally when numbness stopped his shaking, Nogi beckoned him out and wrapped him in a peasant's coarse winter house kimono counseling the virtue of its roughness and simplicity. One of Nogi's rules was "Be ashamed of torn clothes but never of patched ones." Another was "When you order your Western-style clothing, boots, and shoes, have them made larger than your present size, regardless of fashion. You will outgrow them."

Hirohito, for all of his willingness to prove himself worthy of the samurai, labored at a disadvantage. He had inherited from his grandfather Meiji a slight motor dysfunction of the legs, which caused him to walk with a peculiar gait, dubbed by his detractors "the Imperial shuffle." Brilliant intellectually, Hirohito forced himself to reconcile his genetic deficiency only with great difficulty. Not naturally gifted athletically, he applied sheer will. Living in a samurai's world, he put great store in strength, endurance, and agility. With painful effort and arduous determination he became a powerful swimmer, good horseman, and avid golfer, but the pain was ever present. His disability, together with other unusual aspects of childhood, left him with a defensive shyness. He developed an icy poise and a masochistic need to prove himself by living more simply and working harder than anyone else. What he lacked in natural physical ability was more than compensated by a gifted instinct for intellectual maneuver. It was this and his recognition of a built-in edge over adversaries offered by the teachings of samurai that he would mold to his purposes. Bushido, so susceptible by its nature to diverse interpretation, would be adapted, twisted, and perverted. It would become a terrifying instrument of national policy.

Masanobu Tsuji proved to be an ideal evangelist for the new Bushido. Smallish, ramrod straight in his posture, his small, piercing eyes drilling out from a roundish face capped by a bald shaven head, Tsuji was the archetypical staff officer. He stirred reverence in younger staff officers, but some of his military peers regarded him as a clever, fanatic idealist with a touch of madness. With genius came a one-track mind and conviction that his ideals alone were right. Tsuji envisioned himself as the instrument of his emperor's quest for a new Asia under Japanese stewardship. If anyone doubted his imperial mandate, he had only to show his credentials: a set of cufflinks from Prince Mikasa embossed with the fourteen-petal chrysanthemum of imperial princes, and a sake cup from Hirohito with the sixteen-petal chrysanthemum, reserved for the emperor himself.

Promoted to lieutenant colonel, Tsuji made a name for himself by his ruthless, puritanical zeal in Mongolia and China. In 1937 he earned special admiration at court for an act of particular devotion to his moralistic principles, which occurred early in the Japanese campaign in China. One night while stationed in Shanghai, Tsuji turned the rage of his moral indignation on the Chinese brothels, which were supposed to be off-limits to Japanese military personnel but he felt were sapping the fighting spirit of the troops. Lighted torch in hand he charged into the streets, and in a fit of piety burned down some forty brothels, including one filled with his own fellow officers, most of whom perished with their iniquities.

Later while serving in Nanking Army HQ, Tsuji prided himself in living apart from his peers in the squalor of a stable room. Asked why, he is said to have replied disdainfully that "these headquarters officers are all rotten. They work only for medals. Every night they attend parties and dally with geishas. Since the China incident the whole military has gone bad. They hate me because I know these things and speak out against it. They know that I cannot be corrupted." He practiced what he preached, turning "corrupt" fellow officers over to the Kempei-tai's less-than-tender mercies.

In November 1940, Tsuji was transferred to the Formosan Army Command. In January 1941 he was assigned to the top-secret "Unit 82," a special unit of the Formosan Army Research Department created to formulate plans for the controversial Strike South and under the command of Col. Yoshide Hayashi. Tsuji's mentor, General Yamashita, who had originally conceived Unit 82, had been dispatched by Hirohito in November 1940 to study firsthand the German Wehrmacht's preparations for the expected invasion of England. In his absence, Tsuji soon became acknowledged as the driving force of the most difficult area of operations planning for Strike South, that dealing with Singapore, the Philippines, and the Dutch East Indies including Java. The first task was to cull and evaluate the mounds of intelligence that civilian agents of Japan's espionage network had been gathering since 1900 and more intensively since Hirohito's pronouncement in 1934 advocating Strike South. In the Philippines, the Japanese had been amassing details of American military operations and studying the suitability of the islands as a base for attack on Borneo and the Dutch East Indies. Ever since the 1930s they had filtered in by thousands as businessmen, itinerant bicycle salesmen, and photographers. They traveled through every town and barrio noting the smallest details of Philippine life and activities. Their trading schooners and fishing vessels were everywhere, mapping and studying Philippine waters, tides, shores, and coastal installations. The strategically located main San Miguel beer brewery was reputed to be an anthill of Japanese operatives.

Hirohito saw to it that Tsuji and his junior officer colleagues were to have complete access to the intelligence archives. The emperor then went on to delegate his mother's brother-in-law, Count Ohtani Kozui, a renegade but influential abbot of Kyoto's Nishi Hongan-ji, or West Fundamental Temple of Buddha, to shepherd Tsuji and ensure that nothing was denied him. Tsuji's group, all trained in the modern German techniques of blitzkrieg, was quick to find weak points in Allied defenses. They also found gaps in their own intelligence collection, and Tsuji ordered an intensified renewal of data gathering. He and his staff themselves joined in overflights with Japanese commercial pilots and seaborne probes to check their findings. Into the summer they worked to perfect their strategic concept, and in August 1941 Tsuji went to Tokyo where he bulled his plans through the attempted roadblocks of General Staff officers who could only marvel at his mysterious power and influence. After outlining his plans for the army to Hirohito aides and to the officers of the Operations Department of the General Staff in a three-day briefing, Tsuji was congratulated by Chief of Staff Sugiyama for his brilliant presentation and then asked for his estimated timetable of operations.

Tsuji replied, "If we commence on Emperor Meiji Day [November 31], we should be able to capture Manila by New Year, Singapore by National Foundation Day [February 11], Java by Army Commemoration Day [March 10] and Rangoon by Emperor's Birthday [April 9]."

Hirohito gave his full approval to Tsuji's plans and immediately authorized massive troop movements to Manchuria in August, giving an impression that Japan was about to strike the Soviet Union. In reality, these reinforcements freed combat-hardened troops of the Kwantung Army so they could be readied for Strike South. Backed by his approval from the emperor and the princes Takeda and Mikasa, Tsuji used his power to strip choice troops from Japanese divisions and to make the five divisions assigned to the Malayan and Philippine campaigns stronger than any Japanese force that had ever before gone into the field. When he had finished outfitting Strike South, the other fifty-two Japanese divisions in Japan, Manchuria, Korea, China, Indochina, and Formosa had been plucked clean of offensive power. Intensive training and rehearsing of the Strike South force was carried out with emphasis on jungle infiltration and amphibious operations. Always there was the eternal Japanese Army gospel of "ATTACK, and when in doubt, ATTACK AGAIN!" which would later become a predictable and fatal flaw in its war aims.

Tsuji's methods continued to be bizarre. To disprove a theory that it would be suicidal to crowd large numbers of men and horses aboard ship for transport in the suffocating heat of tropical South Pacific theaters of operations, he applied a direct testimonial to his belief that it was simply a matter of discipline and conditioning. Loading several thousand fully equipped soldiers, horses, and heavy equipment into jammed, sweltering ship holds, he ordered them to remain at sea for a week on minimum water rations in temperatures of upward to 120 degrees Fahrenheit. Finally this suffering force was subjected to a full-scale amphibious training assault, landing under the most adverse natural and combat conditions that could be simulated. Tsuji rested his case and preparations continued.

At 7:30 a.m. on 1 November 1941 a meeting occurred at imperial headquarters that would alter the course of history. With the army's Shogun Tojo presiding and the emperor overseeing, the chiefs of staff of army and navy and Hirohito's cabinet ministers convened to choose between uneasy peace or final commitment to war. After grueling debate patiently heard by Hirohito, whose only real concern was how to start a war "with honor," the decision to go to war was finalized at 5:30 p.m. the next day, and the plans so long in the making were set in motion.

On 4 November 1941 the Japanese "Southern Army" came officially into being. Named to take command was an aristocrat, Gen. Count Hisaichi Terauchi, former war minister, founder in 1936 of the Army Purification Movement, and a pious, harsh disciplinarian. His uninspired leadership and martinet spirit would later contribute significantly and with tragic results to the failure and utter breakdown of genuine, traditional samurai chivalry during the Pacific campaigns of World War II. Terauchi was ordered to prepare for operations "in the event that negotiations with the United States were to fail." It was at this very time that preparations and dress rehearsal training operations were fully under way for Japan's historic "Day of Infamy," its surprise air assault on the Hawaiian Islands and the American navy and military installations located there.

Placed under Terauchi's command were the 14th, 15th, 16th, and 25th armies, a force comprising the divisions and an additional three mixed brigades. Under instruction to act only upon direct orders from Imperial General Headquarters, his war mission would be to seize American, British, and Dutch territorial possessions in the "southern area" with greatest possible speed. The individual invasion assignments were divided. Major General Yamashita was ordered to take Malaya and Singapore, and Lieutenant General Homma was to lead the assault on the Philippines. This was probably as close a thing to an advantage that the Japanese would ever concede to Gen. Douglas MacArthur and his Philippine defenders, for it is generally felt that if a general of Yamashita's notoriously aggressive caliber and initiative had drawn the assignment, America's Philippine disaster may have proven a more immediate prospect.

Homma had been given command of the Philippine expedition only after plans had been drawn up by the ubiquitous Colonel Tsuji and his staff in Unit 82. In an unusual departure from standard procedure, Homma was simply summoned before the chief of the General Staff and handed the plans as his orders. The chief of staff at that time was Gen. Hajime Sugiyama, former war minister during the Manchurian Incident and a long-time crony of Tojo. His unfathomable and noncommittal facial expression had earned him the graceless nickname "Bathroom Door." When Homma received the plans from Sugiyama, he was sorely taken aback by this unorthodox treatment and requested that he be allowed to research and make a personal appraisal of the plans for the Philippine operation.

"If you do not like your assignment," Sugiyama shot back without visible expression, "we can give it to someone else."

Shocked and humiliated, Homma bowed quickly but stiffly and from
that day on would follow orders like an automaton, his gifted, innovative
spirit stifled, a casualty of Bushido samurai intrigue.

As Homma approached his invasion force's loading party staff on the
wharf at Kirun, bitter thoughts[1] of the circumstances that had brought him
to that damp, misty waterfront raced through his mind. Accompanying him
were his chief of staff, Lt. Gen. Masami Maeda, his aggressive operations
officer, Col. Nakayama Motoo, and his quiet-spoken staff chaplain, Yoshiaki Nakada. After being briefed on the loading progress, Homma took his
leave to tour the area alone except for his personal security escort. As he
walked among his troops while they boarded the invasion transports, the
full weight of his assignment became a tangible reality. His life's work, his
reputation as a soldier, would now depend entirely on these men and his
ability to lead them.

To accomplish his mission, Homma had assigned to him the Southern
Strike force's 14th army, consisting of the 16th and 48th divisions and the
65th brigade. Among his troops boarding the *marus*[2] that morning were
some of Japan's most brutal veterans. During the campaign in eastern China's Kiangsu Province, the 16th division had been the force left to occupy
the defenseless city of Nanking after Christmas 1937. The unit performed
with infamous distinction its orders to carry out a final five disciplined
weeks of rape and mass executions on both military prisoners and civilian
populace there. Called the "Black 16th" under the command of the sadistic
Lt. Gen. Kesago Nakajima, a secret police specialist in "thought control"
and torture, the division had brought up the rear of the main army to mop
up and carry out a methodical decimation of the Chinese populace and its
will to resist. Under Nakajima's direction, the 16th carried out its assignment in a fashion that defies imagination. Over twenty thousand men,
mostly of military service age, were herded out to areas outside the city
walls where they died horribly as live "dummies" for bayonet practice, targets for rifles and machine guns, and tokens with which young Japanese
officers were enabled to initiate their swords with first blooding. Others
were simply soaked with gasoline and set on fire, the Japanese army quartermasters having a sense of frugality when it came to unnecessary wastage
of live ammunition. Some twenty thousand Chinese women and young
girls were raped, mutilated, and murdered, and tens of thousands of other
civilians were robbed and killed at random. It is estimated that over two
hundred thousand Chinese soldiers and civilians, including women and
children, died in the orgy of slaughter that became universally known as
the Rape of Nanking. It should be noted that many among Nakajima's own
soldiers were sickened by the horrors but were far more afraid of their commander's brutal iron discipline. That such a military unit was included in

the invasion force was to prove an all too ominous portent of the fate that was soon to fall upon the Philippines and its hapless defenders.

In all, Homma had roughly seventy thousand troops to conquer the Philippines within a scheduled timetable of some fifty days, after which the bulk of his assault force was to be required for other campaigns farther south that were considered priority by the General Staff, including such prizes as Australia itself. It was considered vital that the Philippines be completely under Japanese control by March 1942, a schedule destined to be frustrated by the sheer will of a doomed but determined force that refused to acknowledge the possibility of defeat.

The force assigned to the Lingayen Gulf assault landings absorbed over half of Homma's invasion army. Most of the Lingayen force's combat strength had been drawn from Lt. Gen. Yuichi Tsuchibashi's 48th division, formerly the permanent Japanese garrison force on Formosa. Not yet tried in battle, the 48th was composed of the 1st and 2nd Formosa infantry regiments, the 47th infantry, and supporting artillery, reconnaissance, engineer, and transport regiments. These would be followed by a large force of service and "special" troops to consolidate and occupy captured areas. The 2nd Formosa had already been engaged, having made up the Tanaka and Kanno detachments, which had landed earlier at Aparri and Vigan in Northern Luzon. Each infantry regiment had one battalion of bicycle-equipped troops. These were for the purpose of speedy maneuvering in the course of plunging and enveloping tactics so favored by Japanese commanders. Their artillery was the 48th mountain artillery, which employed the pack (horse-mounted) 75mm Meiji-41 mountain guns, eminently suitable to Luzon's rough, mountainous terrain.

Bolstering the 48th's untried force were the veterans of the "Black 16th" division's 9th infantry and part of its 22nd field artillery with horse-drawn 75mm howitzers. Heavier 150mm artillery was provided by the 1st and 8th field artillery regiments.

Finally, there was Homma's armored hammer. A force of some one hundred medium and heavy tanks supported by weapons carriers and mobile antitank guns would provide the steel temper for the 14th army's spearheads and advance columns. The heavy tanks, only medium by American standards, were 18-ton Che He Type 97s assigned to the 7th tank regiment. In turn, light by American standards, the medium tanks—low-slung 14-ton Shiki 95s equipped with short-barreled, armor-shattering 47mm cannons mounted on turrets with sloping sides similar to those observed by Japanese, studying German armor in Europe, to be highly difficult to penetrate with antitank gunfire—were assigned to the 4th tank regiment. The latter were destined to lead the attack from Homma's first beachheads.

As Masaharu Homma watched his troops embark, he was painfully aware of a dismal little manual issued to and carried by each of his men. Authored by Col. Masanobu Tsuji in one of his inspired moments of pious devotion to duty and cause, it had been issued as mandatory reading to all in the Strike South force. Entitled "Read This Alone—And the War Can Be Won" and marked "Confidential," the manual was designed to motivate each and every young knight of Bushido with feverish determination to carry their sacred war to every white enemy and his allies with the solemn spirit and credo of NO QUARTER.

The men of the Strike South forces had been instilled with professional zeal bordering on fanaticism. Japan was the underdog in this multifront war, and every Japanese soldier knew it. Tsuji's peculiar how-to manual endeavored to drive home a spirit of divinely inspired invincibility and was punctuated with grim realism frightening to even hardened veterans. His text rambled discordantly over a wide range of matters, from spiritual respect to care of weapons and health in the jungle to enemy habits and culture. These subjects were punctuated by a grim discourse on preparations for a proper death.

Primarily a document reflecting his own inner rage and racial and cultural prejudice, a sampling of Tsuji's bitter, convoluted wisdom read:

- In the Japan of recent years we have unthinkingly come to accept Europeans as superior and to despise the Chinese and the peoples of the South. This is like spitting into our own eyes.
- Once you set foot on the enemy's territories you will see for yourselves just what this oppression by the white man means. Imposing, splendid buildings look down from the summits of mountains or hills onto the tiny thatched huts of the natives, our Asian brethren. Money that is squeezed from the blood of Asians maintains these small white minorities in their luxurious mode of life [a significantly hypocritical sentiment after Tsuji's tacit, and sometimes active, approval of widespread atrocities committed by the Japanese against fellow Asians in China]. After centuries of subjugation to Europe, these natives have arrived at a point of almost complete emasculation. We may wish to make men of them again quickly, but we should not expect too much.
- Weapons are living things, and rifles, like soldiers, dislike the heat. When soldiers rest they ought to give their rifles a rest, too, offering them, in place of water, large drinks of oil.
- Before going into the battle areas—in the ships at the very latest— you should write your will, enclosing with it a lock of hair and a piece of fingernail, so that you are prepared for death at any time or place. It is only prudent that a soldier should settle his personal affairs in advance.
- When you encounter the enemy after landing, regard yourself as an

avenger come at last face to face with his father's murderer. The discomforts of the long sea voyage and the rigors of the sweltering march have been but months of watching and waiting for the moment when you may slay this evil enemy. Here before you is the man whose death will lighten your heart of its burden of brooding anger. If you fail to destroy him utterly you can never rest at peace. And the first blow is the vital blow.

- Westerners, being very superior people, very effeminate, and very cowardly, have an intense dislike of fighting in the rain or the mist or at night or in hostile, difficult terrain. This weakness is to our advantage. By jungle is meant dense forest in which a large variety of trees, grasses, and thorny plants are all closely entangled together. Such places are the haunts of dangerous animals, poisonous snakes and harmful insects, and since this is extremely difficult terrain for the passage of troops, it will be necessary to form special operation units for the task.
- Beware of poisonous snakes. These lurk in thick grass or lie along the branches of trees, and if you do not watch where you put your feet or hands you may well be bitten. If you discover a dangerous snake, you must of course kill it. You should also swallow its liver raw and cook the meat. There is no better medicine for strengthening the body and your fighting spirit.
- Pineapples and coconuts are good for quenching the thirst, and in mountainous areas you will find that lopping a branch of wisteria and sucking the open end will prove helpful.
- This type of terrain is regarded by the weak-spirited Westerners as impenetrable, and for this reason—in order to outmaneuver them— we must from time to time force our way through it. With proper preparation and determination it can be done.
- Maintenance of direction and good supplies of water are the supremely important factors critical to success.
- You must demonstrate to the world the true worth of Japanese manhood. The implementation of the task of the Showa Restoration [the reign of Emperor Hirohito], which is to realize His Imperial Majesty's desire for peace in the Far East, and to set Asia free, rests squarely on our shoulders.

Tsuji concluded his rambling document with these dreary lines from "Umi Yukaba," a Japanese martial anthem:

> Corpses drifting swollen in the sea-depths,
> Corpses rotting in the mountain-grass. . . .
> We shall die. By the side of our Lord we shall die.
> We shall not look back.

With such cheerless counsel burning in their minds, ancestor-haunted Japanese soldiers, most of them from simple peasant stock, would think and fight like men possessed and would tend to take few prisoners. Those they did would be made to suffer miserably in captivity, being considered beneath contempt for not choosing an honorable death in lieu of lowly surrender. Doctrine such as Tsuji's cultivated a belief that it would be an insult to their emperor's virtue if they did not take more lives than they lost. Conversely, Tsuji's observations on Caucasian arrogance would prove, with disastrous consequences for the Western allies, to be all too intuitive. Complacency in the face of what Westerners so mistakenly presumed to be an inferior, even comic, enemy would explode in their faces. Allied troops' morale would plummet into a mire of guilt and feelings of individual inadequacy as they tried to comprehend the reasons for their initial defeats at the hands of fighting men whom they had been conditioned to think of as little more than trained, nearsighted monkeys in sloppy uniforms.

Whatever the inspirational value of Tsuji's outrageous manual, if any, General Homma, always the professional soldier, despised both the author as a man and his poisonous little document. Far from seeing the manual as uplifting to his soldiers, Homma regarded it as the ravings of a madman and a potential for erosion of genuine military discipline necessary for effective military operations. The mind of the Japanese soldier of the ranks, typically of peasant origin, was taxed enough by concentrating on orders from his immediate superiors. Tsuji's baleful philosophizing could only dilute concentration on soldierly things. This disturbed Homma, who was of the mind that too much spiritual fervor could hinder the functional workings of a soldier's mind and complicate a commander's job—*his* job.

Homma silently cursed Tsuji and his manual. "Damn the man and his power!" he thought (as later recounted in his wife's memoirs). The old soldier was still smarting from his insulting, perfunctory treatment by the "Bathroom Door" and still outraged that he, a general of long, dedicated service to his emperor's army, had not been allowed to even review the plans for his own assignment drawn up by that impudent, outrageous little upstart colonel and his outlaw Unit 82.

At 9 a.m. on 17 December 1941, Homma departed from Kirun on the *Teiryu Maru*, one of twenty-one transports escorted by the Batan Island Attack Force, which had returned to Formosa after its first Philippine assault on 8 December. At noon on 18 December, the convoy from Mako in the Pescadores, the second farthest departure point from the Philippines, set sail with twenty-eight transports escorted by warships of the Vigan Attack Force. The final contingent of the invasion force weighed anchor from Takao in Formosa at 5 p.m. that day with twenty-seven transports escorted by the support ships from the Aparri landings. After rendezvous at sea, Homma's Lingayen force now combined 43,110 men in seventy-six transports carrying two hundred landing craft. The convoy was escorted by two battleships, four heavy cruisers, one light cruiser, two seaplane tenders, and several dozen destroyers and submarines. Some five hundred army and naval aircraft had been scheduled to cover the force from above once in "hostile waters."

There had been a great deal of confusion during the transfer of units to their embarkation points and during the loading. Because of the strict secrecy imposed on the operation, only a select few officers were privy to the plans. These men had to move constantly between the different units and assembly points to oversee and assist in the desperately complicated loading preparations. Officers on unit level, operating with only the most meager information permitted to them, labored virtually blind. Their most crucial orders were revealed to them only at the final moments, allowing little time to assess the problems of logistics and to make proper preparations. The cumulative result was confusion overridden by constant fear of American detection and retaliatory bombing of Formosa and its ports with their vital staging areas. The cloud of secrecy and apprehension followed the men to sea. Even then no one was told where they were going, and the use of maps was restricted to only a select few necessary to direct the convoy's progress. Being kept in ignorance served to sharpen the already edgy nerves of men who knew by all the signs that they were headed for a major combat operation. Homma's own staff was not even allowed to know the destination until he was officially notified to reveal it. Later he noted, while on trial for his life before an Allied tribunal, that "during all my campaigns in the Philippines, I had three critical moments. This was number one." The success of the Imperial General Headquarters' plans for the Strike South force now rested squarely on Homma and the men who sailed with him.

That night, after the convoy's final rendezvous, the husky general stood at the deck railing staring out at the darkness of the China Sea. It was cloudy, and in the blackness even the nearest ships were only dim outlines. Homma sensed someone approach him, and he turned to find his chaplain, Yoshiaki Nakada, by his side at the railing.

"*Gomen nasai*, good evening, My General," said Nakada, making a small, quick bow. "Please forgive me; I did not intend to disturb you."

"*Yoroshiidesu, Nakada-san*, that is all right," replied Homma. "I was just thinking of my *gunjin*, my soldiers out there and of the burden and suffering they must bear soon. It is a most heavy responsibility which our Emperor has entrusted to our hands."

"*Daijobu, tomodachi Homma sama*," answered Nakada gently. "Do not worry so, Homma my friend. I believe you will find that the Crane[3] casts a long and protective shadow over his children."

"*Arigataku omou, Nakada san*," replied Homma with a small bow. He then returned to his quarters to compose a short haiku poem for his wife, Fujiko, and each of his children, as was his habit before retiring.

At the same time that Homma's task force was plowing through rough seas toward their Philippine objective, a massive Japanese air strike force was being organized to deliver a decisive blow to MacArthur's USAFFE air power, naval, and defense installations. Army bombardment formations of bombers and dive bombers, along with Japan's longest-range land-based fighters for escort and strafing assignments, were being martialed at air fields on Formosa. At sea, Japan's most modern naval fighters, Mitsubishi A6M2 Zeros (Navy Type 0 Carrier Fighter Model 21s) and first-line assault aircraft were steaming carrier borne toward launching points to deliver devastating, surprise blows to their assigned Phillipine and American targets.

Army Air Force General Brereton, after the urgent and short warning about Pearl Harbor, had ordered his command to keep as many planes in the air as possible. At approximately noon on 8 December (Philippines time) the pilots who were forced to land for refueling were caught flat-footed at Clark Field by the Japanese bomber assault while eating a hurried breakfast. Their planes were literally sitting ducks for the attack force. The Americans lost twenty-three bombers and most of their effective fighters in the initial attacks, virtually wiping out USAFFE's Philippine air defense force on the first day of hostilities. Brereton had been begging MacArthur to bomb Formosa but was refused. His pleas for some kind of attempt at air retaliation with what he had left of a bombing force were similarly refused, and one by one those remaining warplanes were also either destroyed or transferred to alternative fields on Mindanao or Bataan or flown to safety in Australia. As for most of the Philippine force's airmen, they were ignominiously issued rifles and transferred to the infantry.

NOTES

1. Homma later described his feelings on that night in his memoirs and testimony at his war crimes trial.
2. Japanese merchant marine vessels.
3. A symbol of reference for the Japanese emperor or imperial throne.

6

North to Rosario

16 DECEMBER 1941

Bamban, Pampanga

While the regiment was still in bivouac in Bamban, Maj. Thomas J. H. Trapnell arrived with his command, F Troop, from their detached "palace guard" duty based at Nichols Field just outside Manila. Their forced march of over sixty miles in five days had been a grueling one, having been frequently under attack from the air and having to force their way through hordes of refugees going in both directions in total confusion and chaos following the initial Japanese attacks on Manila and the surrounding provinces. Their arrival was a welcome reconstitution for the strength of the 26th Cavalry Regiment, which had by necessity lost significant numbers because of orders to detached duty of some of its units.

Tom Trapnell ("Trap") was a West Pointer with a notable record, a career soldier and cavalryman of the first order, a rugged individual, and a powerful personality. His presence added steel to the regiment.

Born in Yonkers, New York, on 23 November 1902, one of four brothers, he seemed to be destined to action and leadership. He began making football history in the Mount Hebron Grammar School in Upper Montclair, New Jersey, and learned early to face odds without flinching. His grandfather, a trustee of Episcopal High School in Alexandria, Virginia, got him a partial scholarship when Trap came of age for secondary school. At Episcopal he soon established himself as a leader in sports, recognized as outstanding in track, basketball, lacrosse, and football, which he captained in his third year. During his early days of school, Trap came under strong inducement to become an Episcopal minister and follow in the footsteps of his great-grandfather, grandfather, and two uncles, all of whom were men of the cloth. But both sides of Trapnell's family were also predominantly military people, many serving as rebel troopers in the Civil War. Trap idolized Robert E. Lee, with whom his grandfather served, and it was incurable. Fascination with soldiering won out.

Trapnell was influenced to try for an appointment to the U.S. Military Academy at West Point and devote his life to military service by Maj. Charley D. Daly, a football player and army coach immortal. Trap's first try got him only an alternate appointment for the first year, so he went to work for his brother Joe, who was port steward and purchasing agent for a Baltimore steamship company. On that job, Trap sailed the high seas as an ordinary seaman, but he soon concluded he no more wanted to be a career sailor than a minister and tried once more for a West Point appointment. This time his competitive examination grades were impressive enough to win his place in the "Long Grey Line." At the Point, Trap was well liked, a great athlete, and a serious scholar earning ranking as a Phi Beta Kappa and becoming president of his class for his three final years at the academy. He was outstanding as a football player, lacrosse player, and boxer, his high-water mark being his football performance before 110,000 fans who jammed Chicago's Soldier Field in 1926 to watch Army and Navy battle to a 21–21 tie in a never-to-be-forgotten gridiron classic.

Trap graduated from the Point on 14 June 1927 and was appointed a second lieutenant of cavalry. Until 1930 he served in California, coaching football part time in addition to cavalry duties. In June 1932 he was graduated from Cavalry School at Fort Riley, Kansas, and was promoted to first lieutenant the following February. From 1936 to June 1939 he saw duty at Fort Myer near D.C. and was promoted to captain in 1937. He captained the show horse team and played polo from 1937 to 1938 and then was assigned under Jonathan M. Wainwright to Fort Stotsenburg, where he soon became one of Skinny's favorite officers. He was quick to catch MacArthur's royal eye also. On 20 March 1940 Trap was assigned as assistant to the chief of staff of the Philippine Department, and in January 1941 he was promoted to major. He was assigned to a 26th Cavalry (PS) troop stationed at Nichols Field just outside Manila where between numerous ceremonial duties and parades he became a star army polo player and enjoyed the high life of Manila. Oh, but it was a grand time then. War changed that in a hurry.

On the night of 16 December the 26th regiment, now minus Fitch and his artillery train, gathered its gear and resumed the march north, this time with a heightened sense of urgency pervading the ranks.

At around 2:30 a.m., they made camp north of Capas and remained there during the day. That night the march was again resumed and the column rode into the town of Gerona just before daylight on 18 December. All that day, the regiment rested and fed themselves and their mounts in a thick coconut grove west of the town. After dark, they started north again toward the town of Rosales, Pangasinan, about a twenty-five-mile ride, which they made by around 3:00. The saddle-weary regiment set up a fairly well covered bivouac area, and the 26th lay low in Rosales for two days. While it was in part a time of freshening up, their time there was made less restful than needed because of constant, heavy Japanese air activity overhead. No American aircraft had been seen for several days, which did not contribute to calm. Nerves were on edge and, although security was always routinely posted at night, it was now strengthened. Tension was running high from the numerous reports that kept coming in from advance scouts and other units that the Japanese columns had definitely shifted directions and were now pushing south down along the west coast toward Lingayen. One positive note was that there was no difficulty with supplies and food. Everything was coming up from Stotsenburg, the trucks moving regularly at night. Hay and grain were dumped off the regimental supply trucks at points along the road nearest the bivouac area and then hauled by hand to the horses. Supply, forage, and mess were still regular. When the column arrived at Rosales, kitchen trucks were waiting, and the veterinarians and blacksmiths efficiently set about checking every horse for sores, chafing, illness, and loose or missing shoes, which were replaced immediately. An additional boost to morale was that a section of two SPMs (self-propelled vehicular mounted artillery) were attached to the column for support.

General Wainwright had by now moved his headquarters up to Santo Tomas near Rosales at Alcala on the Agno River. He called in the senior regimental, squadron, and troop officers for briefing on the latest developments with enemy movements. Navy PBY patrol planes had spotted a Jap convoy forty miles east of Lingayen Gulf. General Homma's invasion force convoy was now under sufficient air support from newly acquired forward land bases. The only light note of the meeting was that it was Tom Dooley's birthday, which merited a round of scotch to all present.

On 29 December the U.S. submarine *Stingray* reported a Japanese convoy sailing southward. Early on the morning of the 21st, men on beach defense at Bauang on Lingayen observed a Japanese trawler casually sail in and take depth soundings. The defenders were ordered not to fire. Alarmed at the advance of the Japanese Vigan forces and realizing poorly trained Filipino defenders were overwhelmed just north of San Fernando, La Union, Wainwright ordered a counterattack up the coast. The 26th Cavalry was all he had left to order in support of the counterattack. Wainwright passed the order down to Colonel Pierce and the 26th staff that the regiment would now be attached to the command of the 11th Division, Philippine Army, under Brig. Gen. William E. Brougher. They were to proceed north to the Lingayen Gulf area. These were hardly uplifting meetings considering the fast-deteriorating developments, and the officers found it impossible to keep the scuttlebutt network from sifting the high points of bad news down from officers to noncoms and ultimately to the troopers.

At around noon on the 21st orders came down to prepare for movement again toward Rosario. To the consternation of the cavalrymen, the SPM artillery was transferred away from them to reinforce the crumbling coastal defenses. Once again, the 26th was deprived of any heavy weapons. Their move became a hurry-up process, and few men got a noon meal, a bad sign that heightened the general sense of foreboding among the troopers. Most of the men got hastily prepared lunches to eat while in the saddle. By contrast, it was a standard rule of practice that grain bags on the saddles should be kept full at all times. Readying for the move took only about half an hour. In the midst of all this hurried activity, another disquieting wrinkle in the order of things came about. The big, popular, red-headed Capt. Ralph Praeger's Troop C, with junior officers Lieutenants Tom Jones and Warren Minton and their crack riding first sergeant, Tom Quiocho, were ordered to dismount, take arms and essential gear that could be carried by hand or on their backs, and load up on familiar red Pambusco public buses waiting for them. They had been ordered north overland to the Baguio area where the troop was to patrol on foot (the men were all wearing their riding boots and leggings, not suitable for any extensive infantry activity) north in the mountains to intercept any enemy movements south down the Central Plain and, when and if possible, to plug any runaway retreat of Philippine Army forces. The hastily drawn plan was for Troop C to carry out their orders and to rejoin the regiment in Rosario, La Union, or somewhere in the area near Lingayen. In the meantime Troop C's horses and tack were turned over to Troops A and B to be led and cared for until retrieved by the troopers of C. These men were destined not to see their regiment again. The remainder of the now understrength, somewhat dejected regiment rode out of Rosales and marched west, then north toward their destination of Rosario, La Union, along the Baguio highway until dark. After covering some twenty miles, the column was ordered halted at dusk and directed to set up bivouac in a coconut grove in an area just outside the large town of Pozorrubio, Pangasinan, a provincial government center. They received orders to await further orders. That night the horses all had to be watered from a deep well. It took about two hours for Troops A and B to water their animals and those of the absent Troop C using the same well. Fortunately for all, Troop A always carried one collapsible bucket per squad, two if available, a trench shovel, and a lariat. It was a practice that had proved valuable frequently.

The kitchen trucks, however, did not get to the area until well after midnight, having had to duck Jap air patrols repeatedly all the way. But there were shovels to dig foxholes and slit trenches, and the horses had grain and enough grass and forage to keep them going in decent shape. The men, however, had to go with nothing to eat. This was considered by the troopers to be an ill omen. There had been no time to prepare meals to be carried on the march, and in the hot, humid, and debilitating Philippine climate, it was impractical if not impossible to keep sandwich meals on hand as they would so quickly go stale. Though there was ample room in the saddlebags for them, no compact, boxed field rations were available in that period in history, only a few canned rations (to be used only when severe emergencies demanded it) and some rare, preservable fresh foods. In hindsight, pack animals carrying field rations would have been invaluable. December 21 started off no better. The order to saddle up came long before dawn and too quickly for the kitchen trucks to be able to get breakfasts ready in time. Unknown at this time to the troopers of the 26th was that this was the morning of the Japanese invasion in Lingayen by General Homma's overwhelming assault. In Pozorrubio, however, one of the few good things about the morning was that the day came up cloudy, ideal for marching and good for retarding activity by enemy aircraft. However, hunger was beginning to demoralize the men.

When dawn broke, the regiment was riding north through rolling countryside toward Sison, Pangasinan. En route, the regiment passed a group of American M-3 light tanks of the 192nd National Guard Battalion parked under the cover of trees on the roadside. The tankers, many of them eating canned rations, waved cheerily to the passing horsemen.

The presence of National Guard tank units in the Philippines had considerable significance with regard to the history and gradual shift of American cavalry from horses to armor. A chain of events that would lead to the first actual tank-to-tank combat involving American armored forces in World War II was set in motion in 1921. Under a congressional act in 1920, the reorganization of the cavalry was put into effect and the number of horse-mounted regiments in the U.S. Army was cut from seventeen to fourteen. Ironically, one of the last three horse-mounted regiments that was added— the 26th Cavalry PS—would also be the last regiment of the U.S. Cavalry to go into combat horse mounted as an integral fighting unit.

Little did the tankers on the Northern Luzon road realize that their fate would forever be entwined with that of the horse cavalrymen who passed them that day on the way to Sison.

The thrust of the reorganization was intended to reduce overhead costs, eliminate units thought to hamper a regiment's freedom of movement, while at the same time add firepower across the board and still preserve the valuable mobility of cavalry. It was during this search for the right balance of mobility and weaponry that a then-radical train of thinking, kept carefully quiet until then by its proponents, began to surface. While Gen. Billy Mitchell of the Army Air Corps made headlines in his sacrificial championship of a separate air force, another group of equally dedicated officers began to exert more subtle pressure to achieve what they saw as a vital need for the army. They wanted a mechanized force even though they knew it would spell doom for their beloved horse cavalry with its cherished traditions. Thus, the battle between dedicated horse cavalrymen and proponents of mechanized warfare was joined.

In the vanguard were Brig. Gen. Samuel D. Rockenbach and Lt. Col. Daniel Van Voorhis, who would be dubbed, respectively, the "Great Grandfather" and "Grandfather" of the armored force. Perhaps it was prophetic that they and numerous of their fellow cavalry officers had some service and seen action in the Philippines prior to WWI. History would prove repeatedly that those troubled islands with their complex and unstable terrain had instilled lasting and hard-learned lessons in the virtues of fluid maneuver backed by superior firepower.

In 1917 AEF commander General Pershing (who had served with distinction at the head of the famed all-black 10th [horse] Cavalry "Buffalo Soldiers" in American southwest Indian wars and at San Juan Hill in the Spanish-American War) chose General Rockenbach to head the newly organized American Tank Corps. Pinned down by the administrative load of his new command, Rockenbach tapped veteran horse cavalryman George S. Patton Jr. to oversee training the Tank Corps' twenty light tank battalions. In August 1918 Rockenbach was made Chief of Tank Corps, 1st American Army. His tanks and men won high praise from Allied commanders for their roles in the battles of St. Mihiel and the Meuse-Argonne. Their fighting, however—to the chagrin of all—was done entirely in French- and British-made tanks, the most popular of these being the French Renault light tank. America's own tank production hadn't enough lead time to get this strange new and complex machine to war on time.

General Rockenbach, now reverted to his peacetime regular rank of colonel, returned to the United States in 1919 and remained Chief of the Tank Corps until June 1920 when Congress decreed that tanks would merge with infantry. Never giving up his vision of tanks as a separate branch of the army, Rockenbach transferred to the infantry and assumed command of the tank school at Fort Meade, Maryland. Promoted to brigadier general in 1924, he returned to the cavalry in 1927. By then the advocates for mechanization had persuaded the army General Staff to put their ideas to the test.

Initial maneuvers utilizing obsolete WWI Renault-type tanks at first convinced the General Staff that tanks were too slow to operate with the horse cavalry, but the seed was sown to study further development of an independent tank force and to argue for funds for new equipment. By 1930, Army Chief of Staff Charles P. Summerall, convinced that tanks must be part of any effective artillery-infantry-machine gun team, decreed, "Assemble that mechanized force NOW and station it at Fort Eustis, Virginia. Make it permanent, NOT temporary!"

Commanding the new Fort Eustis force was the mechanization crusader Col. Daniel Van Voorhis. The long-awaited separation of mechanized from the mainstream of infantry and cavalry was short-lived, however. In 1931 a new army chief of staff, Gen. Douglas MacArthur, another Philippine veteran, dissolved the Fort Eustis force and directed that in its place all branches of the army were to adopt mechanization and motorization "as far as is practicable and desirable" and be given free rein to conduct appropriate research and experiment to that end. By 1933 the mounted-horse cavalry's destiny was set on an unalterable course toward complete mechanization with MacArthur's stinging declaration that "the horse has no higher degree of mobility today than it had a thousand years ago. The time has therefore arrived when the cavalry arm must either replace or assist the horse as a means of transport or else pass into the limbo of discarded military formations." He continued, "There is no possibility of eliminating the need for certain units capable of performing more distant missions. . . . The elements assigned to these tasks will be the cavalry of the future."

Fort Knox, Kentucky, was selected as the center for development and testing of combat vehicles. The Fort Eustis force was transferred and formed the nucleus of the new command. In 1933 the 1st Cavalry was ordered to Knox from their base in Marfa, Texas. The Fort Knox command decided to turn the transport of the 1st into a large-scale training mission utilizing all their wheeled equipment and most of their personnel. V Corps HQ disapproved this, but still a large contingent essential for the move was ordered to Marfa. The round trip, made in midwinter, became a memorable cross-country march, unprecedented in its time. The motley array of vehicles covered some 3,240 miles in thirty-one days, from 17 December to 16 January, with only six days of layover. Only one vehicle was lost. The men who made the long march in subzero weather camped in pyramidal tents heated by small Sibley stoves and slept on what straw or dry grass could be procured locally. All arrived at Fort Knox in good order. So it was that the replacement of horses by machines in old cavalry units had begun and American mechanized cavalry passed from its infancy.

In 1938 the two cavalry regiments were joined with other Fort Knox units to form the reorganized 7th Cavalry Brigade (Mechanized) under the resumed command of now Brig. Gen. Van Voorhis. His guidance proved a major factor in forming armored doctrine for the future. The 7th was the beginning of the first total armored divisions. Later that year Van Voorhis was succeeded by Col. Adna R. Chafee, formerly second-in-command of the Fort Eustis force. Chafee was recognized already as a pioneer and strong advocate of mechanization, and his leadership earned him succession in the armored dynasty as "Father of the Armored Force."

The 1939 German blitzkrieg in Poland altered military thinking forever. The Fort Knox tankers seized upon the opportunity arising from the shock created by the Wehrmacht's armored successes and began to openly push for what had been until then a carefully veiled heresy—the creation of full-scale armored divisions with complete supporting elements of their own. Their plea fell on deaf ears until the 1940 Louisiana maneuvers, when an improvised armored division formed by the 7th Cavalry (now reinforced by the 6th Regiment Motorized Infantry) and the provisional tank brigade from Fort Benning, Georgia, stole the show. The mechanized units, haphazardly organized and equipped as they were, dominated the massive military exercises. Louisiana, adding to the alarm raised by the blitzkrieg, carried the argument for the value of armor, and on 10 July 1940 the armored force was created ("for the purposes of a service test") by the War Department with Chafee, now a brigadier general, in command.

From the beginning, the new force struggled to overcome its makeshift, experimental character and the drag of obsolete equipment. As early as 1931 at Eustis when cavalrymen were first launching mechanization, they favored the light tank in keeping with the traditional purpose and maneuverability of light cavalry. Their experiences of success with the Renault reinforced this attitude, which largely carried over to the new force in 1940. In early October 1939, initial orders for tanks in the WWII era called for no less than three hundred light (eleven and a half tons) M2A4 tanks. By 1940, a much improved light tank, the M-3A1, was adopted. It was first furnished by lend-lease to England where it was dubbed the "General Stuart" and later nicknamed "Honey" by British tankers in North Africa. While similar to its predecessor, the M3 was three and a half tons heavier, longer, and had better suspension and flotation (low ground pressure). Manned by a crew of four, its main armament was a new and effectively antiarmor 37mm main gun and had a maximum speed of 35–40 mph. Later, in the Philippines in 1941 the M-3A1 "Stuart" would be the first tank driven by American tankers into WWII combat.

Summer 1940 found Chafee's fledgling armored forces with real problems. When the new arm was established, the 70th General Headquarters (GHQ) Reserve Tank Battalion at Fort Meade was its only separate or non-divisional battalion. It was the armored forces' only reserve and it was short of personnel. When Chafee learned that War Department planning called for use of many such reserve units as special task forces but that no provision had been made to organize such units, he was horrified. He protested to Chief of Staff George C. Marshall that without authorization for such reserve units, his armored divisions would be chopped up piecemeal "to fritter them away for small purposes." Chafee's repeated pleas for additional GHQ reserve units bore fruit, and by early 1941 four additional separate tank battalions, the 191st through the 194th, were organized from eighteen scattered National Guard tank companies. These units would always be referred to as the army's "orphans" because they didn't fit into the T/O (table of organization) of divisions.

On 25 November 1940, the first of these, the 192nd GHQ Tank Battalion, was inducted into federal service at Fort Knox. The 192nd would also be the first U.S. armored unit to experience direct tank vs. tank combat in WWII. The bulk of the 192nd's HQ company and one tank company, B, were all guardsmen from Maywood, Illinois. The remaining companies were from Port Clinton, Ohio, and Jamesville, Wisconsin. About 65 percent of these men had participated in the recent Louisiana maneuvers. The remainder were young guardsmen who had never seen the inside of a tank and whose only training had been from manuals and mockups. Most of them were childhood buddies, and every casualty in their coming ordeal would represent the loss of a friend or relative.

The other three tank battalions were organized soon after—the 193rd at Fort Benning, Georgia, the 194th at Fort Lewis, Washington, and the 191st at Fort Meade, Maryland. Because these newly inducted reserve battalions were expected to be in active federal service only for one year, no effort was made to standardize them or have them conform to any established T/O or equipment. Only two of the units had participated in maneuvers with tanks, the 192nd in Louisiana and the 194th in minor exercises with the 4th army on the west coast. Both had utilized early models of the obsolete M1 light tank.

In August 1941, with war tensions fast building between the United States and Japan, Gen. Douglas MacArthur, now commander of the newly formed USAFFE, requested an armored division for his forces in the Philippines. The reply was piecemeal. On 26 September the first installment debarked on the docks of Manila in the form of the 194th GHQ and the 17th Ordnance Company (Armored). Upon movement to their port of embarkation from the United States, the 194th (as would the 192nd, which followed it in November) was ordered out of its vintage M1s and hastily reequipped with the new M3 light tanks and armored half-tracks. The newly issued heavier tank and its equipment were totally strange to the personnel. The 37mm cannon, the main turret battery, was accompanied by a coaxially mounted .30-caliber machine gun. Two remote-controlled sponson guns, which could be fired by the driver, and a .50-caliber antiaircraft machine gun completed the firepower. The first surprise that confronted these new M3 crews was the tank's power plant. Lifting off the covers, they (as had astounded British tankers before them) found, rather than an expected diesel, a gasoline airplane engine simply stuck into a tank. It had radial cylinders and a big fan looking every bit like a propeller. Fuel would later prove a major problem because the seven-cylinder, air-cooled Continental W6–70 engine ran efficiently only on high octane aviation gas!

The weaponry and the improved radio facilities were also new to the crews. Time and instructions were so sparse in the haste for departure that the bewildered and frustrated tankers made the disastrous mistake of thinking it necessary, in order to install the strange communications gear, to remove the right sponson gun to make space. They then spot-welded plates over the now-empty gun port with the result that their tanks were not only deprived of one needed gun but now had a "soft spot" in their frontal armor! Once seaborne en route to the Philippines there was no opportunity to engage in hands-on training with the M3 as the turrets had to be removed to fit the vehicles into the ships' storage holds. To add to the confusion, the tankers were ordered to apply a heavy coat of Cosmoline (protective grease) to all guns and ammunition to prevent corrosion during the long Pacific voyage. The last of the thick mess was still being cleaned off when the first Japanese bombs struck Clark Field on 8 December. It was indicative of the slap-happy, tragicomic way much of USAFFE went to war in that fateful year.

The 192nd shipped out from San Francisco under the command of recently appointed Col. Theodore F. Wickford from Maywood, Illinois, who had been a major only a year serving as second in command to former Bn. CO Col. Bacon Moore, who had been declared overage and relieved. Moore, a fine leader and military teacher, was highly regarded by his troops, who petitioned vigorously to prevent his transfer. Moore argued hard to accompany his men to the Philippines, but he was turned down cold, as were others of the original hometown groups for the same reasons of age. It was a dispiriting touch and a loss of experienced officers. Some comfort, however, was taken in that the gaps were filled with replacements from the original companies' home states.

To preserve maximum secrecy, the various 192nd companies traveled different, sometimes circuitous, routes to the embarkation point. It added an air of suspense to the confusion already caused by coping with unfamiliar equipment. They were staged at the island installation of Fort McHenry and debarked from San Francisco on a former excursion liner converted to a troop transport. The voyage took twenty-two days, of which four were spent in Honolulu to off-load some cargo and pick up other material bound for the Philippines. At sea they traveled the whole way in black-out conditions and under war alert. This was explained to all personnel simply as training for war condition preparations. There was considerable overcrowding in the troop areas, but the seas were kind, with only a few moderately rough days when the portholes had to be closed in quarters just above the water line. The troops in the latter were envied by those in the holds as having "the bridal suite." In all, the general feeling was that the roll of the dice sending them to duty in the fabled Philippines was strictly sevens.

When the 192nd arrived in port in Manila on 20 November 1941, the impression was quite different. The customary welcoming band and ceremonies for new arrivals were replaced by a port detachment under Col. E. V. Miller of the 194th on the docks with weapons at ready. The air was electric.

"Draw your firearms immediately," rang out the terse order. "We are under full alert. We expect war with Japan at any moment. Your destination is Fort Stotsenburg and Clark Field." The men soon learned that Fort Stotsenburg, adjacent to Clark Field, was about fifty miles northwest of Manila in Pampanga Province.

After initial arrival and off-loading the ship, most of the personnel proceeded immediately via Philippine narrow-gauge railway to Pampanga. The details left behind to finish off-loading went via road convoy two days later. On 21 November the Provisional Tank Group USAFFE was organized under the command of Brig. Gen. James R. N. Weaver. In what was to later prove to be a high point of friction between General Wainwright, NLF field commander, and General MacArthur, the tank group was made a separate tactical command answering to HQ USAFFE at No. 1 Calle Victoria in Manila. The 192nd, 194th, and 17th Ordnance would comprise MacArthur's entire armored force, as events turned out. The final elements for MacArthur's requested armored "division," a medium tank GHQ and supporting units, never arrived.

Completely readied for departure for Manila, its orders were canceled on 10 December. By then the Japanese had shut the door to the Philippines for any reinforcement.

Once at Stotsenburg, the tankers soon learned that this was also the base for the 26th Cavalry Philippine Scouts, who were operating in Northern Luzon as the cavalry reconnaissance for Gen. Jonathan Wainwright, commander of that sector of defense. Until the scheduled arrival in November of the provisional tank group's CO, General Weaver with the 192nd, the 194th engaged in limited recon in Northern Luzon in cooperation with 26th Cavalry recon units. The tank group was not given the benefit of any firing problems or cross-country driving because fuel, spare parts, and ammunition were being tightly reserved and all gunnery ranges were restricted to them. One of the results of all this was that the tank crews still had no opportunity to familiarize themselves or qualify in any manner with their new weaponry, especially the 37mm main guns.

Weaver and his group HQ detachment took up residence in tents at Stotsenburg pending completion of semipermanent housing to be constructed of "sawali," a native-style siding of two-inch reeds woven onto bamboo frames. The only activity for the tankers at this time, other than trying to learn the workings of their new equipment and constantly cleaning the greasy Cosmoline off everything, was some limited recon duty, which took them as far north as Lingayen Gulf and Baguio, the Philippine "summer capital" in the mountains to the northeast. The most important experience gleaned from these forays was to familiarize tankers with the deceptive and treacherous hazard of dry-appearing rice paddies, which, under the surface crust, were dangerous quagmires—natural death traps for the thirteen-ton M3s. They quickly learned the road-bound nature of their area of operations and held new respect for the necessity of horse-mounted recon troopers of the 26th Cavalry.

Some of the humor and frustration of those first days in the Philippines and the opening of hostilities were related by Sgt. Forrest Knox of Company A, 192nd Tank Battalion, to Donald Knox, author of the book *Death March*.

Pearl Harbor ruined the best joke we ever had cooking. Our little bit of Army was different from the regular Army. Ours was a family, a National Guard unit. Everybody knew each other and everybody had a nickname. We had one guy, Bernard Shea, we called "One horse" who took the brunt of many of our jokes. He was a little different from the rest of us and it was a dirty rotten shame they ever took him overseas. He was used as an officers' "dog robber" (go-for) and in that capacity he functioned fine. But I knew, because he didn't have enough smarts to survive what was coming. Poor Bernard was dead the day the war started.

Anyway, outside Clark Field where we were, we could walk to a barrio called Sapangbato. We called it "Sloppy Bottom." Most evenings we'd go down and get into these little Filipino bars. In them they served little duck eggs called balots (pronounced baluts). Just before a duck is ready to hatch, the Filipinos hard boil or bake the egg. To the Filipinos it's a great delicacy. The joke was that you were a true native if you knew which end of the egg to break to avoid biting the duck's ass. Well, One Horse went ape shit the first time he saw someone eat a baby duck. So we coaxed him over to a corner table and got him pinned in there. We wouldn't let him go and everybody just leaned on him while the barmaid ate baby ducks. Finally, he wriggled loose and crawled out under the table. Well, we couldn't pass this up, so we bought two baluts and next morning, which was December 8, the cook who was of course serving hard boiled eggs, was going to put two baluts in One Horse's mess kit. I tell you, nobody in the company was going to miss One Horse cracking open his eggs. Then those rotten sonuvabitchin' Japs bombed Hawaii and we didn't have breakfast. Our reaction to Pearl Harbor was that those bastard Japs ruined the best gag we ever thought up. It seems like a silly reaction now.

We got over losing our duck gag when we were immediately ordered to scatter our tanks in the brush outside the Clark perimeter. We realized we didn't have any ammo loaded, and when they couldn't find our machine gun belt loader they told us to load the damn stuff by hand. I avoided that duty for a while and instead was told to clean the cannons. "Christ," I said, "you have fifty-four tanks and only one rammer staff. Besides I don't even know where the staff is!" They said, "Clean them damn cannons!"

"OK, OK," I said and went and cut a piece of bamboo and wired a chunk of burlap to the end. An absolute no-no in the Army—one thing you never do—is wash a barrel with gasoline, because it removes the oil, permitting the barrel to rust. By God, I cleaned seventeen cannons that morning. Just zip, zip with a bucket of gasoline and my piece of burlap. Each tank commander yelled at me, but I told them I was cleaning out the cosmoline so they could fire the cannons. It was up to those jackasses to put the oil back in so they wouldn't rust.

On 27 November a general alert had been sounded for all forces in the Philippines, but in the confusion of the new command structures of USAFFE, someone omitted including the tank units in the warnings. General Wainwright arrived at Stotsenburg on 28 November to take over the NLF command only to find that Weaver's tanks were still only to answer to Manila. The commanding officer of Clark Field, however, had been ordered by Far East Air Force to execute by 2 December two alerts, one by day and one by night. One of the executive air officers, Major Daley, asked for the tank group to participate. Thus on 1 December, Weaver's force moved into battle positions for the defense of Clark Field.

When in the early morning hours of 8 December (still the 7th in Hawaii) news of the Japanese attack on Pearl Harbor reached the Philippines, crews were already manning their tanks at 3 a.m. At 8:30 word was passed that Japanese planes were only forty minutes away. Clark Field's planes by then were already in the air and ready, but no attack came. Weather in Formosa had delayed the plans of the Imperial Air Force. At 11:45 the American pilots were ordered to land to refuel. Their planes were parked in neat rows being maintenanced and the crews were in the mess halls when the first wave of attackers came over at twenty thousand feet, just out of range of American antiaircraft fire. Japanese intelligence on the range of U.S. ordnance had been frighteningly accurate. The bombers blasted MacArthur's air force to a pulp at will. It was not until the Japanese Navy Zeros came in low passes to complete the devastation with strafing runs that the tankers could bring their guns into play. Technical Sgt. Temon "Bud" Bardowski, B Company 192nd, is credited with the first enemy plane downed by U.S. armor in WWII.

No one had ever bothered to tell the tankers how to lead high-speed aircraft targets, but after so many repeated passes by overconfident Japanese pilots, American marksmen's instinct began to take a toll. After that, low-level strafing and incendiary runs became fewer as Jap pilots became wary of tank presence. Another, sadder precedent is credited to Pfc. Robert H. Brooks of Company D 194th, who was the first American armored soldier killed in WWII combat. He was hit while manning a sandbagged antiaircraft machine gun emplacement in the tank park. Today, the main parade field at Fort Knox bears his name.

7

First Enemy Contact at Lingayen

21 DECEMBER 1941, MORNING

En route to Sison, the 26th Cavalry column moved along the paved road in formation—strung out, single file on both sides of the road—employed to minimize grouped targets when a route passed through an area with barbed wire bordering both sides of the road or trail. A little past first daylight, the alarming sound of aircraft engines was heard fast approaching the column. The planes came into sight flying low along the strung-out regiment. The signal for an air attack (troop leaders waving hats) came just ahead of the planes, so every man was already set to dive for whatever cover was available (in this case, shallow ditches along the roadsides). By this time the troopers were all too well educated in what it would be like to be surprised by enemy strafers. Horses were pulled into the bordering ditches and the men hit the ground making themselves as small a target as possible. To the joyful relief of the men, the planes turned out to be two lonely American P-40s on patrol, both giving them a friendly waggle of their wings as they passed overhead. The dash for the ditch, as it would prove all too soon enough, had been a valuable practice exercise.

Meanwhile, Japanese invasion commander General Homma had been given reports that elevated his fears concerning the notoriously common, treacherous Lingayen tides, which would be encountered by his landing forces. Homma was to later recall that this was one of the most serious times of concern for him in the Philippine campaign.

At about 9 a.m. the 26th column reached the junction of the highway where the Kennon Road goes on to Baguio and Highway 3 turns west toward Rosario. Ominously, the sky was beginning to clear, and the regiment was dangerously exposed in the open. Japanese planes were increasingly scouting overhead in all directions but had not yet attacked. The regiment was ordered halted and moved off the road to rest while a company of light tanks from the 192nd moved by them and went on ahead to Rosario. Lt. Clint Seymour of B Troop dropped wearily, his back against the base of an acacia, and looked skyward, scowling at an insolently circling enemy plane. "You son of a bitch," he muttered, reminded of scavenging buzzards back in his native New Mexico, "we're not dead meat yet, you bastard!"

"Hey, Clint," called out the cheery voice of Hank Mark. "Maybe some of this will cheer you up! Come and get it before I eat it all!"

Seymour looked up to find Mark calling his attention to a beaming little Filipina girl who was holding out a large banana leaf on which there were several pieces of freshly cooked *lumpia*, a stuffed, fried thin pastry similar to a small egg roll. These were filled with fish.

Mercifully, during this brief rest period, civilians ventured out to move about the troopers opening coconuts with machetes and offering other bits of local food items they had prepared for their protectors. These horsemen were their soldiers and nothing could be too much to offer. It was little yet it was everything, and the tense, hungry troopers were grateful to the point of tears. For some of them, it would be their last meal on earth before that day was finished.

"No three-star restaurant in the world could serve up a meal so welcomed and delicious as the offerings of *bibinkas* [small rice cakes], fish wrapped in banana leaves, small, freshly fried bits of *lumpia*, bits of fruit, sweet bread, and other local foods, which were everyday stuff to the locals but world-class delicacies to our tired, hungry men that morning," mused 1st Lt. Arthur K. Whitehead of A Troop, a man who would in the coming months learn only too well how to live off the land in the Philippines.

The regiment remounted and resumed the march west toward Rosario. At 10 a.m. the first elements of the 26th Cavalry trotted into Rosario. A company of light tanks of the 192nd were already parked and spread out throughout the town. Earlier, just before dawn, Lt. Johnny George and his section of scout cars had passed through Rosario on their way to the coastal village of Damortis. They had been sent ahead of the main column and ordered to reconnoiter what was taking place along the coastline of Lingayen Gulf. George shivered as he hunched his shoulders and tucked his chin deeper into his shirt in a vain attempt to ward off the damp chill from an intermittent rain that was falling at the time. The whine of the heavy Dodge engine was beginning to numb his senses as his driver, Corporal Millado, strained in the darkness to keep the bouncing, lightly armored scout vehicle on course in the pitted, rocky road. The windborne rain lashed mercilessly into the forward compartment making the cold, metal interior and the steel-framed seats with their thinly padded, heavy canvas covers all the more cheerless. George hated the cold. The cavalry had rescued him from the bitter winters of his native Indianapolis, Indiana, and he thought back to more pleasant times at Fort Riley and of his wife, Hazelbel, who now waited with their infant son in the small house not far from the post. She was to have joined him in the Philippines, and they had both been excited by his assignment to such a coveted duty station. But anticipation of an exotic life together in the islands had been short lived. Being among one of the last contingents to be shipped over, George had literally arrived in time to see the families of his fellow Americans being shipped home on the very ships he had arrived with. He and his family would never share the pleasures of warmth again—anywhere.

In the equipment bed of George's vehicle, Pfc. Felix Lenardo pulled a damp blanket tighter around his shoulders and tried to wriggle into a more comfortable position on the steel ammunition boxes that served as his seat next to the .50-caliber machine gun mount. Across from him the radio operator, Private 1st Class Umguin, shared his fate as they felt the slam of armor plate with every bump in the road.

The little column was now on the final stretch of road leading west from Rosario to the coast. In the second car was platoon sergeant Domingo de Mesa, the best baseball player in the regiment. He shared the car with three close friends from his home town in Pampanga—his driver, Corporal Laago, his radio operator, Corporal Miole, and the young gunner, Private 1st Class Camplon. De Mesa, too, was thinking of better times. He remembered a particularly sunny afternoon back at Stotsenburg. It now seemed like a century ago. Baseball practice was in progress at one end of the parade ground. A trooper in a jersey inscribed "26th Cavalry" was batting easy grounders to the shortstop, who scooped them up and fired them to the first baseman. "Hey, Demi," someone called. "Sergeant Masiclat wants you right away."

With a final toss to the baseman, de Mesa headed for the regimental HQ, wondering what the hell he'd done now and hoping it wasn't a chewing out from Masiclat, a fairly formidable personage. Lieutenant George had put the scout car platoon through a stiff tactical problem during the previous week's field exercises, and the men were still sweating out the results. Once in the office, he reported stiffly to Sergeant Masiclat, who, not bothering to look up from the mail he was reading, acknowledged with a stern, "Take a seat, Corporal." Placing the papers in his "out" basket, he finally swiveled to face de Mesa.

"Do you know why I asked for you?"

"No, sir."

"Here, take a look at this," Masiclat said, thrusting a paper toward the worried-looking corporal.

De Mesa tried without success to suppress a wide grin as he read. "Gee, Sergeant Major, I thought I'd flunked the field problem!"

"Well, you didn't," growled Masiclat. "You deserve an extra stripe—and, de Mesa," said Masiclat with mock sternness again, "consider yourself lucky. Some others got themselves busted down to buck private on that exercise. Congratulations, Sergeant."

De Mesa smiled as he recalled hurrying home. He had encountered his eldest son, Arthur, first.

"Hi, Pop, where's the fire?"

"Come on, Son, I've got news!"

As they burst into the little house, Felicidad de Mesa was sewing. Her maiden name was Mitchell. She was the daughter of a U.S. Army Air Force master sergeant, Henry Mitchell. She and her young cavalryman had been married in 1928.

"Mommy, I've got good news for you," beamed de Mesa. "You are now looking at Sergeant de Mesa of the Scout Car Platoon."

"Oh, Demi, that's wonderful," she bubbled, jumping up to embrace him. Suddenly he was almost smothered in hugging arms and small bodies leaping against him as Domingo Jr., aged nine, Joe, six, and Louise, four, all vied for a better hold.

"What in the world is happening here?" demanded de Mesa's mother, who emerged from the kitchen carrying Demi's youngest, Jessie, two, in her arms.

They celebrated that night, and de Mesa remembered still another celebration later on. In the spring of 1941 still another son was born. It was all the excuse needed for friends, mostly fellow scouts and their families, to descend for a feast. He remembered a table piled high with roast pig, *loppa-loppa*, spicy chicken, *sili*, *buco* pies, *mutche* rice donuts, *lanzones*, and every other conceivable treat that could be brought in. The San Miguel and rum punches flowed freely, and one trooper, Sergeant Ysmael, puffing heartily on one of de Mesa's cigars, slapped him on the back and boomed, "Well, compadre Demi, this blessed addition goes to show that you're now well on your way to fielding your own baseball team!"

Someone else chimed in, "Yeah, he has five now—lacks only four, the outfielders and a third baseman!"

As de Mesa hunched over the wheel of his scout car, he reflected that the safety of his family was entrusted to his father-in-law, now retired near Clark Field but recently recalled to active duty because of his critical skills. De Mesa's in-laws would continue to watch over them for the duration of the war, evacuating from one place to another to survive.

As false dawn slowly gave way to the first light of the day, the scout cars pulled into the little town of Damortis at the junction of the coast road where Highway 3 turned north. The name Damortis was Spanish, literally "crack in the wall," suggesting a place of passage. That was one thing Skinny Wainwright dearly hoped it would not be that day.

George and his men found two companies of Philippine Army infantry occupying the town. No real defensive positions appeared to be in evidence. They were just there. After checking the area, George called a brief conference of the car commanders and ordered the section to start moving north on the coast road.

Acting as the point scout on his motorcycle was Cpl. Eulalio Arzaga, who had driven Mark's detail to Manila. George ordered him to move on well ahead and check out the road as far as the coastal town of Agoo, six miles away. In the cold, heavy morning fog, Arzaga rode the big Harley-Davidson with caution. He had gone about four miles when the first rays of sun began to break through the mist. Damp and miserable since he had left Pozorrubio, he started to feel warmed for the first time. He began to relax, almost fatally.

Rounding a slight curve blinded by a bank on one side, Arzaga suddenly found himself in the midst of a sea of mustard-colored khaki and conical helmets. His reaction was instantaneous. The Japanese dispersed like a covey of flushed quail. Fortunately for Arzaga his shock did not freeze his reflexes, and he made the first move. Jamming the Harley's throttle wide open he spun the cycle violently to the right, spraying the Japanese *gunjin* (soldiers) with a shower of dirt and gravel. With a roar he plunged into the low underbrush that grew along the road and headed south at maximum power. For about fifty yards the shaken scout, tangled branches whipping and slashing at his legs, tore through the roadside cover. By now the Japanese had recovered from their initial shock. Officers and noncoms shrieked commands and bullets began to snarl past Arzaga, who by now felt as though his pounding heart would burst through his chest wall at any moment.

Uninjured except for his lacerated legs, he met the scout cars after about a mile and a half. Breathlessly he reported to George what had happened. By now the mist was breaking up rapidly and George bounded off the road to the crest of a low hill to try and get some kind of view offshore. Sergeant de Mesa was right behind him. George clawed for his binoculars and wheeled toward the shore. The visibility had by then become surprisingly good. What Johnny George saw was not.

"Oh my God Almighty," he gulped, "I never knew there could be that many Japs!"

He handed the binoculars to de Mesa with a choked groan. "Sergeant, can you get any kind of count?"

"It's hard to say sir. There's still a lot of fog farther out. I make it about twenty transports, escort warships, and very many landing craft coming ashore."

As far north as they could see, landing craft were shuttling back and forth between the transports and the beaches. Ashore they could make out enemy units forming up and moving inland unopposed. The whole scene had almost the deceptive appearance of some huge peacetime industrial operation in its efficiency. There had been no warning sounds of naval bombardment to reveal the operation because there had been no bombardment. There was no opposition to bombard. The Japanese, utterly confident of their superior strength and in the weakness of the defenders, had simply concluded that a covering barrage for the landings would be an unnecessary waste of ammunition. The audacity of it was an added slap in the face of the already stunned and frustrated defenders.

Lieutenant George motioned to de Mesa and started back down the hill. "Sergeant, we'd better get 'em saddled up and turned around if we don't want to get cut off. This place is going to be crawling with Japs in no time."

As they withdrew southward, George began radioing his report back to the regimental HQ. They had gone only about a half mile when suddenly there was the *whang* of bullets against the scout cars' armored plates. George yelled at Millado to floorboard it as he felt himself involuntarily scrunch down deeper in the hard seat. Now the sharp popping of small-arms fire seemed to come from all around them as the Dodge engines roared to life and the heavy cars lurched forward gathering speed. Then a heavy staccato boom began to answer the hostile crackling around them as the gunners in the rear of the cars frantically worked the retractor handles cocking the heavy, mounted .50 calibers, pressing the trigger mechanisms and putting the big machine guns into action while small-caliber bullets whined and snapped angrily around their ears. Arzaga, now for the second time in minutes, was bent over riding for his life on the Harley.

They had run into a party of advance scouts from the Japanese 48th reconnaissance regiment, commanded by the daring and aggressive young Lt. Col. Kuro Kitamura, one of Homma's favorite officers. The 48th had been moving south fast on both sides of and well off the coast road, probing to see how far south Homma's first flying columns could seize ground before hitting any respectable resistance.

They now had found it in the form of Johnny George and his 26th Cavalry scout cars. Now the glove was down and the fight was on.

The 26th Cavalrymen raced on until they crossed a bridge over a creek about a thousand yards north of Damortis. Here George signaled his drivers to halt and ordered them to split their force and take up positions on both sides of the road, thus setting up for a straddling crossfire to block the enemy's route of advance. With the deep slash of the creek, it was an ideal lay of the land for the cavalrymen to adhere to Col. Clint Pierce's regimental Plan 1 for delaying maneuver.

De Mesa hunched over his heavy, mounted .50-caliber machine gun and thought dryly, "You'll have to pay a toll to cross this bridge you motherless bastards."

It would be only the first of a long trail of bridges where the Japanese *gunjin* would bleed tribute to the 26th Cavalry and its dedicated troopers.

8

Pause and Preparations before the Storm: The 26th and 192nd Join to Face the Impossible

22 DECEMBER 1941, 10:30 A.M.

Rosario

Back in Rosario, the rest of the 26th column had settled into town to await further orders. The light tanks, which had passed the 26th on the road to Rosario and now shared the town with the horse cavalrymen, were Company B of Gen. James R. N. Weaver's 192nd National Guard tank battalion. While this company, short of enough gas to field the whole unit, was a meager reply to a desperate plea by Wainwright to MacArthur for tank support early that morning, 22 December marked the beginning of an intertwining combat relationship between the 192nd and the 26th Cavalry, which would be shared in blood in one battle after another starting on the Lingayen coast and continuing down the length of Luzon southward and on into Bataan. It would prove to be a brotherhood forged in steel, tears, and blood that would cost the Japanese a high price for conquest.

In the days following the Clark Field debacle, General Weaver's tanks had been redeployed to provide wide defense coverage against additional air attacks and potential paratroop assaults (widely rumored but which never took place). They were supported from the start by horse-mounted 26th Cavalry troopers patrolling areas too difficult for tanks to traverse. By the end of the day 10 December, the Japanese landings in the extreme north at Aparri and Vigan were consolidated and now spreading southward in a pincers to converge at the expected primary invasion site—the beaches of Lingayen Gulf. With only three ill-trained and poorly equipped Philippine

125

Army divisions, and one battery of field artillery, a few invaluable self-propelled 105mm field guns, and several big 155mm guns of the 86th battalion Philippine Scouts that were emplaced for coastal defense, which constituted his only heavy artillery, a Philippine Scout infantry battalion in Baguio and his prized 26th Cavalry horse soldiers, General Wainwright (himself the consummate, eternal cavalryman by nature and profession) had to defend an area about 625 miles long and 125 miles wide at its broadest point. His plight was made worse by the absence of headquarters personnel and corps troops necessary to direct and support operations in so large an area. It was a strategic, tactical, and logistical nightmare.

By 20 December, Gen. William Brougher's 11th division (Philippine Army) and the few 105s were Wainwright's only hope to defend the northern Lingayen beaches already threatened by a Japanese breakthrough moving down the west coast. First sightings of a huge invasion force confirmed the worst predictions, and Wainwright desperately began to seek means to counterattack up the coast to prevent link-up of the two enemy columns and take the pressure off Brougher. On 22 December, Japanese invasion commander Gen. Masaharu Homma's main force landed, and Wainwright's beach defenses were fast being overwhelmed. The only resort now was counterattack. Wainwright hoped to use Gen. Clyde Selleck's 71st division (Philippine Army) supported by Weaver's tanks with the 26th Cavalry in reserve.

22 DECEMBER, 7 A.M.

Wainwright's HQ near Alcala on the Agno River

At about 7 a.m., while the 26th was still on the march to Rosario, Skinny Wainwright could stand no more of the waiting, reviewing useless maps and listening to the ragged flow of disconnected information.

"Let's get the hell out of here and take a look for ourselves at what's going on," he barked at the members of his staff.

Leaving his chief of staff Col. William F. Maher to tend shop, Wainwright and his G-3 CO Frank Nelson piled into the general's battered 1936 Packard. The big, off-green car was being driven by his devoted orderly, Sgt. Hubert "Tex" Carroll, a tall lanky Texan who had been with Wainwright since he'd been at Fort Clark in 1938 (and who would remain with him steadfastly until his retirement from the army). Next to Carroll was a Filipino orderly, Corporal Centino. Wainwright's two aides were Lt. Col. John Ramsey "Johnny" Pugh (Wainwright's senior aide), a cavalryman who had accompanied Wainwright to the Philippines from Fort Myer, and Major Thomas Dooley (junior aide), an officer from the 26th Cavalry who Wainwright had taken a liking to for both his affability and his ability. They were instructed to follow in the G-2 car with Sergeant Franko, a half Moro detached from NLF from quartermaster, and Corporal Munoz, a Manila taxi driver, at the wheel. The sharp-eyed Franko acted as the group's air spotter, riding most of the time with his door open watching in all directions for enemy planes, which were becoming more active in the area by the hour. For lunch, the group was carrying meat (of unknown origin) sandwiches wrapped in toilet paper. "They finally wrapped them right," quipped Wainwright.

Their first stop was 71st division (Philippine Army) HQ in Urdanetta, where Wainwright called a conference with Gen. Clyde A. Selleck to discuss his counterattack plans. The conference was held at Selleck's HQ in Urdanetta, where they were joined by provisional tank company Gen. James R. N. Weaver, who had set up his own command post nearby. Weaver told them he was headed up to confer with his 192nd battalion commander with the force MacArthur had finally just released to support the NLF. This was news. The 192nd at last had been taken out of reserve at midnight 21 December and assigned grudgingly by MacArthur to the defense of Northern Luzon, while the 194th tanks were to act as combined reserve and armored defense for Southern Luzon.

The brief conference over, Wainwright indicated for Weaver to accompany him on leaving. Telling his driver to follow, Weaver joined Wainwright for the trip as far as Manauag where Brougher's 11th division HQ was located and the tank group was bivouacked.

On the way, Wainwright stressed to the tank commander his dire need for battalion-strength armored support and pleaded that since the tanks were still under USAFFE command in Manila, the closest possible cooperation between the two field commanders was critical. Weaver assured Wainwright he would do all he could to persuade MacArthur—at the same time recalling that just one week before, his recommendation to move the 192nd to Lingayen was met with the USAFFE chief's curt reply that NLF "had too much up there already!"

At Manauag, Weaver departed on his mission and Wainwright met with Brougher, who was not a favorite of Wainwright's. He disliked Brougher for being a chronic complainer and lacking in the leadership needed to inspire his green Filipino troops. Here Wainwright did get updated information of the Japanese landings, and the news was all bad. Despite Brougher's excuses and rhetoric, it was plain to see that the 11th was crumbling at every point when hit, and the NLF's beach defenses were badly threatened with being cut off completely. His counterattack plans were fast going up in smoke. He had no choice now but to ask Col. Clinton Pierce and his 26th Cavalrymen to do the impossible—hold a line along the coast road and the intersecting Route 3 road to the key junction town of Rosario, about seven miles inland, and keep open the strategic Kennon Road south from Baguio. Thus to the small, understrength horse regiment fell the responsibility of being the linchpin protecting the entire northern flank of NLF. They *had* to have tank support from Weaver!

As soon as he sent his messenger off to Pierce with these fateful orders, Wainwright directed Tex Carroll to a public phone booth on the roadside. Such telephones had been his only reliable communication to HQ Manila for days! Now he borrowed still another nickel from Carroll and once again frantically tried to get through to MacArthur. The best he could do to crack MacArthur's royal inner circle was to get through to the general's chief of staff, Gen. Dick Sutherland, a man known as a dedicated and tireless worker but aloof and protective of MacArthur to the point of obsession. Not a politician to begin with, Wainwright was in no mood for Sutherland's usually pompous and condescending manner. Skinny cut straight through to the point.

"Brougher's being cut to pieces, and I need a tank battalion—NOW! Give it to me or the Japs are going to be serving tea in Manila before you can spit. All I've got is Pierce and his 26th Cavalry to hold them long enough to get my people off the beaches. *I* can't give Weaver the order—he's still under your direct command. I need armor—NOW!"

Echoing MacArthur's latest decree from Manila, Sutherland answered imperiously, "I am unable to authorize that. At present, we are committed to defend every inch of our sacred soil in the Philippines, and we cannot carelessly expend our reserves."

Now near apoplexy, Wainwright shot back, "I'm the goddamned corps commander, and if you don't let me fight the way I see it from here in the field, those little bastards will be in your lap in hours. Until then, for God's sake give me permission to utilize these forces up here as I see fit."

Nonplussed, Sutherland replied coolly, "I will ask the general," and abruptly hung up. Shortly after, a call came in on Brougher's main communications line. The communications sergeant called for Wainwright to take the call.

"This is Sutherland," said the flat voice. "The general has already instructed General Weaver to dispatch a company of tanks from the 192nd to the Rosario–Damortis vicinity to support your defenses."

"A company!" exploded Wainwright. "I'm facing maybe two entire Jap divisions, maybe more, with one depleted regiment of horse cavalry!"

"I'm sorry, General Wainwright, but that is all we can commit to you at present."

Sutherland continued in his condescending voice, "General MacArthur wishes me to express his confidence in you and your command. I'm sorry but the situation is very tight everywhere. Good luck to you all."

Skinny Wainwright handed back the phone and turned to his aides, grim faced.

"One tank company is the best we can give Pierce. Let's get the hell over to San Fabian and see what the artillery is doing."

The fact was that up to now the big 155mm guns of the 86th field artillery battalion Philippine Scouts was the only segment of the defense force that was giving Homma anything to be nervous about. They had two guns at their forward position at San Fabian on the Lingayen Bay and two more farther south at Dagupan. When the rough seas had forced many of the Japanese ships to shift anchorage farther south than intended, they moved into the range of the 86th gunners who opened fire. The scouts reported having sunk up to three transports and two destroyers, but in reality other than some light damage and a lot of near misses, their main accomplishment was inciting the jittery Japanese commanders to concentrate a rash of air strikes on Wainwright's only heavy coastal batteries at Lingayen.

As Wainwright and his party approached the site of the batteries about one and a half kilometers south of barrio San Fabian, the ever alert HQ sergeant Franko suddenly shouted, "Nips! Get off the road!" Franko leaped from his perch on the running board of Wainwright's Packard being driven by Carroll, who careened the Packard toward the ditch, and the G-2 car with Skinny's aides Pugh and Dooley followed suit. Instantly, men were diving out of the doors for the mucky shelter of the roadside drainage ditch where they huddled until the Japanese dive bombers completed their run. Wainwright could feel the brutal slam of the concussions go through his body and hear the rattle of debris flying through the trees.

"Gentlemen, I believe we're getting close to the problem!" he shouted. Now Skinny Wainwright was in his element.

When the raid was over they moved forward again and reached the artillery men under the command of Lt. Col. Donald Van N. Bonnett, whose position was still intact and going into action again. After a few words with the battery commanders and satisfied with what he saw, Wainwright returned to his car and announced he was going to Rosario via the back way. Johnny Pugh and Tom Dooley were joined now by an 11th division regimental commander, Colonel Fipps, and were told to make a swing by a place called Tabu where a Filipino battalion was operating under command of 1st Lt. Frederick Thomas, one of the all too numerous 26th officers detached to the Philippine Army to be of any help to the regiment. Thomas had an observation tower built at his CP, and from it Wainwright's two aides had their first actual look at the horror of the Lingayen invasion. They stood for a time trying in vain to get a count of the ships through field glasses, then, thoroughly sobered, they left to join Wainwright in Rosario.

Meanwhile, B Company 192nd under the command of Capt. Donald L. Hanes was racing to Rosario to rendezvous with the 26th Cavalry. He and his unit had left the barrio of Dau outside Clark Field at noon on the 21st with orders to refuel en route at Gerona. There was no fuel there to meet the M-3's requirements, so the company proceeded on to Manauag, where they joined other elements of their battalion.

Lt. Benjamin R. Morin, commanding B Company's 2nd platoon, later recalled, "We arrived about midnight of the 21st. All motor movement after dark was done without lights. I believe this was an unnecessary security measure considering the cloud cover that night. It caused great inconvenience and delay, both on the march and in taking position at Manauag. Corporal Vertuno arrived with our gas truck, and several men from my platoon unloaded the drums and refueled the tanks immediately. It started to rain rather heavily at about 0300 hours, so my crew and I retired for the night inside our tank. It was a damp, brief, cramped sleep we had, too. About 0600 the company began to stir. I reported to Captain Hanes. I don't recall any breakfast there in Manauag, and I'm sure there was none later that morning."

Ben Morin would never eat chow with his battalion again.

At about 8 a.m. on the 22nd, B Company's M-3s rattled past the 26th Cavalry column just outside Rosario. The young National Guardsmen waved and shouted good naturedly at the horsemen, who reined their startled mounts off to the roadside to give way to the tankers. Together they were now pawns in the hoped-for miracle needed to stem the avalanche gaining speed on Lingayen's beaches.

Once in Rosario, the 192nd M-3 light tanks were dispersed in the town under the cover of large trees along the narrow streets and in the shadow of buildings to seek as much as possible concealment under the circumstances from ever-present Japanese aircraft on the hunt.

At around the same time, Pierce arrived in Rosario with his HQ staff and received a message informing him that General Wainwright was en route to Rosario to meet with him. At about 8:30 Wainwright, followed by Pugh and Dooley, skidded into Rosario and met with Pierce immediately. Wainwright unloaded some ominous news on the cavalry commander. The regiment was now ordered relieved from 11th Division and attached to the 71st (Philippine Army) under Brig. Gen. Clyde A. Selleck. Skinny's new orders were given reluctantly, knowing what he was asking of his beloved 26th. He stated that their mission was to prevent the enemy's Lingayen force from coming south of the Rosario–Damortis line, prevent enemy advance along the same road, and also protect the eastern flank of the NLF. It was a formidable order for the now severely understrength 26th. In truth, it was an order tantamount to the impossible. After wishing Pierce the best of luck under the circumstances, Wainwright and his party left to check on what was happening to Bonnett's more northerly force, which was being driven hard by the Japanese column coming south from Vigan to take Baguio and the key Kennon Road—Bonnett's escape route. But Bonnett, in his evasion of the enemy force, had halted his force in Baguio for food and rest, thus giving the southbound enemy time to gain momentum. Wainwright's plan, even if he had to sacrifice Bonnett's way out, was to hit the south-bound Japanese spearhead with some of his "best-seasoned men in my command—the 26th Cavalry." His problem, however, was that the 26th also had to hold the line at Damortis. In short, it was a nightmare. Troop C under Praeger was the only 26th unit headed in the vicinity of Baguio, and one troop of cavalry on foot was most surely not enough to stop the enemy column heading toward them.

At 8:45 Clint Pierce called a hasty officers' conference. Having just received Wainwright's latest orders, he and his staff were trying to digest the enormity of their situation. To add to his concerns, Lieutenant George's advance reconnaissance party had just radioed that contact had been made with advance Japanese patrols probing the coast road. The 26th recon unit had already set up a roadblock position in view of the beaches. At this point Brigadier General Weaver, commanding officer of the Luzon tank battalions, arrived with his recon officer Captain Morely and B Company 192nd Battalion commanding officer Captain Hanes and joined the conference. Weaver addressed Colonel Pierce and informed him of his orders to put the tank company now present in support of the horse cavalry. He went on to explain dismally that fuel trucks carrying aviation gas for the armor had not caught up with his tanks as yet. He went on to say that his tankers were now pooling their remaining fuel in order to put one platoon—five tanks—on the road to meet the enemy advance. For lack of gas, Wainwright's urgently requested armored battalion had already dwindled to a company and now down to a mere platoon!

Tank Lt. Ben Morin was peering over at Colonel Pierce's spread-out maps. "What magnificent maps," he later recalled. "They showed where everything was. Those things they gave us didn't show half this stuff. Hell, they were even better than those Texaco road maps everyone was trying to get their hands on!"

"Lieutenant Morin here will take his platoon out first, Colonel," said Hanes. "We'll follow up with the rest when the fuel gets here."

"ENEMY PLANES!" somebody suddenly yelled. Morin looked up abruptly and counted perhaps three Japanese fighters circling for a run. He bolted for his tank, which was parked nearby. General Weaver ran right behind him ordering him to site his tank for a high-angle shot with his still untried 37mm cannon. Morin, who had never yet even fired the gun, muttered that this was not a great idea but, nevertheless, shouted at his driver, Private Zelis, to get out of the way and man the controls. Vaulting up to the turret, Morin hunkered down behind the sights, getting only a glimpse of the diving plane in the crosshairs and holding his fire as he couldn't bring the gun to bear. The Japanese, unmolested and apparently not seeing anything to shoot at, passed on. Morin sagged on the gunner's step and let out a deep sigh of relief.

Captain Hanes came up and told Morin to get his platoon ready to move out and to ready all guns for action. Morin rounded up his tank commanders, pointed out as best he could possible points of encounter on his rather incomplete map, and assigned the order of march and formation for their "assault." Then he briefed them on their objective and what he knew of the mission in general. Doing his best to convey an air of confidence, he ordered his men to get their tanks ready to move out. At 9:10 a.m. General Weaver briefed Morin on his final orders, which amounted to "proceed at once to the coast road and push north to Agoo to attack Japanese forces in that vicinity. That's about twelve kilometers north and west from Damortis on the road north to Vigan and Laog. Then go ten kilometers farther to barrio Aringay and destroy enemy forces there. The enemy should not as yet have been able to bring his tanks and heavy guns ashore."

It was a mission assigned for a tank regiment, not a platoon, but Lt. Ben Morin accepted his commander's orders without comment or question and signaled his crews to mount up. Then, his tanks—all five of them—coughed to life and went off to war.

22 DECEMBER 1941, 9:35 A.M.

Rosario

The main column of the 26th, which had begun its march at 7 a.m., arrived in Rosario at around 9:35 a.m.

Upon the main column's arrival, Pierce now ordered the regiment's rear echelon be established in the town of Rosario and detached "F" Troop to cover the trails leading from that vicinity to the north and west. The rest of the regiment would make preparations to leave Rosario for Damortis. While in Rosario, the tired 26th cavalrymen settled into town to check equipment and horses and get as much breather as possible while awaiting the order to move out again for Damortis. Some of the light tanks which had passed the 26th on the road to Rosario still remained to share the town with the horse cavalrymen. These were the rest of Company "B" of General Weaver's 192nd National Guard Tank Bn. still waiting for fuel to arrive. These last tanks of Company "B," short of enough gas to field the whole unit, was all that remained of the slim reply to Wainwright's desperate request to MacArthur for major tank support that morning.

Thus it was that December 22 marked the beginning of an intertwining combat relationship between the 192nd and the 26th Cavalry which would be shared in blood in one battle after another starting on the Lingayen coast and continuing down the length of Luzon southward and on into Bataan to the end. It would prove to be a brotherhood forged in steel, tears, and blood that would cost the Japanese a high price for conquest.

22 DECEMBER, 9:50 A.M.

That morning in Rosario, Sgt. Maj. Eliseo Mallari of the 26th's second squadron had a problem.

Lt. Mat Zerfas, the regimental chaplain, was making the rounds offering spiritual strength to the troopers, most of whom were devout Catholics and all of whom now knew that they would soon be in combat. The problem was that Zerfas himself, being young and untried in battle except for the air attacks since 8 December and especially the one close call in Manila with Mark's detail, was finding it difficult to keep his hands from trembling and his voice from quavering as he recited general confession and gave benediction to the religious cavalrymen. Mallari could see that the chaplain, despite his best intentions, was only making the men nervous as hell instead of bolstering their courage and giving them inspiration. When Zerfas got to the point of being literally difficult to understand, Mallari, as quietly and courteously as he could, sidled up to the youthful padre and whispered, "Father, I know you do your most kindness for the men, but I can see also that this will be the first time that you will face the death game. Please, Father, let the men make their own peace with God now. You can do no more for them."

Zerfas nodded to Mallari gratefully and gently retreated.

10:15 a.m.

A gunning of engines and the rattling of treads on Rosario's main street signified the departure of the remaining 192nd tanks. The 26th Cavalrymen were adjusting the buckles on bridles and girths and checking pack gear and weapons in final preparations for the march.

"PREPARE TO MOUNT. MOUNT," came the familiar order, yet somehow this time it had a different, more abrupt, urgent ring to it.

The order of march was led by B Troop, whose first sergeant, Justin Bulawan, and six troopers moved out as point for the column. Next came a platoon of machine gun troop led by Capt. Jack A. Ford and platoon commander 1st Lt. Paul N. Allen. A Troop under command of Capt. Leland W. "Jack" Cramer followed with the remainder of the machine gun troop behind them. Capt. John Z. Wheeler brought up the rear with his E Troop. Vance, "trooping the line" like a mother hen, had positioned scout cars at intervals along the column. Their .50-caliber machine guns, all tilted skyward now, constituted the regiment's only significant defense against the freely marauding Japanese war planes that the cavalrymen had been observing all morning, swooping and diving on unseen targets whenever one looked toward the coast. Up to now, the planes and dull thumps in the distance were the only signs of war that day to those riding in the column, but every man sensed that he would soon face the Japanese in close combat. The real enemy being fought now was fear—how to subdue it, how to hide it, bury it, keep it under control, and, most of all, how to cover all signs of it in the eyes of others: comrades-in-arms, superiors, and subordinates. Each man fought this private battle in his own way, in different ways, some silent and resolute, some talking too much, too loud, with forced and false bravado, some nervously chewing or spitting to show that his mouth was not too dry to do so—but inside, fear itself was the same. It knotted the stomach; it raced the heartbeat; it turned the mouth dry as dust and fouled the breath. Oh yes, it is fear that makes itself felt by every living soul in the presence and awareness of danger—fear—not the face-saving rationales tagged with bogus names and catch phrases such as "nervousness," "butterflies," "pregame jitters"—just fear: real, natural adrenalin, a chemical reaction, and God-given as a protective instinct. What separates the brave from the cowardly is not an immunity to fear, such an immunity being in itself an unnatural state or absence of normal consciousness, but the measure of one's capacity to control fear and to prevent it from paralyzing the thoughts and reactions and actions necessary to cope with what is required at any given moment of threat to existence, to life itself. Fear is an enemy only if allowed dominance of all other instincts, and, like so many other dangerous forces, its power can be harnessed and channeled into positive strength if one has the will and the discipline to do so. Few who have ever been brought by circumstance to a place or state on the edge of the abyss, where death's nearness can be tangibly sensed, can deny the sharpening of the awareness of all about them, all that is a part of them. It is an adrenalin-induced state in which a single grain of sand or blade of grass can be isolated by the eye and seen in stark, blazing clarity if kept in control. It is a common experience for those who trade in danger such as racing drivers, bull fighters, veteran professional soldiers, and, not the least to mention, riders who engage in risky endeavors on horseback. They survive in what they do because they are able to unlock the power of fear and employ positively the keen-edged reflexes, the lightning-quick wits and responses, and the adrenalin-sharpened senses that are fear's chief products.

The Japanese soldiers whom the 26th Cavalrymen were riding to meet in mortal combat had been trained from birth to harness and suppress fear. They were conditioned to readily accept as beyond their control that which is karma—preordained fate. This East Indian word was readily adopted by Japanese from Indian influences in governing Buddhist philosophy fundamental to Japanese conventional beliefs, but especially so in the mutated tenets of Bushido, the "warrior's code" so persistently prevalent in the demeanor and performance of the World War II Japanese serviceman. Courageous and disciplined to a fault, his most dangerous flaw lay perhaps in that sometimes his resignation to his karma prematurely replaced last-ditch initiative to solve a given predicament. That was one of the few aspects Americans and Filipinos had going for them in this stage of the conflict. They were just brought up too damned dumb to know when their luck had run out. Oh, make no mistake, the Japanese would fight you ably to the last with all the *hara-gei*, innermost energy, he could summon, but if it entered his mind that his perceived karma was to die now rather than later, he was apt to lapse into senseless recklessness or give in to the urge to simply commit seppuku, honorable suicide. The Americans and Filipinos, on the other hand, would prove for all time that they had a prevailing respect for life and a habit of hoping to the last moment that something could still be done to retrieve the situation. It was an edge that would provide a margin of survival for a lot of the men who rode toward Damortis and their fates on that cloudy morning.

9

The Blooding of American Armor at Lingayen

22 DECEMBER 1941, 9:20 A.M.

The winding road from Rosario to Damortis was a distance of about seven kilometers, or six miles, a long line of defense for the reduced 26th to cover, even with the mediocre-sized support from the 192nd. Well surfaced by Philippine standards, being a mixture of macadam and gravel, the road ran first over the rice paddy flats outside Rosario and then entered the foothills of the mountains to the north. The first part was hemmed in by drainage ditches and paddies. Once in the hills, steep banks rose up on the north side in all but a few places, and along the south side, most of the ground beyond the drainage ditch fell steeply away to wooded hills and rice paddies. Barbed wire livestock fences followed the south side almost continuously except in a few places where the road passed through high-sided cuts or over deep ravines. The route offered little maneuvering room and few places to set up effective delaying positions with sufficient view down the road for efficient fields of fire against an approaching enemy. A unit in column literally had no place to go if it came under attack. It was a cavalryman's or tanker's nightmare and a strafing warplane pilot's dream.

The Japanese Imperial Staff had decreed everything north of a line drawn from Lingayen Gulf east to Baler Bay on Luzon's Pacific coast to be the exclusive hunting domain of 5th Army Air Group under the command of Lt. Gen. Hideyoshi Obata. Reinforced just before invasion by the 24th Air Regiment, Obata's array of 307 first-line aircraft included Mitsubishi Ki-30 Type 97 light bombers (slow, ponderous, code-named "Ann" and reputed among U.S. fliers to be "easy meat"), Mitsubishi Ki-21 heavy bombers (code-named "Sally"), Kawasaki Ki-15s, and Aichi D3A Type 99 dive bombers (code-named "Val" and dubbed "Washing Machine Charlies" by their American and Filipino prey because of the clattering sound their obsolescent radial engines uttered during their ponderous and noisy ascent after an attack dive; the nickname, however, was the only humorous thing about this bomber to those who had to endure, virtually unprotected from air attack, the Val's savage forays).

Lt. Ben Morin, perched in the open turret of his M3, was dividing his attention between watching the twisting bomb-pitted road before him and casting a wary eye skyward for signs of sudden, unwelcome attention from any of the enemy aircraft that dotted the skies in every direction he looked. His little column was traveling at about 25 mph, keeping intervals of about 50–75 yards between tanks. In Morin's M3 were his gunner, Cpl. James Cahill; driver, Pfc. L. Zelis; and loader, machine gunner Pfc. Steve Gados. Following his tank were M3s commanded by Morin's platoon sergeant, Staff Sgt. Al Edwards, a Chicago policeman, and Sgts. Willard Von Bergen, Lawrence Jordan, and Ray Vandenbroucke.

Roughly half way to Damortis, Japanese pilots decided to give Morin the attention he had dreaded. A couple of Aichi dive bombers peeled off and began their run. Morin ducked down the turret like a startled turtle into its shell and slammed the hatch behind him.

"Weave, dammit, Zelis!" he shouted at his driver, "WEAVE!"

As the tank swerved, the concussion from a bomb hit rocked through the crew pit. The men could hear the sharp *WANG!* of shrapnel hammering the armor, and Morin later recalled, "Apparently it was a fragmentation bomb and hence a light one." What really unnerved the tankers during the attack, however, was that in several instances of close hits, rivet heads from the tank's construction began to pop out from the bulkheads and whiz around the interior of the crew pit. They seemed to loosen with the slightest impacts on the armor and became more of a menace to the crews than enemy bullets and shrapnel outside. The M3 had now revealed another of its dangerous eccentricities.

When the Aichi's attack subsided, Morin ventured topside again. He shouted at Zelis to watch out for shell holes and pick up speed if he could. Morin now hoped they wouldn't lose a tread. This was another of the M3's annoying charms. Its tracks, newly designed with each link mounted in solid rubber blocks, had a bad habit of jumping off the sprockets under little more than ordinary stress. Skilled drivers quickly learned to give an M3 extra throttle and keep the power up when turning to ease pressure on the treads. Those who failed to learn this dodge were apt to spend a lot of time on the side coping with breakdowns. Under fire or in the middle of an air raid was no place to expose oneself fixing flats.

The tank column reached the little coastal town of Damortis at about 10:25 a.m., and, encountering no sign of American or Filipino units supposedly in the area, Morin signaled a right turn northward on the coast road toward Agoo as ordered by General Weaver. This was to be unfortunate for Morin, who was unaware that he had just missed a 192nd Battalion motorized recon group ordered from battalion HQ to rendezvous with him. This additional force might have changed the outcome of Morin's fateful day.

Just to the north outside the town Morin spotted a 26th Cavalry scout car under a big tree by the side of the road and signaled a halt. He saw a tall, handsome cavalry officer who reminded him somewhat of a movie star type standing by the car examining the road ahead through field glasses. This was Lt. Johnny George, whose advance recon group had made first enemy contact earlier that morning. He had just returned down the hill where he had gone on foot to confer briefly with Colonel Pierce and Major Chandler at their temporary observation post. He had informed the CO and his S-3 that his cars would maintain the roadblock until relieved or forced to withdraw.

"Hey, Lieutenant," called Morin, "how far up ahead are the Japs?"

"About a half mile," answered George. "You'll come to a bridge over a big creek. That's where my scout cars have a roadblock set up. After that you're definitely in Indian country, Lieutenant."

Morin waved a casual salute and motioned his column forward. A little farther up, they encountered Sgt. Domingo de Mesa in charge of the 26th's roadblock. The troopers, manning machine guns, waved silently as the tankers passed through their position at the bridge. Morin felt his stomach tighten as they clanked over the gruesome carnage the 26th machine guns had produced earlier in their encounter with a reinforced Japanese advance patrol. Private Zelis had slowed the tank to 15 mph. There was a metallic *CLACK* as Corporal Cahill pulled and released the retractor handle of the bow machine gun. Morin was tense now, poised to drop into the turret where Private Gados crouched ready to load the 37mm main gun as soon as Morin fired the first round. In the hip pockets of his coveralls were stuffed two more shells for quick access.

Morin saw the first enemy tanks at about five hundred yards. They were low silhouetted with sloping sides and at first sight appeared to have no turrets. They were unlike anything Morin had ever seen. These were the newly redesigned Japanese Type 97 light to medium tanks, the Type "i" or Chi-He model, mounted with the latest, viciously effective 47mm cannon as main guns. They belonged to Homma's 4th Tank Regiment, which had gotten some fifty tanks (about half of his armored contingent) ashore that morning despite foul weather and rugged seas. Most of his armored force were the improved Shiki M2595 light to medium tanks and the heavier Chi-He 97s, all mounted with the deadly 47mm. In support were more 47mm cannon mounted on low-slung gun carriers (tracked) for antitank work (these were probably the apparently turretless armor first seen by Morin). Homma's intelligence had far overestimated Fil-American tank strength, and he was taking no chances. In contrast, Morin's M3 with its perpendicular sides, squarish lines, and high profile (observed by British tankers in North Africa to be "straight from Texas and tall in the saddle") presented an uncomfortably inviting target for penetration by the high-velocity 47mm manned by the Japanese gunners. The Japanese 97's slant-ing surfaces offered less prospect for an effective hit by the American gun-ners. Japanese observers of Germany's panzers during the blitzkrieg had done their homework well.

Morin slammed down the turret hatch and settled in behind the aiming device of his 37mm. He decided to fire a trial shot straight down the road beating the Japanese gunners to the first shot. Taking about four seconds to train the crosshairs on his target, he pulled the trigger for the lanyard. A bull-whip *crack* slashed into his ears as his brand new cannon fired its first—and last—shot. "The gun jammed in recoil, evidently locked out of battery, and it stayed jammed," remembers Morin. Another oversight in the hasty indoctrination of the GHQ tankers was to forget to insist they check the hydraulic fluid in the recoil mechanisms. For some unknown reason, many of the 37mms were dry as bone when they went into combat. For Morin, no amount of fiddling, banging, cursing, or cajoling would change the situation. All that were left now were the machine guns against 47mms.

Through the M3's slits, Morin and his crew could see Japanese infantry deploying off the road like ants from a kicked-over hill. "They were hitting the dirt very, very fast," recalled Morin. Zelis sent the tank into a weaving motion in an attempt to achieve maximum coverage of the roadside ditches for his fixed remaining guns. Morin, now steadily firing the coaxially mounted machine gun in the turret, tried repeatedly to signal Zelis to sound the tank's emergency battle siren to alert the rest of the tanks in his column to take battle formation. Corporal Cahill was firing the bow gun as fast as he could while having to cope with the weapon's repeated jamming. Even so, Morin was to observe, Cahill managed to go through several hundred-round belts of ammunition with killing effect. Throughout it all, Private Gados worked desperately to keep Cahill's fixed guns loaded and passed fresh belts to other gunners. By now the M3's interior was a suffocat-ing hell of smoking, acrid cordite and oven-like heat.

Morin was now operating the turret machine gun almost entirely manu-ally. The cover latch and belt-holding device was malfunctioning and forc-ing him, in the midst of firing, to frantically extract ruptured cartridges by hand with an armorer's tool. Finally and desperately, he was forced to pull the bolt manually for each shot.

The five American M3s with their fledgling warrior crews continued to push ahead against the superior Japanese armor, whose surprised occupants had initially actually given ground. The sharp cracks of the 37mms, which still were working, dominated the initial sounds of the fight with a comforting racket, and long white fingers of machine gun tracers arched out only to suddenly dance straight upward as they ricocheted off enemy armor. It was heady stuff for the Americans at first, but about two kilometers south of Morin's objective, Agoo, the Japanese tankers, now over their initial shock, stabilized and struck back with devastating accuracy. Now the ear-splitting crescendo became one of hostile fury.

With a sickening *BANG!*, Morin's M3 took a hit on the hull of its right side, knocking the hatch door loose in front of Cahill's bow gun position. Within seconds another direct hit tore the door away and left it dangling over the front slope plate of the hull.

"The gunfire of the enemy was awfully accurate," recalled Morin. "I signaled Zelis to pull off the road to the right and out of the line of fire. I wanted to put the door back in position in front of Cahill's face before continuing the attack."

While the M3 stood immobilized in the ditch with Morin and his crew struggling to implement makeshift repair of the exposed hatch, a Japanese Type 97 tank exploded out of the high cogon grass, which had concealed it beside the road, and charged down on the hapless Americans. As Morin and his men dove to their stations, the Chi-He slammed into the M3, striking it full on the left bow, dead center in the driving sprocket. As the Japanese tank, apparently undamaged, reversed itself in order to gain firing room, Zelis scrambled at the controls to get the M3 back on the road again. When he tried to go forward, to close with the maneuvering enemy tank, the battered little M3, its left drive sprocket sprung out of line and jammed in the track, could only lurch to the left, driven by the still operative motive power of its right track. Once more, Morin and his crew found themselves defenseless and stopped dead, this time in a rice paddy. Now shells from the 97 began to crash into the right side of the helpless M3's hull and in the right rear. Then a 47mm shell pierced the armor and entered the M3's battery case. The M3's engines abruptly stopped and the radio and forward guns went dead, deprived of power. Suffocating smoke began to curl into the fighting compartment as the engine caught fire.

"I shouted, 'GAS!'" recounted Morin. "We put on our gas masks. Zelis climbed out of his bucket seat and turned on the fire extinguishers. Within a few minutes, the heat and fumes became almost unbearable."

The other tanks in Morin's column had met with little more success. Time and time again, the gunners whose 37mm guns had not jammed observed, with a growing feeling of impotency, that most of their shots were simply ricocheting harmlessly off the enemy's sloping armor. These new Japanese tanks, even at close range where normal impact of a 37mm gun would ordinarily pierce tank armor of the day with ease, seemed to defy penetration.

Morin's platoon sergeant, Al Edwards, the Chicago policeman, his own 37mm now jammed, could see that his CO's tank was down and in trouble. As he and the other M3 commanders tried to continue pressing the attack with their four remaining tanks, all now damaged, with only two main cannon operational, the Japanese 47mms, both tank mounted and antitank-carriage based, increasingly zeroed the Americans in.

Sgt. Ray Vandenbroucke's driver managed to maneuver their M3 close enough for a shot at the Chi-He 97, which was now systematically demolishing Morin's tank. With one of the 37mm's few effective hits of the day, Vandenbroucke succeeded in disabling the turret of the Japanese tank, giving his beleaguered commander temporary respite. From just behind him, Sgt. William Von Bergen's M3, with the platoon's only other still-operational 37mm, disabled the 97's left track. The other two M3s, all remaining guns blazing, followed doggedly in support. This was to be the last relief the American tankers could give their stricken platoon leader, however, because by now the volume of enemy fire was driving them back with a literal wall of 47mm steel.

Sgt. Al Edwards, crouched in his gun turret, felt his tank shudder sickeningly. All hell seemed to break loose in the crew compartment below, and he ducked down to see what the commotion was. Nausea hit him like a sea wave. His assistant driver, Pvt. Henry Deckert, had been decapitated by a direct hit, which had penetrated the forward deck of the tank at the vulnerable ball and socket joint of the bow gun mounting. Private Deckert had just achieved the gruesome, dubious honor of being the first American armored soldier killed in WWII direct tank-versus-tank combat.

Ben Morin later remembered the sinking feeling he had at the time. "Through the smoke I could see four tanks of my platoon retiring to the south. That was *not* encouraging. I had hoped Edwards could have broken through the Nip guns on the road and that the Second Platoon [which was then still in Rosario waiting for fuel!] would be overrunning the landing area at Agoo." This brand of forlorn, almost outrageous hope would soon become all too typical with the ill-fated defenders of Luzon.

At about 11:30 a.m. things around Lt. Ben Morin and his desolate crew became ominously quiet. "Within a few minutes, the engine was smothered with foamite extinguisher, and the fire died out. The tank was heavily damaged. The doors on our right side above the bow gun had been torn off. The engine, radio, and fixed guns were out of commission. Both the bow gun and the turret machine guns were sluggish. Worst of all, the 37mm main gun was useless. Enemy firing had ceased. After about fifteen minutes, a platoon of four Japanese light tanks [high silhouetted Shiki M2595s] came into view on the road. My tank was about fifty to seventy-five yards off the road in a dry, hard-packed rice paddy. I saw the enemy tanks as they cleared the last clump of trees and scrub brush, which lined the road very thickly on both sides. As they came abreast of our open patch of ground, their tank column pivoted to the right and approached our M3 in line abreast. As yet, they did not open fire, but I figured it was only a matter of time before they chose to."

To prevent the Japanese from firing into the badly exposed right front of his helpless tank, Ben Morin climbed out of the turret and, with raised hands clutching a dirty white handkerchief, surrendered himself and his crew.

It was a strangely ludicrous scene—four bedraggled young National Guardsmen in grimy, sweat-drenched coveralls standing helpless in a rice field covered by cannons and machine guns of four tanks and the weapons of a large number of approaching Japanese infantrymen. In one violent morning, these newcomers to war had been transformed from confident new troopers on the attack into a state that is about as abandoned and alone as any human being can feel—captivity. But they had fought and they had survived. On this one day, at least, the veteran Japanese combat soldiers, ingrained as they were with the merciless code of Bushido, treated Morin's little group with respect. They smiled and offered cigarettes and canteens in simple recognition that these *gaijin*, these barbarians, had qualified as warriors. There was that morning a spirit of fundamental combat brotherhood between foes. Such feelings were not to last long in the bloody months to come in the Philippines.

From that day on, the tankers of the 192nd and 194th, along with the intrepid, gutsy horsemen of the 26th Cavalry, would fight an uninterrupted series of violent, brilliant, and desperate holding actions, which would buy time for Generals MacArthur and Wainwright's forces to shatter the Japanese war timetable and to withdraw to that most infamous military rat trap in U.S. military history—Bataan.

10

Lieutenant George's Roadblock

22 DECEMBER 1941, 8:55 A.M.

That morning, prior to Lt. Ben Morin's departure from Rosario, the 26th Cavalry advance recon section of three scout cars under command of Lt. Johnny George had established a roadblock on the coast road leading from Damortis to Agoo. After initial contact had been made by Cpl. Eulalio Arzaga while on point riding his motorcycle and his subsequent harrowing escape from advance Japanese patrols, George organized his roadblock with Sgt. Domingo de Mesa straddling the road at a bridge over a large creek intersecting the coast road. After supervising the positioning of two of his three scout car sections and tactical emplacement of his heavy machine guns to cover approaches to the bridge, George kept his remaining scout car with its primary communications equipment in position to direct any action and stationed it to the side of the road beneath cover of a large acacia tree, where he could readily keep 26th HQ in Rosario informed of the Lingayen developments.

At about 8:30 a.m., Sergeant de Mesa had checked and rechecked the positioning of the two scout cars and their heavy machine guns left under his supervision at the bridge by Lieutenant George, who returned to the position after placing the communications car. There was no sound in the shade of the mango trees that covered their position. Steam was beginning to rise from the macadam of the road, wet from the previous night's storm, as the morning sun began to burn away the last of the clouds and heat the day. Only the dull rumble of explosions far to the north and the faint throbbing of engines from Japanese landing craft in Lingayen Bay about a mile west of them broke the silence—that is, except for the occasional, hostile drone of prowling Japanese aircraft. The tranquility of it all belied the gut-wrenching intensity of the cavalry troopers peering over the sights of

143

the six machine guns, two .50-caliber and four air-cooled .30-caliber, cocked and ready to shred anything that moved on the road, which was the focus of their attentive muzzles. Any fear in these men had already been sufficiently replaced by cold anger. They and their families and friends had been surprised, bombed, shot at, and chased by people who had no business in this familiar countryside, their homeland. Now they were ready to collect heavy toll for the first bridge.

As soon as they had swung into their delaying position at the bridge, Lieutenant George gathered his car commanders and ordered them to site their weapons for maximum effective fields of plunging fire at anyone approaching their position. At the same time, he ordered the scout cars to be positioned for instant departure in the event of urgent withdrawal. Once in place, they were to cover up, maintain silence, and avoid detection of their position by enemy observation, either on the ground or from the air. They were to commence firing only upon his signal. Open radio contact between cars was to be maintained to receive his firing order and any maneuvering instructions.

Back at the roadblock, it had now been almost three quarters of an hour since Johnny George had gotten his message through to Pierce about the initial contact by Arzaga, and the suspense of the waiting was beginning to play on the nerves of George's tense gunners. They began to see phantom enemy moving in the wisps of steam and heat devils rising from the hot, damp roadbed. A gust of wind in the tall cogon grass became an enemy scout. A clump of brush or a mound of earth, stared at long enough, changed shape or shifted position ever so slightly. Such hallucinations are common to a soldier at war, observed Siegfried Sassoon, the Englishman of gentry background who became known as the "soldier's poet" of World War I. "If one lies long enough, waiting, in a dark hole, listening to the sound of one's own breathing, inanimate objects may come to life; bold rocks may be transformed into men's pates; bare sticks and pinnacled stones may become witches' fingers."

Suddenly, movement on the road ceased to be illusion. The cavalrymen were not quite prepared for what they saw.

A man on a bicycle came into view. He wore loose, mustard-colored clothing, accented by oblong red tabs on his shirt collars, and a camouflage netted pith helmet that looked as though it belonged in a Saturday afternoon B-grade Tarzan movie. His *zatsuno* (haversacks), *hango* (kit bags), bedding, and rain gear were hung from every part of the bike that would hold them, and his bolt-action, Mauser-type Arisaka rifle lay across the handlebars. He was no tourist, and neither were the score of others who followed. The nonchalance of their approach was startling to the point of insult to the waiting 26th scouts. Fingers tensed on triggers, but discipline held. "Wait," murmured the almost soundless voice of George to the radio men.

Like so many young men who had played football in their school days, George tended to gauge distances in terms of the lengths of playing fields or fractions thereof. "They're not near the far goal posts yet," his mind clicked. "Wait."

Now foot soldiers could be seen approaching on the sides of the road, their netted, conical helmets bobbing as they jogged along at double time.

"OK, you bastards wanted to find out how far you could get before you stubbed your toes," muttered George. "Now I'm going to tell you."

They passed George's imaginary goal posts—one hundred yards—now eighty—"Wait"—sixty—fifty—"FIRE!" bellowed George into the microphone.

As one, six machine guns exploded in a drum roll of point-blank devastation, the distinctive, deep-throated *chuga-chuga* roar of the heavy .50s in a crescendo accompanied by the sharper staccato of the lighter .30s sounding out a symphony of death.

In spite of their training, their anger, their exposure to death in the past weeks, the troopers were momentarily stunned by the violent convulsion of horror that erupted at the touch of their fingers. The Browning .30-caliber machine gun delivers its payload at a velocity that will tear a human body to pieces. The Browning .50-caliber machine gun simply pulverizes a human target into nonexistence. Three of each type gun ripped into the advancing Japanese in a blood-red cloud. The lead cyclist simply disappeared in a burst of crimson mush. Those who followed became a hideous circus of grotesquely dancing caricatures of what had been men, now obscene, capering puppets manipulated by the shattering, multiple impact to perform ever so briefly on a grisly stage before dissolving as if on cue into shapeless heaps of bloody rags and entrails. Bodies whose heads had vanished or whole limbs had been shot away struggled and stumbled stupidly to carry out the last messages from now-dead brains. Others whose minds had simply not received the message that the body was smashed beyond life flopped like beached fish trying to escape the rending, searing storm that engulfed them.

The big .50 bucked and thrashed with berserk rage in de Mesa's hands, the recoil pile-driving its death message into his very soul. He and the other gunners around him crossed an abyss from which there is no return, for there is an irreversible shock when a rational human being first takes the life of another so violently. Dead, however, that other person ceases to be an enemy. The corpse now simply becomes a lifeless, inanimate counterpart of one's self, an intimate and frightening reflection of one's own mortality. As he continued to fire, de Mesa gritted his teeth and felt himself wishing desperately that he could cross himself.

The Japanese then tried an enveloping attack, but it was caught by de Mesa's sharp eyes. The scout car guns traversed toward their flanks, and the

Japanese attempt was stopped bloodily in its tracks, producing yet another gory pile of dead and mortally wounded enemy.

"Cease firing—cease firing!" broke in George, shouting the order until all guns quieted. Ears ringing in the sudden silence, the newly blooded men of the 26th avoided one another's eyes, hands still frozen on the grips of the now mute, smoking weapons, conscious only of the writhing butchery before them.

It was quiet again there in the shade of the big mango trees by the bridge on the Lingayen coast road, and Johnny George calmly began to radio in his report. "Am maintaining a delaying position north of Damortis. Enemy contact—probably reconnaissance probe by advanced elements—some troops on bicycles—advance repulsed—no casualties our people—expect attack in strength at any time—enemy now observed to be landing light to medium tanks—will maintain position pending orders or until forced to withdraw—sender proceeding to meet CO as ordered—George." It was now 10:15 a.m.

At 10:20 a.m., upon receiving George's terse and alarming message, Pierce, without hesitation, ordered Bill Chandler to immediately get motorcycle transport prepared. The 26th CO wanted to make his own visual reconnaissance of the Lingayen landings from a high ridge overlooking the gulf to confirm for himself the accuracy of the dire reports received from George's scout cars. The two officers, Chandler at the controls and Pierce in a sidecar, roared off toward Damortis. With Clint Pierce holding on for dear life in the rattling sidecar, Chandler swung the Harley off the road and gunned it in a bouncing course up rocky ground to a high, sparsely covered rise overlooking the coast road and Lingayen Bay beyond. From where they dismounted they could see as far north as Agoo. Even though they had known they would see the Japanese invasion force for the first time, they were stunned by the awesome panorama of hostile power that confronted them.

"Jesus, Bill, look at the size of it," Pierce gasped as he groped for his field glasses and scrambled farther up the crest for a better view. Chandler could see small, fast boats maneuvering right off Damortis just out of range for the .50-caliber machine guns on the 26th scout cars. Eyes riveted to his binoculars, Bill Chandler was already counting.

"I make it, uh, 24 transports . . . a cruiser, I think . . . and, uh . . . looks like one, two . . . no, four destroyers. I can't be sure. They're spread out as far as I can see. They must have some carriers out there somewhere judging by all the aircraft around here, but I can't see any."

The latter observation was the same assumption made by American naval airmen and submariners who had searched in futile disappointment for Japanese carriers in the seas off Northern Luzon. The fact was that Japanese air strike planners had been allowed only one small carrier, the *Ryujo*, from the Pearl Harbor strike force, and it was being utilized to permit Japanese naval fliers, assigned central and southern Luzon targets to achieve the range necessary for their southernmost operations. What American observations and intelligence was not yet aware of was the manner in which Japanese planners had divided their naval and army spheres of operations to specific zones on Luzon and the extent to which forward-located air bases were being utilized by the attack force. The planes that Pierce and Chandler were now seeing were all land-based Japanese army aircraft operating from newly captured fields in Northern Luzon, Camiguin Island, and the Batan islands. An overall total of 751 combat planes made up the Japanese air strike force allotted to the Philippines. Their planners had calculated this number to give them the three-to-one ratio they believed sufficient to give them absolute air supremacy. With the American and Philippine air forces now literally decimated as a serious factor, the skies over Luzon belonged to Dai Nippon. By now, any movement on the ground by any Fil-American units was perilous. The skies had been, for all practical purposes, Japanese since 10 December. The few remaining American and Filipino aircraft, mostly a few P-40s and rickety Philippine army P-26s, were now restricted to flying from hidden, emergency "rice paddy airfields" on Bataan to perform sneak reconnaissance and courier missions. They were seldom seen and were able to offer virtually no support to Luzon's defenders against the freely roving enemy aircraft, which was limited only by the Japanese high command's imposition of a rigid quota of logistics on air operations to conserve aviation fuel and bombs in their broad, ambitious campaign of Southeast Asian conquest.

At around 10:40 a.m. the deathly silence around George and his men was broken by a sudden outbreak of sharp cracks, the sound of cannon fire from tanks. This was Lieutenant Morin and his platoon encountering the Japanese tanks farther north toward Lingayen. The firing lasted for some thirty minutes or so and then came to an abrupt end. Soon after, four tanks, all hit, the remnants of Morin's battered little force, limped back through George's bloodied position toward Damortis, some of the badly damaged tanks having to be towed. A fifth, the platoon commander's tank, had left the road to attempt to maneuver out of the trap. It was hit and burned, becoming the first U.S. tank to be lost in WWII. It was later learned that the surviving tanks of Morin's ill-fated foray managed to be returned to Rosario. There they were assessed for repairs and/or salvage. All damaged, one had a hit through the main drive; another had a hit completely disabling its oil system. All four tanks had to be towed out, but all were lost later in the day to bombing and salvage mishaps. A grisly demonstration was organized by Captain Hanes of B Company 192, on orders from the 192nd Battalion CO, Theodore F. Wickford. The tankers who had not yet seen action were made to form a line and climb one by one into Platoon Sgt. Al Edwards's tank and observe to their horror the bloody interior of the turret and the pathetic, decapitated remains of Pvt. Henry Deckert. This exercise had the dubious intent of hardening the men. Nausea was the primary result.

Now on the hill overlooking Damortis, Pierce and Chandler turned and watched as Japanese planes began making repeated dives in the hills toward Rosario. With a sinking feeling, they feared the object of those attacks was their own column moving westward on the treacherous road to Damortis.

At the time Pierce and Chandler were watching from the ridge, George called Sergeant de Mesa over and ordered him to take command of the roadblock. "I'm going back down the road about five hundred yards," he said, pointing toward a clump of trees at the foot of a hill. (It was here that Ben Morin and his tank platoon had encountered George earlier that morning at about 10:30 on the way to their disastrous engagement with Japanese tanks.)

"I'll meet with Colonel Pierce and try to get back up here to you. My radio man will keep a line open to your man Corporal Miole in case you need me quick. My guess is they'll make another try at us as soon as they get some of those tanks off the beach and on the road, so just stay ready to move fast if we have to."

"We'll hold them as long as we can, sir," answered de Mesa.

"Fine, but I need you alive, de Mesa," said George with a grim smile.

George then returned to his command scout car and moved back his intended observation position. Leaving his crew and radio man with the car, he then made his way up the ridge where Pierce and Chandler were observing the landings.

On greeting George, Pierce expressed his consternation at the developments and told George to radio back to Rosario to order the regiment to immediately gear up to march toward Damortis to take up defensive fighting positions. After informing the CO and his S-3 that his cars could advance no farther than their present position at the bridge, having encountered heavy enemy pressure, George departed down the hill back to his position on the road to order his radio man to relay Pierce's orders for the regiment to get on the move. He then settled down with his scout car unit at their roadblock to wait for the next enemy probe.

Pierce and Chandler remained on the ridge a while longer to keep a watch on the progress of the invasion force. They then readied to make a hasty return to link up with the regiment to supervise displacement of the regiment's fighting positions along the ridge. Before leaving the hill overlooking Damortis, however, Pierce and Chandler turned again to watch in dismay Japanese planes making repeated attack dives in the hills toward

Rosario. They were now increasingly certain of the target beneath those attacks. They realized with increasing dread that they could almost follow the progress of the regiment by the closing range of the moving aircraft. However, little did they know of the horror that was taking place in that deadly six-mile march.

11

The Longest Six Miles

22 DECEMBER 1941, 10:20 A.M.

Vance now received the message from Pierce ordering the 26th Regiment to make a fast, forced march to the Damortis area to go into defensive fighting positions. At about that same time the fuel trucks arrived to service the remaining 192nd tanks in Rosario. At around 10:20 a.m., following an air raid on Rosario by enemy dive bombers, the 26th column, now down to fewer than 650 effective personnel available for combat, mounted and began the six-mile march out of Rosario to Damortis, with the several remaining 192nd light tanks leading off, preceding the horse cavalry.

Upon reaching the edge of the relatively slim protective cover of the trees on the outskirts of Rosario, the 26th main column broke into horse cavalry's universal choice for the pace of a long, accelerated march, a mile-eating trot. Once outside the shelter of the town and its trees, the regiment broke into the open, and the world turned instantly perilous. Before the now tense troopers lay the frighteningly open expanse of the broad, flat plain of the Apangat River Valley, which seemed to stretch endlessly and nakedly into the haze of the mountains to the north and the rolling coastal hills to the west, the direction of the column's march. Beyond those hills lay Damortis and the war, but at least this would be a more personal kind of war, one in which a man could fight back rather than being simply a helpless target for enemy airmen.

Thinking of this, the horsemen now peered through their own sweat and over horses' necks down the seemingly endless black ribbon of rough tarmac where steam rose from the previous night's drizzling rain. Heat devils played tricks on men's eyes, causing the road to appear to be undulating, and rice paddies off to the side and beyond seemed to shimmer like some great, eerie sea. The only sounds now were the steady rattle of hooves on the hard road surface, occasional snorts of horses as they cleared their nostrils in the humid, stifling air they were breathing, and the jingle and rustling of tack and equipment. There was absolutely no conversation from the men and no sounds of nature anywhere. It was an oppressive, unsettling quiet.

The nerves of the riders in the column were raw and strung almost to the breaking point. These were nerves of men who had been intensively trained, drilled, and prepared until they had developed an army's most professionally administered and instilled conditioning of reflexes, nerves that had been trained by methodology developed from generations of experience that now dictated that adrenalin-fed reflexes were to serve only as triggers for flawless, unquestioning, and disciplined reaction to instant commands. Nevertheless, the nerves of these men were as human as the men they belonged to, and on this day they were twisted and raw with strain. Muscles were gradually knotting into near paralysis but for the almost automatic motions of riding and handling the horses that carried them to whatever awaited over those hills. Except for an occasional, quiet, soothing reassurance to a mount, most likely uttered as much to calm the man as his horse, there was no talk of any kind. There was no usual joking or griping on this day, just the steady drum of hooves, the faint jingling and the rustling. The column was fully in the open now, and seconds became eternities. Time seemed to stop completely.

The first Japanese dive bombers screamed down on them out of the sun at their backs. The thunderous, numbing hammer blows of bombs drilled into the very core of men and horses alike. The effect was beyond terror and shattered both minds and bodies at once. Men instinctively tucked their chins and felt their bodies contract and draw into themselves in nature's most primordial reflex to external threat and danger. Beneath them, the cavalrymen felt the terror-stricken squatting and weaving motions of their horses as they crouched, feet lifting and falling in a stationary, quivering dance of raw fear. Only a rare few of the well-conditioned cavalry horses reacted by bolting or lunging. Those few that did had no place to go, hemmed in as they were by wire, irrigation ditches, and embankments. The simple truth of the matter was that the road across the Apangat River Valley was a virtual death trap.

Hemmed within an expanse of only fifty feet side to side, the road gripped the helpless 26th column in position like so many target figures in a shooting gallery. The only hope for the road-bound cavalrymen to make themselves more difficult prey for the relentless Japanese bombs and aerial gunners was to disperse in depth, stringing the column out into as long and thin a line as possible.

Lee Vance, the eternal soldier, instantly recognized the need for change in deployment and sent his orderly, Pvt. Artaero Leonardo, racing back along the column yelling to the troop commanders to lengthen their ranks as much as possible yet keep the interval closed on the unit directly in front of them to avoid disintegration of the integrity of the regimental column. Vance shouted to the scout car between the head of the column and the point to get their machine guns in action and radio the same orders to the other cars farther back along the line. Taut anticipation was replaced by the release provided by action and instant response to the bark of commands. Gradually getting their wits about them once more, the 26th troopers began to put their disarrayed column back into some form of order.

Their tormentors that day were the Vals, the Japanese Aichi Type 99 carrier-based dive bombers mentioned earlier. Again and again these Washing Machine Charlies swooped down like awkward, marauding birds of prey, their bombs ripping into the roadway in deadly eruptions of dirt, stone, and pavement. At each onslaught, troopers spurred their horses to the shoulders of the road and dismounted in attempts to make themselves as poor targets as possible. Some of the hapless, terrified horses lost their footing or misstepped into irrigation ditches, where they floundered and sank belly deep in filthy, sucking mud. With much pulling and shouting, most could be coaxed back on to firm footing. Sadly, some had to be abandoned, thrashing in the muck. The column could not wait for them under these circumstances. Horseless troopers grabbed for their weapons and gear and either scrambled aboard scout cars or caught mounts of less fortunate comrades who were now casualties. Each time as a Japanese pilot pulled out of the dive of a bomb run and began to ascend again in the characteristic, slow, grinding fashion typical of a Washing Machine Charlie, the gunner in the aft of the open cockpit would open up with his machine gun as the angle of the climbing plane brought his gun to bear on the carnage below. Charlie's deadly combination strike, unlike its name, was no joking matter.

Sgt. Patricio Ubarro, a communications specialist assigned to the lead scout car, which seemed to be drawing special attention from the attacking Aichis, was working the car's .50-caliber as fast as he could manage. The regular gunner was dead. On the first few passes the Japanese dived in to daredevil low altitudes to give their gunners almost point-blank target opportunities. When the 26th Cavalrymen in the scout cars along the bloody corridor blasted away with their .30- and .50-caliber guns, they didn't succeed in downing any of their tormentors, but they did instill some startled respect in the pilots. With each attack the Aichis pulled out of their dives at higher altitudes, keeping a safer margin of range between themselves and the 26th gunners, thus also giving their own rear gunner reduced opportunities for a kill. The planes spent less time over a column, which now was showing signs of being not as helpless as it first appeared, but the killing went on.

One by one, the men in Ubarro's car were killed as the attacks continued. Now twice wounded himself, Ubarro had become the car's driver by default. Bleeding and in pain he tried to keep the now badly damaged scout car moving forward with its valuable communications equipment. The sputtering vehicle was down to a crawl, however. Ubarro, knowing that neither he nor the car was going to last much longer, made the difficult decision to turn back for Rosario to try to save the car and its equipment. As he attempted to turn the car around, it coughed to a stop. More Aichis began to whine downward for another pass, and Ubarro struggled out, abandoning the smoking car and trying for the ditch. Just as he touched the ground a bomb strike blew him off his feet. Trying desperately to rise again, the sergeant realized he had been hit once more. This time bomb fragments had shattered his legs. Again he tried for the ditch, crawling, tearing his hands on the hot rubble of the tarmac. Nothing he could do seemed right. There was a loud buzzing in his ears and he swirled into unconsciousness, his mind telling him hopelessly, "This is it, Patricio. You're finished." Then there was a hazy sensation of people around him and of being loaded on what seemed to be a tank. His next conscious memory was of being carried into the field hospital in Rosario.

The Japanese attackers were relentless. As the bombing and strafing continued, the cavalrymen's problems multiplied. Now the column had to zigzag and detour constantly to avoid dead and wounded men and animals, bomb craters, downed telephone poles, and sputtering live electrical wires. The terror of being entrapped on that deadly road would sear itself forever into the memories of the men who rode there.

Lt. Clint Seymour later recalled muttering to himself repeatedly, "No cover, no cover, not even a blade of grass! Horse, why the hell don't *you* cover me?" When asked later in jest, "What did the horse have to say about it?" Seymour replied, "The SOB just rolled his eyes and looked at me like I was crazy."

Cpl. R. B. Kausin, the regimental personnel clerk, sat strangely calm at his field desk in one of the scout cars. As he watched the Japanese planes dive, climb, circle, dive, and climb again, he wondered almost as if in a dream, "Who will be the next one to get it?" It simply never occurred to him that he, too, was a target.

Lt. Arthur Whitehead remembered later that not all enemy efforts were efficient. "One bomb that I judged to be a fifty-pounder landed within about fifty feet of some troopers, but because it drove deep into the ground the fragments flew almost straight up at a high angle and inflicted no casualties. Then in strafing the Jap guns had little dispersion and caused only slight damage or delay to the column. As soon as the planes passed over, the troops mounted up and rode on."

Not all Whitehead's memories were so placid, however. "While assembling after having made a quick dash off the road to get away from a strafing attack, I noticed that my platoon sergeant Lomboy was missing. Looking over I saw him dismounted trying to get his horse out of a carabao wallow. The horse was up to his belly and couldn't move. I rode over with the idea of finding a way to get the horse out, and suddenly I realized we had more important things to do. We caught a loose horse whose rider was killed, got my sergeant mounted and resumed the march."

Dead men lay now in the shapeless heaps that seem to be the universal pose of combat dead, losing with death the appearance of their mortal selves, their personal identity now only a caricature, at best, of the former person. At worst, identity was limited to some separate remnant, left recognizable in the scattered display of darkening, congealing blood, scattered array of gore, body parts, and the ever-present sour-smelling excrement such violence produces to accompany the finality of the human state. Only surviving dog tags, personal papers, or other pitiful scraps of identification made recognition of what were once men at all possible. More traumatic for survivors, however, was last-resort ID by fragments of human features or body components. Still, amidst the pervading grief and horror, a kind of protective mental foxhole persisted in the litany that "It's the other guy; it will always be the other guy. I am still here and this will not happen to me." At worst, survivor's guilt finds its way into the minds of those left alive and feeling; but even this does not sharpen clearly the truth of mortality and the inevitability of ultimate death. If this last shield was simultaneously let down by all men in the face of combat's horror, then war would probably cease by default on the spot, for its true pointlessness would be revealed for what it is. But the machine persists, fueled by other mortality factors of men's character, some programmed, some instinctive—anger, pride, fear of peer condemnation, or inspired patriotic competiveness. The rebellious impulses that translate as courage and bravery, once acted out, become pathological urges to commit mayhem in a perverse tribute to the human spirit. The true tragedy of war is the blind willingness of human beings to endure its mauling, albeit motivated, activities. One man's evil is another's virtue, and the differences of opinions on such matters will continue to cause men to perform that glorious travesty perceived as valor. The Japanese soldiers hurling themselves in all their samurai-fortified fervor at the enemy of the Bushido creed, and the Americans and Filipinos driven by their outrage and horror at an enemy—who has physically assaulted their beliefs and homeland and who is perceived as a dangerous, brutal animal—instinctively trust the right that lies in their sights aimed to destroy wrong, which is in turn shooting at them. All of these passions would meet head-on at the ridges of Damortis on the terrible, coming December day, and who can measure the proportions of valor of either foe in the coming suffering that would result?

When the remainder of C Company, 192nd Tanks, now finally refueled, went forward toward Damortis they began to encounter a great number of dead and wounded 26th Cavalry troopers and a large number of dead and dying animals. The dead men had been pulled to the side of the road, dragged there by wounded comrades. The driver of the lead tank, Cpl. John Minier, felt his stomach churn at the idea of running over the dead horses and brought his tank to a stop. His gunner, Pfc. Elton Dudley in the turret seat, viciously kicked him repeatedly in the back, urging him on.

"Go on! Go on!! Christ, if we stop here we'll be sitting ducks for goddamn Zeros! Haul ass, you dumb sonuvabitch!"

Minier clenched his teeth and grimaced until tears rolled down his cheeks. He rammed the gears and as the tank lurched forward he tried desperately to shut out the awful sounds of steel treads grinding over the big bodies in their path. He would never forget the noises of ribs and limbs snapping or the bumping of the M-3 passing over the pitiful carcasses. His mind screamed, "Oh, God, HORSES! They shouldn't have horses in this stinking death trap! This is crazy. They belong in beautiful green fields and horse shows and cowboy movies—but *not here! Oh, God, not here!*"

Private Bonifacio of A Troop lay in the ditch next to a rice paddy as the tanks ground by in their grisly advance. His bleeding, smashed ribs were on fire with pain, but his shrieks of agony were not caused by his wounds. He had just watched his beautiful horse's head disappear into a shapeless, bloody pulp under the grinding treads of one of those coughing, clanging devil machines.

"You have no right! You have no right," he croaked. "We're the cavalry," he sobbed. Then he rolled onto his back and screamed himself hoarse at the sky. "You bastards! You bastards! I'll never stop killing you! My beautiful horse! I'll make you Jap bastards pay as long as I live!"

Bonifacio survived his wounds and managed to rejoin the regiment later in Mexico, farther south. The catharsis for rage would continue for years for Bonifacio and men like him. War was no longer as impersonal as airplanes in the sky. It would become an arena of vengeance versus vengeance and would wreak terrible things. The Philippines would become synonymous with suffering.

About 10:30 that morning the 26th column finally crossed the wooden bridge over the steep-banked little Apangat River where the road now took them into the hills they had looked to as haven during the eternity they had spent in the open on the tormented flat plain. Now at a walk, the hooves clattering on the planks of the bridge lent a temporarily reassuring sound of the familiar, of peace, drowning out the residual roar in their ears from shrieking dive bombers and the awful crash of bombs in the road now behind them.

The shaken cavalrymen relaxed momentarily from their thoughts of the horrors just past and those to come and let the soft song of normalcy wash over them. After the naked flats, the road ahead with its narrow, tree-shaded borders gave the impression of sheltered sanctuary from all the violence. Only as 1st Sgt. Justin Bulawan of B Troop and the riders of the regimental point entered a steep cut on a curve in this pleasant road did it reveal itself to be just another lethal trap. This time when the Aichis dove at them there was no fifty feet of road width. There was no shoulder either, and no protective ditches. Hemmed in by steep banks on both sides, Sergeant Bulawan's point detachment was mauled. Bulawan was riding his favorite and beloved horse.

The sergeant was a man who had loved soldiering since the time he was old enough to remember. He deeply admired all things courageous and soldierly. From the time he had met the shipment in Manila of remount horses from America in 1936 after their long journey from Fort Riley, he had known that this big chestnut thoroughbred with the star on his forehead, the soft, expressive white nuzzle, and two white socks on his forelegs, which he carried high on parade like regimental decorations, was the horse for him to love above all others. It had taken some sharp garrison training and maneuvering to assure that this eye-catching young cavalry horse would be posted to permanent duty with B Troop, but Bulawan, then wearing the stripes of his brand new sergeancy, was an experienced hand at such military matters. The problem of a name for his new charger was solved one evening at the Stotsenburg post theater. Deeply moved by Gary Cooper's classic portrayal of a courageous foreign legionnaire who selflessly gave his all for his comrades in arms, Sergeant Bulawan greeted his horse at stable call the next morning with the most fitting name he could bestow: Beau Geste.

On that awful morning on the road to Damortis, the big chestnut proved himself worthy. Bulawan had ridden forward from his position near the head of the column to check on his advance point detail. On rounding the bend in the narrow, curving road, Bulawan and the six men on point found themselves in a treacherous defile (defilade) formed by a deep cut through a hell that revealed its hazard by high, steep banks on both sides of the passage. It was while in this deadly position that a lone, prowling Aichi Val spotted them and dove in for an easy kill.

At the instant he realized the lethal potential of the situation, Bulawan spurred hard and bellowed the order for all to run for it. They had about forty yards to clear the trap and reach the protective ditches beyond, but the Val's dive was too fast for them. The dive bomber's two antipersonnel bombs struck as one with a vicious crash, and a murderous spray of metal fragments ripped through the point detail with devastating effect.

Beau Geste had responded instantly to Bulawan's first touch of the spurs and had lunged forward as if from a racetrack starting gate, lending his rider the lifesaving benefit of his thoroughbred heritage. A steel shard sliced across the big chestnut's rump, tearing into Bulawan's blanket roll. He ducked low over the horse's neck with his face buried in the beautiful chestnut mane, fully expecting to feel the bite of hot steel in his back, but it never came. Beau Geste's great, running lunge carried them clear of the explosions and into the depression of the roadside just beyond the deadly defile as the Japanese pilot pulled out of his dive and the tail gunner routinely machine-gunned his helpless targets.

On the ground behind was bloody chaos. Five of Bulawan's six point troopers lay dead and dying along with their mounts. The sixth sat stunned and bleeding in the road next to his dead horse. Bulawan looked back in stark horror at the bloody piles of rags that had been his comrades, and his heart tore as horses thrashed and screamed in their pathetic and unearthly death throes. Without hesitation he ran back to the carnage to check futilely for life among his downed troopers. Finding all but one of the men beyond help, he then unholstered his .45 and put a merciful end to the suffering of those good, loyal creatures with whom he had lived and for whom he had cared for so long. Two dazed, bleeding horses were the only other survivors of his point detail. There would be no more parades, no more monkey drills, no more polo games. The true, awful purpose of the cavalry horse in war was upon them now, and the dying had begun in earnest.

As the rest of the column made its way past the shattered remains of the point, Captain H. S. Farris, the 1st Squadron executive officer, stopped to check the casualties. "As I examined the bloody mess where the bombs had hit the advance guard," Farris recalled years later, "I particularly noticed where a piece of shrapnel had gone entirely through one of the horses and broken the saddle in half. All but one of the entire point guard had been killed, so we ordered a new one out." He continued, "While I was standing there, Major Hubert Ketchum rode up to me and said, 'Don't worry, it's only six miles from Rosario to Damortis.' I thought to myself, Farris, this is going to be the longest six miles in the world before it's done."

Bulawan, never idle, had rounded up the point's two surviving mounts and quickly assigned them to some B Troopers who had lost their own horses in earlier attacks. "Keep it moving, keep it moving—you haven't got time to stop and stare at these poor fellas unless you want to be like them." The eternal Sergeant Bulawan knew only too well the cost of any delays now. Flesh and saddle leather were no match for dive bombers and shrapnel. The rest of the column wound its way past the fallen men and horses, each man soberly taking in the sight of what remained of six of their own. Still, however, war was not yet a face-to-face encounter for them—it was still just cruel, impersonal terror from the skies above them.

When the 192nd tanks crossed the Apangat, the road narrowed, and periodically they pulled to the side and camouflaged as best they could with big banana leaves and other foliage to take cover from roving Japanese dive bombers. It was with sinking heart that they came across the scene in the narrow cut where Sergeant Bulawan and his advance party had been shot up.

As the 26th progressed along the twisting road, the prospects for dispersal and refuge from air attack improved slightly. There were fewer irrigation ditches and swampy rice paddies, and in many places, there were gaps in the ever-present roadside wire fences. About three miles from Damortis, the point topped a ridge and they got their first look at Lingayen Gulf in the distance. It was a sobering moment for all of the troopers as they saw for the first time the formidable magnitude of their objective. As their commanders and the advance party had before them, they began counting ships and speculating on the size of the invasion force they were about to face.

Sgt. Eliseo Mallari of 2nd Squadron later remembered the gloom of the day. "It was a damp chill and the skies were dark. An intermittent rain was still falling." While the accounts of what they saw before them in the gulf varied, there was general agreement later that they were facing a fearsomely overwhelming force. Mallari recalled, "Eight troop transports, destroyers and small cruisers, and in the distance, an aircraft carrier. The troop ships were spilling out landing craft which were speeding to the beaches in successive waves."

Mallari and the others could even see that many of the troops in the initial waves carried bicycles, so sure that the opposition would be so lightly organized that they could just ride right down the road through them. The men of the 26th were not yet aware that Lt. Johnny George and his recon unit had at their roadblock at the bridge already bloodily dispelled such notions for Japanese advance parties.

Lt. Arthur Whitehead of Troop A, 1st Squadron, pulled his skittish black horse, Crow Flight, out of the column to have a look for himself at the view. As he reined up to a halt, an army sedan drove up and stopped nearby. Captain Dooley and Major Pugh got out and approached him. They had been sent over to Lingayen by Wainwright to survey the situation. As they ran to the high vantage point on the ridge where Pierce and Chandler had gone earlier, Whitehead concluded, "Skinny must be hard up for intelligence to send two of his key people up here."

The ridge was a bare, exposed place, and the two staff officers were casting nervous glances upward at the free-roaming Japanese planes. Amused by Dooley's obvious discomfort, Whitehead called out jokingly, "Better be careful, Tom!" Dooley turned and shot him an annoyed look, then turned to continue sweeping the area with his field glasses. Whitehead watched the scene for a short while longer and then wheeled his horse back toward the column to catch up to his platoon. As he did, he looked back to see Dooley and Pugh run back to their car, make a quick U-turn, and roar back east.

Just after the column passed through the little barrio of Cataquintingan, just a little more than halfway to Damortis, Vance received a radio message from Pierce ordering him to place one troop in position just west of the barrio to serve as a second delaying position. Vance sent Private Leonardo to Maj. Tom Trapnell and to Capt. John Z. Wheeler with orders that they report to him on the double. Vance told Trap he was to place E Troop in position at a road cut that offered the defenders a tactically advantageous defilade. Trap then had Wheeler pull his Troop E out of column, and as they trotted back to take up their position, the young troop commander remarked disappointedly to E's first sergeant, Amigable, "We may miss the fighting stuck way back here." Little did John Wheeler know how mistaken he was and how many of his men would die there in the road that night.

E Troop set up its positions and got its horses under cover with horse holders. Wheeler then sent out small patrols to reconnoiter their general operations area, and opportunity was taken to water, feed, and check the condition of their horses after the brutal morning. As the troopers watched the animals eat, their own stomachs growled with awareness that they themselves had not properly eaten since leaving Rosales two days before. Based on intelligence gathered by his returning patrols, Wheeler made his final dispositions of weapons. He sent the second platoon and a light machine gun section under command of Lt. Robert L. Carusso into position about half a mile west covering Route 3, the Damortis road. As soon as Carusso was satisfied with the placement of his men and guns, he let his platoon sergeant, Mascancay, send out a foraging party to look for food. To their delight, they found the civilians in the area very generous. These were people whose lives were in the direct path of holocaust, and they regarded these cavalrymen as protectors.

During a rare lull in Japanese air activity in their area, Wheeler used the respite to check Carusso's positions. As the captain, 1st Sergeant Amigable, and Cpl. Felipe Fernandez approached the hill occupied by the 2nd platoon, they were struck by the aroma of chickens cooking. On arriving at the base of the hill and Carusso's CP, they found, tucked away under the cover of several deeply shaded acacia trees, a group of troopers lovingly cooking small chickens over hot, smokeless fires in small pits. Mouths watering, Wheeler and his inspection team dismounted and gratefully shared a few welcome bites before returning up the hill.

At the top of the hill, Wheeler and the others could see through binoculars the ominous mass of Japanese ships offshore and the constant stream of landing craft shuttling back and forth with men and equipment.

Only then did they fathom the extent of the gravity of the regiment's situation. The faint crackling of almost continuous small arms and machine gun fire drifted back from the direction of the coastline, punctuated occasionally by the deep thumps of artillery shells and bombs. Every shot seemed to drive the nails of foreboding deeper into their consciousness. Even the delectable little chickens began to sit like lead in their tightening bellies. It was their first real look into the mouth of hell.

By 11:45 a.m., the rest of the regimental column was continuing toward Damortis. The roadsides now offered much readier access to cover from air attack, and they made good time. After about a mile from where they had left Wheeler's troop, orders came for Colonel Vance, squadron commanders Majors Ketchum and Trapnell, and Capt. Jack A. Ford, CO of Machine Gun Troop, to report to regimental commander Colonel Pierce immediately. The four men moved out at a gallop and a short time later joined Pierce at his hilltop observation post. They gave Pierce the dismal reports of the past hour and a half's heavy casualties from bombing and strafing and then summed up the present conditions of their respective units. The colonel received their reports in silence, and then he remarked that he was just thankful that their losses had not been even heavier.

It was hard news for a man who loved his regiment as Pierce did and who knew practically every man in it by name as well as many of their families.

Later, Jonathan Wainwright would receive the heartbreaking news that his beloved horse Little Boy was among the casualties. He had died from a bullet through the head in one of the strafings.

Pierce then explained that George and his scout cars were now under heavy enemy pressure, and the situation was fast becoming critical. (Pierce was not yet aware of the disastrous engagement between Lieutenant Morin's five 192nd light tanks and advancing Japanese armor and that now nothing stood in the way of the massive Japanese advance except Johnny George's ferocious but thinly manned roadblock at the bridge on the coast road.) Pierce emphasized that the regiment had to occupy the fighting positions that he had selected as quickly as humanly possible or the Japanese would overrun Damortis in short order. This would give the enemy immediate tactical use of both Route 3 to the east and Route 7 to the south.

Now the burden of defense fell fully on the few, steadfast troopers of the 26th Cavalry to stem the tide.

12

Stand on the Ridge at Lingayen

22 DECEMBER 1941, 11 A.M.

Lingayen Gulf, west coast of Northern Luzon

The deadly encounter of Lt. Col. Kito Kitamura's advance reconnaissance elements with Lt. Johnny George's scout car roadblock at the bridge caused a quick reappraisal of the situation by Japanese officers, now already under pressure from Homma to regain valuable time lost too early in the game. The consensus was that aerial reconnaissance and aggressive attack by dive bombers was needed to sufficiently clear the coast road before further advance could be judiciously made by their main force with tank-supported infantry. Now Johnny George's hand was to be called, and the price of his successful delaying action was going to be high. Nipponese hell was about to give his small force vicious attention.

When the air attacks on his position began and the sounds of advancing armor supporting a second wave of assault on his position became audible, George sensed that he had no time to lose in ordering withdrawal. He ordered a preplanned, full fallback maneuver, but because of the noise of the guns of the scout cars now opening up on the renewed attack, the men in the other two scout cars were unable to hear George's commands for withdrawal being relayed by his radioman. George jumped down from his vehicle and, waving signals to break off and retreat, he rushed to the other cars to alert them physically, shaking de Mesa on his shoulder in the process. He urgently pointed back at his own vehicle, which was now slowly getting under way, and then returned to it. Before the other two cars could get fully maneuvered around to follow, a Japanese dive bomber swooped down to score a direct hit on George's car. All of his crew members, including troopers Lenardo, Millado, Heroka, and Bandelman, were killed instantly, and George was literally blown to bits.

Now Sgt. Domingo de Mesa had no choice but to take charge. He began commanding his driver, Corporal Lago, to steer their vehicle in a series of violent evasive maneuvers while Corporal Miole, the radio operator, and gunner Private Camplon manned the machine guns against the attacking aircraft. With quick reflexes much conditioned by his considerable experience as a baseball player, de Mesa directed the surviving cars in a wild stop-go, zig-zag, leapfrog retreat to foil the accuracy of the bomber pilots and escape the same fate as George from the now furious enemy air attack. De Mesa later recalled that he felt angry and torn. He did not at all like the idea of leaving George and his other fellow troopers behind and having to make a run for it, but as he commented in characteristic Filipino style prose, "I wanted to stay put and battle the enemy to the last bullet in our guns, but I knew this was the fruit of war and protecting my regiment came first at all cost."

Many of the rest of the regiment, now in the urgent process of taking positions on the high ground overlooking the coast road, witnessed George's horrific end and the hair-raising retreat of the surviving scout cars. Incredibly, the cars evaded destruction by Japanese planes, which literally exhausted their ammunition in the attempt to destroy the fleeing vehicles and their occupants. De Mesa's car was hit several times, but the scout car machine gunners with their weapons literally in vertical position put up a withering hail of antiaircraft fire, which served to somewhat discourage and spoil the aim of the Japanese pilots in their final strafing runs. De Mesa and his driver were slightly wounded and their vehicle was damaged beyond repair. After dismantling machine guns, radio, and critical spare parts, the car was destroyed to deny it to the enemy. The survivors continued back toward Rosario and took up a rear guard position with the remaining scout car to support the 26th troopers on the ridge. Later that day, under heavy fire but with the desperate instinct born of long conditioning of loyalty to the regiment that none should be left behind, de Mesa led a small patrol in a daring foray downhill from the 26th defensive positions on the ridge. Carrying shelter halves, they made a frantic effort to recover what little they could of the shattered remains of George and his crew for return to their own lines. All they could find that was identifiable of the late, handsome, and affable Johnny George was one of his legs encased in its custom-made cavalry boot with his name stamped inside.

THE 26TH'S STAND AT DAMORTIS

At the outset of hostilities on 8 December, the 26th Cavalry had its authorized troop strength of 838 men consisting of 54 officers, including veterinarians, medical officer, and chaplain, and 784 enlisted men (a general, available roster of the regimental makeup can be found in the epilogue). By the morning of 22 December the strength of the regiment had been significantly reduced by a combination of casualties and detachment of troops to assignment separated from the main body (for one, Troop C was assigned to the northern central highlands of Luzon to guard the critical mountain road that afforded the enemy the ability to connect its Aparri invasion force with its Vigan assault force and to counter enemy advances in that sector and southward toward strategic Baguio). The detachments of G Troop to the Baler Bay area and C Troop north left a balance of 699 men and 28 officers to move on toward Rosario. Additional dents in the main body of the regiment took place with the detachment of some 85 key officers and NCOs for various command and staff duties with other Philippine Army units. Also, that morning, Colonel Pierce gave orders to Troop F to detach at Rosario and take up patrol duty on the five main trails north of that town to block the threat of Japanese advances that risked the regiment being cut off from their withdrawal route back through Rosario. The remainder of the regiment then had to move toward Lingayen on the dangerous Rosario–Damortis road to carry out their formidable assignment from Wainwright to hold open the coast road and the critical junction at Damortis so his main defense forces would not be cut off. These forces were located north around Agoo and south around Dagupan (where the heaviest artillery was positioned), and they had the task of holding back the invasion force from the Gulf. Roughly translated, this meant that the severely understrength 26th was the only finger in the dike.

The most dangerous problem facing the 26th in holding the Rosario–Damortis line was the road between the towns. Hard surfaced and winding through foothills, curves interfered with efficient observation and fields of fire. To the north loomed the highest mountains of Luzon. To the south the ground was heavily wooded, rolling terrain. The five separate trails, all coming south from the now Japanese held region around Agoo, posed the danger of infiltration to the regiment's rear. This was the concern that prompted Pierce to chance the loss of Troop F to cover the trails with three strong patrols, each reinforced by a much needed machine gun section. They were ordered to focus on three largest trails until they made enemy contact. They were then to fight a delaying action back toward the main road, falling back only under extreme pressure. Smaller patrols were picketed along the two smaller Agoo trails.

At around noon when the remainder of the regiment finally reached the approaches to Damortis and joined Pierce at the ridge overlooking the coast road, they were then down to a force of around six hundred men and their surviving officers. Nevertheless, forced to cope with what they had, Pierce and Chandler began relaying orders to the squadron and troop commanders to dismount and fight on foot, designating their fighting positions on the ridge. The plan of defense was a roughly semicircle perimeter with the long side facing the coast road and the right flank bending back to face north and deny the regiment's flank to the enemy. Elements of the regiment went into line much according to the order of march to the position.

The 1st Squadron, which had a platoon of heavy machine guns (Troop B, MGs) attached, was ordered to take up defense positions about six hundred to eight hundred meters north and five hundred meters east of Damortis itself. The squadron also consisted of Troop A (under command of Capt. Leland Cramer from Maguon, Illinois) and Troop B (under command of Capt. Joe Barker, a tough, affable soldier's soldier from Birmingham, Alabama). About one half of Machine Gun Troop, the heavy machine gun platoon, under command of 1st Lt. Paul K. Allen (from Tucson, Arizona), was concentrated on the left flank nearest the coast road to cover any enemy approach from the direction of the road and Damortis. Another section of Machine Gun Troop was placed in the center of the line in support of the regimental command post (CP) on a hill about half way between the 1st and 2nd squadrons. The remainder of Machine Gun Troop was dispersed among the troops holding the right flank sector of the line. The 2nd Squadron, along with the machine gunners, had part of troop E (under command of the gentlemanly, quiet-spoken John Zachary Wheeler from St. Paul, Minnesota), which had been split. Part of E was on line and part of the troop was placed on the Rosario–Damortis road to guard any enemy approach on the road to the rear of the regimental MLR (main line of resistance). The other part of Troop E (under command of Capt. John W. Fowler) was joined on the line by part of Troop G. Troop F, as mentioned previously, was detached to guard the Rosario–Agoo trails.

Downhill, behind the ridge where the regiment was taking up positions, was a valley where the troops had dismounted. In it was a rice paddy that had been recently harvested and was now a hard, broken field covered with rice stubble. A stream bed running down the center of the field had a generous growth of tall cogon grass about ten feet high, and as many horses as possible were hidden there. Others were put under cover here and there where clumps of small trees could be found. As the dismounted regiment took up its positions, horse holders (average one trooper to four or five horses and mules) from each troop were positioned about a hundred yards to the rear in classic cavalry fighting routine to safeguard the mounts and pack animals. The dismounted men assembled in columns of troopers and moved up under cover to the brow of the hill where their troop commanders were waiting. A few of the men had taken their canteens off their saddles and hooked them to their belts by use of the small chain attaching the canteen cover. Those men who did not do this would sorely regret it later that day. All the men were tired and hungry and, most of all, hot. Few of them truly realized the gravity of what was happening.

While the regiment was going into line, the men were able to witness the awful fate of Lt. Johnny George and the brilliantly elusive withdrawal of the remaining scout cars directed by Sergeant de Mesa. It was a sobering sight in addition to the view of the huge Japanese landing forces, but the primary reaction among the troopers was only a more hardened resolve to hold their ground at any cost. Japanese planes were actively at work all over the area but had not yet turned their attention on the regimental defense line for the moment.

The following are Japanese monographs from 22 December 1941 on the progress of the Lingayen operations.

> The main force of the invasion army was very complex, since the assembly points were separated into KIRUN, TAKAO and MAKO. Because of this, the order in which the units boarded the ships did not run smoothly, and some mistakes were made. However, the preparations for departure were completed through the efforts of each organization. Thus, the 3rd convoy left KIRUN at 1700 of 17 December. The 2nd convoy left MAKO at 1200 of 18 December, and the first convoy from TAKAO left at 1700 of 18 December.
>
> These large convoys (totaling 71 ships) sailed south toward LINGAYEN (the designated landing point) under the escort of the main force of the 3rd Fleet.
>
> The 16th Division left AMANI-OSHIMA at 1300 of 17 December with a convoy of 14 ships and sailed south toward LAMON BAY (their designated landing point) under escort of a portion of the 3rd Fleet.
>
> The commencement of landing operations by the main invasion army force took place at 2300 22 December. The convoy for the main force reached LINGAYEN BAY at midnight of 22 December without encountering enemy air or submarine attacks and reached its anchorage at 0210 hours. At this time, they were bombarded by a few shells from shore batteries, but no damage was inflicted.
>
> At dawn, the weather became worse and there were waves two meters high. Very strong running tides. Since landing barges utilized by the first landing units could not return to the ships, the landing was expected to be difficult. These circumstances were a matter of grave concern to command. However, in spite of weather and tides, the landing was carried out according to plan.

The Advancement of the 48th Division into Damortis and Rosario

The 48th Division (6 infantry battalions, 3 mountain artillery battalions, 2 tank regiments, two 15 cm. howitzer battalions, two 10 cm. cannon battalions, and support units) a total of about 28,000 men, after eliminating light resistance offered by a portion of enemy beach defenses (Philippine Army and American shore batteries) began landing operations in the southern area of AGOO, TUBAO (about 6 km. east north east of AGOO), PUGO (about 6 km. east of TUBAO) and ROSARIO. The 48th Division was gradually joined by the now combined northern invasion forces of Col. Toru Tanaka (Aparri landings) and Lt. Col Kanno (Vigan landings), increasing the Lingayen area troop strength to some 40,000 troops total.

Advance probes were initiated southward on the Lingayan Gulf coastal road by patrols of Lt. Col. Kuro Kitamura's reconnaissance force. These patrols encountered heavy resistance on the coast road and withdrew for reinforcement and to call for air attacks on the stiffening enemy defensive positions. Then with infantry and mountain artillery units as their main force, one unit resumed advance southward on the coastal road and others took the route southward through AGOO, TUBAO and PUGO toward ROSARIO. An enemy force of about 10 tanks was encountered north of Damortis but was destroyed. At 1200 hours, infantry and tanks attacked toward Damortis but encountered determined brigade strength resistance north of the town.[1] This battle continued until 1900 when 48th Division forces advanced into DAMORTIS about 10 km southeast of AGOO. The unit which advanced into DAMORTIS then changed their direction toward ROSARIO. This unit, supported by tanks encountered withdrawing tanks and cavalry and pursued them to a crossing at the APANGAT River where they were delayed when the bridge was temporarily destroyed. The other 48th Div. unit and supporting detachments from AGOO took a mountain path in the PUGO area and advanced into Rosario where they encountered considerable resistance from mounted and dismounted cavalry. ROSARIO was cleared of resistance by 2100 hours, 22 December. Enemy defense forces withdrew southward toward BUED. Resistance at DAMORTIS caused considerable concern at command level because of significant delay in planning timetable.[2]

Other Occurrences of concern: 21 & 22 December: The landing of the KAMASHIMA Detachment and other units under direct control of the Army and the occupation of NAGUILIAN airfield. The KAMASHIMA Detachment (1st battalion of the 9th Infantry Regiment) and a reserve unit (2nd Battalion of the 9th Infantry Regiment) began landing operations in the western area of BAUANG at 0730 and 0930, respectively. Cooperating with each other, they destroyed strong enemy forces [Note: These were mostly Philippine Army and some U.S. Army coastal defense forces.] and expanded the position. After driving the enemy eastward at 1400, the KAMASHIMA Detachment contacted the TANAKA Detachment (main force of the 2nd FORMOSA infantry regiment and one mountain artillery battalion) which had advanced to the southern edge of SAN FERNANDO that morning. The reserve unit occupied BAUANG at 1700 hours, SANTIAGO at 0830 and, after eliminating enemy resistance, advanced to the northeast and captured the Naguilian Airfield.

It was necessary to travel a long distance in landing barges to reach the designated landing beach (southern part of San Fernando) because of the shifting of the anchorage to the south. Therefore, the landing barges reached the beach after dawn and received heavy damages from the bombardment of the coastal batteries.

Changing of the Landing Point and Difficulties in Landing of the Army

In this landing of the main force of the army on 22 December, the 48th Division was only able to land its infantry, most of its mountain artillery, and a portion of its tank unit. Although weather conditions were comparatively good, the tides were treacherous, and units under the direct control of the army encountered great difficulties. [Note: This was the time that Homma in his recollections referred to as the first of his three most critical moments.] Homma later recalled, "All of the boats which went ashore did not return to the transports. Owing to the conditions of the sea, we referred to it as 'the rolling waves.' I do not know what or how to explain it, but on the beach, many of our boats went up on shore only to be buried in the sand and could not get out. It took us a full day to dig them out and bring them back to their mother ships. So the landing schedule was not carried out as previously set. In the morning fighter planes came over the transports, and there was fighting over our heads. After sending the first landing party, we could not send a second. I was worried about the situation because only a part of my infantry went ashore while the rest remained aboard ship. If we were counterattacked, we would be helpless. We did not know when the sea would be calm enough to land next day, so during the night of the 22nd, I shifted the anchorage of my boats south so we could land between Damortis and Agoo. We were able to land troops the next day, but it took us two extra days to land all our force." At 1730, the Army decided to change its landing point of the remaining units of the 48th Division to the vicinity of DAMORTIS and ordered the changing of the anchorage of a portion of the 48th Division to occupy SAN FABIAN (where the bulk of Wainwright's heavy shore batteries were positioned) as quickly as possible in order to protect the new anchorage from enemy fire. (More delay in the Japanese timetable and worry for Homma.)

On this same day, one transport (having field hospital units on board) was sunk by a torpedo from an enemy submarine, but the majority of the personnel were saved. At dawn of 22 Dec. a few enemy planes bombed and strafed our ships and troops on land but inflicted light damage only.

The above Japanese reports indicate the gradually accumulating chinks in the Nipponese timetable, which ultimately caused Homma to be replaced as Japanese commander in the Philippines. The 26th's stand at

Damortis played a significant role in this even if circumstances and overwhelming odds did not allow them to fully accomplish Wainwright's prayed-for miracle for the Rosario–Damortis line.

ON THE RIDGE AT DAMORTIS

22 December 1941, 12:15 p.m.

First Lt. Arthur K. Whitehead, of Troop A, First Squadron, commanded by Capt. Leland Cramer, sharply recalls his two platoons going on line. "The 1st Platoon was already in position on the hill facing the coast road. The Light Machine Gun Platoon went into position with them. The 2nd Platoon, with Lt. Fred B. Evans, was ordered to send one squad of riflemen mounted to the high ground to the east to cover any hostile movement attempting to get in our flank and rear. The other squad of 2nd Platoon was sent dismounted to occupy the part of the ridge just east of the right flank of the 1st Platoon position. Two heavy machine guns attached to the troop also occupied this part of the ridge. I was placed in command on this section and given instructions to keep in contact with the mounted patrol on our right flank to the east.

"The troop commander's CP was on the ridge occupied by the 1st Platoon overlooking Lingayen Gulf and the vicinity of Damortis. This ridge, which ran north and south parallel to the shore of the gulf, was one half to three fourths of a mile long, forming a cut for the highway on the west and petering out into a gully on the north. A short distance from the northern end of the main ridge, a narrower ridge of about the same elevation ran perpendicular to it. This furnished a fair field of fire for 1000 yards to the north toward another group of hills. The shore of the gulf was about one and a half miles away. From the shore in, for about three quarters of a mile, the land was level. From this plain to the 1st Platoon's position, there was a gradual rise made up of billowing hills covered with tall cogon grass. Lingayen Gulf seemed choked with Jap warships and transports. There was a heavy haze in the airless heat, and the sun was already low enough in the west to make seeing in that direction very difficult. We watched the Jap landing barges bringing men and supplies ashore, but we could do nothing to stop them. There was an empty pit in everyone's stomach at that point."

The Japanese had amassed some two hundred landing craft of various types. Sixty-three were the regular workhorse Daihatsu landing barges; some seventy-three were larger of the same; about fifteen to twenty were extra-large landing craft called Tokubestu Daihatsu. The remainder were light, motored sampans. Despite their numbers, the enemy landing force was vulnerable prey to American and Filipino gunners waiting onshore, and the toll was heavy.

To the south of the regiment's positions, the remaining company of 192nd tanks were stationed to block any enemy advance on the road from Damortis. Farther to the rear, two or three of the 26th scout cars were using their .50-caliber machine guns for antiaircraft fire at the Japanese planes now busily trying to wipe out anything on the road.

Far to the left of Whitehead's flank, Troop B and the heavy machine gun platoon under Lieutenant Allen were settled in and waiting for the first enemy ground probes. All along the 26th line, their defensive positions were almost devoid of any overhead cover. They were at the full mercy of an increasing storm of bombs and bullets from strafing aircraft, but the ingrained discipline of the scout cavalrymen held firm, and no trooper broke under the continuous, heavy air attacks. By 12:30, all of the regiment's assigned positions were occupied, and the pitifully thin line of cavalrymen now settled in to do mortal combat with the entire brunt of the Japanese invasion force.

Their wait was not long. Shortly after 1 p.m., high-pitched cracking sounds overhead signaled the initial enemy attack. At first, the noise was puzzling and somewhat confusing, but it soon dawned on the men that it was the sound of bullets overhead making a noise identical to that heard in the target pits of the rifle ranges as firing passed on the target levels above. Japanese machine gunners with highly effective Nambu Type 99 automatic rifles—modeled after the previously used Hotchkiss and modified by Gen. Kirijo Nambu, this was a bipod-stand-mounted weapon resembling the British Bren Gun (originally, like its Japanese counterpart) modeled after Czechoslovakian ZB26 auto rifles captured from the Chinese in the early 1930s—had somehow maneuvered themselves in alarmingly close to the 26th positions and were laying down a heavy preparatory fire for their infantrymen to make an assault. The Nambus fired a rimless 7.7mm cartridge, a little larger caliber than the smaller .25 caliber or 6.5mm cartridge used in the Japanese Mauser type Arisaka standard infantry rifles. Use of different calibers for basic weapons was a troublesome supply disadvantage to Japanese troops, unlike the American standard use of .30 caliber for its main infantry weapons. The advance attackers were also using portable, lightweight, smooth-bore Model 89 50mm (1.97 in.) mortars (more grenade launcher than mortar, really). These handheld ten-and-a-half-pound, short-range (from 140 to 700 yards, Model 89 shell, less with other type ammunition) weapons, a simple twenty-inch tube with a sliding range device on its side, were commonly known as "knee mortars" and used with great effectiveness by Japanese troops, who seemed to have an uncanny sense of accuracy with them. There were frequent leg casualties among Allied defenders who made the mistake of taking the term "knee" literally and tried to fire some of the captured little mortars by placing the base on their knees instead of correctly on the ground in front of them.

Two or three hundred yards beyond and to the north and west the men caught glimpses of Japanese helmets and sometimes heads and shoulders of enemy soldiers bobbing up and down just beyond the crest of a group of hills facing the 26th lines. The 26th light machine gunners and riflemen wriggled low on their stomachs, sweat burning their eyes, muttering to one another where the next target might pop up over the ridge to their front.

On the left, closest to the coast road, the 1st Squadron caught the worst of the first Japanese assault, and it was not long before it became apparent that they could not hold for long despite the terrible punishment they were inflicting on their attackers. Advancing Japanese troops tended to be somewhat overconfident; many of them had experienced only the relatively weak resistance put up by inexperienced, poorly armed Philippine Army troops. Here, against the 26th, was a different matter entirely. The Japanese were stunned by the ferocity of the withering fire delivered on them from the keen-eyed 26th Cavalry marksmen, seasoned with months and years of devoted time on the ranges honing their marksmanship, both for status, rank, and increases in pay. Maj. Bill Chandler felt a rush of pride as he watched troopers calmly and professionally adjust slings and sights in preparation for their deadly work. This day marked the first-time use in World War II combat of a deadly new American infantry weapon, the Garand M-1. Until now, the volume of rapid fire put down by the new .30-caliber semi-automatic rifles was unheard. They fired nonstop, eight-round clips at a time with only a split second reload for a new clip, shocking the Japanese with a hail of fire that they felt could only come from a brigade, not an understrength regiment. A formidable number of them got acquainted with their ancestors that day before they got any wiser. This factor afforded the 26th a brief respite as the Japanese initially hesitated, their confident attack temporarily blunted by the unexpected storm of lead. But the dye was cast by overwhelming numbers, and enemy pressure on the scout lines began to build and take a painful toll.

Shortly after 2 p.m., firing commenced heavily toward the right flank where Japanese were now trying to make an end run to roll up the 26th line. Now, the air along the line was a storm of lead, but still the heavy volume of fire from M-1s and machine guns held the attackers firmly at bay. By about 2:15 the center of the 26th line and the 1st Platoon of HQ Troop began taking artillery fire. Slowly, the 26th line became heavily zeroed in by fire from Japanese 75mm Type 94 mountain guns from the valley toward the gulf where the enemy was concentrating for an all-out assault. The Japanese commanders had taken measure of the situation and mistakenly, but unfortunately for the 26th, concluded that they were facing brigade-strength resistance and were mustering enough force to subdue it. Soon, Japanese light tanks, firing their small cannon, began to show themselves over the ridge. Under their cover, moving in columns of squads, Japanese infantry began to move toward the center and right sectors of the 26th line. Soon they had heavy machine guns joined in the assault as well as knee mortars, whose small shells made a terrific racket as they tumbled end over end in flight. The Japanese assault force was now roughly a thousand yards to the front of the 26th heavy machine guns, and their troops were scrambling down into the defilade protection of a gully. The 26th heavies took a terrible toll, but the tenacious Japanese kept coming.

Lieutenant (later a major) Whitehead of A Troop on the sector of the line facing the coast road recalled, "Watching the firing of the heavy machine guns was engrossing. The first man to see a target would try to show it to the gunner. If the gunner was unable to find it, the man who saw it would aim the gun, then the gunner would do the firing. Realizing there was else to do rather than just watch two guns, I crawled back to where my squad of riflemen had been put into position and found them behind the crest of the ridge lying prone doing nothing.

"Then Corporal Abad told me that he did not know where he was to get into position to fire. After getting the men into a good firing position in front of where they had been lying, they started up a heavy volume of fire and stayed there without any trouble throughout the rest of the action."

At around 2:40 p.m., Japanese tanks and infantry had formed and were advancing aggressively from the direction of Damortis against Major Hubert W. "Hank" Ketchum's 1st Squadron, with particular focus on 1st Lt. Paul Allen's Machine Gun Troop. Ketchum sent a messenger to B Troop and its attached units of MG Troop with orders that they were to withdraw immediately. He also ordered their animals be brought to the foot of the hill to meet them. A Troop was to cover B Troop, and the reserve part of MG Troop was to cover A Troop's withdrawal. But before the messengers could reach the troop, the Japanese began their assault. Led by tanks, they hit the 26th's left flank on the low ground near Route 3, the coast road. The two squads of MG Troop's .50-caliber guns, which were positioned astride the road, tried desperately to stop the tanks, but even at point-blank range they had little effect on the enemy armor. The 26th lacked any real antitank weapons or ordnance, and even though a .50-caliber machine gun could frequently blow treads loose on a tank at close range, it was hardly an efficient antitank weapon.

Slowly, Japanese artillery fire began to blanket the whole line. Jap tanks, firing their small cannons, begin to appear. Jap infantry moving in columns of squads went up under cover of the tanks and soon had their machine guns blanketing 1st Platoon's positions and left flank and the heavy machine guns under Allen. At the time, incoming artillery fire was causing increasing casualties, and the few men of the medical detachment found it impossible to evacuate them from the area. To add to the difficulty, enemy aircraft were now bombing and strafing everything that moved on the road behind the 26th lines.

Before the withdrawal could be executed, Lieutenant Allen's two squads of MG Troop's .50-caliber guns, which were positioned astride the road, caught the full brunt of the combined tank and infantry attack. The full fury of Japanese attention was now turned on Allen's gritty little band of machine gunners, who had been sweeping the road with concentrated MG fire from their horrifyingly exposed shallow gun pits and ditches. The cause for this deadly attention was that Allen's troopers were screwing up what might have been an easy execution of the Japanese passion for end runs.

Now aware of the situation, commanders of the ponderous Japanese Shiki 97 medium tanks turned the full fury of their armor on Allen's positions and began to rumble steadily, inexorably toward the hapless cavalrymen whose heaviest counterweapons were .50-caliber machine guns and hand grenades. The acrid smoke and smell of cordite engulfed the troopers, and they were immersed in the drum roll crack of 47mm cannons and the shrieking of oncoming Japanese infantrymen shepherding the mechanical monsters.

Even engrossed as they were with their own pitched battle farther up the ridge, other 26th troopers looked down on the scene with gut wrenching horror as the tidal wave of fire and metal swept over Allen and his men, with whom they had shared so much.

One by one Allen's machine guns fell silent as the troopers manning them died where they fought, not giving an inch. Troopers were ground to bloody pulp as the enemy tankers wheeled their vehicles in circular maneuvers over the strong points. The 47mm cannons and machine guns on the tanks had literally massacred Allen's force as they tried point blank to hold their position. They were virtually run over, causing terrible casualties among the gun crews and B Troop. Among those killed were Lieutenant Allen and a number of senior noncoms. Japanese infantrymen who had survived the murderous fire from the ungiving cavalrymen wreaked terrible vengeance with their bayonets on the few troopers who had lived through the armored onslaught. But some of them died also, as they found that the stubborn cavalrymen did not die easily or willingly, and hands strong from work with horses and training closed around the throats of their tormentors and razor-sharp machetes flashed, cleaving Bushido warriors from collarbone to belly in their own time-honored fashion. The end was brief and nightmarishly violent for Allen and his gunners, and the defenders up on the ridge sensed that time was running out for the 26th at Damortis.

By what could only be described as a miracle, about a dozen battered, bleeding survivors of Allen's stand managed to extricate themselves and tried to make their way back to the regiment, which was now in the process of phased withdrawal. A few others fled straight down the coast road and were unable to rejoin the regiment for several days. Still the troopers on the ridges continued to take a vicious toll of the assaulting Japanese with murderous, disciplined M-1 fire so long nurtured on the ranges at Stotsenburg. The extra five pesos a month for marksmanship was proving to be one hell of a profitable investment for the U.S. Cavalry on that terrible afternoon.

Pfc. Eduardo Lagaspe thought over and over as he aimed and fired: deep breath; let it out a little; squeeze; recoil; deep breath; no hate, no fear, just targets, their little red collar tabs and yellow stars on headgear, bobbing, teasing, inviting the seasoned marksman's concentration. The ceaseless din and crack of weapons and the burning fumes of smoke and cordite blotted out all awareness of battle, the yells of the attackers—intended to strike fear into the hearts of the defenders—and the shrieks of pain and terror as men felt their bodies being ripped and torn by vicious, impersonal, invisible metal. The 26th was making the ridges of Damortis costly real estate for Homma's troops.

BIRTH OF A CAVALRY LEGEND

Major Ketchum ordered the withdrawal to continue but authorized a daring counterattack in a desperate attempt to rescue or give the survivors of the overrun units a chance to escape. A composite mounted platoon from Troop A then made a hell for leather, surprise cavalry charge, which temporarily stunned the Japanese. In their ferocious horse-mounted attack the 26th troopers attacked tanks with a tactic that, in itself, would appear suicidal; but these men, most of them devoted Catholics, were not suicidal people. The motivation was just simple, unquestioning courage and righteous anger. In a maneuver that they later perfected and that would become a Bataan legend often told to illustrate the bravery of the 26th, the mounted cavalrymen charged with hand grenades, pistols, their only anti-tank weapon, makeshift as it may have been, being Molotov cocktails made up of San Miguel beer or Coke bottles filled with gasoline and fitted with a gas-soaked rag wick. The procedure employed was four men, two two-man teams, who would attack a tank from two sides knowing the tank commander could only focus his defense to the left or right at one time. One team might go down, but the other would reach the tank to jam grenades down the hatches or explode the Molotovs on the tank's forward surface or rear radiator vents, roasting the vehicle's occupants alive or forcing them to exit to their deaths from the unerring gunfire of other scout troopers. It was a costly but effective way to eliminate enemy armor, and throughout the coming campaign, a significant number of Jap tankers met such a fate at the hands of the 26th Cavalry.

The surprise charge allowed some survivors of the overrun machine gun platoon to rejoin the regiment and the remainder of the 1st Squadron to withdraw at a full gallop past the regimental CP toward the 26th main line of resistance. The cost had been high for Troop A, for it had lost almost half of the counterattacking force. However, the Japanese tanks halted in shocked confusion. Meanwhile, Colonel Pierce found it hard to hold his position but was reinforced by a retreating company from the 71st Infantry (PA) and the remaining five tanks of 2nd Platoon, Company C, 192nd Tank Battalion. These tanks started eastward down the road toward Damortis to support the 26th but would arrive too late to help. The regimental CP was now fighting a rear-guard action against the Japanese, who had once again begun to advance. However, Troop A's daring, aggressive charge had made the enemy hesitant about entering the draw through which the 1st Squadron had escaped. The Japanese, now far more respectful of the cavalry than earlier, feared another attack on their armor while in such a confined area. By around 3 p.m. Troop A had successfully slipped west and was headed cross country to rejoin the regiment, leaving only the CP and the machine gun section to guard the left flank.

At around 3:30, Lieutenant Whitehead could hear increasing artillery fire zeroing in to his right and rear in the area where he had sent his mounted squad. Not getting any information back about his mounted contingent, Whitehead crawled to the backside of the slope only to find to his consternation that the Japanese had gotten up to the rear of his mounted squad's position and were advancing west up the 26th line. In spite of heavy losses from 26th machine gun and rifle fire, the Japanese had managed to get over the ridge and down into the defilade of the gully about seven hundred yards to the front of Whitehead's position. The awful realization sank in that they had been flanked. Around 2:40, he had started moving to the Troop CP to inform Major Ketchum of the threat but was stopped by the troop commander, who, seeing the desperation of the position, had obtained permission from Colonel Pierce to withdraw all of his command, including Whitehead's platoon and the mounted squad, immediately. They were ordered to take up a new position on a hill about four hundred yards to the south to cover the withdrawal of the rest of A Troop. Whitehead had checked the line during a slight lull in the incoming fire. He was concerned that he had not heard from his mounted squad, and he could not find them with his field glasses. He sent a runner to find out what was happening with them. During his line check, Whitehead found one of his machine gunners firing at aircraft and stopped him. They were low on ammo and had been previously warned to refrain from this practice and concentrate on ground attack. The gunner had been told specifically that the MGs were not to be used for antiaircraft fire. Whitehead crawled back to his rifle squad and verified that they were still firing effectively. Then he returned to the machine guns and found one gun firing at airplanes again. "It was not that I thought the gunner was deliberately disobeying. I believe the idea of those planes always overhead had preyed on his mind to the extent that he could not think of anything else. From time to time he would point at streams of smoke from our tracers and say that the Japs were dropping gas. I felt compelled to relieve him to the rifle squad and put the assistant gunner to firing."

In contrast to the gunner described by Whitehead, there was a different story with another gunner. On one of his light machine guns, the gunner and assistant gunner were cousins. The gunner in the course of the afternoon was hit in the chest. He fell away from the gun and rolled down the hill a short way. The assistant gunner, without giving his cousin a look or a thought, immediately got behind the gun and calmly continued firing. The 26th was a family as a whole, in truth, but they were also highly trained professionals at what they often and quaintly referred to as the "death game."

Colonel Pierce now directed the remainder of his immediate force back toward the preplanned second position. By 3:30 the regiment was in place in secondary positions halfway between Damortis and Rosario. Five 192nd tanks then came up and moved past the 26th's new defensive position, headed back along the road toward Damortis. Somehow they ended up a little north of Damortis in the thick of things and tried to head toward Agoo. Then the lead tank was destroyed by enemy tank fire and the remaining four, each struck several times by light antitank fire, quickly retreated back toward Rosario. The Japanese tanks followed.

This sequence of the tank maneuvers was to cause chaos on the Rosario–Damortis road later that evening.

At 4:30, squads of Japanese were noticed about one and a half miles to Troop A's right rear working their way behind Whitehead's holding force. The enemy troops could be seen for only seconds at a time as they passed in squad columns over a piece of high ground. It was unknown to Whitehead and his men how long this had been going on, and this posed a serious threat. The troop's horses were in the valley to its rear. South of the Valley was more high ground, which overlooked the troop's position. Captain Cramer ordered Whitehead to move two heavy machine guns to the hill to cover the withdrawal of the rest of Troop A. One heavy MG was withdrawn immediately from action, and the route to and exact locality of the next gun was carefully explained to the gun crew. The new position could be seen plainly, and the second gun and its crew were sent back to occupy it. The corporal of the rifle squad was instructed to stay in his present position for ten minutes after the second machine gun pulled out, and then to withdraw his squad to rejoin the machine guns at a designated point at the new position only about a quarter of a mile away.

The first gun had ample time to get settled in, yet could not be seen by Whitehead. After a short time, he started back with the second gun and had it in position within minutes. The first gun, however, still couldn't be located. It was later learned that on seeing the troop pulling out of position in front, the crew had taken it on themselves to pack the gun and take it to the place where the troop was assembling. The rifle squad also never got to its second position. Later the corporal explained that he had believed it necessary to get the horses out right then or they would have been lost, considering the Japanese movement on the ridge to their rear.

The one heavy machine gun left to fire had too much to do because it had an area of over ninety degrees from northwest to northeast to cover. Thus, after each burst was fired, it was necessary to traverse a full ninety degrees in order to fire on any enemy movement in the opposite direction. During the full hour (from 4:30 to 5:30) it took to get Troop A out of action, get horses and equipment checked over, and get back on the road saddled up and mounted, the single heavy machine gun kept up an incessant covering fire.

Toward the last stages of the withdrawal, the Japanese had worked their way up into positions overlooking the troop's movement and put down considerable fire on the unit. However, it was in large ineffective, either because the enemy soldiers couldn't shoot fish in a barrel or because the lone heavy machine gun was succeeding in keeping them down. Somehow, in the confusion, the pack horse of that last machine gun in the second position had disappeared. The gun and its crew were finally able to withdraw to a scout car waiting on the road to make their hasty exit. After Lt. Johnny George had been killed, 1st Lt. Russell Bowers of HQ Troop took command of the surviving scout cars brought back by de Mesa. His daring and effective performance in effecting delaying action using all remaining guns of the last two scout cars with maximum, devastating impact on the Damortis road earned him a commendation for the Silver Star from Maj. Lee Vance. But by now, despite the stiff resistance from the cavalrymen, it dawned on the Japanese that the 26th was in a phased withdrawal, and they began pushing forward with renewed determination.

Troop A proceeded to march roughly three miles back to a river (the Apangat) to water the horses, which, incidentally, had been faithfully fed during the action. The Japanese planes had now paused in their bombing and strafing (probably to rearm), but scout planes were still constantly overhead. Now the remnants of the 192nd light tank company were between the cavalry troopers and the enemy advancing from Damortis. After watering, the troop marched a half mile back toward the enemy and dispersed under cover along the road. Roughly half of Troop A was missing by now and most of its ammunition was exhausted. Whitehead's platoon sergeant, Nicholas Mendoza, who had been sent with a squad to protect the right flank, was the only man of the squad to return to the unit. His face was caked with blood from a shell wound. The squad had met with a considerable force of Japanese sent around in an enveloping maneuver, and although the Troop A squad had held up the enemy progress for a significant time, it was ultimately wiped out by fire from knee mortars and 75mm mountain artillery. No one from that squad was ever sent to notify the troop commander that contact had been made, because the squad was too heavily engaged and pinned down. Also, no one ever knew what had happened to a messenger sent from the troop to contact the squad.

Meanwhile, always gutsy Capt. Joe Barker's Troop B on the right flank of the main line of resistance was also withdrawing in stages back toward the Rosario–Damortis road where the horse holders were stationed with their mounts and pack animals. The indomitable 1st Sgt. Justin Bulawan was everywhere, calmly seeing to it that the officers' commands were being carried out to the letter. The formerly stoutish 1st Lt. Henry Mark had burned up considerable poundage that day in his tireless efforts fighting shoulder to shoulder with his courageous Filipino scouts. There was little or no Hollywood left in Hank Mark's system that afternoon. The Japanese, at the same time, were pushing hard to get around the 26th right flank hoping to roll up the line; but as Troop A and HQ Troop had done on their left, the stubborn B Troopers maintained a steady, deadly volume of fire from M-1 rifles and light machine guns. All afternoon, the 26th had been holding more than ten times its number almost to a standstill. Indeed, the Japanese commanders had convincing good reason to assume they were up against a considerably larger force than merely fewer than six hundred men.

Gradually the whole remainder of the regiment made its way back to the road behind them and to their horses. Troop E under the gentlemanly John Wheeler had been doing a yeoman's job of covering the road and protecting the 26th column as it gradually organized to break contact and withdraw toward Rosario. For all practical purposes, the battle of Damortis could have been assumed ended at 7 p.m., when the Japanese finally took control of the little town and the surrounding area. The now exhausted 26th Cavalrymen had held them at bay for more than six hours, ten if counting ill-fated Johnny George's courageous action at the bridge on the coast road. The enemy commanders had ample reason to be furious at what the 26th had done to their urgent, planned timetable. Further, the road to Manila had been denied to them, and they had been prevented from overrunning Wainwright's coastal defenses below Damortis. Although the 26th had sustained severe casualties in the course of their baptism of fire, morale remained high as they prepared to dig in at new defensive positions to await further enemy advance. Skinny Wainwright had prayed for the impossible and the 26th had damn near given it all to him. The regiment had fought with a stubbornness never before encountered by Japanese troops, and for a time the invaders actually found themselves being slowly pushed back by the 26th Cavalry horsemen. The 26th had left one indelible impression on the Japanese in that first full-scale collision on the ridges. The soldiers and commanders alike of Nippon found that an underdog in the uniform of a U.S. Cavalryman bites viciously when pushed.

However, the day was far from over for the dogged troopers of the 26th.

DEBACLE ON THE ROAD AND
A BRIDGE IS BURNED

22 December, 5:30 p.m.

By this time, the 26th regiment had completely closed on its second defensive line, which was now about five kilometers west of Rosario, with Troop E still astride the road guarding the route of withdrawal. Maj. Tom Trapnell was riding with Wheeler and E Troop to oversee the rear guard and make sure it withdrew immediately on receipt of information that the rest of the regiment was organized and in the process of moving out toward Rosario.

Pierce prepared to move his CP back to Rosario and direct the continued delaying action from there. At this time, the four surviving 192nd tanks were returning to Rosario, and on their way paused to check in with Pierce on their movement. Their crews informed the cavalry commander that they had been ordered by General Weaver, the provisional tank brigade commander, to operate forward of the 26th Cavalry to provide early warning until 8 p.m., or until the regiment's reorganization was completed. However, no mention had been made that the tankers were also to cover the roads on which the 26th would withdraw toward and from Rosario to a new defensive line farther south, which appeared to be the basis of the newest orders from Gen. Clyde Selleck, commander of the 71st Infantry Division (PA), to whom the 26th was now attached. Contact with Japanese forces along the 26th's western front toward the gulf had now been broken off, but in the meantime, Troop F was heavily engaged resisting increasing enemy probing pressure along all five of the Agoo–Rosario trails, which the troop had been assigned to defend. Colonel Pierce told his squadron commanders to quietly prepare to withdraw, for he knew that with Troop F slowly being pushed back by heavily superior numbers of enemy and massive firepower, their current positions north of Rosario could not be held.

At around 7:00 the 71st Division HQ contacted Pierce with orders from Selleck for the 26th to march to Agat and guard the right flank of the 71st along the Bued River. The four 192nd tanks were to position themselves behind E Troop to act as rear guard for the regiment. Colonel Pierce was ordered to report to Selleck for a briefing and then was to link up with the regiment at Agat. Troop A was to deploy on the road at 7:30 in columns of twos and proceed at a slow walk while Troop E moved in behind them. The only fly in the ointment was that the commanders of the four 192nd tanks had not gotten the word. They had already moved through the regiment, headed toward Rosario.

Lt. Col. Lee Vance, the 26th regimental executive officer, stopped the tankers and informed them that their new orders were to rear guard the 26th. The tank platoon commander replied that he could not disregard his original orders to depart for Rosario at 8:00 and that he and his tankers did not belong to the 71st Division but rather to the Provisional Tank Brigade. Colonel Vance then asked him if he had been in contact with the enemy and was told that the tankers had not seen anything and that the enemy must still be milling around Damortis. Then, with 26th regimental S-3, Maj. William Chandler in hot pursuit on a motorcycle intent on getting the rear guard tank support straightened out, the 192nd tanks rumbled on toward Rosario.

What happened in the next few minutes was an exercise in pure chaos. Trapnell and Wheeler, who had been informed that the 192nd tanks would be bringing up their rear, heard the sound of armor treads on the road.

They rode back waving flashlights in the darkness to tell the tankers to slow down and give the mounted cavalrymen time to get their horses to the sides of the road and out of harm's way.

Trooper Felipe Fernandez recalled vividly what happened next. "I heard vehicles with a sound different from the noise our own tanks made. I knew that we were supposed to have tanks coming from our rear, but this sound, like that of loose tracks, was audibly distinguishable, like a mispitched chord struck by mistake in the midst of a melody."

What Fernandez heard with his perceptive hearing was a sound caused by the mechanical nature of Japanese light and medium tanks, which have only one or two idler wheels on top of looser treads.

The moon was fairly bright, being just a few nights before an oriental full moon. The air, except for the sound of tank treads, was quiet and tense as if something ominous was going to happen. The men spoke in whispers and even the horses had their ears pricked in alarm.

Then, what Trapnell and Wheeler heard was the guttural sound of Japanese orders being shouted, and what they saw in the dim light of their flashlights were not American M-3 tanks but Japanese Shiki 94 light tanks. Suddenly there was a *Boom!* followed by the rattle of machine guns and more booms over the continuous rattle of automatic weapons. Upon seeing the American cavalrymen on horses, the Japanese tankers immediately and without warning opened fire with every gun they had from point-blank range.

All hell broke loose as the cavalrymen made desperate attempts to get off the road and into ditches or low ground offering some semblance of cover from the onslaught. Attempts by the stunned regiment to get off the road were thwarted by barbed wire south on their right and combined barbed wire and steep embankments north on their left. Near universal panic broke out as troopers tried to control their terrorized horses in the darkness, lit only by muzzle flashes of the Japanese guns. Some troopers died literally trying to hold the enemy armor back with their bare hands. Others were unhorsed and trampled by terrified mounts running completely amok. More died from relentless streams of enemy tank fire. With barbed wire on both sides of the road, there was no place to deploy or get into defilade.

Fernandez shouted at his first sergeant to get into the ditch with him, but his bucking horse fell dead under him. "I attempted to get my horse, Dayang Dayang, to climb the embankment to pick up the fallen sergeant, but before I could negotiate the bank, somebody—it was the bugler, Pfc. Magbanua—stretched out his hand and the sergeant mounted double with him, and they galloped away to the rear. Men without horses scrambled through the barbed wire fences and headed across country toward Sison. I followed the ditch and a few hundred yards down the edge of the road, I saw Pfcs Tamayo and Lazo, both machine gunners of my troop, each dragging mules with light machine guns on them. I yelled at them to follow me, and a little while later I saw riflemen from my troop who I told to join our group. Then I saw two .50-cal. machine guns on either side of the road covering our rear and a sergeant motioning us to hurry to the rear and join the retreating column. There was a bottleneck ahead, which was caused by everybody trying to pass over a bridge at the same time. I went back to get my men over to the right side of the road and ford the river where it wasn't so deep. I'm sure this was the Apangat because there is no other river that side of Rosario."

Whitehead later recalled the chaos. "At about 2000 hours Troop A was still waiting for the order to mount and withdraw to its new positions when suddenly all hell broke loose. Small cannon, machine gun, and rifle fire came over us and into us all at once. Machine Gun Troop, already mounted, stampeded through us which caused a number of A troopers to lose their horses. The men who still had mounts had trouble getting the reins over their heads, and then in mounting. As the firing became stronger, the horses got crazier. Jap tanks followed by infantry came right through our rear guard which had nothing heavy enough to stop them. In mounting, my horse bolted, dragging me for some distance and knocking me out cold. Later when I came to, the firing had subsided, forms could be seen moving down the road from the direction of the enemy, and there were no cavalrymen around. I jumped a fence and got into a bamboo thicket by the side of the road."

Meanwhile, Tom Trapnell and Johnny Wheeler succeeded in making their way to the bridge over the steep-banked little Apangat River. Horses could cross the stream and negotiate the banks, but vehicles could not. Trapnell realized this and knew the river could be the only thing that would stop the Japanese tanks from overrunning them even further. His first thought was to defend the bridge, but no one else seemed to be in sight. He and Wheeler seemed to be the only ones left. At that very moment, Capt. Clayton E. Michelson of the Veterinary Corps came up with the veterinary truck. The three officers proceeded to manhandle the vet truck, which had now stalled, on to the bridge. Grabbing jerry cans of spare fuel, the three poured gasoline on the truck and on the bridge. Trapnell then shot off the carburetor with his .45 pistol and set the whole thing afire. The crossing was now denied to the fast-approaching Japanese. Later, for their action on the bridge, the three 26th officers were each awarded the Distinguished Service Cross for valor, the first of these medals cited in World War II.

Meanwhile, the other survivors of the regiment had scattered and were making their way west toward Rosario and Bued any way possible. Miraculously, so were the large numbers of loose 26th horses. No one will ever be able to explain what drew the horses and troopers in the same direction to be so incredibly united a day or so later in locations around Agat and the Bued River, where the regiment would manage to accomplish an admirable degree of reorganization after the melee on the Damortis road.

Lieutenent Whitehead had managed to get off the road about fifty yards into a bamboo thicket and took cover there, dazed and exhausted. The firing had stopped, but from the distinct sounds of tanks and guttural shouting in an unfamiliar tongue, it was quite apparent that Japanese were on the road where Troop A had been surprised. Whitehead pondered his next move. The river where they had watered the horses earlier should not be more than a mile away to the east. He reasoned logically that the 26th would destroy the bridge and then take up positions east of the river. He decided to get farther off the road and then work toward the river in hope of finding a crossing and eventually hooking up with the right flank of the regiment. The terrain was hilly, covered with thick underbrush and occasional clumps of trees. It seemed likely that enemy patrols would be in the area. Just before pulling out, A Troop observation posts had reported sounds of Japanese voices and the rattling of equipment nearby.

The pitch darkness made it necessary to feel for each step, so the going was slow. He found it wise to stop and listen for a minute or two after each short distance was covered. During his slow passage, Whitehead heard the sound of a sudden burst of machine gun fire from the road, a pause, and then another burst. With horror, he wondered if the Japanese were doing away with prisoners they had caught. Just then, he saw a red glare fill the sky ahead of him in the direction of the river. As he went over the crest of a hill, he saw that about three hundred yards away, the bridge across the Apangat River was burning in the center. From the light of the fire, he could see several low silhouette tanks parked on the road and Japanese soldiers on the bridge examining it. Shots were being fired from the river bank on both sides of the road from the Japanese side, but no firing was coming from the opposite bank. Before long, the Japanese on the bridge hurried back. Then two of them climbed into the leading tank, and, driving onto the bridge started through the fire. As they reached the center of the bridge there was a loud sound of cracking timbers and the tank could be seen to ease over on its side and crash into the water. Trapnell's fast-thinking fire brigade had done its job well.

Whitehead was never able to rejoin the regiment, but he did manage to hook up with some 26th stragglers and make their way into the mountains toward Baguio. Along the way, Whitehead encountered 1st Lt. Archie M. Hendricks of E Troop near Tayug, but they got separated. Subsequently, Whitehead heard from Filipino guerrillas that Hendricks was killed in a fight with a Japanese patrol. Later, Whitehead, constantly moving south with the periodic aid of civilians, Igorot Indians, Philippine Army stragglers, Filipino guerrillas (some trustworthy, some not), and native fishermen, obtained a small, crude sailboat and made a Homeric journey through the southern islands, which finally landed him in Australia in 1943, after an epic trek of almost a year and a half.

The other survivors of the regiment had hoped to regroup in Rosario, but upon arriving there, they found F Troop fighting for its life in the town square.

NOTES

1. Note Japanese command impression caused by 26th!
2. Note here concern about the 26th.

13

Miracle on the Bued River

22 DECEMBER 1941, AROUND 9 P.M.

The exhausted and fragmented 26th Cavalry troopers who had survived the all-day fight at Damortis and the following, terrifying melee with Japanese tanks on the road were now attempting with all their remaining strength to make their way back in fearsome darkness (broken only by a half moon largely obscured by clouds) toward Rosario, the appointed rallying point for the regiment. Some of the men were moving in small groups of twos and threes who had managed to connect in the confusion, some with horses, some without. Many were simply trying alone to rejoin the regiment. Most of the horses that had thrown or were let go by their riders, frightened and shaken by the devastating terror on the road, were now milling around the countryside between Damortis and Rosario. They had, however, gotten over to the Rosario side of the Agno River and away from the probing Japanese and somehow, incredulously, were moving in the same general direction as the scattered members of the regiment.

Sgt. Domingo de Mesa made his way back toward the Agno to find and guide more troopers and to observe the progress of the Japanese at the river. What he saw was Japanese troops and their commanders in confusion and frustration attempting to negotiate the steep banked river with its destroyed bridge. He saw two tanks plunge into the water and then others doggedly attempting to make the crossing using the wrecks as bridge support. It was a vital delay permitting the disheveled 26th to struggle back toward Rosario.

One of the troopers making his way back was Pfc. Alejandro Abad of E Troop. Typical of the family nature of the 26th, his father, Sgt. Pedro Abad, had fought with Whitehead's A Troop that day, and his brother Salvador, a radio operator, had been with HQ Troop in the fight. Alejandro had lost contact with E Troop and his pack horse and mules at "Trap's bridge" over the Agno but had the luck to be picked up by one of the surviving scout cars headed toward Rosario. His father had been wounded, survived, but never got back to the regiment. His brother, also wounded, was able to rejoin the regiment.

Rosario, however, had become a perilous haven for the disorganized regiment. F Troop, which had been assigned by Colonel Pierce to cover the trails north of Rosario against any Japanese movements south toward the town, had run into serious, heavily supported enemy contact on the trails, and troopers were now fighting for their lives on Rosario's outskirts trying to keep the town open. Meanwhile, the remnants of 192nd Battalion tanks, which had followed its orders from Weaver to withdraw from Damortis to Rosario, now found themselves in the midst of an all-out brawl in the town square between the F Troop cavalrymen and advance elements of the Japanese under the command of Colonel Yanagi. The arrival of the 192nd tanks was a godsend. Using communications telephones mounted on the rear of tanks, outnumbered, dismounted troopers were able to amplify their firepower against the advancing enemy and stiffen their resistance.

The critical mission of the 26th now, dictated by hopeful minds of the NLF staff, was to hold open the junction of the Baguio and Rosario roads so the Philippine defense forces under Colonels Bonnett and Horan could accomplish their withdrawal south. Bonnett, unaware of the perilous situation at Rosario, chose to hold his ground at Baguio. Later, finding he had no other choice, he moved east over the mountains into the Cagayan Valley. Horan held his positions to 23 December until the situation was untenable and finally withdrew, thus giving up the summer capital and its military installations to the enemy.

In the ferocious delaying action at Rosario, F Troop proved itself a company of valiant soldiers in anyone's book. One example was Cpl. Florencio Diaz, who was awarded the Silver Star for his part in the desperate holding defense of the critical town.

As related by Diaz, "Our platoon was designated to meet the Japanese north of the town [of Rosario]. My squad was ordered to a certain hill to cover the right flank of the troop. When we saw the Japanese coming up, they saw us and everyone seemed to freeze and wouldn't move. So I got a light machine gun off a mule and moved about 150 yards in front of the platoon."

Diaz then continued his advance and fired his arm-held machine gun for nearly a half hour, blunting the forward movement of the enemy on his designated trail. Diaz's commendation remarked that "his action delayed the advance of the enemy and was crucial to the mission of F Troop being accomplished successfully without casualty, an act of heroism which reflected the highest traditions of the military service."

Slowly but steadily, the fragments of the 26th converged on Rosario only to find themselves caught up in yet another fight for survival. In the midst of the fighting, the disorganized troopers were joined by a steady, milling stampede of loose horses and mules in their equally instinctive search of some semblance of familiar order. As more and more of the small groups and stragglers converged on the town, officers and noncoms shouted orders and passed the word that the men of the 26th were to pass through Rosario, break contact, and make their way south toward the Bued, where it was hoped that the regiment could be reorganized. Meanwhile, F Troop and the few 192nd tankers of B Company continued their vicious rear guard action until they got word that Rosario had been cleared.

One tanker, Sgt. Albert C. Allen from Mansfield, Ohio, recalled his fearsome experience in the terror of the Rosario holding action. Earlier in the afternoon C Company of the 192nd tanks had arrived at the outskirts of Rosario and moved to support B Company. They had been ordered at around 3 p.m. to proceed west on Route 3 for about three kilometers. They moved to a position just short of the Apangat River and pulled to the side of the road, unaware of what was happening to the 26th farther back on the Damortis road. For an hour or so little happened except a messenger passed them on a motorcycle and three riderless horses galloped past them headed for Rosario. There was an occasional communication on their radios that broke the silence, but the reception was so poor they could barely understand half of what was said. Allen cursed such lousy radio equipment, muttering that it must have been built during the Civil War. The tank crews were getting restless with the waiting and wanting to get at the Japanese.

Abruptly, about a thousand yards north of the road, they started taking machine gun fire. The tankers swung their turrets in the direction of the fire and opened up with their 37mms. Before long, a series of explosions silenced the machine gun fire. What they didn't know was that the fire was indication that Colonel Yanagi's southbound troops were now just over two miles from Rosario, and the trap was fast beginning to close on the 26th Cavalry and the two companies of 192nd tanks.

Darkness was fast closing in, and C Company's tankers received orders to withdraw to Rosario. Having taken part in the sharp, losing battle between the little American M-3s and the Japanese medium tanks earlier that day, Allen, his tank now put under the command of another sergeant, was ordered by his CO, Lieutenant Collins, to mount a motorcycle and act as reconnaissance for the remaining tanks. At first he found the motorcycle missing, but it reappeared in the hands of Major Vance, who had been using it trying to coordinate the elements of his regiment. "I was happy to see that the tommy gun was still in the saddlebag. I talked briefly with Major Vance about how things were going and was told that the 26th Cavalry was receiving pretty much of a beating and were withdrawing from Damortis. I figured that those poor cavalrymen were catching hell because I kept seeing loose horses coming toward me and felt terrible about it." They were still unaware of the terrible debacle on the Damortis road between the 26th and the Japanese tanks.

Allen recalls, "We were hearing very little about Philippine Army troops except that as ill equipped and trained as they were, they weren't seeing much action. They were picking up their mess kits and taking off, so the 26th Cav. were the only ones doing the fighting around us along with what tanks we had left. At around 8 p.m. it was getting really dark. I was really tired by then and I lay down on the back of my cycle for a break. My tank company was now lined up heading the other way toward Rosario. I saw a lot of tracers arching through the air over our heads but not near enough to be of too much concern. It was then I began seeing loose, scared horses and mules passing by us on the road. It really bothered me because I love those animals, and I could see they'd been in hell back where they were coming from. It was hard to tell really how many we saw going by us. I don't want to exaggerate, but it seemed like fifty or a hundred or so coming through in groups of twos, threes, sometimes fours and fives. We knew those cavalrymen didn't just let horses and mules loose unless they'd been killed, wounded, or some way in a position where they had to turn loose and fight the enemy. Anyway, it was a sure thing that some kind of a hell of a fire fight was going on back toward Damortis.

"Then, pretty soon, troopers began to show up in various sized groups— squads, platoons, some just making their way alone. A lot of them were wounded or cut up and bloody. It was really kind of a rout, but they were all headed the same way like they knew where they were supposed to go. At the time, I don't know what our tanks could have done to help. It was pretty much pitch dark and the last place a tanker wants to be when you have enemy moving up on you unseen. We knew we couldn't just stay put and be sitting targets. It was obvious there had been some mix up about protecting the rear of the cavalry so the tanks headed on into town. There we found ourselves in a fight along with the cavalrymen who were holding the north end of town and had to go into action against the Japs at our end of town. They were able to fight their way to the town square, but that wasn't much relief. The thing that was bad for me was being on that damned motorcycle with Jap machine gun fire all over the place. But I had to get out, and the only way was to follow the tanks to where the 26th Cav. was in action. You learn as you go in combat, and right then I was feeling closer and closer to those cavalrymen. I got about a hundred feet more to a building on the corner where there was about four or five 26th horses and men firing at Japs up the street. I started talking to one of the Filipino troopers, a sergeant, just as a Nip machine gun opened up on our corner. The next thing I knew two of the troopers fell out of their saddles. I couldn't really believe what had happened, thinking they were just slipping off their horses to fight. But, sure enough, they'd been hit. I didn't know just then if they were wounded or killed. Then two other men ran up and began dragging them back to cover. Two more men turned their horses and began to move away. One trooper, about twenty yards away, was picked off and immediately went down. Then about four more troopers came flying around the corner with the Nips hammering away at them. I think the only thing that saved me was, riding beside them, my cycle put me about four feet lower than those poor guys on horses. It was an experience I'll never forget. I stopped and ran over to the sergeant I'd been talking to. He and another guy were down but seemed to be okay. They had pulled out their rifles and were firing back as fast as they could with those M-1s and were bent on holding their position. They were calm and collected and didn't seem taken back in the least by the situation."

Allen had encountered Sergeant Bitenga of F Troop, whose patrol had been forced back to Rosario after several of his men had been hit or cut off. Now, like wild Indians, they were fighting house to house at vicious close quarters constantly moving toward the center of town. The indomitable Corporal Diaz had followed them in still carrying his light machine gun by hand and wondering if they would ever be able to rejoin the rest of the troop, or what was left of them, in the town square.

Allen took stock of the situation. "There was no question in my mind though that there was soon going to be another rout. The Japs were pushing at us hard and fast dodging in and out of doorways, shooting and hollering and heaving grenades. All I could think was that if the cavalrymen didn't get the hell out of there fast, there wasn't going to be any of them left. It was awful to think about having to leave wounded and dead behind for the Japs, but the volume of fire being put down on us was like a hurricane and there were no vehicles of any kind to take out the casualties. But those scouts were stubborn and risked their lives to drag or carry out their buddies. One thing I noticed in amazement. None of the horses were getting hit in all that fire, just the men riding them. I felt like it was the closest call I ever had. If the Nips had aimed better, I was a goner. There was really nothing more I could do so I moved fast to get over to a couple of tanks covering the withdrawal and found Lieutenant Collins who told me we were waiting for orders!"

Collins, now acting CO of C Company, said he had received information from General Selleck earlier that evening that the Bued River bridge was going to be blown at midnight, but he had decided to hold in Rosario to help the cavalry delay the Japs coming from the north. What happened next, however, changed his plans. The tracers that had been going overhead of the tanks stopped. The Japanese machine guns now concentrated their fire on Collins's tanks. C Company rapidly returned fire with their 37mm main guns, but it soon became evident that their fire was having negligible effect on the attackers. The M-3s had no high explosive shells, only armor piercing, which were proving quite ineffective against advancing infantry and machine guns. As the Japanese drew closer, Collins was compelled to make a hard decision for the safety of his tanks. The limited visibility from inside the tanks left them vulnerable to enemy troops charging in and placing explosive charges on or under them, especially in such darkness as then. The only solution for such a problem was infantry support, which Collins didn't have. He ordered withdrawal.

Allen followed. "Finally what was left of C and B Companies went into gear and pulled out. The recall took place around 9 p.m. When we moved out, things were getting really hot all around in town. We fought our way out east through Rosario and made it to the junction of the Baguio Road. The cavalry and some Philippine infantry were fighting a delaying action to hold open the road from Rosario. At least they could withdraw cross-country. Our tanks were road bound and had to go straight through. By now most of the tanks were just about out of gas and running on fumes. There was only a kitchen truck with us, no gas truck. I asked a nervous captain what we should do about it and he ordered me to go find one and ordered me on a hair-raising trip I'll never forget. I had to go all the way back to Carmen to the battalion HQ area to get gas. The guy in charge of the gas trucks was a real jerk, and I had to dig up Colonel Wickford personally to get permission to take at least one gas truck back to our tanks stuck on that damned road. An HQ lieutenant in a jeep accompanied us." Allen is more than modest in his account. The ride back to Carmen was a horrendous one, but it literally was the salvation of 192nd's C and B Companies. Allen, for his courageous ride to save his company, received a commendation for the Silver Star.

Steadily, while F Troop and the 192nd tanks desperately held the enemy back, a semblance of order was being quickly restored in the rest of the regiment moving through. This was brought about largely by the calm efficiency of Maj. William Chandler. He moved briskly up and down what was gradually becoming a column again, giving encouragement and instilling a renewed sense of confidence among the men that they still had leadership. Chandler had returned to the town riding a motorcycle but was knocked off it by a riderless horse. Wrestling the frightened animal under control, Chandler mounted and, constantly trooping the column, continued directing the withdrawal and commanding from horseback.

When the Japanese tanks had clashed with the 26th on the Damortis road Capt. Joe Barker and his B Troop were approaching the Apangat bridge. After they crossed it they rounded a slight curve and pulled up in a holding position out of the line of tank fire. While there, Maj. Harry Fleeger, the regimental G-2, roared up on a motorcycle and told Barker that

F Troop was under heavy pressure on the outskirts of Rosario and that Barker and his troop should avoid the town. About that time, Lt. Clint Seymour's platoon caught up with the rest of B Troop after barely escaping the disaster with the Jap tanks. Barker knew they couldn't stop the tanks unless the bridge could be blown, but part of the regiment (he didn't know how many were left) hadn't gotten to the river yet. Also, there was no time to set demolition charges. He decided right then to have his troop cut cross-country toward the barrio of Esperanza on Route 3 south headed for the Bued. There they would be only about fifteen hundred yards from the river and the Bued bridge. First Sgt. Justin Bulawan was directed to the column's left flank, and Barker led the rest of the troop south and forded the Bued River south of Agat, which had been designated as the secondary rallying point for the regiment.

In his diary on the regiment, Chandler observed, "Major Trapnell's action at the Apangat bridge, together with the naturally superb discipline of the Scouts and the actions of the noncoms and officers throughout the column, turned what had all the ingredients of a panicked rout into an orderly withdrawal. Captain Paul H. Wrinkle's F Troop, driven from the mountain trails leading south and east from Agoo by strong enemy pressure, was still on the job of covering our northern flank. Wrinkle held his line on the northern edge of the town until assured by Vance and Trapnell that the last man accounted for had passed through. He then fell in and covered our rear for some three miles until we reached the Bued River position just before midnight, still December 22. To most of us it felt like next week."

The road to the Bued, like the road from Rosario to Damortis, was bordered by wire fences and gave rise to dark memories for the troopers of their bloody ride toward Lingayen. Nerve-wracked glances skyward were constant, but their luck held. When the first group arrived at the Bued bridge, they were met by Colonel Pierce and Capt. Paul Jones, who was back from detached duty with the Philippine Army. Most of the first arrivals were members of A Troop, and they were promptly placed in position on either side of the bridge. Sgt. Lomboy's light machine gun squad was placed in position to cover the bridge from the east side. As 192nd tanks arrived they were emplaced on the left of A Troop. E and F Troops were positioned on the right flank. B Troop was the last unit to arrive at the Bued. Their movement across country had been slow, and part of the troop had taken the wrong turn at a fork in the trail. The second section under 1st Sergeant Bulawan had arrived at Esperanza as planned, turned south on Route 3, and in minutes crossed the bridge. Bulawan was directed to the left of the line. Shortly after, Captain Barker rode in with the remainder of B Troop. He had taken another trail and had forded the river south of Agat.

At around midnight a general count of regimental strength was made.

To Chandler's dismay, Colonel Pierce informed him that the regiment was almost destroyed as a fighting force. "As we set up defensive positions, we found that we could place only 175 effectives on the line."

This grim picture only lasted a few hours, however, as groups of scouts and single stragglers who had been cut off north or south of the Damortis road continued to steadily trickle in and rejoin the regiment by moving cross-country. Many of them had figured Rosario lost and chose to go the roundabout way. Chandler observed with both amazement and pride, ". . . every man with his mount and his weapon, mounts tired but field-groomed and weapons clean and oiled." In the face of terrible odds, the 26th was actually regrouping.

Upon the outset of reorganization it was calculated that the 26th had suffered actual losses of some 150 men killed and wounded on 22 December at Damortis and around Rosario. The scouts had almost unbelievably gotten every man out of Rosario except two. Even more miraculously, over 80 percent of the regiment's horses and mules found their way back and were recovered. It was quite a Christmas present for the regiment. A number of the troopers who had lost their mounts were remounted on horses left behind by C Troop upon its detachment north several days before. Around 522 effectives had met the Japanese at Damortis while F Troop held north of Rosario. After their losses of some 150 men killed or put out of action, the regiment, with the addition of the rejoined stragglers, was able to muster around 400 surviving effectives in the reorganization at the Bued. Other troopers who had been cut off took the trail south to Sison and reported to the regiment's rear echelon at Pozorrubio. Still others on foot were able to make their way south to Bataan with Philippine Army units. But still, the real miracle was the rejoining on their own of so many horses and mules after all the chaos.

During the early morning hours of 23 December, the regiment was finally able to pause for a few hours' break along the Bued River line. General Wainwright had been able by luck and good strategic ability to extract the main of his other forces and was now again ready to oppose the Japanese advance with what he perceived to be a unified line. He instructed Colonel Pierce to have the 26th hold the river crossing at Agat and keep the old road to Baguio open to allow any cut off troops to rejoin friendly lines. Some intact units of the 71st Infantry Division (PA) did come through during the night but did not join the defensive effort at the Bued. They continued on south. The tired and depleted 26th was left to cover the 71st withdrawal until around 9 a.m. on 23 December.

The bridges on Route 3 and Route 11 were prepared for demolition by the 26th's Scout Car Platoon now under command of Lt. Russel Bowers.

One Scout Car section under Sergeant Masiclat had been patrolling the Kennon Road since about 6 p.m., vainly looking for the return of C Troop from the Baguio area. They never showed. Unknown to Masiclat, C Troop was now hopelessly cut off in the mountains north of Baguio. After the main of the 26th regiment passed through the junction, Masiclat sent his cyclist, Private Soloman, back east toward Rosario to scout out the Japanese movements. Shortly after, Solomon skidded back in with the alarming report that Jap patrols were only a half mile from the junction. This information was reported to Bowers, who ordered the scout cars to immediately fall back just south of the junction of the old and new roads south. During the night several busloads of Philippine Army troops and new inductees passed through on their way from Baguio. They were directed to take the old road, narrow and crooked but usable. Bowers had his scout cars maintain a heavy patrol all night to ensure that the Japanese would not cross the river and hit the 26th lines from the rear. Troops of the 71st Division (PA) also passed through on their way south to Sison. As the dim light of false dawn began to rise, Bowers ordered his scout cars to withdraw to the 26th line on the Bued.

As the first light of dawn came, Cpl. Felipe Fernandez, company clerk of E Troop, heard the sound of a truck approaching from their left flank. Alarmed, the men got a welcome surprise to find it was Sergeant Valenton with a mess truck bringing up breakfast for B Troop. As the exhausted regiment was far from full strength, there was enough for everyone. Since most of them had not eaten since 21 December, the chow was savored as one of the best meals they had ever had.

As daylight increased, Sergeant Lomboy appraised their position and concluded that they held excellent defensive ground. "The water was about only waist deep, but the river is about 150 meters wide with a high, steep bank on our side and a low one on the opposite side giving us an ideal field of fire."

Full daylight had come when the advance Japanese elements first appeared. A large number of them were approaching the river on bicycles when Sergeant Lomboy and Cpl. de la Cruz opened up on them with their light machine guns before the enemy could disperse. The 26th gunners and riflemen inflicted a substantial tally of Japanese casualties before the enemy could begin building up a line on the west bank.

The time had come, and Lieutenant Bowers shouted the order to activate the explosives. With a gratifying roar followed by splashes in the river from falling timbers, the 26th said good morning to their tormentors.

The Japanese advance had fast approached in pursuit from Rosario only to have the Bued bridge blown up right in their faces by 26th troopers who had their demolition charges ready for the occasion.

With tenacious and stubborn discipline, Japanese engineers appeared and amazingly attempted to repair the bridge under heavy fire. One after another they were shot into the churning, bloodied water, but like determined ants they kept on trying in blind obedience to their Bushido conditioning. Finally, as the 26th and the 192nd tankers continued to pour down a withering volume of fire, the Japanese pulled back.

Shortly thereafter, General Selleck came up to the 26th line. He told Pierce that he was to hold his position at least until 9 a.m. or as long as possible as the 71st Division was being placed in position just south of Sison and needed more time to consolidate their line. Pierce replied that with his present, depleted strength, he was in peril of being flanked at any time. Selleck answered with a plea to hold as long as he could, then withdraw back through the 71st lines toward Pozorrubio.

In concurrence, Pierce held his ground. He ordered the bridges at Camp One and Dongon to the north blown and at around 8:30 a.m. ordered the scout cars south. The 192nd tanks at the Bued also withdrew under orders to Pozorrubio. Pierce now held the Bued line with a skeleton force of mounted patrols, which he instructed to inform him of enemy attempts to cross the river. By 9 a.m., the Japanese lines had been hesitantly but gradually extended and by then were across the river in strength opposite the 26th Cavalry's left flank. The time had come to withdraw. The patrols were pulled in and the regiment's rear guard withdrew with little opposition.

The furious Japanese general staff were like a nest of hornets that had been kicked loose. They were embarrassingly forced to admit later in their reports that their near successful attempt to cut off the defending forces on Northern Luzon before they could move south to the Bataan Peninsula was a dismal failure, and their battle plan was already put four days behind schedule due mostly to the stubborn, gutsy delaying tactics of a brash, understrength, horse-mounted regiment of cavalry who fought like three times their number.

General Wainwright was agonized by what the 26th Cavalry had been forced to endure and was determined to get them out of the line and give them a chance to get some rest and to have some time to regroup and mend their wounds. He issued orders that they be pulled out of the line in the area of Pozorrubio to a position some twelve kilometers farther south near the town of Binalonan, the headquarters of the 71st Division. At around 2 p.m. on the afternoon of 23 December the 26th had arrived in Pozorrubio, where they were to begin reorganization. On the way in they passed 192nd tanks parked under the trees by the side of the road. The tankers called out friendly greetings to the horsemen with whom they had shared so much desperate combat.

Pierce and Vance were surprised by how many men had joined the column during the night. There were some men on foot, some mounted double on horses, many with their individual mounts. But almost to a man, they had their weapons. One machine gun trooper whose pack animal had been killed carried his light .30-caliber across the pommel of his saddle.

Reorganization at Pozorrubio was limited at best. It consisted mainly of combining remnants of squads and platoons into full-strength units and juggling officers and noncoms to fill vacancies in the ranks. Some men were taken out of administrative duty positions and assigned to rifle or machine gun squads. Men without mounts were assigned horses from the now missing C Troop. The troopers got their second hot meal in eight hours, beef stew and fresh bread. It seemed to the men that things had gone from famine to feast. There wasn't much rest to be had though. Routine tasks to maintain animals and equipment had to be done regardless of fatigue. Perimeter security was put out in shifts. They were spared having to dig new fortifications, however, because they had been on this same ground in the past year's maneuvers, so machine guns were able to be emplaced in their same old positions covering the roads and trails. But there was little rest or sleep to be had that afternoon.

Chandler recalled in his diary the travails of the weary cavalrymen. "The days of constant fighting and movement had taken a terrible toll on both men and animals. Men slept at odd moments, sometimes in the saddle, officers almost not at all. Horses and men became gaunt and worn looking. Sturdy field horseshoes were worn thin as racing plates and tired horseshoers, exchanging rifles for hammer and forge at every opportunity, fought a losing battle to keep the animals properly shod. Whenever the fortunes of battle necessitated a daylight move, which was far too often, casualties among the animals from incessant air attacks were heartbreaking. Nonetheless, the regiment continued to fight almost constantly from Rosario southeast to Agat on the Bued, back through Pozorrubio to Binalonan only to have to endure a day-long battle to delay a strong Japanese column driving for the crossings over the Agno River."

During early evening on 23 December a message was received from Wainwright to move on new positions near Binalonan. As the regiment was saddling up, sounds of artillery rumbled ominously from the direction of Sison and a messenger rode in with a frantic message from Selleck saying, "All is lost. Move at once to Binalonan!" (where they were already headed).

The regiment moved out at about 2 a.m., but the seven-mile ride to Binalonan was grueling.

The road was jammed with men and vehicles moving in both directions. Trucks and buses moving the 91st Infantry (PA) were rushing north to reinforce Selleck at Pozorrubio. The 71st Field Artillery was hastening south to take up positions in Binalonan. The weary 26th cavalrymen, choking with dust and swaying in their saddles from exhaustion, had to make their way through this steady, chaotic stream of military traffic the whole way.

The regiment reached the outskirts of Binalonan shortly after midnight, now 24 December, and bivouacked in the southwest corner of town. Someone, either out of real sentiment or with an ironic sense of humor, quipped, "Maybe we'll get a rest now. It's Christmas Eve."

26th Cavalry HQ troop in the easy days.

26th Cavalry official dress pin.

The 26th Cavalry at Fort Stotsenburg (adjacent to Clark Field) in Northern Luzon.
Courtesy of Col. Edwin Ramsey.

The author with a Japanese 75mm howitzer.

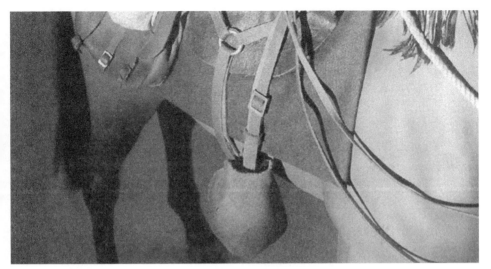

Typical U.S. Cavalry tack.

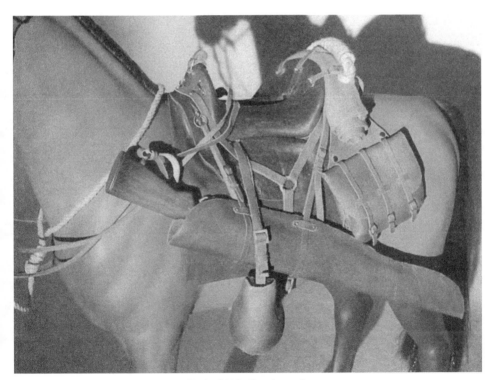

Typical U.S. Cavalry tack.

Philippine troopers—an elite horseback riding group—and their families.
Courtesy of Col. Edwin Ramsey.

Philippine communications personnel of the 26th Cavalry earned the everlasting gratitude
of General Wainwright in the terrible ordeal to come. Courtesy of Col. Edwin Ramsey.

Japanese soldiers and sniper gear.

Edwin Ramsey would escape capture by the Japanese and organize a Filipino guerilla force that would ultimately support the American invasion of the Philippines and the retaking of those islands after Leyte. Among his many decorations, Ramsey was awarded the Distinguished Service Cross and the Purple Heart. He ended his military career with the rank of lieutenant colonel. Courtesy of Col. Edwin Ramsey.

The last mounted charge by an organized regular unit of the U.S. Cavalry was led by Lieutenant Ramsey (shown firing in this official portrait) against Japanese forces in the Philippines on 16 January 1942. Painting by John Solie, reprinted with permission.

Philippine Scout with Browning Automatic Rifle fighting dismounted on Bataan.

American officers (rank of colonel and above) captured by the Japanese.
General Wainwright is seated, wearing shorts.

American prisoners of the Japanese after the surrender of Bataan.

Maj. Achille Tisdale, aide to General King at the surrender of Bataan, after liberation.

Lieutenant Ramsey and guerillas, taken two days after removal of
his own appendix without anesthesia.

14

Christmas Eve Ordeal at Binalonan

23 DECEMBER 1941, MIDNIGHT

Skinny Wainwright was still determined to give his beloved, weary 26th Cavalry some rest and a chance to reorganize themselves efficiently. He ordered them out of the line and to move about twelve kilometers farther south to a position on the outskirts of the big town of Binalonan, a provincial center of government. The movement was nightmarish for the cavalrymen, what with all the military traffic coming and going on the narrow road. The men had been without sleep or real food since 21 December. Civilians along the way eagerly offered what they had in food for the horsemen. Small chickens, balut eggs, rice cakes, lumpia, whatever they could scrounge up and give to the men who were defending their homes. It was an outpouring of heartfelt support for those they perceived were suffering to protect their home ground against a ruthless, merciless invader of the modest but beloved corner of their country.

The 26th had withdrawn from the Bued River about dusk when outflanked by a hard-pressing enemy advance just before noon on 23 December. After a short break at Pozorrubio, they had been ordered south again and, making a grueling night ride, passed through the 71st Division's new lines at Sison and moved on to Binalonan. They arrived at Binalonan just after midnight of December 23, Christmas Eve. The town was crowded with troops, being the 71st Division Headquarters, full of rear echelon troops busily milling about and C Company of the 192nd Tank Battalion.

Vance pulled Hank D. Mark's platoon from B Troop and positioned them at the fork of Route 3 as an outpost. "You're our main fire alarm, Mark," emphasized Vance. "Don't screw it up, Hollywood. I'm counting on you and so is the regiment. Take care of yourself and us, son."

The main of the regiment bivouacked about a thousand yards farther

195

south on the western edge of town. A second outpost was established using a section of Lieutenant Bowers's scout cars under Sergeant de Mesa. It was positioned on the Route 3 bypass (the "new road") just south of its intersection with Route 8, only a short distance from the regiment's bivouac area. By 1 a.m. men and horses finally settled in for their first real sleep in three days.

Bad news came all too soon. At dawn's first light, around 5:00, scout cars from Lieutenant Bowers's main rear guard scout car section appeared at Mark's outpost on the crossroads. They frantically gave Mark the news that Bowers had been captured and that Japanese tanks and trucks were hard on their heels. Mark sent an urgent message to the regimental CP, but the messenger was barely out of sight when Japanese medium tanks appeared. Mark's platoon opened fire with everything they had, but the Japanese swung around them and moved south on the new road. Chandler received another message that Mark's position was being overrun and that enemy tanks and infantry were pushing south on Highway 3 toward Urdaneta.

At the second outpost, the scout car section had been alerted by the sound of machine gun and small arms fire and readied themselves for the assault. When the Japanese appeared, the cars opened fired with .50-caliber machine guns on the tanks from the Japanese 4th Tank Regiment and supporting infantry. Their fire was devastating but failed to stop the Japanese tanks' push toward Urdaneta. Some of the tanks, however, did not bypass the position but turned off the road into a bamboo thicket and opened up on the outpost. Japanese infantry followed the tanks closely in trucks and confiscated red Filipino buses. The fire from the scout cars raked the column with deadly effect, disabling tank treads, destroying several of the troop-carrying vehicles, and inflicting heavy losses on the enemy infantry.

At about the same time the scout cars opened fire on the tanks, Mark's messenger reached Chandler. The regiment hastily organized a defensive perimeter on two sides of a newly mown field. The makeup of the line consisted of positions dictated by each unit's place in the bivouac. The result was a line like a reversed capital L, with the upright extending north from their CP area and the bottom short leg of the L extending west almost to the highway. Troop E was on the left, HQ and CP personnel at the corner, Troops B and A along the upright, with Troop F held centrally in reserve. In spite of the unorthodox shape of the defensive line, the cavalrymen had an unobstructed field of fire for about four hundred yards across level ground affording them choice opportunity to put their finely seasoned marksmanship to maximum use.

There was little time to waste before the Japanese infantry lunged forward in an unhesitating attack, confident of their numbers and showing little respect for the waiting cavalrymen. They first swept south across the open field toward E Troop's line, screaming "Banzai!" with all the bravado of

Bushido they could muster. From a line of trees about three hundred yards distant, E Troop riflemen coolly delivered their answer with a withering, accurate storm of fire from their semiautomatic M-ls and machine guns. On their flank, B Troopers delivered an equally devastating deluge of deadly marksmanship. The Japanese assault was stopped cold in a writhing pile of torn, twisted bodies of would-be samurai warriors.

Before the Nipponese could recover, Capt. Leland Cramer led A Troop forward in a vicious counterattack, which carried everything before them, driving the assault units of the Japanese 2nd Formosa Infantry Regiment all the way back to the cross road. For the first time, a Filipino and American ground unit took the initiative with an effective offensive action. The rout was such that the Japanese were forced to bring up additional tanks to stop the scouts' determined charge. A Troop, under heavy pressure, was pushed back to their line of departure, where they hastily dug in for the next round.

The Japanese, apparently not anticipating such a brutal reception, went quiet for the time being while they regrouped, giving second thought to what they were up against. Once again they overestimated the size of the 26th forces because of the steady and heavy volume of fire delivered on them, still unaware of the significant authority of the new M-1 rifles.

Meanwhile, Pierce, Vance, and Chandler rallied the troop commanders of the main body of the regiment to form a hasty line of defense. During the brief lull, Colonel Pierce felt a puzzling concern. The 26th had been fighting for almost two hours and had received no sign of support from the 71st Division. "The whole damned town was full of troops last night," he commented. "What the hell happened to them all? Dammit, their division HQ was less than three quarters of a mile from here!" He turned to Bill Chandler and told him to go to the 71st and see what was happening.

Chandler hurried over to check what had been the 71st HQ in search of information from General Selleck's CP to only to find that the area was deserted of both military personnel and civilians. The town, so crowded with Philippine army the night before, was now empty and abandoned. Only a few dogs barked as he passed by. The 71st Division's line had obviously been broken, and the 26th officer saw with a sinking feeling that the 71st had also pulled out of Binalonan. On arriving at the town square, there were only a few abandoned trucks and the usual debris left by a retreating army. The cold reality of the situation came down heavily on Chandler. The 26th was again left to hold the line alone, and their left flank was wide open!

Chandler, shaken by what he had found, no sooner delivered this dismal news to Pierce than the Japanese launched another attack. This time, the Japanese had decided to try the other end of the 26th line. Pierce immediately ordered Trapnell to have F Troop, his reserve, pull in its outposts to cover the flanks at the northern and eastern exits from town and the bridges across the Tayumising River, preparing them for destruction if necessary. Trapnell wasted no time putting his orders into effect. One of his scout cars was dispatched to ready the bridges for demolition, and the rest of F Troop took up positions to defend the flank. At this time, Pierce had a radio message sent to NLF headquarters to inform Wainwright of the situation in Binalonan.

There was no letup in the Japanese attacks, and each new one increased in intensity. The enemy was now supported by mortars their line had extended to a longer front. Although the 26th was well dug in, they were now under heavy pressure with an increasingly wide front to defend. It became obvious that any withdrawal could not be executed without heavy losses of men, horses, and their remaining motor equipment. The regiment was down to a strength of around four hundred effectives and were now supported by even their cooks and truck drivers. Pierce and his entire staff were personally filling gaps in the line. Grabbing a carbine "from somewhere," Chandler, who numbered an expert rifleman's badge among his credentials, dropped down beside Pierce and joined in the firefight. It was at this point that Pierce, upon digesting Chandler's grim report and with no contact with any friendly units, chose to engage in a heavy brawl with the Japanese with little prospect of ever being able to disengage his besieged little force. It was then that Pierce, the bulldog from Brooklyn, made a remark that Chandler and others within earshot would remember for the rest of their lives.

Pierce shot a grave look at Chandler and said with conviction, "Bill, I'm getting goddamned tired of running! It looks like right here is where we wind up our ball of string, but before the bastards get us, we'll damned well make them pay!"

Bill Chandler remembers equally well his reaction. "Since no one in the vicinity had a better plan, we settled down to ensure that the Japs would know they'd been in a fight. Perhaps because of this spirit of determination, that latest enemy assault was also repulsed, and the staff was able to pull out of the line and begin to put their minds to making plans again."

Meanwhile, spirits at the second Route 3 outpost temporarily soared as they observed a 192nd M-3 rattle up a short distance behind their position and stop. Corporal Arzaga said delightedly, "Now we'll get the bastards." But the elation was short lived. The Japanese tanks kept out of sight in the bamboo thickets, and after observing the area for a few minutes, the U.S. tank pulled back. Soon afterward, two Japanese tanks crashed out of the thicket. Private Obsena, a .50-caliber gunner on one of the scout cars, opened up on them at about five hundred yards aiming at their treads but had difficulty getting zeroed in on their range. Pfc. Bartolome Geroka of Headquarters and Service Troop, the driver of the car, jumped from his seat, pushed Obsena aside, and got behind the gun and began firing bursts at one of the treads of enemy tanks, managing to disable two.

The Japanese infantry pressed an assault on the 26th left flank. Cpl. Felipe Fernandez recounts that Sergeant Bulawan shouted the order for the troopers to get to the other side of the street one by one. Corporal Thompson was the only one wounded, but he managed to cross near Pvt. Juan Soria of B Troop just a few yards ahead of Fernandez. It was at this time that Private Soria arose to immortalize himself in the 26th's military history annals.

Small, whip-cord lean, and fit, Soria had been an expert in the prewar, fun-filled "monkey drill" exercises. Vaulting onto a horse, armed with grenades and two Coca-Cola-bottle Molotov cocktails, Soria charged in recklessly and leaped onto the nearest tank. He struggled to pry open the turret hatch to drop in a grenade, but while doing so was hit by fire from a second tank nearby. As he rolled off the side of the tank he was on, he managed to smash one of his fire bomb bottles into the slits of its exhaust radiators. Badly wounded, he got close enough to the second tank to disable it with his remaining grenades and fire bomb. Leaving two tanks burning gloriously on the road, Soria crawled back to the 26th lines but not before the stunned enemy could bring fire to bear on him and wound him again. A man on a horse attacking their tanks!? Lt. Clint Seymour saw him get shot. "He was hit just to the right of his spine. Sergeant Bulawan picked him up, put him on his shoulder, got Soria out of the line of fire and put him under cover. We all assumed he was dead, and it wasn't until I was visiting our vet, Dr. Gochenour, on Bataan that I ran across Soria again. He said 'Lieutenant, do you remember me up at Binalonan?' I said, no, so he pulled up his undershirt and showed me a huge scar just to the right of his spinal column. I remembered then, and I swear I don't know how he survived." For this act of unquestioned valor, Soria was recommended for the Medal of Honor. At the time, though, his action was lauded less for bravery but more as a much needed lift to the hearts of all of his imperiled fellow cavalrymen who witnessed it. The 26th Cavalry legend grew another notch. Juan Soria survived the war and retired as a master sergeant from the U.S. regular Army and as an American citizen.

On the 26th left flank there were increasing problems. The Japanese were fast extending their line to the front and threatening to flank Troop E's light machine gun platoon's positions. Corporal Felipe Fernandez had been relieved as troop clerk and given command of the MG platoon. This hadn't set well with the platoon's other two surviving corporals, but Lt. Clint Seymour was out of sight and felt that time was of the essence. He wanted a man he knew he could count on and issued orders to extend the line as much as possible. He implemented this by sending out the number three and four men of each squad as riflemen. During the action, one of the MGs inexplicably stopped firing. Fernandez quickly crawled over to see what the trouble was. The gunner told him the weapon had a separated cartridge case jammed in the chamber and he had no combination tool to clear it. Fernandez "located" a tool and extracted the ruptured case, but before he could remove his hand, his thumb was badly mashed by the bolt being released prematurely by the gunner. He wrapped a dirty handkerchief around the wound and went back into action.

By then, firing had subsided somewhat. The lull had lasted about half an hour, so Pierce, with information that the road to the southeast was still open, decided to attempt to get the wounded on some of his remaining vehicle trains and out of Binalonan. The Japanese by now controlled all of the roads out of the town except the one to Tayug, so that is where Pierce directed them. Good fortune was on their side and the small convoy with the 26th wounded got clear of the town without loss and raced southward toward the town of Asingan. They were led by Cpl. Eulalio Arzaga riding point on his motorcycle. He looked back with deep concern for the rest of his regiment and their slim chances of extricating themselves from the mess they were now in.

The lull in the fighting did not last for long. Several Japanese tanks moved from cover and began to proceed hesitantly south on Route 3 toward Urdaneta. At around 10:30 a.m. the all-out infantry attacks by the Japanese had ceased, but a steady exchange of small arms and machine gun fire kept up. For the first time that morning it appeared as if the regiment would be able to execute a withdrawal. Then suddenly, an enemy tank lunged from cover and began to chew Lt. Hank Mark's B Troop platoon's outpost to pieces. The outpost's heaviest defense was their light machine guns, and it looked certain that they were going to be massacred. Hank Mark, without hesitation, turned to 2nd Lt. Clint Seymour and Platoon Sergeant Bulawan and yelled for grenades and to "Cover me!"

Henry Mark, the jovial, chubby young man from southern California who had joined the horse cavalry with illusions of the glamour associated with the traditions of the much heralded branch of the army, was a changed person. Days of hard fighting and privation had made him lean and hardened him into a warrior. With only his pistol and a shirt full of grenades, Mark covered about fifty yards and charged the tank that was savaging his men. He succeeded in blowing the treads and putting lethal fire through the slits into the tank's interior, but he paid the ultimate price to do so. Before he could get the last of his grenades on to the forward surfaces and into the slit openings of the tank, he was riddled with machine gun fire. But his last conscious, living act put a grenade directly into a vulnerable opening and stopped the tank cold. Hank Mark's premonitions about never seeing Manila again had been tragically correct. He would never again feel the warmth of his home California sun or its pretty girls. His action earned him a commendation for the Medal of Honor in the notebook of his 1st Squadron CO, Maj. Hubert W. Ketchum, a document to be lost like so many others in the chaos of the harrowing months to come.

Private Geroka was still behind the .50-caliber machine gun he was manning on one of the scout cars (T-7). The gun was mounted on a pedestal on one of the vehicle's running boards, and his firing had momentarily stopped the rush of the rumbling Japanese tanks. He was still holding the handles and trigger of his gun when a direct hit by a 47mm tank gun blew his head off. Slowly his decapitated body fell off the running board and rolled into a muddy ditch behind the road. It was typical of the bravery and loyalty of the scouts, who rarely if ever faltered or flinched in the face of sure death.

At about 11 a.m. a measure of salvation arrived on the scene in the form of two 75mm cannons mounted on half tracks. This belated assistance had been sent by General Selleck to support the 26th, which his 71st Division had left behind holding the bag. Major Ketchum was at the regimental CP when the guns arrived and immediately asked Pierce to direct the guns to support his 1st Squadron, which was now fighting for its life against overwhelming assault by Japanese tanks that now appeared to be gathering to overrun his positions in a coordinated assault from their cover of the bamboo thickets directly on the 26th front. Up until then, the 26th's primary defense against the enemy armor was its few .50-caliber machine guns and the unerring marksmanship of its troopers firing through the observation slits on the Japanese tanks. Pierce concurred immediately and Ketchum hurried over to the artillery battery commander, Lieutenant Vandelester, and yelled, "Let's go get 'em!"

Rushing into the street, they boarded the first vehicle. Ketchum perched himself on the running board shouting at the drivers and pointing directions to his beleaguered troops. The half tracks roared north toward the Tayug-Manaog Road in the direction of the action. As they approached the intersection, 1st Sergeant Bulawan leaped out of his foxhole and frantically gestured toward the general location of the enemy tanks. The half tracks then turned west on the road through B Troop's lines and then swung right to bring their guns to bear on the bamboo thickets. Both guns managed to get off a couple of rounds into the Japanese hiding place. Before they could continue firing, however, the American guns were hit in reply with a withering storm of armor piercing and explosive shells from the Japanese. Major Ketchum was blown from his precarious mount on the lead half track and killed outright. One by one the guns and their remaining crews, including Lieutenant Vanderlester, were cut down by enemy fire with only the driver of the second half track surviving. This brief respite was to be the only instance in which the 26th had the support of weapons truly able to stop enemy armor. However, the Japanese had been caught off guard by the appearance of the heavy weapons and, inexplicably, did not press their assault. Instead, they held their positions in the shelter of the bamboo thickets for the time being. This hesitancy would prove salvation for B Troop when the orders to withdraw finally came down to them.

In the meantime, General Wainwright at his headquarters near the Agno was fast coming to the conclusion that nothing could stop the Japanese advance in Northern Luzon. His poorly trained Philippine army units were being outgunned and outflanked at every turn. With only ten weeks of training and armed only with old, unreliable Enfield rifles (which only a few of the Filipinos had even learned to shoot), the defensive picture was grim. It was becoming quickly evident that the old War Plan Orange-3 (WPO-3) with its risky phased withdrawal must go into effect and the NLF withdrawn to Bataan where solid defensive lines might be established and time bought for the Southern Luzon forces to reach the narrow, defensible haven of the Bataan peninsula. However, only MacArthur had the authority to make such a decision. In the meantime Wainwright must delay the enemy any way he could with what he had at hand. If the Japanese broke through now, they had a clear road to Manila and could cut off all of the Southern Luzon defense forces in addition to swamping the NLF.

At USAFFE headquarters in Manila, the air was generally one of turmoil. Communication from Gen. George Marshall had been received that the long-awaited relief "Pensacola" convoy had been diverted to Brisbane, Australia, and that expected air reinforcements in the form of B-24s and B-17s were hopelessly delayed. In addition to this dismal information were reports from Wainwright detailing the strength of the Japanese invasion forces and their progress. Wainwright pleaded for more air support, especially fighters and dive bombers, which had been promised to be made available by aircraft carriers. Desperate messages were sent to Washington from MacArthur asking, "Can we expect anything in that line anytime soon?" USAFFE drafted longer messages describing the situation at hand and the extent of Japanese forces already on Luzon. Eighty thousand to a hundred thousand troops were indicated, vastly larger numbers than Homma's approximately forty-three thousand troops at hand. The American-Filipino forces were likewise underestimated as being only some forty thousand, when the defense forces were actually more like eighty thousand effectives. MacArthur was bent on backing his argument for the initiation of WPO-3 and its risky phased withdrawal into Bataan. Unless resistance could be hardened within days, Wainwright and his NLF had no alternative but withdrawal to Bataan. The plea fell on closed ears in Washington, and WPO-3's need appeared imminent.

Wainwright kept a close watch on the 71st Division's resistance from the morning of 23 December in Rosario and what was developing into a critical defense of the routes south to Sison and the Bued. The 71st's primary mission was to deny Highway 3, the Manila North Road, to the Japanese and prevent a breakthrough at Sison, putting the enemy in position to outflank the 21st Division positioned at the southern edges of Lingayen Gulf. Selleck's 71st mission was the critical key to stemming the tide.

Wainwright ordered the 91st Combat Team to reinforce the 71st, but they would take time to get into position. The Japanese struck first. At first, they were stopped cold by 71st artillery, and by noon they were still held at bay. The next attempt was an all-out frontal assault backed by tanks and air support. This time the Filipino infantry broke and bolted to the rear through their own artillery positions. On hearing the reports, Wainwright still hoped the 91st would get there in time to plug the hole, but because of a bridge blown by enemy dive bombers, they were unable to reach the 71st in time to help stem the rout.

The messages of the breakthrough were increasingly discouraging, and Wainwright concluded that a new line must be organized blocking Route 3 to be held by some unit other than the 71st until the division was able to reorganize. Wainwright, relying on his maps, came to the decision that a stand would have to be established south of Sison near Pozorrubio. He had only the 91st and the battered 26th Cavalry to execute the delay, but they would have to hold the line long enough for a stronger defensive line to be put in place to prevent the Japanese from overrunning all of Luzon. He had only one natural advantage: the deep, wide Agno River, about twenty miles inland from the Lingayen coastline. Once he decided on his course of action, Wainwright telephoned USAFFE HQ in Manila. Sutherland answered his call and upon the information that a stopgap defensive line on the Agno was the only alternative open, MacArthur's chief aide gave his approval. Wainwright then told Sutherland that he had a further plan worked out to launch a counterattack when the Agno line was in position, but with his forces in their present, shattered, and demoralized state, he was too poorly prepared to initiate such an action. To implement his strategy Wainwright pleaded that it was imperative he be given command of his old command, the Philippine Division, which was now being held in reserve to the south by MacArthur. Sutherland replied that he needed Wainwright to submit detailed plans for his attack. In reply, Wainwright said he would outline his plans as quickly as possible, but he had to have a reply on getting the Philippine Division out of reserve. Sutherland hesitated, then answered, "That may be highly improbable at this point."

This came as a blow to Wainwright, whose strategy counted on the Philippine Division catching the Japanese off guard and possibly cutting off their most advanced southernmost forces. This could not be implemented with the meager forces he presently had at hand, but he pressed on with his plans for counterattack. MacArthur, however, did not release the Philippine Division to him, and the decision put in motion the beginning of a hard-pressed retreat to the Agno River. The drastic withdrawal shocked Mac-Arthur into the decision to immediately put the WPO-3 plan into effect. It was a move made too late, and military historians later observed that the delay did more to affect the defeat of American and Filipino defenders of Bataan than any following actions on the part of Homma, his commanders, or his troops.

On the night Wainwright was formulating his plans for counterattack, a telephone call was received from Col. Pete Irwin in MacArthur's headquarters. "WPO-3 is in effect," he was informed.

Wainwright was stunned and could barely reply. "Do you understand?" pressed Irwin.

"Yes, I understand," the general replied dejectedly.

Now, with no reasonable possibility of counterattack, Wainwright was left only with the alternative of trying with his forces on hand to hold back the massive pressure of the Japanese offensive long enough for the main of MacArthur's forces to withdraw to the relative safety of Bataan.

Deciding to take matters into his own hands and assess his options first-hand, Wainwright, accompanied by Col. Frank Nelson, NLF G-3, and Capt. Tom Dooley, Wainwright's aide, drove his faithful old Packard on what seemed at first to be a relatively uneventful inspection trip of the Northern Luzon force's tenuous lines. Primarily, he wanted to get a firsthand report from Gen. Clyde Selleck. The nature of the trip changed abruptly as he approached Binalonan. There were two roads that led to Binalonan: the main highway (Route 3) and a secondary road running parallel to it. Wainwright took the secondary. He then observed tanks moving south on the main highway about six or seven hundred yards to his left. At first he reckoned them to be friendly, but on closer examination through field glasses, they were confirmed to be Japanese! Wainwright urged his party to waste no time getting on to Binalonan. His routine trip had now become a potentially deadly risk for the general.

On his arrival with the intention of conferring with General Selleck, Wainwright was instead greeted with the sound of small arms fire and explosions. Wainwright drove his Packard toward the sound of the heavy firing coming from the northwestern edge of the town, where he found not Selleck's 71st Division Headquarters but instead the weary men of his cherished 26th Cavalry in a desperate, vicious fight for survival. (Wainwright's aide, Tom Dooley, described Selleck with utter contempt in his diary.) They had now been holding the Japanese at bay for almost six hours, even at one point attempting to counterattack only to be driven back by enemy armor. He then came upon Maj. Tom Trapnell's 2nd Squadron command post in the center of Binalonan where the 71st HQ should have been. On being told by Trapnell that the 71st had pulled out during the night without even informing the 26th, Wainwright was first stunned then silently near apoplectic with anger. In a quiet, level voice, with all the restraint he could muster, the general asked to be directed to the 26th regimental HQ. Though seething inside, he paused briefly to have a few words of morale-encouraging conversation with Trapnell, mostly reflecting on happier days that stirred memories for Trapnell when he had served under Wainwright at Fort Meyer, Virginia, and later in the Philippines before the war. Trap then cautioned the general against going to the regimental CP, which was only about four hundred yards from the enemy and under heavy small arms and artillery fire, but Wainwright was adamant. Skinny and his party then moved on to meet with Pierce. In his element under fire, Wainwright had his car parked behind a shack near the CP and calmly walked on to meet with Pierce.

The general's arrival found Pierce and Chandler scratching layouts of their positions in the dirt and trying to figure their next defensive moves. Pierce whipped around in surprise at the sound of Skinny Wainwright's greeting. They then got down to the business at hand. Pierce gave the general a condensed but thorough rundown on what had happened that morning, sparing little detail and with more than a small hint of bitterness on having been abandoned without warning by Selleck's 71st. Wainwright gave Pierce the grave news of WPO-3 going into effect, then wasted few words giving Pierce directions to get the wounded out and withdraw the 26th as soon as he could disengage the regiment. Then Wainwright said he wished to troop the line with Pierce. Having spent most of his military career with horse cavalry, the general felt at home as he and Pierce moved along the line under heavy, persistent small arms fire and shrapnel whistling all about them. The two veteran cavalrymen acted as unconcerned as if they were taking a routine stroll down a post sidewalk. Their demeanor belied the gravity of the situation, and their calm transmitted to the men on the line. Wainwright remained in the area for more than an hour, much longer than necessary to assess the situation. Word passed quickly down the 26th lines that their general was with his beloved regiment, and a new level of resolve and morale settled in knowing he was sharing their peril. Adjusting their rifle slings, they settled down to inflict on the overconfident Japanese a devastating display of sharpshooting. Pierce and Skinny returned to Pierce's command post, and it occurred to the colonel that it was Christmas Eve. He turned to Wainwright and asked, "Would anyone like a small drink of Christmas cheer?"

Wainwright answered with a gentle smile. "Well, that would be a fine thing if you can spare it." Pouring from Pierce's small, hoarded supply of scotch, the two old cavalrymen briefly savored the moment in sentimental camaraderie reflecting on better times past.

While this short acknowledgment of the holiday took place, Colonel Nelson informed Bill Chandler of some grave information. The day before,

MacArthur had instructed all his commanders that the old prewar defense plan known as WPO-3 was to be put in effect immediately. The North Luzon Force would now withdraw as slowly as possible in five successive phase lines into the Bataan peninsula. The first lines called for holding for twenty-four hours, but the last two required holding the Japs north of San Fernando, Pampanga, until Maj. Gen. George M. Parker's Southern Luzon Force could pass through Manila and into the defensive refuge of Bataan. In 1921–1922, when Wainwright had been assigned to the general staff, he had helped draw up the plan. He never really dreamed it would have to be implemented.

As Wainwright prepared to leave, Chandler checked with Trapnell to be certain that the Tayug road was still open. It was, and Chandler informed Colonel Nelson the way was clear. Pierce ordered a scout car to escort the general to the river, but Wainwright refused, saying, "You can't spare it, and we don't really need it." With that, Skinny and his party calmly entered their staff car and proceeded out of town the way they had entered, still without even a motorcycle as escort.

By this time the relative lull in the Japanese assaults had persisted over one half hour. The enemy was in the process of regrouping with the intention of extending its lines with the objective of flanking the 26th lines. The lull had lasted about fifteen minutes more when Pierce and Vance concluded it was now or never. With Wainwright's information that the road to the southeast was still open and the firing subsided for the moment, it appeared to them that there might be a chance to extricate the regiment after all from the mess they were in. A hasty plan for pulling out was thrown together right there and then. Orders were issued, and once again the value of training and discipline would prove to be the saving strength of the regiment.

At well past 3:00 that afternoon Japanese fire began increasing in volume again. All indications were that they were gearing up for another attack, and it was then that Pierce decided that if the regiment was going to disengage, the time was at hand. The word was passed and the 26th began slowly pulling out of their positions with as little sign as possible to the Japanese. Again, the value of training and discipline of the 26th came through. First, all remaining supply and support trains were sent out of town toward Asingan immediately. Then E Troop was ordered to pull out of line to saddle up under the covering fire of armored cars and the other units still in position. When the saddling was completed, E Troop returned to their positions. Then the same process was followed by HQ and B Troops. A Troop, whose position was separated from its horses by the Manoag-Asingan road, was forced to cross the road in a rush in plain sight of the Japanese, saddle up, and proceed directly out of town to the east, becoming the advance guard of the regiment. In only minutes, the balance of the regiment was mounted and on the road behind Troop A, followed by Colonels Pierce and Vance, at a walk and leading their horses. To their great credit, the troopers never got excited or rushed in their movements, with the result that the Japanese remained unaware of the regiment's movement until Troop A crossed the road to its horses. At that, two tanks that had been concealed in the bamboo thicket near the road junction roared to life and began to move in. Lt. Clint Seymour of Troop B and an officer from the staff crouched behind a ditched and burning ammunition truck near the road until the leading tank almost reached them. Then they each threw three hand grenades over the wrecked truck body, ran for their horses, and caught up with Pierce and Vance just short of the bridge out of town. Apparently the grenades, while relatively harmless to the tanks, made them hesitate long enough for the main body of the regiment to get clear. The enemy tanks did not follow, probably afraid of an ambush. Troop F remained as rear guard at the bridge for over one half hour. Once the rear guard scout cars cleared the bridge, Trapnell gave the order to blow it. Then a scout car section settled in and covered until darkness began to descend.

The regiment stopped east of Asingan just long enough to repair a blown bridge for their scout cars and arrived at the Agno River bridge at dusk. The bridge had been prepared for demolition but fortunately had not yet been blown. The structure was actually a series of spans about fifteen hundred feet long that crossed a swamp and both channels of the deep Agno River. About one half mile farther south lay the barrio of Agno and about a mile farther, the 26th's destination, the town of Tayug.

Maj. Bill Chandler, in recalling the withdrawal, marveled at the circumstances. "Why the Japanese did not follow us or why they had not outflanked us to the north or south hours before is a complete mystery. However, we were more than happy that it now appeared that our 'little ball of string' could remain tightly wound for a while longer."

Upon arriving at Tayug, the cavalrymen rode into a scene of chaos. The 71st Division (PA) had been almost hopelessly scattered following its disastrous battle at Sison and the added pullout from Binalonan. Lt. Col. George Ventura, the 71st's artillery CO, had tried the whole day to find enough units and personnel to organize what was now a ragged line on the south side of the Agno. On seeing the degree of confusion, Pierce, Vance, and Chandler came to full realization of how important the 26th's action at Binalonan had been. If it had not been for the cavalrymen, the Japanese might well have flanked the whole Northern Luzon Force and cut off any hope for withdrawal to Bataan. The 26th had effectively, but at tragic cost to the little regiment, refused the line to the attackers.

Casualties in the Christmas Eve action at Binalonan had been painfully heavy. Killed in action were Major Ketchum, CO of 1st Squadron and one of Pierce's most valued officers; Lieutenant Vanderlester of the 24th Artillery (on an SPM); Lieutenant Mark of B Troop; Lieutenant Bowers of Machine Gun Troop; and Corporal Geroaka, scout car driver and gunner. Among the wounded were Capt. Paul M. Jones (a West Pointer), who was awarded the Silver Star and Purple Heart, and the valiant Juan Soria. In addition, the artillery unit had nine men killed and one wounded and lost two track-mounted cannon. The dead and wounded among both men and animals were far more than the depleted regiment could afford, and no reinforcements appeared to be forthcoming. However, the 26th had held up for an entire day the advance of the major element of the Japanese column driving for the critical crossings of the Agno River and prevented all hostile movement to the east from 5 a.m. until 2 p.m., thus providing invaluable time for the hard-pressed Philippine army to organize the strategic D-1 line along the Agno called for by WPO-3.

Once again, the intrepid little regiment of horse cavalry had put a serious glitch in the Japanese timetable and bought time for General Wainwright, who in a later, official report praised the cavalrymen for their costly action at Binalonan. "At daylight on 24 December, Japanese forces attacked the 26th Cavalry at Binalonan. After successfully checking the advance of the Japanese eastward from daylight until past 3:30 p.m., the regiment withdrew at dusk to Tayug." With the exception of one small Japanese tank column, which had bypassed them toward Urdaneta, the 26th horsemen had stopped the enemy cold for more than ten hours.

"I was personally present during a portion of the fight and cannot speak in too glowing terms of the gallantry and intrepidity displayed by Colonel Pierce and all the officers and men of the 26th Cavalry on this occasion. This devoted little band of horsemen of less than 400 men, weakened by both detachments and heavy casualties, sustained at Damortis and Rosario on 22 December, held up the enemy advance guard and caused a premature beginning of deployment of the enemy's main body. It affected a delay of over ten hours and maintained the best traditions of the American Cavalry. I speak of this from the point of view of both an eyewitness and a proud commander."

Once again, infuriated apoplexy reigned in the halls of the Japanese General Staff.

Major Chandler observed in his regimental diary, "The past two and a half days had laid to rest forever the misconception, perpetuated by all too many Americans, that the Filipinos wouldn't or couldn't fight. Trained and well led, they had proved the equal to any fighting man in the world."

At about 10 p.m. Christmas Eve, the 26th Cavalry column passed through the 71st's lines and reported to Brig. Gen. Luther Stevens, CO of the 91st Division (PA). The general's 91st, supported by elements of the 192nd Tank Battalion, at this time were positioned in line east of the 71st. Stevens ordered Pierce to take the 26th on to Tayug for a rest. Fortunately, the bridge at Tayug was mined but not yet blown, so the 26th column was able to cross the river dry shod.

At Tayug the 26th Cavalrymen found a scene of utter confusion. The 71st Division had been hard hit at Sison and was badly scattered. Lieutenant Colonel Venture was doing his best to organize a defense of the river with fragmented parts of numerous units. The 91st Division, however, was occupying their part of the line in good order under the command of Brigadier General Stevens, who ordered the 26th Cavalry into the town to rest. The 26th would take no part in any defense that night but would at least get some respite to prepare for action the next day.

In Tayug, the regiment bivouacked amongst houses in the barrio, received a welcome hot meal, and then deployed their own security outposts. They had learned bitterly in the past two days that they could not depend on other units to guard their safety. After posting their lookouts and caring for their animals, the troopers put themselves down for the kind of sleep that comes only from sheer exhaustion.

During the night, Felipe Fernandez's machine gun squad relieved another unit at outpost. As he sat beside his gun, Fernandez looked up at a clear, starry sky. The utter quiet and peacefulness made it difficult for anybody to sense that there was a war on. Someone who had looked at his watch quietly called out, "Merry Christmas." Fernandez's reply froze on his lips as the memory of his dead and wounded comrades crowded into his mind. He closed his eyes and instead let his thoughts drift to his father and mother, who lived in the small town of San Nicolas only three miles away. For most who lay there that night, Christmas was a distant, hollow concept but for the gift and blessings of sleep and the rarity of a full stomach.

15

C Troop's Saga Begins[1]

On 20 December, toward Rosario at the junction of the road to Baguio, C Troop had been ordered dismounted and embarked on familiar red Pampanga buses to scout out the Japanese progress in the rugged northeastern area of Luzon. Their orders, the first combat mission assigned to a troop of the 26th (overly ambitious orders at best), were to prevent the Japanese moving south from Ilocos Sur from making a surprise dash into the mountains, seizing Baguio, and thus threatening the rear of the Lingayen defenses. They were to rejoin the regiment in the lowlands at Rosario. The troop's horses were put on lead by men of Troops A and B. The men of C Troop began their trek still wearing cavalry riding boots and leggings, hardly suitable for sustained march in the mountains. Their weapons consisted of their M-1 rifles, some Thompson submachine guns, and a few grenades. They were provided with field rations for only three days.

Unknown to all was that C Troop would never again rejoin the regiment.

In command of the troop was Capt. Ralph B. Praeger, who had been burdened with a heavy assignment for a mere, young captain. In the words of surviving 26th Cavalry veteran Col. Thomas Jones (USA Ret.), a 1st lieutenant at the time and Praeger's soft-spoken, reserved, and deeply loyal second in command, observed, "Captain Praeger certainly never considered himself other than an ordinary man. He was not an adventurer at heart; he had no special hatred for the Japanese; and he had no deep feeling about the war as such. In peacetime he had been an isolationist. He was subject to no fervor or passions. Like most of us he had his limitations, made errors in judgment on occasion, and sometimes missed opportunities. Yet alone of the original commanders in North Luzon, he kept his unit intact and operated against the Japanese for nearly two years. When he finally fell, it was in the line of duty. Yet he kept at least a semblance of government alive until the end, long after it had collapsed elsewhere on Luzon. Many a civilian is alive today because Praeger insisted that order be maintained despite the war and the occupation. For a long time he was the only viable link between the Allied world and the chief island of the Philippines."

In the beginning, Captain Praeger was not the only trained commander in North Luzon, but he was perhaps the only one who never considered disbanding his unit, and he never let it slip away from him. In other units, it was usually left to subordinates to put the pieces together and provide some spark to accomplish things. So why was this not the case in C Troop?

Ralph Praeger was not only the leader of Troop C; he was a commanding physical presence who radiated an air of authority and sincerity to all around him. Standing almost six feet four, he towered over the rest of his troop. Although he was only twenty-eight years old, his prematurely balding red hair, scraggly red beard, and persistently furrowed brow suggested to most people that he was at least forty if not older and definitely a figure who inspired respect.

In addition to this, his background had molded him well for his present purpose. Praeger had gone straight to West Point from a Kansas farm that his German-born grandfather had pioneered. His mother's family were of English stock. In this combination of breeding lay the bedrock of his natural, dominant characteristics. Behind him lay a tradition of hard, methodical work and honest dealing. At West Point, Ralph Praeger found the life easy in comparison to working on a farm from dawn to dusk in summers and before and after school in other seasons. He was assigned to duty in the Philippines with the 26th Cavalry in July 1939. He was given command of C Troop on 3 November 1941 pending his orders to sail for the United States in December. On the morning war was declared, he received orders to sail, but along with others due to return to the homeland, he remained in the Philippines.

Praeger was fundamentally lacking in sophistication and worldly wisdom, and he tended to credit others with his own high motives and honesty of purpose. Good natured and trusting, he accepted all men at face value but was likely to be somewhat embittered when forced to recognize that sometimes they fell far short of his initial impressions. He neither understood nor tolerated anyone's shirking responsibility or acting other than duty required. Now, here in the Philippines in a war going badly, his eyes were being initially opened to the fact that not all men in a crisis are motivated to act out of unwavering considerations of duty, and to his deep disappointment, he found that all too often there were men who sought or took opportunity to shrink from steadfast service to their country and to their comrades-in-arms.

In his memoirs, Colonel Jones observed of his captain, "Like many men who are large and strong in body, Captain Praeger had a relaxed and unworried manner about him which inspired confidence in those whose lives depended on him and his decisions. His was a deliberate and always patient way of doing things which reflected his origins from a race of farmers. While not particularly aggressive and certainly not ambitious, he was a hard, diligent worker. At times, he took his own good time to act, especially if the situation was of a secondary priority and could be just as well done tomorrow. This by no means was an inattention to duty. Praeger was conscientious to a fault and a painstaking officer in all he was called on to do. He took initiative when it was called for, but generally, he had an easy approach to matters and rarely got in a sweat about anything. When hard work was called for, he lent full effort to the task, but he was not one for making mountains out of molehills. If anything, he erred toward making molehills out of mountains.

"Praeger's reactions tended to be slow at times, and he was apt to be insensitive to the emotional needs of others. Unimaginative generally, he did lack full comprehension of the effect of the imagination on the minds of his men. Unworried himself, he seldom sensed that other men labored under psychological strains which he himself did not experience. For example, when encamped he would not post a guard unless the situation demanded it, thinking to save the men needless work or lack of rest. But they, with their vivid imaginations, could not sleep knowing there was no protection and consequently arose frequently in the night to insure all was well.

"His intellectual judgments were sometimes erroneous, but he was stubborn in adhering to them. It took a great deal to shake Captain Praeger from his convictions. He enjoyed an argument and would debate upon every subject under the sun—except things in which his knowledge was extensive, such as motors and machinery. On that sort of subject he would listen with polite interest to the opinions of someone who knew little or nothing of the topic and agree if he possibly could.

"He was a simple man, wholly without pretense of any sort. He had little tolerance or understanding why some people regarded Army officers as a race apart. To him, being an officer was a job, like being a master mechanic, or school teacher or lawyer. At Fort Stotsenburg, when he had been regimental motor pool officer, one was quite likely to find him under a truck working on it. He had no aversion or hesitation toward dirtying his hands. Little things delighted him. Even during the war, he spent much of his spare time playing checkers with a nine-year-old Negrito-Filipino boy. Whichever won, the ground nearly shook from the resulting pounding on the table or playing surface. Both their hearts were equally the same and both seemed overjoyed to win. At first sight of his balding head and furrowed brow, people took him to be a deeply serious and certainly dignified man. As they came to know him better, the general impression was, 'Why, Captain Praeger is just a big boy at heart.'"

Praeger had little patience with spit and polish, even the later guerrilla equivalent of it. "I shined so much brass at West Point that I swore I'd never make any man under my command shine anything that wasn't absolutely necessary for a purpose," he remarked.

He believed in calisthenics but had little use for close-order drill. Although he carried himself with generally good posture, his head tended to hang forward a little. Only when he was demonstrating the position of attention was the West Point in him evident.

He enjoyed going barefoot and became more adept at it than any of the other men of C Troop who became eventually shoeless moving in the rugged terrain of the Luzon hills. Less than six months after separation from the regiment and dismounted, Praeger could walk thirty-five miles a day over rough trails barefoot. He had knowledge of the nature of his surroundings and instincts for things necessary for survival in rough country that officers from urban areas and cities would have to learn the hard way. He knew that his men could manage without almost everything except salt in the Luzon climate, and it was seldom a day passed that he didn't mention it, check on how much was available, and watch for probable sources of supply. He understood home medicine and natural remedies. If a man became ill, Praeger tended to him himself. (Many a trooper with intestinal complaint submitted to an enema administered by their captain.)

Colonel Jones went on to recall, "Praeger's mind was primarily technical rather than scientific, dealing in facts not intangibles. Compromise was not his way. In his instinctive reasoning, machines were what one made them. People, however, tended to bewilder him a little by their unpredictability. Yet he instinctively liked people, liked them around him and would rarely stay alone if he could find someone to share the time with. Any defects he had usually stemmed from the limitations of his virtues. His good nature made him err toward trusting others too much, and his strength and solidity made him sometimes insensitive to the limitations of minds more delicate than his own.

"The possibility of defeat disturbed Praeger little. He persistently believed that we would somehow prevail. I doubt that Captain Praeger ever gave up hope until he was led to his grave. Any success in war is dependent on such a positive outlook, and C Troop's survival and accomplishments in the face of frightening odds hinged on that mindset.

"Although the men of C Troop would be in contact, either directly or indirectly with the enemy for three and a half years, their battle record might be considered relatively insignificant in terms of the overall world war. Yet to achieve even this made heavy demands on the leadership qualities of their commander. C Troop's story is not just one of combat successes. Battles cannot be fought nor wars won without materiel. Spirit alone is insufficient. The liberation of the Philippines ultimately could be accomplished only by great forces from outside those islands. But insofar as their task was made easier during 1942 and 1943 by enemy troops being tied down in the Philippines instead of being used elsewhere, and insofar as guerrilla activity contributed to the intelligence that made the invasion by the allies less difficult, the primary credit must go to Filipino and American leaders like Ralph Praeger who kept alive the spirit of resistance in a conquered country."

After being detached, C Troop began its journey up the Kennon Road toward Baguio, the Philippine "summer capital." The troop had the daunting task of covering a mountainous area some sixty miles north of Baguio. Meanwhile, the Japanese landed at Lingayen on 22 December. By the time the first elements of the troop reached Baguio at noon on 23 December their troubles had already begun. The Japanese had penetrated far enough inland to cut the highway leading south, thus isolating C Troop from the regiment. In this American-built city of some twenty-five thousand people, Praeger and his men found no sort of leadership, either military or civilian. Chaos reigned. The senior American officer in Baguio was located in the radio room of the post office. He had in his hand orders from MacArthur to occupy defensive positions, but he told Lt. Warren Minton, commander of C Troop's advance element, that he didn't know where any men of his command were! Minton then ordered the seventeen men of his point detachment to outposts, four men on the Naguilian Road running from Baguio to the Lingayen beaches, and eleven men on the Kennon Road south. They found the Naguilian Road blasted in many places, but only one short bridge had been destroyed on the Kennon Road. Because of the latter, the balance of C Troop had to abandon the buses and proceed on foot.

The other army forces stationed in Baguio had been evacuated some miles from the city and were located resting at the foot of a dead-end mountain road. Later in the day, arrangements were made for them to return to Baguio and reinforce C Troop.

Praeger and the remainder of the troop arrived in Baguio around 4:30 p.m., and the detachments at the road outposts were strengthened. In addition, about thirty Philippine army soldiers who had been separated from their units in the Lingayen debacle the previous day volunteered to join C Troop.

The American civilians were bitter against the U.S. Army. Insults of "cowardice" and "inefficiency" were frequently heard. Yet they calmed down somewhat when C Troop took measures to defend the city, and they offered their assistance. However, when volunteers with automobiles were requested to run messages between the outposts and troop headquarters, they were hard to find. Nearly all the American civilians said family responsibilities prevented them from such services. There were exceptions. Raymond Hale Jr., an American-Filipino who had been working as chauffeur for the Baguio senior officer for the past twenty-four hours, was one. An old man, his son, and a few others also volunteered, but on the whole, the effort was disappointing.

Praeger took prompt measures to provide as much of a defense as possible and prepared to make a determined fight for the city. On 24 December, a five-man patrol led by Pfc. Joaquin Pangalinan made a reconnaissance on foot to the village of Naguilian down Route 9 about five miles from the coast. Although strafed three times by enemy planes, the patrol pushed into Naguilian, which had been occupied and abandoned by the Japanese on the previous day. This mission involved an all-day trek totaling about forty kilometers of march, and the manner of their performance drew great credit for the five men.

At a little after 6:00 p.m. that day an order from General MacArthur was received by the senior officer in Baguio to withdraw the forces in the city and rejoin the North Luzon Force using mountain trails. The senior officer acted promptly to carry out the order, directing destruction of all equipment other than what could be carried by individuals. Praeger objected vehemently to such waste and suggested the equipment be sent to safe places in the mountains where it could be retrieved in the event that the troops in Baguio were unable to rejoin the NLF. He was overruled and all surplus equipment was thrown over a cliff. Morale in C Troop, which had been excellent up to then, was severely eroded by such useless loss of resources.

Then the march into the mountains began, each man carrying his arms, about a hundred rounds of ammunition, a blanket, and a gas mask carrier full of canned food. At midnight Captain Praeger called out, "Merry Christmas, men; pass the word." But the men were so dispirited that the message died out before reaching the end of the column.

Troop C was ordered to march to Aritao in the Cagayan Valley from where it was hoped it could escape via Balete Pass through San Jose and Munoz to the south. The mountains in that area are high and precipitous, and although airline distance from Baguio to Aritao is barely forty kilometers, it took six days to get there.

On the way into Aritao many disbanded Filipino soldiers were encountered moving in the opposite direction. They said they had been ordered by their American instructors to discard their uniforms and arms and return to their homes. It was a disheartening spectacle. Some of the men were glad enough to be free of facing further defeat in battle, but others were bitter that they had been disbanded and said they wanted to continue to fight. Some joined C Troop. These men told of one Filipino private who had refused to carry out the order to throw away his arms and had been shot on the spot by an American officer. The story was greeted with disbelief, but the men who told it insisted it was true.

By 30 December when Troop C, foot sore and weary, marched into Aritao, it had little left but rifles and the ammunition being carried. On arrival they received the dismal news that Munoz and San Jose had been taken two days before by the enemy. The troop had lost the race against time and the Japanese and any hope of rejoining the 26th.

In Aritao they were met by a clean-shaven, smartly dressed Philippine army officer full of vinegar and vitality. He introduced himself as Capt. Manuel P. Enriquez, assistant chief of staff, G-2, 11th Division. He had been sent into the Cagayan Valley a few days before to evacuate as many of the cut-off troops as possible. He confirmed the capture of Munoz and San Jose. He said individuals and small groups might still be able to filter through the lines, but the situation was developing so rapidly that the main American army would be withdrawn into Bataan before a man on foot could reach it.

"I am turning guerrilla," Enriquez said cheerily. He had already gathered together about two hundred disbanded soldiers and now had them fishing arms and ammunition out of the Marang River, where they had previously been ordered dumped. Praeger and his lieutenants reviewed the situation with Enriquez and then questioned some Americans who had tried unsuccessfully to slip around San Jose. Praeger weighed the findings carefully and made his decision without hesitation.

"I'm not going to break up my outfit merely in hope that some of them will get back to the main force. We'll stick together and operate against the enemy up here."

Troop C had present three officers and fifty-nine enlisted men, plus five Philippine army officers with about forty men. The troop's morning report strength was normally eighty-nine men, but two men had been lost near Baguio. The remainder who were either in hospital or on special duty had not accompanied the troop when it had been detached from the regiment. Those men subsequently took part in the defense of Bataan. One of them, Pvt. Jose P. Tugab, who had been wounded on 10 December, escaped miraculously to China after the fall of Corregidor on a Japanese ship, got to Chunking, and fought in the Papua and New Guinea campaigns.

In addition, a few American enlisted men and civilians were picked up by the troop. Among them were two really valuable additions, Tech Sgt. William E. Bowen and a civilian named Francis A. Camp, both of whom had joined the troop during the march across the mountains. Bowen and Camp with another civilian named Dickey had stayed behind in Baguio after the army had withdrawn. On Christmas Eve they had driven by car to the foot of the Kennon Road. They stopped a few hundred yards short of a bridge over which Japanese troops were passing and at dawn the next morning opened fire on the enemy. Several enemy armored vehicles came out in pursuit, but the three Americans blocked the road by blowing up an abandoned gasoline truck in the enemy's face. Afterward, they calmly ate breakfast in their automobile while three enemy planes reconnoitered the road. This incident was indicative of the qualities of initiative and fighting abilities of these men, who seemed to be not at all disheartened at being cut off behind enemy lines.

Upon arrival in Aritao, Praeger made Bowen and Camp acting lieutenants, telling them they would have the responsibility but not the pay of officers. The troop then gathered up field corn growing nearby, boiled it, and had their first relatively square meal in days.

Sergeant Bowen was a professional soldier with twelve years' service. Slight and handsome with black hair turning gray and a carefully trimmed moustache, he looked more like a film actor than a guerrilla. Full of charm, he had a keen, sensitive mind and a rich store of tales and songs with which he was always ready to entertain those about him. The men who had served under him in Baguio were devoted to him, and few could know Bowen long and not know the reason. The well-being of others was one of his first considerations. He was decisive and had a way of getting things done without apparent effort. Camp, a very brave man himself, obviously held a deep admiration for Bowen as a consequence of the fearlessness Bowen had displayed in their Christmas morning fight with the Japanese. In Aritao, Bowen possessed several hundred dollars, and the rest of the men had practically nothing. He gave Praeger the larger part and divided the remainder among the enlisted men, retaining only a few dollars for himself.

Frank Camp was a different type. Although not very tall, he had broad shoulders and a powerful body and impressed one as standing six feet. He had been a member of the 4th Marine Regiment in Shanghai during the battles of 1937 and told of the bloated corpses that the marines nicknamed Joe, Ike, Mike, and so forth as they floated down Soochow Creek past his sentry box. Camp had somehow obtained a BAR automatic rifle, which he carried with ease together with several belts of ammunition. He soon proved he could always be depended on to do any job—except *not* fight Japs. Camp never acquired any particular hatred for them, but he could seldom resist the opportunity when on patrol to open fire on them regardless of orders. Because Praeger, himself a formidable fighter, knew that Camp was one of his most valuable officers, any reprimands were never so severe as they might have been in other cases. If action really was undesirable, it proved better to send someone else to do the job. If there were Japs to be killed though, Camp was the man.

On 31 December, New Year's Eve, the troop moved nine miles north to Bambang, Neuva Viscaya. There they quartered in the rectory of a Belgian missionary, Father Diesnick, who had cared for and fed at his own expense several thousand disorganized troops during the past few days. A poorly clad, big man with a rough voice and large black beard, he nevertheless radiated the quality of saintliness. His entire days were spent finding food, clothing, salt, and shelter for disbanded, lost troops, some moving north, some south, west, or east. The priest was deeply saddened by the sight of these bewildered youngsters, more so because it brought back to him memories of Belgium in 1914. Only the people and place were different.

On New Year's Eve the news came that Manila had fallen. The next morning, Father Diesnick delivered a sermon on the theme that the good soldier must at all times do his duty to his country, regardless of difficulties. Later in the morning, a Philippine constabulary soldier arrived from the north with the information that the enemy had established a large airfield at Tuguegarao 215 kilometers north. This was received with angry delight by everyone. Now here finally was a real way to earn their pay and move toward the enemy for once. The remainder of the day was spent making tentative plans for an attack.

On 3 January, Troop C left Bambang for Santiago, about forty-five miles to the northeast. Lieutenant Minton, the junior officer in the troop, preceded the main body with a patrol to find transportation and repair bridges when possible. Transport, what little could be found, was usually in need of repair, and with one exception, every bridge in the Cagayan Valley had been demolished. Until reaching Northern Isabela, movement was principally on foot. Rare motor transport and calesas (small horse-drawn carriages) were utilized when possible. Shoes and boots were fast wearing out, and by now some of the men went barefoot. Even so, putting bitter memories of the past two weeks behind them, morale began to rise.

The troop arrived in Santiago, Isabela, at about 5 a.m. on 5 January. Progress during the last ten kilometers had been impeded by a particularly balky calesa pony, which the efforts of all Troop C could not induce to move when he wanted to stand still. The pony was finally left to his own devices and the column walked on into Santiago, a painful experience as walking for days in riding boots had given nearly everyone severe blisters.

Santiago is a comparatively large town, and all the citizens who had dared to remain there turned out to greet the troop.

Tom Jones recalls, "We were not a particularly impressive portion of the U.S. Army as we straggled in, but we were all that was available at the time. Important to the citizens there, we were the only troops going in the direction of the enemy to the north which threatened them."

The next day a patrol consisting of Lieutenant Minton, Acting Lieutenants Camp and Bowen, and four scout troopers left Santiago to make a reconnaissance of Tuguegarao, more than eighty miles north by the most direct route. The remainder of the troop spent its time repairing and cleaning equipment and weapons. A Chinese storekeeper contributed about thirty-five pairs of canvas shoes, accepting as payment a voucher to be redeemed by the government at some future date. All food for the troop was contributed free by the people as it had been for the most part since leaving Baguio. As cash was seldom used by officers in the Philippines, no one had much money on hand when the war broke out. The money contributed by Lieutenant Bowen was practically the entire purse available.

Early in the afternoon of 8 January, Pvt. Antero Soriano was accidentally shot by Pvt. Constancio Ocampo while the two recruits were hunting chicken. Soriano died within minutes. Ocampo was discharged and ordered home. Soriano was given a quick funeral, the local carpenter turning out his coffin in about thirty minutes. He was buried at sunset outside Santiago with the troop as escort. Unfortunately, the grave was slightly too small, and 1st Sgt. Tom Quiocho pushed the coffin down with his foot muttering, "Get down there, Soriano, get down." This was everyone's first Filipino funeral away from Fort Stotsenburg.

Fifteen of the older men who were deemed unfit for arduous field service were left in Santiago under command of the first sergeant. They were subsequently attached to the newly organized 14th Infantry as instructors. After the fall of Corregidor, they were either captured or killed. About thirty men of the 11th and 71st Divisions (PA) and Philippine constabulary with Lieutenants DeLeon, Ramos, Diesto, and Villou were attached to Troop C for the raid on the Tuguegarao airfield. The troop, thus now organized, left Santiago at 9:00 the evening of the funeral.

On 9 January they billeted in Cauyayan and at 1 a.m. on 10 January arrived at Mallig No. 2, a resettlement station. Here there was a radio, and the troop got its first outside news since 26 December. They learned that the United States proposed to make 60,000 airplanes in 1942 and 125,000 in 1943. This was of little use to them at the time. There was not much other news, so the situation in the Philippines could not be determined.

At 3 p.m. Lieutenant Minton returned and gave a report on the progress of his reconnaissance. He spoke highly of the cooperation and help he was receiving from Governor Marcelo Adduru of the province of Cagayan and the provincial engineer, a Mr. Imperial. He reported that Adduru had set up his government in Tuao, forty kilometers west of Tuguegarao, after the Japanese had captured the latter town on 16 December. The government of Cagayan had set up a news and propaganda section and was printing emergency money to carry on its work. Lieutenant Minton left for Tuao at 6 p.m. after an officer's conference on plans. The next day the Troop moved to Mallig No. 1. There they met the director of the resettlement project, who was having difficulty with his people, some of whom thought that law and order had ceased to exist with the onset of war. Some of them had been given hand grenades by withdrawing Philippine army units for protection against the Japs. Now they were instead using them to intimidate others of their own race. The director, whose life had been devoted to improving the lot of the less fortunate, was killed a few weeks later when someone threw a grenade into his living room.

Soon after, Praeger and Tom Jones had their first discussion as to measures they might take to maintain some semblance of law and order in this remote part of Luzon.

NOTE

1. Accounts about C Troop are for the most part taken from interviews with and the memoirs of Col. Thomas Jones (USA Ret.).

16

The Long Road to Bataan Begins

25 DECEMBER 1941, CHRISTMAS MORNING

On the NLF D-2 line at Tayug

Upon their deployment at Tayug to join the defense of the south bank of the Agno River, the 26th Cavalry in actuality became the eastern flank anchor for the NLF at the outset of its withdrawal to the D-2 line in its phased withdrawal southward toward Bataan in accordance with MacArthur's War Plan Orange-3. One memorable aspect of the 26th arrival at Tayug was that the exhausted troopers were fed for the first time in three days. The stew was a thin mix of corned beef hash (dubbed by the troops as "corn Willy") and canned vegetables, but it was hot. At Tayug the regiment relieved the 71st Engineer Battalion (PA), which had been covering the Agno river crossing. The cavalrymen now joined up with the Brig. Gen. Luther Stevens's 91st Division (PA) and a scattering of units from the 71st who had set up hasty defense positions on the river under command of Lieutenant Colonel Ventura, F.A. To the west on D-2, holding the NLF center was General Brougher's 11th Division (PA) supported by the 192nd Tank Battalion, still the only armor support in North Luzon.

In the meantime, the 194th Tanks had left Manila on the 24th under orders to take up position around Carmen, just west of Cabanatuan and the Pampanga River, on what was to be part of the D-4 line. Other NLF units were also withdrawing southward toward Bataan, blowing bridges as they retired. During this phase of the withdrawal, there was little or no enemy contact. The stiff defense of Binalonan by the 26th had caused the Japanese advance to falter. However, now that Binalonan had been captured, General Tsuchibashi, commander of the 48th Division, ordered his chief of staff, Col. Moriji Kawagloe, to split the attack into two columns, one south on Route 3 toward Urdaneta and Brougher's 11th Division on the D-2 west flank and one east toward Tayug and the 26th. His western column was composed of the 1st and 2nd Formosa Infantry supported by the 4th Tank Regiment. The bloody fight at Urdaneta lasted all Christmas morning, but the Japanese finally, after taking heavy losses, forced the Filipinos back toward the Agno. Meanwhile, to the east at Tayug, NLF units were hastily being shuffled and regrouped. That afternoon the 26th relieved Ventura's shattered 71st remnants, who were ordered south to San Fernando, Pampanga, to reorganize.

On Christmas day, Clint Seymour happened to walk by George Spies, a 1st lieutenant with F Troop. "He stopped me and introduced himself and offered me some Christmas cheer. I answered I'd give almost anything for a drink of scotch, and he said 'just a minute.' He went into a bahays [hut]) and came back with a bottle of Dewar's White Label and offered it. I took it up, and then Cramer, an A Troop captain, 1st Lt. Fred Evans, also of A Troop, Capt. Joe Barker of B Troop showed up, and we passed that bottle around until it was dead. I never had scotch taste so good to me in my life. I then, a little tight, got sent out on a patrol to the river with my orderly, a corporal, and three other guys. When we got there some Japs were trying to cross. It was a swift stream, and they were having trouble. We opened up and Japs now got across the river on a piece of bamboo with a rail on it. We decided our position wasn't the greatest so I said to the others to follow me. We got out of the area and a couple of miles upriver we ran into a group of Philippine army guys. They joined us and we kept walking. I had a tommy gun, and we laid down some heavy fire. We could tell our troops were pulling out because we could hear them blowing bridges, and we went toward the sound. The Filipinos we'd picked up didn't like my course of action nor did my own patrol. So they left me. I got back to camp and they eventually came in. Joe Barker was irate. He didn't bust them, but he gave them hell. What I liked about Barker was he always seemed to know the right place to go. On several occasions when Japs jumped us at night he'd make us ride like hell and bivouac any place handy. We'd just jerk off the saddle and go to sleep on the damn thing. Later, I can't remember the circumstances, I got dismounted and put to riding a bus."

Upon relieving Ventura, Pierce had Col. Lee Vance order a patrol out under the command of then Lt. George J. Spies. This detail of cavalry was ordered to Asingan to make contact with the Japanese. In the progress of their movement, Spies's detachment destroyed with explosive charges the key bridges along the Carmen–Tayug road to clear a withdrawal route for the 91st Division. Spies's troopers had to swim to the TNT charges carrying boxes of matches in their mouths to keep them dry to light the fuses. The 26th patrol encountered advance elements of Lt. Col. Kuro Kitamura's 48th Reconnaissance Regiment at Asingan, across the river from Tayug. By 7 p.m. Spies's patrol was driven back by superior enemy numbers to the 26th Cavalry lines where the Japanese then proceeded to attack the 2nd Squadron's line in force. (This was while Seymour was on the river with his patrol.) Only the soft mud of the riverbank prevented Japanese tanks from crossing immediately. The enemy laid down heavy fire, mostly with little effect on the 26th positions. They then shifted to launching two frenzied banzai assaults, which earned them only murderous casualties from the disciplined fire of the battle-tested, well-dug-in 26th troopers. The new M-1 rifles were fast gaining respect. The fight raged into the night until about 2 a.m., when the Japanese finally gained the opposite shore. The 26th scouts broke off the action and by 4 a.m. Tayug was in enemy hands. Blowing eight Agno bridges between Tayug and Carmen as it retired, the decimated 26th passed through General Stevens's line at 5:45.

Colonel Pierce withdrew the 26th to the 91st Division line, ten miles to the southeast. As previously ordered at around 10 p.m. on the 25th, the 91st Division (PA) with the 26th Cavalry attached was ordered to pull back to the D-3 line and deploy at San Jose. Acting as a rear guard, the 26th was ordered to hold the river line at Tayug to cover the 91st withdrawal and protect the NLF right flank. The 92nd Combat Team, a shell force from the 91st, was ordered to take position to the left of Colonel Pierce's 26th and delay along the Agno River as far south as Carmen on the D-4 line. Company C of the 192nd Tanks was assigned to support the cavalry defending the Agno River crossing at Tayug. Once again the fates of the 26th and the 192nd were entwined by circumstances of necessity.

During the heavy fighting on the Tayug line, Col. Tom Trapnell noticed that the two heavy machine guns protecting the left flank had paused in their counter-firing, thus causing a severe potential threat on that end of the 26th lines. These were two water-cooled guns manned by Philippine army personnel attached to the 26th. He called out to 2nd Squadron's Sgt. Maj. Eleseo Mallari, an able and dependable senior noncom, and ordered him to get over to the gun positions and see what was causing the stoppage problem. Mallari at this point was exhausted from hunger and lack of sleep. However, he was steadfastly loyal to Trapnell, and, although there were other messengers who could be utilized, his first instincts of training discipline, which decreed "obey first before complaining," got him on the move.

As he got about twenty-five yards from the gun positions, he observed with dismay that the gunners and their commander (a young, Philippine army "third" lieutenant, fresh out of officer's school, his rank being that conferred on fresh graduates from officer training and considered rookies expected to defer mostly to experienced noncoms) had abandoned their guns in the face of the enemy without even destroying their ammunition. Apparently, they were incorrectly anticipating the withdrawal of the 26th. Normally, in such circumstances, when men are unable to carry their guns, they are to disable the guns and dispose of the ammo to prevent them from falling into the hands of the enemy. This is what the commander and his gunners should have done. The inexperienced lieutenant and his equally green gunners had failed. Mallari's arrival pulled them up short. The latter threatened the young officer and his gunners at pistol point to return to their guns and resume their counterfire. In a deadly serious, menacing tone, Mallari told them bluntly, "It is better that all of you get back to your posts or die on the spot. You are threatening the regiment to a slaughter." The young officer recognized without hesitation that the better part of valor was to return with his men to their positions and resume firing.

The Japanese persisted with their futile but heavy pressure until about 2:30 a.m. on 26 December, at which time the planned, phased withdrawal of the last elements of the 26th from the Agno positions was put into effect. Mallari recalled later that the withdrawal from the Tayug line was done in haste because of heavy pressure from enemy tanks pushing across the river. While executing the withdrawal, the 2nd Squadron (at that time composed of Troops E and F only) was receiving heavy fire from the flanks and rear. Under murderous fire, the cavalrymen had to destroy bridges while at the same time struggling to break contact with the hard-pressing, aggressive Japanese. Even in this chaos, the 26th's luck was miraculous, although the 2nd Squadron's men and horses were badly scattered.

However, according to the 26th executive officer Maj. Lee Vance's diary records, the 26th's losses were one horse killed and one enlisted trooper, Private 1st Class Belio, shot in the thumb. The order of withdrawal was: 2nd Squadron, HQ Troop 1st squadron, scout cars, and the attached 192nd Tank Company. En route, the cavalrymen created havoc for the advancing Japanese by blowing eight bridges between Tayug and San Quentin. Two troopers were lost in these risky demolitions. The Japanese later were forced to admit that their attempt to cut off the defending forces before they could move onto the Bataan Peninsula was a complete failure due largely to the stubborn, well-planned and -executed delaying tactics of the superbly disciplined 26th Cavalry. One Japanese officer was quoted as saying, "It was like fighting spirits and devils." Already there was muttering amongst the Japanese Imperial Army Staff that General Masaharu Homma was bungling his assigned timetable for the invasion of the Philippines. Agitating ambitiously on the sidelines for an investigation was none other than the sinister Col. Masanobu Tsuji, flushed with the fresh successes of his planning against the British and Dutch in Malaya and Java and basking in higher than ever favor in the eyes of his emperor.

The regiment marched toward Umingan and arrived there at about 5:45 a.m., 26 December. On arrival, Colonel Pierce was informed that General Wainwright considered the delaying actions of the cavalry so successful that he had ordered the 26th to Santa Rosa to become the NLF main reserve. Pierce was stunned by this, considering the dog-tired condition of his regiment. He realized that Santa Rosa would simply be too far for such worn men on horseback to reach without marching day and night, a demand he regarded impossible considering the present physical state of his men and horses. He ordered the regiment to dismount, disperse, and rest as best they could. They badly needed a respite and a chance to check on the condition of horses and equipment. Then Pierce wasted no time going to meet with Wainwright about the situation. On arrival Pierce found Wainwright gone elsewhere, but he was able to obtain from the general's chief of staff Lt. Col. Johnny Pugh approval for a change in orders. The 26th's new bivouac site would be the town of Mexico, well behind NLF's defense phase line D-5, where the regiment was to hold for several days. Even so, the horses and men were in such worn shape that the regiment was told to take its time getting to the new rest and reorganization position. In addition, Pierce received the welcome news that at Mexico Capt. John Fowler's Troop G and the scout car section under Lieutenant Cunningham would rejoin the main body of the regiment after their detached defensive movements in the Cagayen Valley. With the exception of Ralph Praeger's Troop C, now completely cut off in the mountain province north of Baguio, the regiment would be together again as a cohesive unit for the first time since before the onset of the war.

S-2 Maj. William Chandler in his diary recorded that the 26th moved out of Umingan at 7:15 p.m. on 26 December and arrived in Munoz at around 2:30 a.m. on the 27th, where once again the regiment slipped behind the lines of the 91st Division whose troops had passed them in trucks during the night. Departure from Munoz was made around 7:15 p.m. and the regiment reached San Isidro at 6:30 a.m. on the 28th. It had been a long and exhausting march for animals and men in such poor condition, but finally the 26th had reached a relative sanctuary well behind the front of the 91st lines. There at San Isidro Troop G rejoined from Bongabong, where it had been since early December. Leaving San Isidro at 7:30 in the evening of the 28th, the worn regiment finally reached Mexico at 1:30 a.m. and were met by Cunningham and his scout car section.

Once at Mexico the 26th farriers feverishly set about general refitting and shoeing the horses, many of which were in extremely poor shape. About one third of the regiment's animals had been lost in the past days' fighting and withdrawals, and roughly the same fraction of troopers had also been killed, wounded, or listed as missing. By some miraculous means, most of the regiment's support vehicles and farriers with their equipment had managed to get to Mexico, and on the whole, the 26th was able to mend itself back into a respectable state of operational condition, not to mention receiving some much-welcomed hot meals.

At Mexico, Colonel Pierce remarked to his executive officer, Col. Lee Vance, that it looked finally like the 26th was once more a relatively unified, effective fighting force and that with just a little sufficient rest, the regiment would again be ready to take on any real trouble.

However, fate was not to favor any significant respite for the dogged but battered 26th. The Japanese launched determined attacks against the sector of the D-5 line that ran along the Bamban River. Fearing a rapid, unwelcome breakthrough against the defending Philippine army troops, Wainwright ordered the 26th Cavalry north to Porac, twenty-six kilometers behind D-5.

At about noon on 29 December, Col. Frank Nelson, Wainwright's G-3 for the NLF, arrived at the 26th bivouac with orders that the regiment was to march on Porac that night. This was a dismal blow to the 26th, whose men and horses were still exhausted and battered, and much of their equipment was damaged from the past week of heavy combat and forced movement. The regiment had just begun a basic reorganization to make two full-strength troops out of the three decimated ones in each squadron. Colonel Nelson was shown the situation on the spot. A dismayed Clint Pierce immediately dispatched Major Chandler to accompany Nelson to General Wainwright's headquarters to plead for a few days' delay in order that his weary regiment could more efficiently rest and regroup. There Wainwright's chosen chief of staff, Col. William F. Maher, a veteran of World War I and a thoroughly professional, ascetic, and intelligent officer, sympathized with Pierce's plight and displayed as much consideration as the situation would allow. He gave the 26th a twenty-four-hour extension but said reluctantly that it was absolutely all he could do. It would have to suffice.

A still weary but uncomplaining 26th Cavalry moved out from Mexico at 7 p.m. on 30 December. They marched over sixty grueling kilometers West to Porac, arriving at midnight. At Porac the 26th completed its reorganization throughout the remainder of the 30th and then the 31st. Troops E and F, which had suffered the severest losses, were combined into one troop under command of Capt. John Z. Wheeler and, with Troops A and G, formed the three-troop horse squadron under command of Maj. Tom J. H. Trapnell. Troops B and Machine Gun Troop were dismounted and formed into a motorized unit mounted in buses and trucks under command of Capt. Joseph R. Barker Jr. (which is how Clint Seymour ended up on a bus). Headquarters and Service Troops remained roughly the same with vacancies and gaps filled by dismounted men from Machine Gun and B Troops. This makeshift reorganization was made imperative because sufficient replacements of men and animals were simply not available. One unusual but welcome addition to the regiment showed up in the form of some British Bren gun carriers (small, lightly armored but useful tracked vehicles with a capacity for only four or five men at most but with the ability to haul heavy equipment that would otherwise be burdening tired horses, mules, and men). This orphaned equipment, minus Bren guns, originally destined for ill-fated Singapore, got dumped in Manila in the beginning days of the war and was subsequently offered to and snapped up by enterprising 26th Cavalry scavengers for the regiment's motorized units. They arrived at Porac late on 31 December having been brought there from Manila by a detail commanded by chief regimental veterinarian Capt. William Gochenour and 1st Lt. Robert L. Carusso. They would later prove quite useful on the way to and once in Bataan.

The vehicles also bore a not-too-clandestine supply of wet goods with which to modestly celebrate a New Year's Eve end to 1941, a year thought best buried far and deep in memory by members, to a man, of the 26th Cavalry.

17

Baliuag: The 192nd's Revenge

Control of the USAFFE armored forces was still split between MacArthur's HQ in Manila and General Wainwright's command, thus leaving the latter at a distinct disadvantage with regard to his latitude in use and displacement of U.S. armor in his defense of Northern Luzon. Chain of command was a muddle down the line.

On 23–24 December the 192nd Tank Battalion commander, carrying out his orders to keep one company south of the Agno River, was told at General Wainwright's HQ that "I'm the immediate battle commander and you will take orders from us." And thus that company was sent north. All three of the line companies were operating north of the Agno when the main bridge at Carmen was bombed out. A Company's commander, Captain Wright, was killed at Urdaneta the night of 23–24 December. As only two highway bridges remained, the tanks finally had to make end runs to get south of the Agno on that night, with A Company coming out via Malasique and Bayambang according to instructions "if the bridge [highway] was blown," which did occur. They met Japanese resistance early in the evening and came out the next morning at about 10:20.

As reported by the battalion commander, the 192nd received a written order from one division commander to cover his withdrawal, which it did, the action taking it from a key point when one of the other companies was far better situated to have carried out that particular mission. With his fighting element all north of the Agno in a maze of streams, with his main line of supply and evacuation broken, and the strong prospect of being caught there, and with each general officer encountered becoming his "immediate battle commander," the battalion commander (Maj. Theodore Wickford) needed a free hand to do his best to carry out his mission rather

228

than follow arbitrary orders. He had now lost a ninth of his tanks and two of his company commanders.

On 24 December Tank Group Headquarters was based at Manila and then moved north with the 194th (minus Company C, which was left with the South Luzon Force) arriving with it on Christmas Day. In accordance with USAFFE orders received on the Agno on 25 December to cover the withdrawal of the North Luzon Force on successive phase lines, the south bank of the Agno was to be held twenty-four hours, with withdrawal on the night of 26–27 December to a line (Santa Ignacia–Gerona–Santo Tomas–San Jose) then to withdraw the night of 27–28 to the Tarlac–Cabanatuan line.

Thus it was that the 192nd was withdrawing in phases that kept armored elements roughly in support of the 26th Cavalry in its movements south from Tayug to Porac.

On the night of December 26–27, all hell broke loose for Company A, 194th Tanks. At about 10:30, Lieutenant Costigan arrived with the remnants of his platoon at Rancho Rosario, San Miguel, where Tank CP had been established earlier that evening. Costigan reported that the lines had withdrawn from the right. Threat from the enemy had come in that way and made a roadblock with antitank guns covering at Carmen. Costigan had forced his way through, losing two tanks and three men. The other three tanks were badly hit but were regassed, repaired, and sent back to report to battalion CP at San Miguel on Route 3. He reported the new company commander, Lieutenant Burke, and his sergeant apparently dead near the cross road at Carmen. (Burke, wounded the second time since the beginning, actually survived and was captured, his tank being destroyed.) The balance of A Company of the 194th made a spectacular dash out, one tank at least going across the whole front with hostile fire impact and its own return fire making a pyrotechnic spectacle. Lieutenant Petrie fought his way out and across the river before the bridge was blown, losing but one tank. This was at Bayambang on the Agno. D Company had to come out across country reaching Route 3, North of Moncada, at about 2 a.m., receiving fire from the highway as they approached, paralleling the railroad embankment running NW–SE. The two bridges at Moncada had been blown by the withdrawing infantry division. The major bridge had crossed a stream with high banks, and reconnaissance found no way across. The company commander reluctantly ordered tanks dismantled of guns and radios and destroyed according to standard operating procedure. Fifteen tanks had gotten out and were immobilized on the side of the road (reported later by U.S. airmen as enemy tanks). One platoon commander could not bring himself to major destruction (i.e., shooting into successive tanks with a 37mm, a grenade in the engine compartment, or by fire with a can of gas) and merely pulled out the wiring and rheostats, hoping eventually to salvage the tanks. Unfortunately, the Japanese did so, one of these tanks appearing later just north of Baliuag on 31 December and several more later in Bataan.

Later than night, Colonel Rodman, of one of the divisions being supported by the 192nd, informed Major Wickford that "HQ had changed their plan to a straight line from Carmen to Umingan." This uncovered the river and left the supporting tanks badly exposed.

"On the next order," Wickford informed him, "you had been informed that a new line would not form until 7 a.m. or so the next day." Again checking the CPs of the units on the line, Wickford found they all had orders to be on the new line around midnight and were beginning to send people back by busloads. Wickford later reflected that these buses might better have been used to salvage badly needed supplies. Instead, the tankers had to destroy a major part of forty-four thousand gallons of drummed 100-octane gas at the advanced landing field near Carmen, as they could not get out on 26 December. They also reported several caches of 75mm ammunition on Route 3 that also couldn't be removed. The latter had been designated for use by 75mm SPMs supporting the tanks on Route 3. Five SPMs under Capt. Gordon Peck did manage notable defensive action at the San Manuel roadblock, however. One 75mm SPM had been in a house at the road junction at Carmen when last seen on the 26th. It had been previously pulled out, intercepted twice, then sent back. It was not there, unfortunately, when the Japanese came in and established their roadblock at Carmen at about 9:30 on the 26th.

At 9:30 the right element of the 194th (West of Carmen) received a message from the 11th Division, marked sent at 7:30, that the line was pulling back at that time, uncovering the Carmen–Tayug road and ordering the 192nd tanks in that division zone to withdraw before the bridges therein, clearing the way to the rear, were to be blown at 2330. This presented a literal disaster to Captain Altman of Company D, not to mention leaving the 26th Cavalry, still holding in rear guard, out on a limb. Altman and his surviving men crossed the streams (two of them) at Moncada with their movable weapons, tank and personnel, and some radios, and were reported out to the Group Command at 2:30 in the morning on 27 December. One lieutenant, Hart, and his crew elected to remain on the line instead of coming out cross-country. Hart many days later sent a message to Group Command by a Filipino, reporting himself and crew still, as late as 7 January 1942, "continuing sabotage and harassment in vicinity of Ft. Stotsenburg." Hart was later reported killed as a captain of guerrillas sometime in 1943, according to Filipino accounts after the war. Hart was assisting Major Nelson of Group staff. He was captured and was shot in an abortive execution at the infamous Camp O'Donnell on 14 or 15 April 1942. Major Nelson crawled out of a mass burial pit in the night (rain had delayed the Japanese from filling it in) and escaped, only to die later of other causes.

27 DECEMBER 1941

The D-3 line

General Wainwright was frantically trying to deal with Japanese break-throughs in the center of his D-2 line at Carmen by General Tsuchibachi's 2nd Formosa, a battalion of the 1st Formosa and the 4th Tank Regiment (with air support by twelve planes of the 8th and 16th Light Bombardment Regiments and east at Tayug with Tsuchibachi's 48th Reconnaissance Regiment and supporting armor. In a matter of a few hours, the Japanese raced eastward, leaving Brougher's 11th Division only the Manila railroad line as a means of retreat. With one locomotive and some freight cars, the trapped men of the 11th units escaped to the new D-3 line. The dogged 26th Cavalry rear guard were left to make their epic withdrawal from the Agno south to Mexico and finally to Porac.

Now, on the D-3 Line, Wainwright's force stood at the thinnest, widest, least defensible of the five defense lines of the NLF withdrawal. Catastrophe threatened, but an almost miraculous turn of events changed the situation. There was no attack by the Japanese anywhere along the forty-five mile long, thinly held NLF line. General Homma had decided to pause in his attack in order to reinforce his units, bring up more supplies, and consolidate his lines. His intelligence informed him that Wainwright's forces facing him were badly shattered, MacArthur had transferred his headquarters to Corregidor from Manila, and that, he incorrectly concluded, signified the Fil-American forces planned no more than a minor delaying action for Bataan. Homma met with his staff and formulated a plan to occupy Manila as quickly as possible, and once taking the capital city, his forces would easily conduct mopping up action of the defending forces. He mistakenly concluded that enemy withdrawal on to Bataan would merely simplify his capture of Manila and force the campaign to an early conclusion. He would be made to long regret his error.

Wainwright did not hesitate to make full use of the strange lull. He labored tirelessly at his headquarters with his staff, reviewing maps and defense positions and assessing supplies and the condition of his troops and the disposition of the main of MacArthur's forces and their chances to pull off an effective withdrawal on to Bataan. It was sharply clear that the junctions comprising San Fernando, Pampanga, and the all-important Calumpit bridges had to be kept open at all costs if General Jones's Southern Luzon Force were to have any chance at all of passing through successfully. If any part of these key points was lost or abandoned, the SLF as well as parts of the NLF could be written off. Wainwright felt compelled to alter the original plan for withdrawal, which called only for minimal holding of the D-4 line before moving South to D-5 for an all-out holding action to allow the southern forces through the gate. He decided that his weary soldiers must make a firm stand at the D-4 line, extending twenty-five miles from Tarlac east to Cabanatuan offering maximum delay until relieved, then move back and hold D-5 as long as humanly possible, thus giving the bulk of the withdrawal maximum time to avoid being trapped outside Bataan. Had the 26th Cavalry not made their stubborn, costly stands at Binalonan and Tayug, frustrating the Japanese push, Wainwright's D-4 line would already have been overrun.

The very afternoon Wainwright was shifting his orders, utter chaos began to gather steam on the vital San Fernando road. A huge convergence of NLF units ordered south. Stragglers, deserters, convoys from Manila with troops and supplies, and the first of the southern units all piled together in the bottleneck route through San Fernando, Pampanga, with the goal of reaching the elusive safety of Bataan. Soon the immense logjam of humanity came to a stop. The heat was almost unbearable, and the cold terror of being massacred by Japanese aircraft was widespread. Streets were clogged with every form of vehicle—trucks, ambulances, cars, red and yellow Pambusco public buses, ox and pony carts (calesas). The panic went on until late that evening when finally a military police unit pushed its way in and was able to establish some form of control.

In the meantime on 28 December Wainwright had moved his HQ south near the village of Bacolor to a damp, musty building in a convent, St. Mary's Academy. Skinny and his staff were graciously given mass by the priest and hymns by the choir at the small, nearby chapel.

The Japanese resumed their offensive, and the D-4 line was somehow held by its hungry and exhausted defenders for two days. The attacks seemed to have no pattern, and no one knew where the enemy would hit next. On 29 December, though, the Japanese hit the right flank at Cabanatuan hard and seized it. They then pushed south and west, threatening to flank the 11th Division (PA) holding the D-4 center and move behind the line to cut off much of the NLF defense. But the 11th held tenaciously, and one of its battalions surprised the Japanese with a vicious counterattack. It soon became obvious, however, that the D-4 line couldn't hold on much longer. The 91st Division (PA) had been overwhelmed, and Wainwright had the survivors taken south on buses to regroup. The danger to the critical Calumpit bridges was increasing by the minute, so the NLF units were ordered to withdraw to the D-5 line. Once there, farther retreat was out of the question until the SLF was on Bataan and out of danger. The beleaguered men of the NLF now knew it was hold or die.

AMBUSH AT BALIUAG AND THE
DEFENSE OF CALUMPIT

In the meantime, elements of the 192nd Tanks from Northern Luzon and the 194th Tanks coming north from Southern Luzon and Manila were gradually converging to hold the gates open for the withdrawal of MacArthur's beleaguered forces into the Bataan Peninsula. The defensive lines at Plaridel and Calumpit, both south of the key Angat River crossing village of Baliuag, would be crucial to withdrawal into Bataan. The little town was made up of rambling houses and nipa huts scattered along the strategic Route 5 and straddled the banks of the Angat River. The town commands the approaches to Plaridel, six miles to the south, which is located at the intersection of Route 5 and several secondary roads, two of which extend along opposite banks of the Angat to Route 3 and the vital Calumpit bridges some eight miles to the northwest. The South Luzon Force and those elements of the NLF in the area would have to pass Plaridel and along these secondary roads to cross the bridges at Calumpit. South of Plaridel lay the invader's route to Manila.

Meanwhile, the Japanese at Cabanatuan split their attack force, sending one element westward attempting to get behind and cut off the D-4 defense and the other pushing hard straight down Route 5 toward Baliuag. General Tsuchibashi, commander of the 48th Division, was fully aware of the significance of the Baliuag–Plaridel area and on 30 December had ordered two tank regiments and a battalion of infantry to advance from Cabanatuan to the Angat and cut the route from Manila to San Fernando. This force, commanded by Col. Seinosuke Sonoda of the 7th Tank Regiment and supported by a company of engineers, was marching unopposed down Route 5 toward Plaridel on the night of 30 December.

Baliuag stood smack in the path of the aggressively pressing Japanese forces under Colonel Sonada, which had broken through at Cabanatuan and were now pushing hard down Route 5 east of the Candaba swamp. Once they reached Plaridel, where a road led west to Route 3, it would be only a short distance east of the two important bridges at Calumpit. If the Japanese could secure Plaridel and the bridges quickly enough, they would cut off any retreat of Fil-American troops still south of Calumpit and, by gaining position west of the Pampanga River behind the D-5 line, they could block the Bataan withdrawal. MacArthur had realized the seriousness of this contingency as soon as the Japanese had taken Cabanatuan and had moved quickly to send reinforcements from both North and South Luzon Forces to hold Plaridel and the road north as far as Baliuag. So it was that defending Baliuag became key to holding Plaridel, which had become crucial to both holding the D-5 line and keeping open the bridges at Calumpit, and escape for his forces into Bataan. Failure to hold here literally spelled doom for MacArthur's entire defense plan.

On 29 December orders were received by the Provisional Tank Corps HQ from USAFFE to occupy and hold the line behind the Bamban River. The tank commanders were directed to organize the antitank defense of the Bamban line in collaboration with the NLF commander, Wainwright. The considerable defensive preparations would include fire trenches and tank obstacles, including log barriers, complex wire, and staked areas and cleared fields of fire. The latter involved extensive leveling of sugar cane crops. The Tarlac line was evacuated that night and the Bamban line was ordered held until further orders. For some reason, NLF set up its group command post at an inconvenient location at Magalang, west of Mt. Arayat. The HQ detachment consisted of one general officer, two field officers, two captains, and ten enlisted men. This small group had to drive and service two half-tracks, two quarter-ton C&R cars, two sedans, two motorcycles, six machine guns, and two radios in operation around the clock. There was little or no equipment to properly maintain a command post. There was no mess, quartering was haphazard, and living conditions were bare and almost constantly mobile while attempting to serve what in peace time had been a much smaller force seen to by an HQ staff of some 18 senior officers, 141 enlisted men, 14 radios, numerous half-tracks, quarter- and half-ton C&R cars, trucks, and the like, supported by medium tanks, a force involving some 50 wheeled and tracked vehicles. The vital necessity of coordinating with only two radios, the tank units now covering four divisions of the NLF and two of the SLF, operating over a hundred miles apart, demanded constant movement of the Group Command to maintain effective and physical contact, coordination and cooperation, overall supply, and sufficient reconnaissance for the units under its control in view of the now rapidly changing situation on the line. Obtaining sufficient tank fuel, ammunition, and spare parts from prepared roadside caches presented formidable problems and wasted effort to the limited transport capabilities of the tank units so crucial to the D-5 defense. Efforts to strengthen the supply situation were all but hopeless. The tank radio set-up at Group HQ USAFFE had been abandoned because of the last-minute denial of trucks to transport HQ equipment when Tank Command left Manila on 24 December. All that could be salvaged was what could be jammed into a single extra sedan. The armored Ordnance Company might well have been a more proper HQ location, but its rearward situation necessitated by heavy mobile shop equipment and isolation to enable constantly increasing maintenance work made this impractical.

In the meantime, C Company/192nd Tanks under the command of Lt. William Gentry, from Harrodsburg, Kentucky (all of his original unit, B/192nd, were from Harrodsburg), which had supported the 26th Cavalry in their withdrawal, blasted machine gun nests and blew Agno River bridges, south from Rosario to Tayug and then to Umingan, San Isidro, San Jose, and on down to Bongabon. At this point the 26th, under orders, split from the 192nd to march southwest across country all the way to Santa Rosa on Route 3, well south of the D-4 line. Gentry later related the actions of his C/192nd tanks around Bongabon Kabu to the south: "We encountered the Japanese at Bongabon and then, at Kabu, we blew the bridge and waited for the Japanese to move in. At this particular time, we felt that we needed to gain information as to how the Japanese made their attacks. We camouflaged one platoon of C/192nd just south of the river at Kabu and waited for the Japs to cross. Our infantry troops were then ten or twelve miles further south, and the only thing we had in the vicinity was tanks. Due to the fact that we had them very well camouflaged under *nipa* houses and covered up with brush and clumps of trees, all we had to do was talk, shout and make noise in general to make the Japanese think they had a sizable force of troops in front of them. They hesitated a while and then began their attack when they crossed the river. As they made their river crossing, we could hear them talking and shouting. Then we began to hear their tanks operating on the opposite side of the river. Their infantry came first, and we sat through about three hours of troops streaming by before they ever discovered we were there. In fact, I sat on the front of a tank and described their complete action by radio back to HQ and where they were at this particular time, giving a complete account of it.

"They finally discovered us by a Jap trying to walk through the brush pile I had standing around my tank. On being discovered, the only thing left to do was sound the siren and attack. We had a sharp skirmish in a field just south of the river at Kabu for quite some time and then withdrew down to the town of Cabanatuan [south of the D-4 line]. We still had ammunition left but had to withdraw south to join up with the rest of our forces. But, coming into Cabanatuan, we found artillery and plenty of other equipment there, so we stayed in the town for two hours doing everything we could to chop up the Japanese units and to halt them before they proceeded south. We then pulled back to the town of Gapan where we picked up more ammunition, gasoline and pulled back down to the vicinity of Baliuag [south of the D-5 line]."

While Gentry and C company were racing toward Baliuag, General Weaver on 29 December had ordered D/192nd over from east of the Pampanga, the 192nd axis of withdrawal being Route 5, to supplement the twenty remaining tanks left in the 194th zone, of which Route 3 was the axis. East of Concepcion, Lieutenant Reed of D Company/192nd and his sergeant died under a bridge when their half-track was hit by artillery. Reed, refusing evacuation in favor of the other wounded, was recommended for the Silver Star.

THE 192ND TANKERS AVENGE LINGAYEN

General Weaver reported on 30–31 December: "Hostile action became more aggressive east of the Pampanga. Tank reconnaissance counted 30 medium hostile tanks of 35 earlier reported by our air in the vicinity of Cabanatuan. Later, eight of these medium tanks were ambushed by a platoon of C Company/192nd as they lined up north of the stream north of Baliuag awaiting restitution of a blown bridge. The remnants withdrew east and, as expected, accomplished a crossing elsewhere. At 1700 [5 p.m.] they came into Baliuag and engaged two platoons of C/192nd in a running fight back and forth through the town. Our light tank proved its superiority over the enemy medium tank—in contrast with its difficulty in coping with the Japanese light tank. Our bag: eight medium tanks. None of the rest appeared."

Lt. William Gentry reported on 30 December: "We reached Baliuag late in the morning and had time to make a complete reconnaissance before the Japanese moved in on us. I sent Sgt. Allen on his motorcycle to scout out the edges of the town and the roads north to check on the progress of Jap patrols and south to scout out our route of withdrawal when the time came. At Baliuag we found ourselves confronted by a bridge that had not been blown by the engineers, a narrow gauge railroad bridge. We began digging in and preparing fighting positions at Baliuag while waiting there for the Japanese to advance south. At this particular point, we were given orders to hold at all costs because the troops from the South had to clear the bridges at Plaridel and Calumpit before we could withdraw. We were holding open the only route to Bataan.

"On the morning of December 31st, we made a reconnaissance run north on the route we had retreated on and on which we knew the Japanese were pushing south. We encountered several advance patrols, so we knew that they were well on us. We also knew that the bridge would be the only possible place they could cross the river, so we positioned our defenses in view of the railroad bridge which was in a large rice paddy at the edge of Baliuag."

Once again, C Company/192nd (now assisted by the 71st Field Artillery) ingeniously used town houses and nipa huts to conceal its force from the approaching enemy. Surprise was to be the tankers' most crucial weapon.

Early on the morning of 31 December, an advance detachment of Colonel Sonoda's force reached the outskirts of Baliuag. Japanese engineers, protected by tanks, attempted to repair the bridge north of town but were met by withering fire from the 71st artillerymen. Shortly thereafter, the enemy tanks found themselves under heavy fire from a platoon of C/192nd, which lay in their concealed positions below the stream. Badly mauled, the Japanese broke off the action and withdrew eastward. Shortly after, the enemy engineers were at it again, now putting down planking on the bridge to support tanks, which began to effect a crossing some time before noon.

Lieutenant Gentry: "By late afternoon, the Japanese assembled a considerable number of tanks at the end of the bridge. The enemy now had placed lookouts in the steeple of the town church. We had one platoon under the command of Lt. Marshall Kennedy to the southeast of the bridge. I had my platoon to the south. Lt. Collins was south on the road leading out of Baliuag with the remainder of the tanks. Early that morning, we had sent Lt. Preston south after we had observed the Japanese trying to move across the bridge. We had him go south to find a bridge that he could cross to find some way that he could get back up on the opposite side of the river to surprise the Japanese. He left early that morning and became lost in some way. He never made it back. We did, in fact, have to look him up the following day to find out where he was. We found him still trying to find a crossing, but he and his men were ok.

"Late in the afternoon of 31 Dec., Major Morley came noisily riding into Baliuag in a jeep. At this point, during the day, we had maintained complete radio silence so we would not give our positions away. We had all remained within the houses under which we had the tanks parked and had zeroed all our guns in on the collection of Jap tanks in the field only some fifteen yards in front of us. When Morley rattled his way in, he came directly to our house, came inside; and I informed him in a fairly unfriendly whisper that we were sitting there looking at an unsuspecting collection of Jap tanks out in the field and also that the Jap look-outs in the church steeple were now all excited as to why he was there. We told him that the only thing for him to do was get in his fucking jeep and drive out of town just as though nothing had happened. We said we'd hold until we thought he was clear of the town, and then we would attack before the Nips in the steeple, who were now bound to be curious, would investigate just what was going on in this house. Morley retreated out the door with a sheepish look on his face and took off in his jeep. We waited until we felt that he had enough time to clear and then opened fire with everything we had from the houses.

"Our first round of fire was concentrated on the collection of Jap tanks at the end of the bridge out in the open field. We then immediately pulled out from our position under the house and signaled Kennedy that we were going to herd the Japanese tanks in his direction. He held his position until Jap tanks came within view of his platoon, and, at this particular point, he and his men entered the fight with full force. At our first combined burst of fire, the now dismayed enemy immediately scattered out over the field and headed for the town."

Some of the Japanese also lurched in the direction of Kennedy's platoon southeast of town. In now fading daylight, the Americans were chasing the Jap tanks up and down the narrow streets like stampeded cattle, under buildings, through buildings, in complete disarray, firing into bahays and nipas like so many toy houses and turning the part of Baliuag in Japanese hands into a shambles. Japanese infantry scattered in utter panic, firing small arms futilely at the pursuing tanks. The brief tank-to-tank battle that followed was one sided. It was a welcome sight to vengeance-hungry men of the 192nd. After the two-hour running brawl, the Americans, their main guns almost white hot, withdrew, leaving behind eight destroyed Japanese medium tanks. None others appeared. It was sweet revenge for Lingayen and a satisfying way to celebrate the end of what had been a generally lousy year. When the melee subsided, the 192nd tankers were able to definitely establish that they had put eight enemy tanks out of action before being ordered to withdraw. They had also done considerable damage to the Jap infantry unit, in fact putting them to rout over the bridge whence they came. They left the town burning—the fires, of course, being of great help in chasing Jap tanks in the dark.

The battalion headquarters was naturally tuned in on Gentry's radio frequency and apparently having a picnic listening to the fight. Occasionally, they would break in and give words of encouragement, sort of like cheering on a football team. The only American casualty from the encounter was a sprained ankle when one of the boys attempted to get off his tank in a hurry to tell his part of the story after the fight was over and Gentry's people had been withdrawn to a safe area. They were completely out of ammunition; they had completely outmaneuvered and outfought the Japanese medium tanks. The little M-3 tanks were, of course, very fast and very maneuverable, and the new 37mm guns readily demonstrated that they packed a considerable wallop. It was one helluva New Year's Eve.

Gentry later commented, "We only had armor-piercing ammunition with us, however, the only ammo available for the new 37mm guns in the Philippine operation. There was plenty of high-explosive ammunition available for the old type 37mm guns, and later on we had ordnance take a projectile from old type 37mm shells, reduce the amount of powder in the shell and reinsert the high-explosive in the new type case and recrimp it. We used these to great effect in later operations on Bataan."

Allied artillery commanded by Colonel Fowler and self-propelled guns commanded by Colonel Babcock had remained quiet through the fight, unable to fire for fear of hitting their own people. But when C/192nd finally broke off their action, the big guns opened up on Baliuag and kept firing until 10 p.m., when Fowler and Babcock pulled their men and guns back to Plaridel and then west across the Pampanga.

1 JANUARY 1942

According to General Weaver: "Had it not been for the 192nd's sharp action at Baliuag, the plight of the 91st Division (PA) would have been desperate, even after it was augmented by units of the 71st Division (PA) that day. The 91st command reported that division reduced to an effective strength of only 200.

"The tanks paid for themselves there, although the only credit given them, in a syndicated account, was a statement that 'a company of the 192nd was sent in to help.' At that time, the 192nd [less one company] was in that sector entirely engaged. One company was on the western axis of withdrawal. The 194th [less the company in South Luzon] had been moved by USAFFE orders to a position in readiness at the barrio Apalit, northwest of the Calumpit Bridge [actually a pair of bridges] over the Pampanga River to insure the exit of the South Luzon Force and that part of the North Luzon Force east of the Pampanga."

CALUMPIT AND ESCAPE TO BATAAN

Shortly after their successful ambush, the 192nd tankers were pulled out of Baliuag on orders from General Weaver. They were instructed to pull back to the Calumpit bridgehead and hold there until all friendly troops had cleared from the south and elsewhere. To their dismay, when they reached the Calumpit bridges at 2:30 a.m. on 1 January, they found they had been dynamited by retreating forces. However, the American tanks somehow managed to get across the damaged spans. Just north of the bridges, they now found themselves in an area consisting completely of open rice paddies. The rice had been harvested in the area and had been left in large stacks there. Since Gentry and his men felt that the next attack would probably come at night, they moved into positions with their guns zeroed in on the rice stacks so that the first round of ammunition from their 37mms would be tracer ammunition, which would go through the stacks. The result would be fire to light up the area so the Japanese would be exposed to their guns.

They spaced their tanks about one hundred yards apart or more and, since they were the only troops in the area, kept up a constant chatter of shouting between tanks in order to convince the Japanese that there were enemy troops in front of them to hold up their advance. The Japanese began moving equipment across the bridge and troops from dusk until around midnight. At that particular point, they had advanced up within just a few yards of the waiting 192nd tankers. The Japanese steadily collected behind some houses directly to the front of the Americans until it seemed there couldn't be room for any more. They could be seen setting up mortar positions out a little ways, and the first volley of mortar fire dropped amongst the 192nd tanks, causing some minor shrapnel wounds to four men. At that point the tankers opened fire, setting the rice stacks afire, and opened up with a heavy stream of small arms and machine gun fire. Later, after leveling the enemy troops directly in front of them, the tankers began using their 37mms on the equipment they could see further out. It got to the point that the Americans were literally cutting down single Japanese troops with single 37mm rounds. The toll on the Japanese was fearsome, but by around 2 a.m. the tankers were completely out of ammunition, even though they had started out with more than their normal ammo supply. Finally, under orders, they pulled back to San Fernando, where they refueled and replenished their ammunition. They were then told to proceed to Porac. Withdrawing Allied troops from both the north and south were converging and clearing through San Fernando, and the Japanese were pushing hard in the Porac area with the intention to cut off the withdrawal at San Fernando.

One tragically serious foul-up in the NLF withdrawal occurred earlier on 14 December in the vicinity of Cabanatuan. Several large warehouses at "government central" were bulging with some ten million pounds of freshly harvested, bagged rice. The rice was not to be removed from the province in which it was stored without authority of the Commonwealth government, and that government, through the Civilian Emergency Administration, had notified the governors of the provinces that no rice or sugar was to be removed without authorization. The situation was reported to proper authorities, but no action was taken. There were also huge quantities of canned foods such as meat and fish stored there, which had belonged to the Japanese in North Luzon before the war. NLF advance depot commanders begged for authority to seize these goods but were denied permission. Always oversensitive to political protocol in the Philippines, MacArthur incredibly ordered the rice and other foodstuffs left where they were as private property under Commonwealth control! It was a supply that later on Bataan might have spelled a considerable relief to the prevailing conditions of starvation and related disease destined to hasten conquest of the peninsula by the Japanese. No amount of pleas by Wainwright changed it.

At Porac, the tankers found the Philippine Army having considerable trouble from enemy artillery fire. They wasted no time finding the location of a Japanese artillery battalion, being informed of the exact position by a Filipino lieutenant who was returning from fighting there with the remnants of his platoon. The tankers pulled out and headed straight for the gun positions. When they got there, they were able to knock out three of the enemy guns, but the rest of the Japanese beat a hasty retreat and dispersed. The tanks chased them all over the area, putting out of action a number of Japanese trucks and decimating as much of their infantry as they could locate. After that encounter, the 192nd tanks were ordered to hold up at the Hermosa Bridge until the last Allied troops passed through. After some time there, Major Morely came up and told the tankers it was time for them to back up over the bridge. The Japanese were within small arms fire range at the point when the last tanks crossed over the bridge and blew it.

The Japanese had failed to cut off MacArthur's intended withdrawal into Bataan, and by the time they attacked again a few days later, they ran up against the defenders' first line of defense on Bataan. Homma's tidy, over-ambitious timetable had been badly shattered by a stubborn, unforgiving phased retreat spearheaded by an understrength, tenacious horse cavalry regiment and a wily group of green American National Guard tank soldiers.

The gate had been effectively shut in the face of the invader.

EPILOGUE FOR THE TANKERS

Throughout the next months until the unavoidable surrender of Bataan to prevent a wholesale massacre of allied personnel by the Japanese, the 192nd and 194th Provisional Tank Battalions were in constant action. They were particularly effective covering the phased withdrawal of Wainwright's forces' phased withdrawals southward from the series of primary allied defense lines established across the peninsula and especially in the engagements known as the Battle of the Points and the Battle of the Trails. The Guardsmen squeezed every possible ounce of use that they could out of their dwindling numbers of tanks, steadily being reduced by a combination of attrition from combat damage, mechanical wear, and breakdown from horrible terrain and weather conditions. They constantly cannibalized their vehicles to the extent that at times a single tank might be a combination of three or more wrecks. Ammunition and fuel were simply used as much and as often as they could obtain them. Japanese troops became terrified by the horrific sound of the big airplane engines of the M-3 tanks, knowing the mauling power that was overtaking them. American tankers became both feared and hated by the Japanese, and after the surrender, these men, along with Philippine Scouts, were singled out for particularly brutal treatment in captivity.

It is a monumental and touching tribute to the American and Filipino soldiers' spirit and depth of endurance that any of the cavalrymen of the Philippine defense campaign, horse or tank trooper, survived the ordeal from combat to captivity to liberation and return home (and often to military duty).

NOTE

1. Much of this chapter is derived from the official operations report of Brig. Gen. Jas. R. N. Weaver, CO Provisional Tank Group, USAFFE, 1941–1942.)

18

Manila Abandoned / Return to Stotsenburg/Layac Junction/Culis

25 DECEMBER 1941

Gen. Douglas MacArthur closed down his opulent penthouse apartments in the lovely Manila Hotel, leaving most of the furnishings and extensive library of some eight thousand books in immaculate order, with valuable furniture and ornamentation carefully covered with sheets and netting, as if the family were simply leaving for an extended vacation. At USAFFE's heavily guarded headquarters at No. 1 Calle Victoria, there was a beehive of frantic activity as staff prepared the huge accumulation of files, documents, office furniture, and all the other trappings of command control for immediate transfer to the new headquarters location in the fortified tunnels of the island fortress guarding any intruding entrance to Manila Bay, Corregidor (referred to generally as "The Rock").

MacArthur, his senior aides (frequently snidely referred to by subordinates and troops as his "court," senior of which was his tireless chief of staff, aide-de-camp, and confidant, the brittle, often arrogant, and aloof Lt. Col.—soon to be Maj. Gen.—Richard K. Sutherland), MacArthur's wife, Jean Faircloth MacArthur, and their small son, Arthur, with his doting Chinese amah, Ah Cheu, had already been transferred to Corregidor and were settling in as best they could in far less elaborate quarters.

On 26 December 1942, Manila was publicly declared an "open city," and the news was broadcast on Radio Tokyo. General Homma, however, appeared to be in no pressing hurry to actually occupy the capital city. Regardless of the accepted practices of war, raids by roving Japanese aircraft continued to bomb and strafe "targets of opportunity," which, roughly translated, amounted to anything visible that moved. In the meantime,

General Homma had established his 14th Army headquarters at Cabana-tuan, where by 31 December his staff received the detailed declaration of the surrender of Manila. He was content in a sense of false complacency. Intelligence reports of his subordinates and field commanders assured him that the Americans and Filipinos were being readily herded into a bottle-neck before the entrance to Bataan, where they were being cut off and trapped. One of them, Lt. Gen. Sasumu Morioka, quipped smugly that Wainwright's forces were "like a cat entering a sack." Homma at that point was feeling a complete, although to be proven mistaken, confidence that his forces were poised to tie the sack closed and thus bring about an early conclusion to his Luzon campaign. He had not yet been apprised of the stubborn, overwhelmingly effective Fil-American holding actions at Bali-uag, the Calumpit bridges, and Porac, allowing both the Northern and Southern Luzon Forces to escape to the deceptive haven of their new defen-sive positions on the dangerous peninsula.

On Christmas day, the USS *William L. Maclan*, a hospital ship based in Manila Bay, steamed out for Australia with 224 wounded Americans aboard. It was the last ship to escape.

In Manila itself, the municipal government under Mayor Jorge Vargas had made preparations for a peaceful entry by the new occupiers with all intent that there would be no incidents to incite retaliation against the citizenry. At strategic points around the city's outskirts, there had been prominent posting of notices declaring "OPEN CITY! NO SHOOTING OR RESIS-TANCE!" Radio broadcaster Don Bell, a West Coast American émigré, kept up repeated caution messages on Manila Station KGEI to the citizenry to remain calm. This was mixed with his ongoing, continuous daily stream of positive, encouraging mix of news and rumor, reassuring the Fil-American defenders that they would not be forgotten and that the people, both Fili-pino and American, were fully aware that they were putting up a magnifi-cent fight.

Don Bell was summarily shot dead by the Japanese on the first day they entered Manila.

In the course of overall allied military exit from Manila, the big, military Sternberg General Hospital, with a capacity of more than a thousand beds, was evacuated with all its personnel and patients. Many of the patients, most of the ambulatory, military personnel, returned to their units, whether fit for duty or not, when they learned of the gravity of the overall situation. In addition to Sternberg, a steadily increasing overflow of incom-ing wounded were hospitalized at Manila's once fashionable Jai Alai Club. The incoming patients there, for a first few days, were treated to luxurious meals prepared by the club's staff chefs and served by nattily dressed wait-ers, complete with white linen tablecloths and silver utensils. That state of luxury was short lived, however, when everything reverted over to a more mundane diet of military rations.

The evacuating military and volunteer nurses for the Manila medical facilities, some two hundred or so of them (the patient load per nurse would prove staggering), led by Capt. Martha C. Davison, were ordered to pack only their bare necessities for transfer to the newly set-up field hospitals on Bataan. They could take only a small, light bag with duty-white uniforms and essential items. They were assured that their other packed possessions would be sent on to them later. The bulk of these nurses were sent to "Hospital #1," located just outside Limay on Bataan. The "wards," with an official capacity of only around a thousand beds, were set up in nipa houses, Philippine dwellings six to eight feet off the ground on poles with split bamboo flooring spaced about three-quarters of an inch apart to allow food waste to fall through for domestic animals below to scavenge. There was a second hospital (#2) set up in the foothills at the base of Mt. Mariveles at the south end of Bataan. This so-called hospital consisted of tent shelters, at best, and open, unsheltered ground for litters. On arrival, the nurses, to best protect them from jungle insects and conditions, were issued army fatigue overalls, all of them male size 40–42. These unflattering garments swallowed the generally petite females directed to don them, but they served their intended purpose.

Upon arrival, Col. James Duckworth, commanding officer of the Limay medical facilities, gave nurse Lt. Juanita Redmond, from South Carolina, the task of setting up and organizing the operating rooms. When she opened the doors of the designated sites, she was assaulted with the smell of stale beer and the litter of empty cans. She enlisted the help of two American and two Filipino nurses assisted by several corpsmen and put the area in shape to do a grisly task far beyond its capacity.

All of Bataan was urgently digging in for what was all too soon to come.

30 DECEMBER 1941

Porac

While the 26th Cavalry was just south of Porac on Route 74 for rest and refitting, they were also near Route 3, just a few miles southeast of Fort Stotsenburg. They were positioned as force reserve on what would be the west flank of the eventual D-5 line. While a brief respite was at hand, Major Fleeger decided to make a reconnaissance to Fort Stotsenburg to ensure that secret maps were destroyed and vital papers recovered. He was joined by a general proposal that someone should accompany him to Stots to retrieve some of the more needed and valued belongings left behind by the officers. The same was true in the ranks of the troopers. Lt. John Wheeler and Cpl.

Eulalio Arzaga volunteered. Keys to quarters, foot lockers, cabinets, and the like were handed over with name tags on them. The most prevalent requests were for clean underwear and boots if there was room. Footwear was getting severely worn.

One particular request was made by Capt. George Kauffman, a handsome New Yorker, an heir to the Kaywoodie Pipe fortune who dearly loved and had raised thoroughbred horses. He also loved show girls, especially the exotic Russian Eurasians he encountered in Manila. His prime asset in attracting these priceless beauties was his beloved, fire-truck-red Buick convertible, which he'd had shipped from the states for stalking sensuous quarry. The gentlemanly and quiet Johnny Wheeler and a fun-loving staff officer at Stotsenburg, Lt. Gary Anloff, had been his favorite hunting companions. Privately, Wheeler sought favor (in the face of much competition) with a pretty, auburn-haired nurse lieutenant from Swansea in the coastal "low country" of South Carolina, Juanita Redmond. The latter, who spoke in the soft, alluring patois of her origins, had captivated Wheeler from the start. The attractive young woman thoroughly and frequently enjoyed afternoons at the Manila Polo Club watching the dashing young officers and various opponents playing the fast, hard-hitting game, not to mention the splendid, gala evenings after the games.

Kauffman pleaded with Wheeler to find someone to protect his priceless Buick until things died down. Fleeger and Wheeler commandeered a small supply truck while Arzaga followed on one of the motorcycles with sidecar scavenged in Manila. They made the trip fast, wary all the way of roving Jap planes. When they arrived they split up, Fleeger and Wheeler to Stots and Arzaga to Sapangbhato to check on his fellow troopers' families and collect any presents for them from loved ones.

Fort Stotsenburg was like a ghost town and manned by a skeleton force of maintenance troops, clerks, and a few headquarters staff officers. MacArthur had ordered the post abandoned on 24 December over the objections of some staff and line officers who thought this premature and the rush would cost the loss of much valuable equipment and needed gas supplies. On Christmas day, Lt. Col. Gyles Merrill, Wainwright's supply officer, informed Lt. Col. Charles S. Lawrence, CO of the big supply depot at Tarlac, Pampanga, that it must be evacuated to clear the area for the imminent move of the NLF to the D-4 line, which would run right through it. Again the defenders were forced to abandon or destroy large amounts of vital, strategic materiel, which would have hugely altered the desperate circumstances that would soon develop on Bataan.

At Stotsenburg, the lovely parade and polo fields were already overgrown with native grass and weeds, and the 26th stables were empty and silent. The houses on officers' row were showing signs of neglect but were still there and securely locked. Wheeler trooped the lonely line and, using his keys, heaped the small truck with requested items of clothing, especially fresh underwear, special mementos, and his prized pair of custom Peal boots. He went up to the headquarters building and by pure luck found Gary Anloff. Together they went down to have a look at Kauffman's precious red Buick. Other than a thick layer of dust, the car was in fine shape. Wheeler told Anloff it was his until Kauffman reclaimed it somewhere.

After about three hours, Fleeger and Wheeler rendezvoused with Arzaga, who had the motorcycle's sidecar and saddlebags stuffed to overflowing with fruits, cooked fried meats, cooked rice, homemade breads, and desperate messages from families for the 26th troopers. They looked sadly around the place, which offered up many good memories, and then gunned it back to the regiment.

John Zachary Wheeler would never see Fort Stotsenburg or its playing fields again.

Anloff kept his word. Not finding a key, he hot-wired the wonderful red Buick, which went with him back and forth to Bataan ferrying communications and office equipment and a few remaining personnel from Stotsenburg. He also gathered up some more of Wheeler's personal clothing and possessions. Anloff encountered him again at Isobela, about ten miles south of Stotsenburg, and gave him his possessions, including his treasured custom Peal riding boots. The ever gentlemanly Wheeler commented characteristically that at least now he could start the New Year dressed properly for war. The splendid red car survived Bataan to the very end at Mariveles. There Anloff sabotaged it, and its Japanese captors never could figure out how to make the beautiful vehicle run for them.

Out of frustration, they simply blew it up.

The next time Wheeler would encounter Anloff, they would both be fighting for survival as POWs in the cargo hold of a Japanese *maru*, one of the "hell ships" trying hurriedly to transfer all Caucasian Allied prisoners to Japan to prevent their liberation by forces recapturing the Japanese-occupied southern pacific islands and countries.

30 DECEMBER: THE LEFT FLANK OF THE D-5 LINE

Since arriving at its position on Route 74, south of Porac at midnight on 30 December, the 26th Cavalry regiment had been refitting while acting as reserve to General Capinpin's 21st Division on the left and General Brougher's 11th on the right holding the D-5 defense line north of Clark Field and Stotsenburg, running from the Zambales Mountains on the west (left) flank east to Aryat.

Seven miles south of Porac, at San Jose, the 26th, in force reserve, was at least partially rested and reorganized from its series of desperate fights. The regiment was now assigned to cover the left flank of the 21st Division and extend it west to the Zambales Mountains. The purpose was to protect the extreme west end and rear of the D-5 line. Colonel Pierce dispatched Troop G, equipped with pack radio, forward toward Porac to a position left of the 21st. He held the rest of his regiment in readiness at San Jose, also the location of the 192nd Tank Battalion and 21st Division HQ. Although the 26th engaged in a number of minor skirmishes, the Japanese seemed to concentrate their primary effort in repeated head-on assaults against the main line. Inexplicably, no determined attempt was made to turn the left flank.

On 31 December the two steel bridges spanning the Bamban River, one highway and one railroad, had been blown by engineers, but due to the dryness of the season, this presented no great obstacle to the advancing Japanese, who could ford the shallow stream with infantry and light vehicles. In order to strengthen the river line, Company C, 23rd Infantry, took position on the high ground north of the Bamban with support from the 21st Field Artillery. This paid off at about 1:30 New Year's morning when a company of enemy bicycle troops, an advance point from the Kanno detachment, were caught in the open and mauled by punishing fire from Company C. By 9:00 the remainder of the Kanno force reached Bamban and began to assault the river line. They were met by Company C and the artillery, and after an afternoon of sharp fighting with heavy shelling on both sides, the Japanese were forced to withdraw late in the day after failing to dislodge Company C.

The Japanese 9th Infantry and supporting units were reported moving south from Tarlac to reinforce the Kanno detachment, joining them at about 4 p.m. As their force came within range on the north side of the river, they were brought under fire by the 21st Field Artillery and failed in an attempt to cross. At nightfall, the 21st Division (PA) began withdrawal with Company C wading the Bamban to rejoin the main body. The entire division then went down Route 3 and turned southwest on Route 74 toward Porac.

Having received an unexpected bruising by the Filipinos, the Japanese now followed with caution, and it was not until 11:30 of 2 January that the Kanno detachment reached Angeles. The Japanese now finally had possession of Clark Field and Fort Stotsenburg.

Toward the east, the time had now come for the 11th Division (PA) to clear its D-5 positions and withdraw into Bataan. Early on 1 January 1942, the 11th CO, General Brougher, had ordered his field commander, Colonel Townsend, to have the 11th to begin withdrawal at 10:00 that evening. They were to retire by a route along the Magalang road through Mexico and San Fernando to Guagua, only some fifteen miles from Bataan. While the 11th was beginning its move, a reinforced Japanese infantry battalion with artillery support was pushing along the Magalang road in an attempt to cut the 11th's withdrawal. They hit Townsend's line just befgore 5 p.m. and were stopped cold by Maj. Helmert J. Duisterhof's 2nd Battalion, composed entirely of fierce, never conquered little Igorot troops from mountainside tribes. Despite meeting repeated attacks, the Igorots, supported by two 75mm SPM guns, did not budge and savaged the attackers. Another ploy by the Japanese to outflank the 11th by pushing through dense sugar cane fields also failed dismally. At the planned 8 p.m. deadline, the 11th Infantry broke off contact with the enemy and withdrew through the 194th Tank Battalion rear guard position. By 2 a.m. on 2 January, they reached Guagua, and during the night were joined by the remainder of the 11th Division. With the completion of this successful retrograde, the defenders of the D-5 line had escaped through San Fernando, yet again frustrating Japanese entrapment.

At the same time, the blowing of the Calumpit bridges marked the escape of the Southern Luzon Force, thus ending its separation from the NLF and blending MacArthur's forces as a single defense force for the battle of Bataan. The increasingly infuriated and frustrated Japanese commanders tried with renewed determination to cross the wide, swift, unfordable Pampanga River in pursuit. But when the bridges had been blown, the Americans and Filipinos sent back a covering force of 71st and 91st Division elements to assure the delay of any Japanese crossing. A second force consisting of the 23rd Infantry and a battery from the 21st Field Artillery moved into position farther north on the west bank of the Pampanga. The Tanaka detachment—2nd Formosa, less 3rd Battalion—and a battalion of the 48th Mountain Artillery, which had moved with caution from the debacle at Plaridel, reached Calumpit on the morning of 1 January only to find themselves facing a renewed covering force blocking their crossing of the Pampanga. Nerves on both sides were frayed. Green, but now blooded, Filipino troops were shaken by such a large Japanese force facing them at close quarters. Neither were their spirits lifted by swarms of Japanese bombers passing above on the way to pound Bataan. Nevertheless, when the Japanese repeatedly attempted to push across the uncooperative river, the Filipinos held. Finally, now disorganized and badly short of equipment, the last of the stubborn defenders were allowed to pass through San Fernando. The last elements of the rear guard, the tankers, reached the town at about 2 a.m. Finding it a ghost town, they blew the last bridge across the San Fernando River and sped down Route 7 in the darkness toward Guagua and then south to the junction at the small village of Layac.

Meanwhile, MacArthur communicated repeated pleas to Washington for a major effort by the United States to address the war in the Southwest Pacific and to reinforce the Philippines. His entreaties were greeted with solemn but superficial sympathy, but the president and his joint chiefs of staff were all in agreement that the threat by Germany superseded all else and that Winston Churchill's direct requests to alleviate the pressure on Great Britain and North Africa should have precedent in America's war effort. MacArthur, for all apparent purposes, was abandoned and, with his valiant but forlorn Philippine defense forces, left with little hope. All he and his staff could do was to try their best to cover up the realities of the denied Philippine relief.

On 2 January 1942 General Homma received an alarming communication from Imperial General Headquarters in Tokyo. He was informed that the whole timetable for the invasion of Java had been advanced by a month and because of this, his 48th Division, not scheduled to go to the 16th Army until the end of the Philippine campaign, was now needed immediately along with its 5th Air Group. In its place Homma was to receive the 65th Brigade, commanded by Lt. Gen. Akira Nara with a strength of about sixty-five hundred troops. This was a blow to Homma, who was just about to commence a vital attack. Now he found himself inflicted with a change-over of units, which not only reduced his number of available troops but gave him a force that had been raised only a year before as a garrison unit and was made up largely of untested enlisted men with only a month's training. Its three infantry regiments—the 122nd, 141st, and 142nd—were composed of only two battalions, each with few vehicles and no field artillery. These units arrived on 1 January and were moved at once to the Tarlac area in preparation to be put into battle. The crucial delaying actions of the 26th Cavalry and 192nd Tanks had cost Homma far more than mere time delay in his battle plan.

However, Homma did not need the additional forces yet. He was already in the process of putting heavy pressure on the Guagua–Porac defense line. The initial, expected assaults against that line began on the afternoon of 2 January from an advance detachment of the Japanese 9th Infantry coming down Route 74. Though fairly small, the enemy force pushed the weakened and thinly spread 21st line back about two thousand yards toward Pio to the southwest. There, bolstered by reserve troops, the 21st held. Attempts to regain their lost ground failed with the result that their artillery was badly exposed to attacking enemy infantry who had gotten to dangerously close quarters. The 21st Division HQ made hasty plans for counterattack using a battalion of their reserve 23rd Infantry regiment. Before the counterattack could be executed, darkness fell and the 23rd was ordered to advance at dawn and restore the left of the line. The 21st was directed to regroup on the right to shorten its front. All through the night, the quiet was broken by Phillipine artillery, which had pulled back some six hundred yards. In the morning, the Japanese were gone and the original line was restored without counterattack. The evening before, the main body of the Takahashi detachment had moved from its positions between Bamban and

Angeles toward Porac. The 8th Field Artillery Regiment (less one battalion) supported the movement with 105mm guns to augment the infantry attack. Thus the advance of the 23rd Infantry was met by sharp infantry small arms fire combined with 105mm bombardment. At this time also, three Japanese fighters flew in low to strafe the road in support. The momentum of the thrust carried the Japanese below Pio, where determined resistance finally stopped them. The most alarming aspect of the attack to Wainwright was appearance of Japanese medium artillery, thought to be heavy artillery, on the left of the American line, posing serious peril.

General Capinpin's 21st held from the western mountain foothills east along the flatlands along the south bank of the Bamban River. Now they were given strict orders by Wainwright to hold the enemy north of Layac Junction for a minimum of five days "if it costs the life of every man in both divisions." Capinpin was stiffened with resolve. The 26th Cavalry was still to cover the left of the 21st Division to the Zambales Mountains and would constitute the only reserve force north of Bataan. This was one time the Philippine Army finally showed it had teeth.

S-3 Maj. Bill Chandler of the 26th Cavalry recorded that "the 21st and 11th performed valiantly, though at times confusedly, falling back stubbornly in the face of repeated Japanese attacks. At times, the 21st's artillery batteries were firing muzzle bursts at charging Jap infantry less than 600 yards away. Could poorly trained troops become battle-hardened veterans in two weeks? These men certainly gave the best performance I had seen to date, and, despite heavy losses, they effectively held back a determined enemy for the required five days."

Colonel Takahashi kept up a determined push against the 21st lines, and had it not been for the desperate, incessant, and effective pounding from the 21st Field Artillery's guns firing at close range to stop Takahashi's ferocious attacks, the 9th Infantry might have achieved a rout. For six hours, until darkness descended, the left portion of the 21st Division line was held entirely by the guns of 21st Field Artillery, firing at close range across open fields and breaking attack after attack until their gun barrels were literally white hot. Col. Richard C. Mallonee of the 21st Field later wrote that he knew what Cushing's artillerymen must have felt with the muzzles of their guns in the fore as Confederate waves came on and on and broke on the high-water mark at Gettysburg. Takahashi, his attack shattered by the terrible toll inflicted by the artillery, could only pull back and assess the awful damage to his force.

On the afternoon of 4 January, because of heavy pressure on the 11th Division to the east, Wainwright ordered the 21st Division at the west end of the line to break contact with the enemy and withdraw at dark to a line along the Gumain River about eight miles south of Porac. After some confusion in making the move during the night, the 21st dug in on their new

line with the 26th Cavalry still covering their left flank. Their HQ and those
of the 23rd Infantry, other special units, were set up at Dinalupihan. The
21st Field Artillery took up position just east of town.

3 JANUARY 1942: GUAGUA

The eastern half of the Guagua–Porac line was being held by the 11th Division in contact with the 21st only through patrols. The 13th Infantry held
Guagua and was positioned across the strategic Route 7 south. The 12th
Infantry extended the line to the southeast. In support of the division was
the newly arrived 11th Field Artillery, part of Weaver's 194th Tanks and
Company A of the 192nd.

The now reinforced Tanaka detachment had probed carefully down
Route 7, and on 3 January at around 4 a.m. their point made contact with
a tank platoon from Compnay C/194 about a thousand yards north of
Guagua.

Coming under sharp tank fire and pinned on the road by marshes on
both sides, the enemy advance force signaled the main body to come up.
Under increased Japanese pressure, the 194th tanks fell back slowly to Guagua. The Japanese were forced by the difficult terrain to attempt a frontal
attack on Guagua. Slowed down by a cluster of small villages along their
line of advance, the Japanese found the progress of their advance was getting bogged down. They called up artillery, and their 75mm guns went into
action in the afternoon, scoring at least one hit on the 11th Infantry CP.
Then the defenders heard their own 11th Field Artillery answering from
their positions at Guagua. The green PA artillerymen displayed more enthusiasm than skill but gave the Japanese pause. The Japanese continued to
pound Guagua through the night and intensified their bombardment in the
morning when a battalion of their 150mm howitzers were brought to bear.
In the early afternoon, spearheaded by armor of the 7th Tank Regiment, the
Japanese broke through the 13th Infantry on Route 7 and bulled their way
into Northern Guagua. Another column on the left hit the 3rd Battalion
and 11th Infantry, which suffered some 150 casualties. Those two units
clung to their ground long enough to allow the 11th Division's 1st and 2nd
Battalions to avoid being overrun. Then the survivors broke off and withdrew behind the two battalions.

In the meantime, Company A/192nd Tanks and part of the 11th Division
tried to counterattack by hitting the Japanese flank before they reached
Guagua. This move was nearly a disaster. Infantry on the line mistook their
own tanks for enemy armor and began to lob mortar shells on them. General Weaver, who was in a jeep attempting to coordinate the attacking tanks

and infantry, was almost hit. Fortunately the error was seen in time and damage avoided.

SUNDAY, 4 JANUARY 1942

After news of the Japanese overrunning Guagua reached Wainwright, he knew it was time to fall back once again. He chose the south banks of the Gumain River about eight miles south of Porac as his new line and directed both the 11th and 21st to withdraw there that night. On the afternoon of 4 January, because of the heavy pressure on the 11th Division to the east, Wainwright ordered the 21st Division on the west end of the line to break contact with the enemy and withdraw at dark to the new line along the Gumain River. When all reconnaissance laid out the situation, the division commanders reasoned that the only recourse left to them for any semblance of orderly withdrawal, in order to avoid a confused rout, was to traverse a circuitous, thirty-mile route through San Jose and then down Route 74 to Dinalupihan. The force could there turn southeast toward Layac Junction and then north along Route 7, where they could establish a line to stop the oncoming Tanaka detachment.

All through 4 and 5 January, the 11th, 21st, and 192nd tanks and the 11th Field Artillery tenaciously denied the enemy its advance down Route 7. In the meantime at San Jose, 11th Division commander General Brougher was frantically gathering everything on wheels to send forward to extricate his force. With this transportation, the 11th was able to block Route 7 between Santa Cruz and Lubao. By about 6 a.m. on 5 January they had established the line they had sought to occupy. Troops arriving on this line found themselves under heavy small arms fire from the Tanaka detachment now holding Lubao.

On the previous afternoon, just north of the line blocking Route 7, Brougher had set up an outpost line with the troops who had been able to withdraw down Route 7. For fourteen hours, from the afternoon of 4 January until the morning of 5 January, the small force under command of Capt. John Primrose, about two hundred infantrymen supported by ten guns of the 11th Field Artillery and several 75mm SPMs, stalled the Japanese advance. When he received word that a new line had been formed below San Jose, Primrose withdrew his people to the main body of the division.

The 194th Tank Battalion was able to withdraw from Guagua only after a vicious brawl with the advancing Japanese column. Col. Ernest B. Miller, the tank CO, had ordered his tanks to pull out on the morning of 4 January. Peeling off one at a time, the tanks began a slow withdrawal covered by several tanks of Company C/194th and some SPMs from Capt. Gordon

Peck's provisional battalion, which had set up a roadblock along the Sexmoan–Lubao road. At around 4 p.m. Peck and Miller spotted a large Japanese force of some five hundred to eight hundred men supported by machine guns, mortars, and artillery advancing on their position. The column was led by three obviously terrified Filipino civilians, undoubtedly hostages, carrying white flags. Having no choice, Miller's tanks and the SPMs opened fire, cutting the Japanese column to pieces. The 194th then left the burning Guagua and Lubao and pulled south to new positions just above Santa Cruz. The retrograde was covered as long as possible by the SPMs and remaining tanks at the roadblock.

Around 2 a.m. on 5 January, the rear guard covering force was hit again by enemy infantry and artillery with the Tanaka detachment. They attacked across an open field in bright moonlight but came under devastating direct fire from the American guns. Suffering heavy casualties they were driven back. Tanaka ordered more attacks and again and again they were driven back with horrendous casualties until dawn. Later that day, Tanaka's force, now cut to pieces, was relieved by Col. Hifumi Imai's 1st Formosa Infantry, which was attached to Tanaka's remaining tanks and artillery.

By early morning of 5 January, after two days of bloody fighting, the last of the Guagua–Porac line was abandoned to the new line south and west of the Gumain River. Farther west the 21st Division and the 26th Cavalry on their left flank were digging in along the river about eight miles south of Porac. The stand on the Guagua–Porac line had paid off big. The Japanese had been made to pay dearly for the ground gained and still had been denied their objective of closing the gateway to Bataan. Just as important was the time gained by those already in Bataan to fortify defensive positions.

All that remained to hold the final line before Bataan were the 11th and 21st Divisions, the 26th Cavalry, and part of the 194th Tank group. The eight-mile line stretched along the Gumain River approximately eight miles above the main access road to Bataan and blocked any enemy approach to the peninsula through Dinalupihan and Layac Junction. After some confusion in making the move during the night, the 21st dug in on their new line. The 26th Cavalry had to pack up, abandon its reorganization position, and rapidly move south in a forced march to cover the 21st's left flank. The 21st HQ and those of the 23rd Infantry, other special units were set up at Dinalupihan. The 21st Field Artillery took up position just east of town.

Both Dinalupihan and Layac Junction lie along the key Route 7, the 11th Division's route of withdrawal. The road extends southwest from San Fernando to Layac. There it joins with Route 110, the only road into Bataan. At Layac, Route 7 turns sharply northwest for a little more than a mile to Dinalupihan, the southern end of Route 74 down which the 21st Division was withdrawing. Route 7 then continues west to the town of Olongapo adjacent to the important American naval base on Subic Bay. The road then goes north along the Zambales coast all the way to Lingayen Gulf. This was the southward route that the Japanese had, luckily for the Fil-Americans, chosen to ignore in favor of blasting down the central plain of North Luzon, which they surmised to be the most direct course to Manila, their main objective.

Layac Junction, for the allies, was the key point on their route of withdrawal. There all roads to Bataan joined. Through it and over a single steel bridge across the Culo River, the entire, combined American and Philippine forces, not to mention thousands of civilian refugees, would have to pass to get to Bataan. If the enemy were able to break through and make an all-out attack on such a bottleneck, Layac could be a disaster. It had all the makings of a major nightmare unless timing and route discipline were kept under tight control.

On the eastern end, the withdrawal from the Gumain River line, with the exception of a few skirmishes, had been executed without any major engagement with the Japanese. General Brougher's 11th Division, reinforced by a battalion of the 71st Infantry, were on their way to Layac.

On the western end of the Gumain line in the 21st Division area, there was considerable confusion and poor communication of orders. General Capinpin was unduly alarmed about the 11th Division's ability to hold and protect his eastern flank. He ordered a pull back to just north of Dinalupihan and had begun the move when General Wainwright firmly ordered him to hold where he was until further orders. Capinpin's sector of the line was thin in one place and overcrowded in others. Fortunately for him, the Takahashi Detachment on Route 74 hesitated its advance at Pio. This failure to press home the attack was later attributed to caution on the part of the Japanese colonel who had been assigned to the 65th Brigade for operations on Bataan and had overestimated the strength of the enemy and their capacity to fight. This hesitancy was a godsend to Capinpin and his force, for if Takahashi had chosen to launch an all-out attack on the 21st sector at that time, he might well have put "the cat in the sack" before Bataan.

The 26th Cavalry was ordered to protect the left flank of the 21st during its withdrawal. In the meantime, one 21st battalion was moved east in front of the 11th to protect its own pullout from the Gumain line. The maneuvers were complicated almost to the point of impossible, but somehow the entire combined force vacated the Gumain line and reached Layac in a classic traffic jam.

During all this time, it was not until the afternoon of 2 January that the Tanaka detachment with its artillery finally effected a crossing of the Pampanga River. Colonel Tanaka then pushed his force quickly to San Fernando, where at 5:30 p.m. he linked up with the Kanno detachment, which had made all haste down Route 3 from their capture of Angeles. The Japanese columns then succeeded in taking Guagua and Porac and pushed hard south in pursuit of a stubborn enemy. Their costly advance was to no avail. The trap had snapped shut on an absent prey. In the few days from 30 December 1941 to 4 January 1942, the combined Luzon defense forces had, in a complicated and difficult series of maneuvers, succeeded in leaving Lt. Gen. Sasumu Morioka's cocky, allegorical "sack" empty of the "cat," which was still free and had claws. His battle plan timetable now a shambles, a disbelieving and irritated Gen. Masaharu Homma, his plans to cut off and entrap MacArthur's retreating forces thwarted, now faced a difficult, protracted campaign to conquer Bataan.

A small force of obsolete, impudent horse cavalry, perceived by his commanders as a flea to be brushed aside, had instead shown themselves to be a viper in his path.

MORNING, 5 JANUARY

General Wainwright now issued the final orders to all commanders to initiate the last withdrawal movement into Bataan at dark, putting WPO-3 now into full effect and some thirty-five thousand regular Philippine Army troops, about ten thousand untried Filipino reservists, and about twelve thousand to thirteen thousand American military servicemen into the intended defensive shelter of Bataan. What had not been counted on in terms of food, shelter, and medical supplies were thousands of civilians crowding onto the peninsula in their frantic flight from the Japanese. MacArthur's planners in Malinta Tunnel on Corregidor laid out the grim statistics of the food supply for Wainwright's already hungry forces. If the Philippine forces were not resupplied from outside, Bataan could not hope to hold out for more than two months unless the troops were put on half rations (about thirty ounces, or two thousand calories a day per man) and less as they went on. That did not take into consideration the masses of some twenty-six thousand civilians fleeing along with the military. (Homma had seen the cynical advantage in this and forbid any interference with refugees moving toward Bataan.) All reaching Bataan were tired, hungry, and in danger of disease. The peril of malaria presented a disaster. Many vital supplies left behind included most of the available mosquito bars/nets available and quinine, already in dangerously short supply. This all proved a lethal oversight and incompetent neglect by those in charge.

Still, the phased withdrawal had been no less than a brilliant, complicated maneuver to organize the massive combining of the Southern Luzon forces in their link-up with Wainwright's NLF with tremendous credit due the SLF commanding generals Albert M. Jones and George M. Parker Jr. in their remarkable retrograde north through Manila to the final rallying point at the critical Layac Junction. Amazingly, WPO-3 had worked.

In the course of the now completed withdrawal to Bataan, the rear guards of the North Luzon Force, especially the 26th Cavalry and 192nd Tanks, had done their work superbly. Not one major unit had been lost and only at Cabanatuan had the NLF line failed to hold long enough to execute the phased withdrawal as planned.

The cost of the withdrawal movement had been high for both sides. Since the initial combined Japanese landings of over 60,000 troops (43,110 of which had landed at Lingayen alone), their losses were far more than they, especially Homma, had bargained for. Their total casualties in that time were over 2,000 men, including some 650 men killed and 1,300 wounded and missing. Wainwright's far smaller NLF force of some 28,000 had total losses of some 12,000. Only a small, unknown number of these were battle casualties or captured by the Japanese. Most of the reduction was caused by desertion of green, poorly trained and poorly equipped Philippine soldiers, many of whom were literally cadets and school boys who simply went back to their homes. The South Luzon Force had fared better. Of General Parker's original force of 15,000, about 14,000 remained when he reached Bataan.

At twilight, with the 26th Cavalry (now down to some 650 men) covering, the Southern forces, the exodus to Bataan, led by the exhausted 11th Division, began making the jumbled, often disorderly crossing of the steel bridge across the Culo River at Layac Junction. Even in view of the mass confusion, Wainwright's task demanded precise timing if it were to succeed. As military police struggled to maintain some semblance of column order, the remaining elements of the American 31st Infantry and 21st Division PA made up the final elements of the congested throng making the crossing over the final bridge to Culis on the south bank, where the now entangled thousands of both NLF and SLF were massed in a great, milling flood of humanity, vehicles, and equipment.

Major Lee Vance, the 26th Cavalry executive officer (and later commander), recalled in his memoirs that what happened at Layac Junction was "beyond imagination." He noted that, as usual, the 26th was "riding drag" for two Philippine divisions and a mass of civilians, all tired and barely moving along. "They would stop and move and stop again, and we just herded them as best we could. When they stopped, I would simply have a scout car fire a few shots in the air to get them moving again, and they did. How we ever untangled that mess is a miracle."

Col. Ray M. O'Day, senior American instructor for the 21st Division, observing the horrendous crossing, wrote in his records, "It was a painful and tragic sight—our soldiers trudging along, carrying inordinate loads of equipment and personal effects. Many had their loads slung on bamboo poles, a pole between two men. They had been marching almost since dark the night before."

5–6 JANUARY 1942

Layac Junction

The 26th Cavalry was directed to cover the withdrawal of the last units across the Culo River Bridge at Layac Junction. The cavalry was finally cleared to cross at 1:00 in the morning, closely followed by the last of General Weaver's rear guard tanks. General Wainwright himself was there waiting at the crossing to personally cheer on the rear guard, especially his beloved 26th. He then, with obvious relish, gave the order to blow the Culo River bridge, thus effectively dropping the latch on the gateway to Bataan.

Maj. William Chandler entered into his 26th Cavalry regimental notes, "The 26th Cavalry (PS) is at last behind friendly lines, having marched more than 200 miles since leaving Rosales on 21 December 1941, having fought numberless delaying actions and one pitched battle, and covered the withdrawal of four divisions from Lingayen Gulf into Bataan. The regiment has lost nearly half of its men and animals in the process, killed, wounded and missing."

Chandler's satisfaction with a job costly but well done would be short lived. Culis would prove to be a terrible and devastating ordeal for the regiment.

A new defense line had been prepared along the southern banks of the Culo River at Culis. On 28 December, after WPO-3 had gone into effect with MacArthur's approval on the 23rd, the 31st Infantry (AUS) was sent to Layac by General Parker, commander of the Bataan Defense Force, to cover the strategic junction. Col. Hugh J. Casey, MacArthur's chief engineer officer, pointed out to Dick Sutherland that defense lines already being prepared on Bataan left enemy control of the narrow, paved Route 110, the only road running north to south to the bottom tip of the peninsula where, at Mariveles, it curved back north again up the west coast to Moron. He recommended that the Japanese be denied access to that road as long as possible by a strong delaying position at Layac–Culis. This was approved, and on 3–4 January, the 31st assisted by elements of the 71st Division under Gen. Clyde Selleck went into position below the Culo and began entrenching positions and stringing barbed wire. The work was slow because the NLF 71st Engineers were assigned to preparation of lines farther south. The result was that the Culis line was far less than top grade.

6 JANUARY 1941

Culis

The Layac–Culis defense line had the 31st and Selleck's 71st spread thin along the narrowing Route 110, which ran southeast between Layac and Hermosa. On the east was the 71st Infantry holding a front along the south bank of Culis Creek (not to be confused with the Culo River just to the north). This line, parallel and north of Route 110, ran from Almacen, northeast of Hermosa, to a point just northeast of Culis where the creek turned south to cross Route 110. On the east flank, the 71st Infantry sector was protected by swamps and a wide river. On their left was the 72nd Infantry straddling the now narrow, single-lane Route110, and to the left of them was the 31st Infantry with its 1st and 2nd Battalions extending the line to a gap of some three thousand yards to the nearest foothills of the mountains. It was to be the job of the 26th Cavalry to plug that wide gap. Armor was to take up supporting positions southwest of Hermosa with the 194th to the west and the 192nd to the east. Spaced along the line to counter enemy tank assault were 75mm SPMs. To General Parker and others of the staff, the line appeared to be a strong one, mainly on high ground with good fields of fire and a sufficient force to hold it. General Selleck did not agree. He felt that the front was too wide and that all units, except the 26th Cavalry, were overextended. He also felt that both the right and left portions of the line were faced in such directions to be vulnerable to enemy enfilade fire. The prevailing argument, however, was that the enemy would likely hesitate when encountering an organized defense line and wait for supporting heavy weapons before making an organized attack. By then the purpose of the Layac–Culis line would be accomplished—a delay to buy time to fully prepare the stronger defense lines to the south on Bataan.

6 JANUARY

The Layac–Culis Defense Line at the Gateway to Bataan

Upon arrival at the new defense line south of the Culo River at about 2:30 a.m., Pierce and his staff were met with orders to take up position to the rear left flank of the 31st Infantry (U.S. Army) and cover the extreme west end of the line, covering the wide gap between the 31st and the densely jungled slopes of Mt. Santa Rosa on the northern end of the rugged line of the Bataan Peninsula's central spine of ragged mountains and extinct volcanic peaks. The highest of these are mounts Natib (about 4,222 ft.) in the north; Samat (1,920 ft.) about midway down the peninsula overlooking the one, rough east-to-west road running from Pilar to Bagac; and the Mariveles mountain group, dominated by the highest of the range, Mt. Bataan (about 4,722 ft.), which overlooks the harbor town of Mariveles at the southern tip of the peninsula. The range became all the more rugged the deeper the approach into the malaria-infested, steamy, canopy-covered jungles, which in 1942 covered at least 90 percent of the entire of Bataan from its Manila Bay coastline on the east all the way across the peninsula to its west coast on the China Sea. Most of this jungle terrain could be negotiated only by narrow trails cut with razor sharp machetes or bolos. The whole interior is crisscrossed with cold, deep streams and unnegotiable gullies and ravines. Some thirty miles long and only fifteen miles wide at its narrowest point in the middle, Bataan, a deceptive, primitive paradise, appeared to present an ideal military defense location. With the exception of narrow, tortuous roads and a few small openings offering locally cultivated clearings and coastal meadows, mostly of tall cogon grass and New Guinea *kunai* grass (tough, saw-edged, and best avoided), Bataan was an almost endless, impenetrable tropical forest based in two main, prevalent types of soil—rich, black humus in the jungle areas, and red clay-like dirt in the coastal and central hills, which turned to choking white dust when dry. Sugar cane fields and graceful coconut palms, which grew in orderly rows (not safe to recline beneath as many an injured head experienced), flourished near beaches. The Bataan of that time was a dark, jungle forest whose endless variety of huge tropical trees blotted out the sun and sky (not to mention offering welcome shelter from the eyes of predatory Japanese airmen) with their almost impenetrable ceiling of enormous leaves and thick strangling vines lacing through groves of huge banyan trees with trunks so large that shelters could be cut into them and whose thick roots spread out above ground. The variety seemed endless—clumps of huge nara or luan trees, source of renowned, hardwood Philippine mahogany; big, tortured-looking banyan trees (especially good lairs for snipers); big mango trees with treasured purplish-red fruit showing through their huge leaves; amlang trees with big, twisting roots at their base large enough to conceal men; acacias with lacy, frond-like leaves; thick groves of incredibly tall, elegant bamboos; and dao. The ground was an endless entanglement of matted creeper ferns, endless rattan vines laced in kava brush, abaca (hemp), gobi plants with big, waxy elephant ear leaves, interspersed with small palm-surrounded cool springs and quiet pools in grassy clearings. Everywhere there was an endless variety of riotous color from bougainvillea, red hibiscus, fragrant frangipani, and wild sprays of pink and white spider orchids. Poisonous plants abounded, tempting to the starving men who would fight on Bataan, such as tree nettles and *cowhage* with stinging hairs that caused unbearable rashes and itching; physic nuts causing dysentery; *carut* (called "tugui" by native Negritos); and other roots looking much like potatoes and causing severe gastroenteritis. This deceptive, dangerous tropical paradise was also an enticing and overwhelming haven for snakes of all kinds, including deadly, small rice cobras and huge pythons, which lurked in plentiful *alang* grass. Monkeys of several species, voracious insects of every description, and armies of lizards abounded. The most prevalent were geckos, which had the virtue of preying on mosquitoes, making them welcome household guests and a taboo if harmed. Outside they preferred to dwell in palm and fruit trees, and in the evenings the night air was filled with their shrill two-syllable scream, which sounded not unlike "Fuck you!" A legend from the Spanish-American War holds that one night, as American and Aguinaldo troops faced one another in fighting emplacements near Manila, the darkness was filled with insults shouted across the lines. Suddenly when the geckos opened up with their characteristic cries, the Americans took it as a taunting "F—you" from the enemy and charged from their trenches in a rage in reply. On Bataan, dwindling food rations soon removed the gecko's sheltering taboo, and it frequently became just another rather repelling but still edible stew ingredient. Those on Bataan, foe or friend alike, learned the hard way that, when faced with starvation, you cannot be picky.

At about 3:30 a.m. on 6 January the 26th Cavalry began designating the order of line for its units in their assigned position extending the western flank of the 31st Infantry. Pierce and his headquarters staff set up a CP to the rear of roughly the center of the line. The first squadron, less C Troop, went into line on the right flank nearest the 31st end of line in right to left order of A Troop, and B Troop supported by machine gunners interspersed among them and scout cars to their rear. Second Squadron took up position in the left sector of the line extending westward into the rolling foothills of Mt. Santa Rosa. They had machine gun support, but the terrain was impassable for the scout cars to back them up. Four cars and their communications equipment were sent to the rear, closer to the 31st Infantry, to help maintain sufficient coordination between the regiments. By around 4 a.m. the 26th was in place. Pierce knew his line was thin almost to the point of invisible, but they were on good fighting ground for defense. Now his tired troopers had just to wait.

At 6 a.m. on 6 January, when he was satisfied that all the designated troops were on the line, General Wainwright, without reservation, relieved General Selleck from his command of the 71st and put him under General Parker's control. The NLF had now completed its mission. After notifying MacArthur of the situation at Layac, Wainwright withdrew south to new headquarters near Abucay below what was to be the first main line of resistance on Bataan.

Now only the thinly stretched covering force at Layac Junction and Culis stood in the way of Japanese free entry into Bataan.

19

The 26th Gets Left Behind at Culis

TUESDAY, 6 JANUARY 1942

At 9 a.m. the beginning of the battle for Layac Junction and Culis was heralded by an incoming Japanese artillery barrage. Contrary to the reasoning of General Parker and his staff, the enemy had not hesitated at the sight of a fixed defense line at Culis and waited to bring up heavy weapons support and reinforcements. Already frustrated at having been stymied out of their hoped-for entrapment of MacArthur's forces before Bataan, the Japanese were wasting no more time in commencing their all-out assault on the Culis delaying line. Buying time for MacArthur and Wainwright was going to be expensive.

Lt. Col. Katsumi Takahashi, frustrated that the enemy had eluded the Japanese pincers at Layac, was pushing with determination down Route 110. His ferocious banzai attacks on the Culo River line were heavily supported by incessant air attacks and part of the guns of the 48th Mountain Artillery.

At about 10 a.m. forward observers reported Japanese infantry and heavy weapons were already advancing down Route 7 toward Layac Junction. The column they saw was the forward elements of Col. Takeo Imai's detachment, consisting of the 1st Formosa Infantry, a company of the 7th Tank Regiment, two battalions of the 75mm-armed 48th Mountain Artillery, and one battalion of the 1st Field Heavy Artillery Regiment with eight 150mm howitzers. By 10:30 a.m. the enemy column came within artillery range of the Culis defensive line. The 1st battalions of the 23rd and 88th Field Artillery regiments then opened fire. The Filipino Scout gunners' first salvo was dead on target. The scouts then immediately switched to rapid fire and were joined by 71st Field Artillery gunners. Their salvos saturated the road areas from front to rear and drove the Japanese back nearly five thousand yards northeast of Layac.

The Japanese then put their own artillery to work. The 75s of the 48th Mountain and the 1st Field Artillery's 150s, aided by unhindered aerial direction, laid down concentrated and accurate fire on the Culo River defense line. One member of the hard-hit, defending 88th Field Artillery (Philippine Scouts), Jose Calugas, the unit's mess sergeant, exposed himself repeatedly, directing his fellow scout gunners during this punishing Japanese firestorm. On his own initiative, running zig-zag about a quarter of a mile to the friendly battery position then passing through no-man's-land, he rallied a few men huddled in nearby foxholes to hurriedly repair the only remaining workable gun back into action. Calugas fired all the remaining ammunition at advancing Japanese infantry while a Filipino officer directed his lethal fire. This handful of survivors with their repaired gun destroyed some sixty enemy vehicles and killed hundreds of Japanese. For his action, Calugas was awarded the first Medal of Honor of the campaign.

With no air cover, General Selleck was unable to interfere with the deadly accurate Japanese air spotting for their guns. The Japanese 150mms were able to stay out of American artillery range and pound the defending infantry positions at will. At around noon, Selleck directed the Fil-American artillery to change their positions. The Japanese air spotters simply reported the shifts and the Jap artillery followed accordingly. Their devastating fire enfiladed the American 31st Infantry positions and heavily battered the 71st Infantry and the 23rd Field Artillery's 1st Battalion, destroying all but one of their guns. The 88th had been able to situate themselves in more-protected positions and fared a bit better. Total Japanese control of the air was telling heavily.

Sgt. Sabiniano Ibanez of Capt. John Fowler's Troop G observed, "The Japanese had a spotter plane over us, and then they got an observation balloon up, too. Then they started hammering us with their artillery. [Thirty-first]st troops started using small arms against the aircraft, but it was like trying to hit an eagle with a slingshot. The next thing I knew, they had our positions bracketed."

At around 2 a.m., combined masses of Takahashi's and Imai's infantry were busy forming their lines for an attack in strength against the artillery-weakened defense line. The remaining American and Filipino commanders and troops alike could clearly hear the noises of preparation for assault but could do nothing but ready their weapons and brace for the storm to come. In between barrages, there were strong enemy probes to feel out the weak spots, and these were met with firm small arms and machine gun resistance. All during 7 January and into the small hours of the morning, sharp fighting could be heard up and down the line east of the 26th as the probes were countered and heavy assaults began.

Throughout the day, the 26th Cavalry suffered heavily under aircraft-directed artillery shelling, taking casualties of some twenty-five animals lost and a number of men wounded by shrapnel. Many men literally bled from their noses and ears from the awful concussion. Fortunately for the thinly stretched 26th sector of the line screening the 31st, the Japanese, for reasons unknown, did not make any concentrated ground assault there. However, that was to be the only thing resembling good fortune for the 26th at Culis. Troopers on the end of the line closest to the 31st Infantry, and where some of the 26th scout cars were positioned behind the 31st for communications purposes, had some sightings of Japanese bicycle-mounted infantry approaching down Route 110 and going into position to assault the 31st and the 71st lines. For some reason, there were no ground probes to the west where the tense cavalrymen were stretched in their extension of the line toward the mountains.

The Japanese commenced their main attack at about 2 p.m. pushing several battalions of infantry across the Culo River below Layac Junction, forcing that section of the American line to give ground. During the whole day of 6 January and into the small hours of the morning, sharp fighting could be heard up and down the line east of the 26th as the probes were countered and the heavy assaults began. Another assault force turned north at Layac and advanced toward undefended Dinalupihan, taking it at about 3 p.m. The Japanese, who had advanced south from Layac, hit Selleck's line about an hour later driving between the 31st Infantry and the 72nd Infantry. Col. Harry Skerry, chief engineer of the NLF, had strongly opposed the positioning of the 31st sector of the line. The 31st's performance to date had not been outstanding, and they were now situated on ground with little natural concealment or commanding terrain. Accurate enemy batteries with longer range and unmolested air observation had almost pulverized the American batteries and troops. In addition, the 31st line and protecting ridge faced northeast, effectively permitting enfilade fire from the west. The Japanese were quick to exploit this factor with withering, length-wise shelling. On the right of the 31st line, B Company, which had been badly hurt by the shellings, was pushed back about eight hundred yards in disorder to higher ground in the rear. This opened a hole in the line between C Company/31st on the left and the 72nd Infantry on the right. The Japanese wasted no time pushing into the gap, which the remainder of 1st Battalion/31st tried unsuccessfully to plug. Regimental CO, Col. Charles Steel, hastily brought up his 3rd Battalion from Selleck's reserve to hold the line. But the Japanese, backed up by artillery, still widened the gap, assaulting the right end of Company C/31st and Company A/72nd on the left of the hole. The CO of 3rd Battalion, Lt. Col. Jasper Brady Jr., ordered I and L companies/31st into the sector formerly held by Company B in an attempt to stem the tide. Company I was cut up by enemy artillery and, badly disorganized, was forced back. However, Company L was able to continue its push forward and in about a half hour was able to restore the broken line. For a time the situation seemed back in control, but by the afternoon of 6 January, General Selleck was in serious trouble. The Japanese attacks had wedged a gap between the 31st Infantry and the 72nd Infantry and were exploiting the penetration of Selleck's overextended line. If they were to break through the 72nd line, they could control and cut off Selleck's route of escape. The enemy penetrated his overextended line. He had no reserves left, and his artillery had been in large put out of action. There was no letup in the Japanese pressure to ford the Culo River and gain control of the road, thus cutting off Selleck's last route of escape. Selleck had committed his last reserves and, under advisement of his aides, concluded that he must withdraw. He pleaded to General Parker that without artillery and infantry reinforcements, he could not hold and that a pullback in daylight invited disaster. At 1:30 a.m. on 7 January, under the cover of darkness, Selleck was permitted to order his force to withdraw, leaving three companies of the 31st as a rear guard shell. The 71st was able to make an unhindered withdrawal. After delaying for about an hour, the 31st shell began its pull out. At that same time, the Japanese assaulted Hermosa, cutting off Company E of the American 31st and almost completely chopped it to pieces. By 5 a.m., the Japanese secured their objective, but the survivors of the decimated Company E were not able to rejoin their regiment for several days.

Neither side had used tanks, the Japanese because of a lack of bridges over the Culo River. Col. Ernest Miller, senior CO of the American tanks, many of which were hit by artillery, was hesitant to commit because of "unsuitable terrain," much to the disgruntlement of Selleck, who felt the 31st counterattack might not have failed had it been supported by armor. Miller pulled back his tanks to the highway, where at about 9 p.m. they were directed by General Weaver's executive to withdraw south into Bataan. They were on their way when other units on the Culo line got orders to pull back.

All during the primary assault on the Culo line to their right, the 26th Cavalry stayed in their western screening position but were not attacked on the ground. What they did not know was that they were being isolated by the long day's action. In the night, things began to come apart.

26th Exec. Lee Vance recorded, "On 4 January, the motor squadron had left San Jose via Florida Blanca and on 5–6 Jan. moved into bivouac just south of Layac. Their CP set up about two km. southwest of the 31st with four of its cars for communications and staff work attached to the 71st Division. At about 3:30 a.m. 7 January a code message was received from 31st HQ. It was garbled and undecipherable. What we didn't know and no one had informed us was that the radio codes had been compromised and had to be changed. The problem was that nobody informed the 26th Cavalry of the switch. During the night of 6 January and wee hours of the morning of

7 January, the 26th's repeated attempts to establish contact with the 31st on their right were met not only with enemy fire but 'friendly fire' from nervous 31st Infantry troops who were fearful of enemy infiltrators and were shooting at literally every shadow. Only luck saved the 26th troopers from any casualties. The 26th CP continued trying desperately to contact the 31st by radio but evoked only gibberish in reply, except for one message in the open from Captain Barker, whose motorized unit had been left behind where the road turned into a trail impassable to vehicles. Barker reported his belief that the line would break before daylight. Then Chandler finally learned of the code change and that no one had thought to notify the 26th. It was a snafu beyond comprehension. At 0430 Colonel Pierce was informed that the scout car section had been ambushed, and three out of four cars were lost. Now it was confirmed that the 26th was hopelessly cut off behind enemy lines and had no choice but to strike out across country over trackless jungled mountainous terrain previously declared impassable by mounted troops. It was to be an agonizing trip for the regiment, for the troopers had neither food nor water for themselves nor their animals."

Chandler recorded, "The following three days were the most physically grueling so far. It was necessary to make our way by game animal and foot trails along the precipitous and jungle-clad slopes of Mt. Santa Rosa toward Luzon Force's main battle position running from Abucay Hacienda on the east coast of Bataan west to Moron on the coast of the China Sea. This we managed to do only through Herculean effort; sometimes hauling animals up and down virtually vertical slopes by ropes and manpower alone; crossing the Abucay-Moron line somewhere left of its center and reaching the Pilar-Bagac cobbled road just before noon on 10 January after a heart-breaking climb out of a deep ravine where we had to literally carve a trail with hand tools up the steep south wall. At the top we were met by Capt. Joe Barker's motorized unit which had been patrolling all day and night looking for us to appear.

"With the exception of one poor, wounded mule which we had to kill and eat the day before, every man, every animal, and every piece of equipment that had left Culis four days before was hauled up the south wall of that last damned ravine. The regiment was, once more, together again, though somewhat worse for wear and very, very hungry."

Earlier, on 7 January at around 3:30 a.m., after receiving the undecipherable code messages from the 31st, Capt. Joe Barker of B Troop, who at that time had charge of a motorized unit of scout cars, sent out a message in the clear advising the Culis road would be closed by 4:30 a.m. Attempts by his unit to physically make contact with the 31st were met by "friendly" fire from confused 31st patrols. Barker sent four scout cars out at 4 a.m. to seek a route of withdrawal, but they were fired upon from both sides of the road near Culis with terrible losses. Barker put in his report to Vance: "Only one car returned. Three cars were lost; 1st Lt. Carol I. Cahoon, 2nd. Lt. Stephen Graves; U.P. correspondent Mr. Franz Weisblatt wounded and captured; and eighteen enlisted men killed, missing or captured. Moved out with the 31st Inf. and moved down to Km. marker 139 on the Pilar-Bagac road. Commenced search for rest of regiment."

A particularly tragic incident in the 7 January ambush was a direct hit on the car carrying Sgt. Felipe Bato of HQ Troop, who was assigned to be official custodian of the regimental colors and files containing irreplaceable historical accounts and organizational records of the 26th. Bato survived and escaped into the bush with the 26th's American flag standard. Sadly, the other precious artifacts in his keeping were lost, including the regimental flag and records. Sergeant Bato tied the rescued flag around his waist and made his way cross-country to his home, where his family hid him. His wife sewed the treasured American flag inside a pillow to keep it from the Japanese. A short time after the fall of Bataan, Bato went back into the hills and joined a group of guerrillas. An air corps major, Henry Clay Conner Jr., an escapee from the Bataan Death March, was among them, along with seven other Americans, a score of Philippine troops and scouts who had been cut off and had taken to the hills, and a number of civilian volunteer fighters. Most of them were armed with only bolos, wooden spears, and whatever enemy small arms they could capture, but they raised hell with the occupiers. The 26th flag was "our symbol of faith in God and country [and] became known as 'the flag than never touched the ground.'" Over almost three years, the band grew to almost three thousand in number, joining up at times with outstanding leaders like Maj. Claude Thorpe, Maj. Robert Lapham, and Capt. (later Col.) Edwin Ramsey (fomerly of G Troop, then E–F and leader of the very last horse cavalry charge) from the 26th Cavalry, who had refused to surrender, went into the hills, and was now commanding some eight thousand guerrillas in the hills above Manila. They fought and daily defied the Japanese behind the national colors from the 26th Cavalry. Connor felt the flag deserved better than being sewed hidden in a pillow, and each morning it was cautiously and ceremoniously raised in the sunlight of Luzon and reverently lowered every evening until liberation in 1944. Many times in those years the flag and its keepers were in jeopardy, but Connor swore later, "Not only did we keep it safe, but never let it touch the ground even once." Connor survived to return the historic flag to the United States.

7 JANUARY 1942

Near the Pilar-Bagac Road across central Bataan

Vance later put in his report, "<u>7 January</u>: The regiment moved out with the 31st Inf. and moved down to Km. marker 139 on the Pilar-Bagac road.

The regiment, less motor elements, formed up and marched cross country on Abucay Hacienda at 7 p.m. No guides available and no one in regiment knew trails. Regiment lost its way and by noon was half way up Mt. St. Rosa. Turned back and night found us near previous bivouac."

Cpl. Felipe Francisco of the Barker's No. 2 Scout Car Section heard the communication come in to notify the regiment that the road was no longer open for retreat. "We had received previous word that the road would be open until 0500 [the morning of 7 January] but it was about four o'clock when we got to Culis and found the town occupied by the Japanese. I really don't know what happened, but I remember we were able to turn around and warn the regiment the Japs had closed the road. I was in the second car in line when a 37mm Jap anti-tank gun hit one of our front wheels. The car went out of control and I was thrown out of the open rear into a rice paddy. When I came to, I was in rice paddy water, and I could hear the Japanese talking. I crawled out of the rice paddy away from the direction of the Japanese I heard and kept going east until I reached a village on Manila Bay. I met a civilian there and the town mayor. I told them I was with the 26th Cavalry and needed some kind of transportation to rejoin my outfit because the war was already way inside Bataan. It took three or four days. They told me to just hold on and they'd have some kind of boat shuttling back and forth. I guess they knew what I didn't. There were a lot of stragglers. I met a man from the 31st Inf. who told me everything had come apart. After about three days, I think, a boat got us inside Bataan along the Bay not too far off shore. I don't know exactly where we landed, but I found an outfit that knew where all the units of USAFFE were. They told me to wait, and then we hitched a ride to where the 26th Cavalry was located. I was a corporal then, so they assigned me to another scout car section. My new assignment was to patrol the west coast road. Pfc. Castronubo was my driver. We left that night to go from the west coast to the east coast, down through Mariveles and then north again. It was about a fifty mile patrol along lonely coast and not knowing what we would run into."

Cpl. Salvador Abad of HQ Troop (the youngest of three Abads in the regiment: father, Cpl. Serapio "Pedro" Abad, oldest corporal in the 26th, and older brother Alejandro with E Troop) was with Felipe Francisco when their scout cars were bushwhacked outside Culis. Salvador recalled later, "At Culis, Captain Wheeler sent me about a hundred yards from a forest clearing to set up an outpost. We were told the 31st was in front of us. About an hour after Wheeler left, a 31st Inf. man came by and we challenged him. He told us it was getting very hot on the line, so we let him go by. We stayed there thinking the 31st would stand fast there all night. At about four in the morning, four 26th scout cars tried to move forward from the forest. In the second one was my brother Alejandro. I told him to take care of himself as they went by. About a half hour later, only one of the scout cars came back and Pvt. Hill told me the second car in line took a direct hit, but Hill's car was able to get turned around and come back. I didn't know where Alejandro was."

Alejandro knew. "I was in the car behind Felipe's when we were ambushed in the morning. We got ready at four a.m., I think, and we had to cross a bridge. The people we thought were guarding the place [the 31st Infantry] had pulled out, but we didn't know. Nobody told us. Getting caught like that wasn't our fault. They should have notified us. When they blew the bridge, we were about a mile, I think, from it. Suddenly there was a tank right in front of us and we got hit with a 37mm I think. We stopped behind Francisco's car and started firing. You could see Japanese on both sides. Our guns fired for two or three minutes. Then somebody shouted for us to jump and save ourselves. There was a lot of fire slamming into the lightly armored metal sides of the cars, and we didn't know where it was coming from, so you couldn't raise your head without getting hit. We started jumping out of the right side (the scout cars were open vehicles). I hit the ground with another guy where there was a creek on the right side of the car about a foot deep with a rice paddy on the other side. We started running until we heard somebody out there after about a mile shouting and talking Filipino/Tagalog. We found they were friendly soldiers, and we told them we'd got ambushed. After that we reported to the CP thinking everybody was killed, but later somebody told us some other guys had also made it back. Only one car made it back. Sgt. Major Masciclat was in that last car. Later on we hitched south with the 91st Engineers who were blowing bridges and eventually got down the highway to Bataan where we finally found the rest of our regiment."

Maj. Lee Vance notes, 8 January, 1942: "Our elements of the regiment present moved out at dawn for a fresh start; soon became lost; made two false tries. At 10:00 a.m.—halted in hills and sent out 5 patrols in different directions to locate the trail we needed to reach Abucay Hacienda. Being short of rations, reluctantly killed and ate one of our wounded horses. Two patrols located the trail we desired. One scout car which had returned was abandoned as it could not negotiate the trails. Continued the march and at 5:00 p.m. arrived at left flank of 51st Inf. P.A. outpost. Negrito guides then led regiment over very rough ground to main line. Capt. Cummings, 26th Cav. on detached service with P.A. had the left flank Battalion. We were informed that horses could not get out of the ravine we were now in. This was unacceptable.

"9 January: Moved out at daylight and took until 2:00 p.m. to get out of that damned ravine. On arrival at Abucay Hacienda we were met by Captain Walter J. Buboltz, S-4, with forage and rations. C.O. and S-3 went to Hq. I Corps [former NLF] for orders. Regiment, less motor elements, marched at 7:00 p.m. on Km. 139 on Pilar-Bagac road. Motor Sq. moved to bivouac 3 km. north of Bagac on the Moron road [on Bataan's west coast]."

(It should be noted here that since the initial movements north to Lingayen, the red-haired and -bearded 26th S-4, Capt. Walter J. Buboltz from Milwaukee, Wisconsin, had tirelessly and often at the risk of his life kept the regiment's supplies, including ammunition, rations, and fodder for the animals, constantly flowing to the beleaguered regiment. Buboltz was awarded the Silver Star for constantly exposing himself at Binalonan distributing supplies and ammunition under fire. During the worst of the combat conditions on Bataan, Buboltz continued his dedication to meeting the regiment's supply needs under fire. For his courage and persistent performance under fire, Captain Buboltz was recommended by Col. Lee Vance for the Distinguished Service Medal, which was awarded him posthumously. Tragically, while a POW, Captain Buboltz was killed in bombing by American aircraft while aboard the infamous Japanese transport *Oryoku Maru* on 14 December 1944.)

Major Lee continued: "10 January: Regiment, less motor elements, marched to bivouac 1 km north of Bagac on Moron road.

"11 January: Arrived at Bivouac north of Bagac. Troop "G" [Capt. John W. Fowler and 1st Lt. Edwin Ramsey] attached to 1st Regular Div. P.A. [Brigadier General Segundo] and ordered to Moron. Troop marched during the morning.

"12 January: Rest; shoeing horses and reorganization."

Lt. Ed Ramsey of G Troop had developed jaundice during the Luzon withdrawal and, suffering and ill during the grueling move cross-country from Culis, expressed particular joy when the lead elements of the regiment finally reached the Pilar–Bagac road and were met by Lieutenant Cummings of the Scout Car platoon with news that Capt. Joe Barker and the Motorized Squadron were bivouacked just a few short miles away. After the remainder of the regiment finally struggled clear of the deep gorge, they were greeted by the regimental supply officer with a field kitchen with hot food for the troopers and forage for the animals. The horses were fed first and then the exhausted, nearly starved men scraped the bottoms of the cooking pots. The column then mounted up and made their way to Barker's bivouac near Pilar.

On 10 January, Fowler's Troop G and Ed Ramsey were assigned to support the 1st Division (PA) on Bataan's west coast, where they commenced reconnaissance patrols north to Moron until G Troop was relieved by combined Troop E/F commanded by Capt. John Z. Wheeler. Ramsey was ordered hospitalized and returned to his unit only after the jaundice had subsided and his strength regained. He was taken to the No. 1 field hospital at Limay, halfway down Bataan's east coast. Under the command of able chief army medical surgeon Col. James Duckworth, the hospital had been hurriedly set up in a collection of screened, battered barracks-like sheds and leaky nipa huts that had been evacuated by the 12th Medical Regiment.

Some of the personnel had stayed behind to familiarize the newly arrived staff with the setup. At least the cots were well covered with mosquito netting. The smells were an awful mixture of blood, gangrenous wounds, and disinfectant. Infection was rampant in the Philippine jungles. Ramsey was constantly awakened at night by the cries of the wounded, which remained indelibly in his memory for the rest of his years. He also had two close calls while there. The first was when the hospital was mercilessly bombed, causing heavy casualties, and again when a huge python dropped out of a tree one night on the cot next to him. No one was injured and the snake went on his way in the dark. Among the some fifty nurses who had arrived on open buses in a harrowing trip from Manila and Stotsenburg was the pretty South Carolina redhead Juanita Redmond, now dressed in baggy, unflattering but practical fatigues. She recognized Ramsey and asked him about some of the officers of the 26th whom she'd known and associated with at Stotsenburg. She asked especially about Johnny Wheeler and reminisced about polo games and fun evenings at Jai Lai and the Wack Wack club. It was the only pleasant interlude there for Ramsey, who was only too grateful to return to duty.

Back at I Corps, an anguished General Wainwright had feared the worst when he got the disheartening news that the 26th Cavalry had been cut off by the foul-up at Culis. Though some of his staff assumed that the regiment had been destroyed, he never lost faith that somehow the gritty Clint Pierce would bring his troopers through despite the awful odds.

The evening of 9 January, after initial fighting on Bataan had begun, Wainwright and Parker received orders from Corregidor to assemble all general officers to receive "an important visitor" the next morning. At first light, General MacArthur and Maj. Gen. Dick Sutherland arrived at Mariveles on a PT boat. Their entire day was spent inspecting as much of the line as possible, first II Corps positions and later Wainwright's I Corps sector. It would be MacArthur's first and only visit to the Bataan area of operations during the campaign, and a tiring day for the harried Wainwright.

However, 10 January had an unexpected happy ending for Skinny Wainwright. The tough but sentimental fifty-nine-year-old soldier almost shed tears when his confidence in Clint Pierce was rewarded as the 26th Cavalry finally reappeared at Bagac around midnight. As tired as he was, Wainwright personally took time out to meet them. Among the haggard group was his surviving, beloved horse "Joseph Conrad," whom Sergeant Major Masiclat personally led over to greet the weary but grateful general, who one more time leaned to put his face affectionately against the animal's soft muzzle.

Somehow, the resilient little regiment had once again pulled itself together out of the jaws of a nightmare, but at terrible cost. Bataan would soon prove not to be a place that favored togetherness, regardless of the depth of devotion. The time of ultimate testing had arrived.

20

The Battle of Bataan Begins: The Abucay–Mauban Line and the Bridge of Dead

7 JANUARY 1942

Bataan

General MacArthur now tensely awaited his forces to take position on his first main line of resistance (MLR) on Bataan. Prepared by tenacious efforts of U.S. and Philippine Army engineers, U.S. Marines, and civilian volunteers during the long withdrawal of the Luzon forces, it comprised a twenty-mile-long line across the northern part of the peninsula from Abucay (a cluster of nipa shacks for sugar cane workers, to the east flank on southbound coastal Route 110 to Mariveles) to Mauban (on the west flank coastal Route 110 leading north to Moron). There was a ragged break almost in the center of the line, except for patrols and outposts, made necessary by the rugged terrain of the Santa Rosa mountains capped by two high, extinct volcanoes, Mt. Santa Rosa and Mount Natib. Defensive positions on the main heights in this area were considered ideal by the infantry commander, but in reality, they made any truly effective mutual support between the east and west Bataan Defense Corps all but impossible. But then, minimal threat was anticipated from any significant force crossing over this forbidding spine of Bataan.

MacArthur had ordered a "defense in depth" of the new line. A strong outpost line of resistance was established in front of the main battle line and additional defense positions were prepared covering several miles to the rear. The prepared defenses were as formidable as the builders could make them. Spike log roadblocks reinforced by barbed wire, deep ditches, and blown bridges awaited tanks and vehicles. Double-depth barbed wire entanglements of concertina rolls and crisscrossed wire staked about one foot above ground spanned the fields of fire in front of the infantry positions. Bunkers, dugouts, trenches, and foxholes were positioned to deliver maximum small arms, machine gun, and artillery fire on attackers from every possible angle, including beaches. Both coasts were covered by troops posted to fend off any attempts of amphibious flanking by the Japanese. But the backbone would be measured by the strength of the men on the line.

Eight miles behind the MLR, a secondary line of defense was still being prepared as a fallback position. This was parallel to the cross-peninsula Pilar–Bagac Road. In prewar planning, this line had originally been intended to form the main Bataan defense line. The USAFFE reserve forces, the Philippine Division, the tank group, and a number of 75mm SPMs—this line was considered as a potential last-ditch defense and was to be completed while the forward MLR held the enemy back.

The Luzon Defense Forces were now designated the Bataan Defense Force and divided into two corps: I Philippine Corps of some 22,500 men under General Wainwright to the west and II Philippine Corps of about 25,000 men under Maj. Gen. George Parker to the east. The division of the two sectors was roughly designated by the mountain area in the center. The southern tip of Bataan south of the Mariveles Mountains was organized as the Service Command Area and main concentration of supply and ordnance depots under command of Brig. Gen. Allen C. McBride. Both corps were under supreme command from MacArthur's headquarters on Corregidor.

The remainder of the 26th Cavalry Regiment was assigned to be included in Wainwright's western I Corps, which consisted of three Philippine divisions—the 1st, the 31st, and the 91st. In addition were the 26th, one battery each of field artillery and 75mm SPM guns, and some additional, miscellaneous units. The cavalry was put in position between Mauban to the north and Bagac to the south directed to patrol and guard that sector of coastline and the poorly surfaced Route 110, now northbound toward Moron above Mauban. The sector assigned to I Corps was densely wooded, the ground largely made up of steep, high-timbered banks and virtually uninhabited. Movement on foot, for the most part, called for the use of machetes and bolos to facilitate any kind of appreciable headway except where there were existing trails. Communications conditions in the area were dismal. Wainwright's engineering officer, Col. Harry Skerry, remarked, "By and large, this was an area where an American needed a map, compass and bolo even in the dry season." I Corps MLR ran along the Mauban Ridge eastward to Mt. Silanganan. As the western anchor, Mauban presented an ideal defensive anchor with a fifty- to seventy-foot ridge commanding a clear field of fire along the beaches for hundreds of yards. The rest of the line, with the exception of only the portion held by the 3rd Infantry with reinforced positions fronted by a double apron of barbed wire, was almost totally unprotected by any kind of obstacle other than that provided by dense jungle and rough terrain.

Farther north, Moron offered long stretches of beach with a dangerous potential for envelopment from the sea. Early in the planning stages, MacArthur had been urged by his engineering advisor, Col. Hugh Casey, to place the western MLR farther north at Moron with the Mauban axis as a secondary position. The 26th Cavalry would soon find out how right Casey was.

On the right of the line to the east, Parker's II Corps was made up of four more Philippine divisions—the 11th, 21st, 41st, and 51st; units of the American 31st Infantry; supporting artillery and 75mm SPMs and the 57th Infantry (Philippine Scouts), which included one personable 1st Lt. Lloyd Mills of Company C/57th, who had pleasant memories of playing polo and riding in dress parades leading his men with the 26th Cavalry. He would survive to be a living testament many years later to the horrors of Bataan and Japanese captivity.

Most of the east coast terrain defended by II Corps tended to be flat, low, and swampy, much of it having been used to cultivate rice. The cleared ground offered broad, open fields of fire, which favored the defenders. Unlike the rough western coast road, 110 on the east was a comparatively excellent highway, making it a potentially ideal route for Japanese advance. It was here that the enemy was expected to make the initial attempt to breach the II Corps line. In view of this probability, Parker positioned the fresh, superbly trained 57th Philippine Scouts to straddle the sector from Manila Bay across Route 110. Lloyd Mills would soon be in the forefront of the battle for Bataan. Although the prepared fortifications of II Corps were stronger than those to the west, the scouts and other infantrymen on the line still had to labor frantically with just a small number of picks, shovels, and axes. When these weren't available, bayonets, small entrenching tools, and mess and kit covers were resorted to for burrowing as best they could into foxholes and dugouts. However, camouflage was thoroughly prepared and communications networks had been well and efficiently laid. Only as II Corps line extended into the rugged foothills of Mt. Natib did the efforts to prepare adequate fortification become virtually impossible. But, again, planners saw slim peril from any attack across the forbidding mountains. Patrols, operating with great difficulty and some high-ground outposts, would have to suffice.

To the extreme south, McBride's Service Command Area was manned by a variety of units, composed of remaining elements of the 71st Division (PA), the newly organized 2nd Division of Philippine constabulary troops, and provisional units formed from grounded air force troops, a battalion of beached navy personnel, and U.S. Marines from Subic. The supply situation was questionable at best. Originally, Plan Orange called for supplies for forty-three thousand men for six months to be in place on Bataan. Not only was the amount of supply short of the plan, but the combined number of troops and miscellaneous personnel had swelled to a staggering eighty-thousand with an addition of some twenty-six thousand civilian refugees fleeing the Japanese. A large-scale movement of supplies to Bataan and Corregidor did not begin until after 23 December. Corregidor, already with rations stored for seven thousand, was stocked first with reserves sufficient for ten thousand people for six months. Bataan presented a far more difficult problem, mainly transportation. The limited land routes were already being choked by withdrawing defenders, and the usually ample sea routes across Manila Bay were being cut by bombing. In addition, debarking and docking facilities on Bataan were few and primitive. Also, the pressure of the Japanese advances had bred an epidemic of "withdrawal fever" causing many of those retreating into Bataan to abandon even the most basic necessities. A great deal of food, clothing, and other supplies were retrieved and brought in by more disciplined defenders in the withdrawal, but it was far from enough. By 3 January, inventories indicated roughly only a thirty-day supply of varied field rations for about one hundred thousand men. The food included canned meats and fish for fifty days, canned milk for forty days, flour and canned vegetables for thirty days, and only a twenty-day supply of rice, the main staple of the Philippine diet. The abandonment of the rice at government central at Cabanatuan in deference to civilian government relations was a disaster with far-reaching consequences and one of Douglas MacArthur's most devastating administrative blunders affecting Bataan's defense.

In view of the situation, MacArthur's quartermaster recommended immediate, drastic measures be taken to conserve what little was available, and on 5 January the order went out to put both troops and civilians on Bataan and Corregidor on half rations. This was translated into roughly two thousand calories a day, about half of what an active person required normally. For combat troops working up to twenty hours a day under dangerous conditions in brutally enervating, almost unbearable climate and in difficult terrain, this constituted a punishing existence. As soon as the order was announced, troops began making every possible effort to augment the miserable allowance. Many had saved, purchased, or accumulated food of various sorts over the past weeks in Luzon, which helped out for a time. Luckily, it happened to be the season for rice harvest, and much of the crop was ripe in the paddies. It was gathered by all hands available and taken to mills hastily built in Limay by engineers. Veterinary personnel supervised establishment of a substantial abattoir operation for the purpose of butchering and preparing whatever fresh meat could be obtained. This consisted mainly of carabao draft oxen, regardless of ownership, and whatever wild animals, including even monkeys, men could kill or capture for food. Every man became a hunter when he wasn't fighting, and shots were often heard far from the lines. Edible reptiles were not excluded, although some fatal mistakes were made in that category. Pythons were considered a delicacy and became almost extinct on Bataan. At Lamao, a fishery processed all the local fishermen could catch. They went out almost always at night to avoid Japanese fire until this, too, became too hazardous. Every possible natural food resource was utilized, such as edible plants, roots, and salt from boiled seawater. Shortage of clothing and shoes also soon became a serious problem. All of these deficiencies combined with the hostile weather contributed to lowering immune systems and making everyone increasingly vulnerable to the ravages of disease and infection. Malaria, dysentery, hookworm, beriberi, and a host of other tropical ills soon became universal.

Clint Seymour of B Troop/26th fared pretty well. "My mess sergeant, Valenton, knew every edible root there was, and we ate plenty of iguana right down to the tails!"

Elmer Long of the 4th Marines later recalled the best way to prepare normally tough, stringy carabao. "When they killed carabao, mules or horses, we dug a hole, put a fire and rocks in it, then put the meat, ground, in sacks and laid it in the hole. We'd cover it all up with rocks and dirt, leave it overnight and dig it up next day. The meat was still a little stringy but tender and juicy that way. It was same with monkeys and other wild animals."

The island fortress of Corregidor, "The Rock," was being defended by the American Regular Army 31st Division, Coastal Defense Forces, 4th Marine Brigade elements on beach defense and some ten thousand Filipino troops. On the Bataan MLR at Abucay, Parker had a stronger force under his II Corps command because MacArthur's intelligence sources were sure the initial Japanese push would strike the eastern sector of the line. They would soon be proven right.

For several days following the battles for Layac and Culis, however, there was a lull in the fighting while the Japanese planned and regrouped. This brief respite was used to the utmost by the defenders to prepare and strengthen their fortifications as best they could. On the Japanese side, there was both fury and frustration at a once again missed opportunity to trap MacArthur's forces and bring a close to the campaign. Recrimination from the highest military echelons was fast in coming, and General Homma was in slim favor for the delay in the Japanese timetable for conquest, which had originally called for his campaign to be completed in fifty days. Numerous documents later revealed Japanese admission that their complete failure to cut off the defenders from escaping into Bataan was due in large part to critical delays directly caused by the stubborn holding actions of the 26th Cavalry at key points. A few hundred horsemen with light weapons and sporadic support from a small force of aggressive National Guard tankers in light tanks had succeeded beyond imagination in altering the face of an entire invasion strategy.

During the Bataan defense preparations, in keeping with the original Japanese schedule, Homma's best units, the 48th Division and the 5th Air Group, were to leave the Philippines for operations in Java. (In late December, Gen. Count Hisaichi Terauchi, southern army commander, recommended that the invasion of Java be advanced about one month in view of Homma's optimistic expectations about finalizing the Philippine conquest.) They were to be replaced by a combat-shy garrison force composed of the 65th "Summer" Brigade from Formosa and the 16th Division was designated for "mop up" operations. On 2 January, Homma received word he was prematurely losing command of his best units while still engaged in his attempt to trap the withdrawal into Bataan. Although both the southern army commanders and Imperial General Headquarters saw the risk to Philippine operations by this early deployment, they went forward with the plan to hasten the fall of Java and prepare for any potential move by the Soviet Union. On 27 December, an overconfident Homma had ordered Lt. Gen. Akira Nara to sail from Takao with his 14th Army to take Southern Luzon and Manila. The belief of Homma and his commanders was that any resistance on Bataan would be weak and, therefore, quickly concluded. Fortunately for Homma, the 65th Brigade had departed earlier than planned, or he would have had only the untried 16th Division (which, he commented with disdain, "did not have a very good reputation for its fighting qualities") to initiate his assault on Bataan. The day the 65th landed on Luzon, it was ordered to force march by foot to Tarlac. General Nara, a stocky, middle-aged man who'd spent many years in the United States, attended Amherst College and graduated from Ft. Benning Infantry School, boasted that his troops had made the march on time but were "foot sore and exhausted." Nevertheless, he felt trepidation about his assignment to replace the vaunted 48th.

Nara said that his 65th Brigade, which was replacing Homma's prized, well-trained, and well-equipped 48th Division, was "absolutely unfit for combat duty." Organized in early 1941 as a garrison unit, the 65th had a strength totaling sixty-five hundred men. It was formed as three infantry regiments, the 122nd, the 141st, and the 142nd Infantry, consisting totally of only two battalions, each organized into three rifle companies and one machine gun company. There were few vehicles and no organized artillery unit, although one regiment was supported by a battery of field artillery. Logistical support consisted of a field hospital, one unit of engineers, and a signal unit of little more than platoon strength. The majority of the enlisted personnel were poorly armed, much older troops and fresh conscripts with but one month of inadequate combat training on Formosa.

Even with this weakened force at his command, Homma remained optimistic that enemy resistance on Bataan would be weak and that he would be able to conclude his operations in short order. Despite setbacks and delays in Luzon, his plan for attack was characterized by assumption of rout by a fleeing foe rather than attacking head on into a strongly fortified line of resistance in depth. His miscalculation was reinforced by his own faulty intelligence sources, who portrayed the defense as consisting of only a few thousand Philippine troops and no strong, constructed fortifications to speak of. They were assumed to be starving and demoralized, and Homma's conclusion was that MacArthur might make a stand at Mariveles to implement a withdrawal to Corregidor but that taking the rest of the peninsula would be a virtual pushover. Accordingly, Homma assigned the conquest of Bataan proper to the green 65th Brigade, having it advance in two columns, one down the east coast through Abucay to Balanga and the other down the west coast through Moron and Bagac. Then both would converge on Mariveles with orders to "annihilate the enemy."

For General Nara's planned operation, the 65th had infantry, artillery, armor, and miscellaneous service units. The 9th Infantry and a battalion of 75mm field artillery, an engineer regiment, and medical units were assigned from the 16th Division. From the remaining elements of the 48th Division came two battalions of 75mm mountain gun artillery, which were pulled out soon after the fighting began. Armored support was provided by the 7th Tank Regiment. Artillery support was drawn from the 14th Army's 1st Field Heavy Artillery Regiment 150mm Howitzers and army service and support units. Air support was to be provided by Col. Komataro Hoshi's unit now based at Clark Field, which was to commence attack on I Corps artillery positions, enemy air strips on Bataan, and installations in the Mariveles area starting 10 January through the 13th. The 16th Division was to support the 65th Brigade by sending part of the division to occupy the south shore on Manila Bay to cut off communications between Corregidor and the Luzon forces.

By noon on 4 January Homma had ordered the 65th Brigade to move down Route 74 to their main battle position to relieve the 48th Division and take command of the Takahashi detachment and the 9th Independent Heavy Artillery Battalion. It became clear to Nara that his unit was to relieve the 48th Division and that his force—and his only—was to destroy the enemy, advance toward Balanga, and send a secondary force toward Olongapo on Subic Bay. Final relief of the 48th by 8 a.m. of the 7th was ordered, and General Nara was ordered to move on Olongapo and Balanga. By 6 p.m. on 8 January, relief of the 48th was completed, and the brigade was then concentrated between Dinalupihan and Hermosa, readying to attack. The main attack would commence the following afternoon.

This period of the struggle to defend the Philippines from the Japanese had an ironically tragic aspect to it, which has been perceived and argued by a number of serious military historians. The radical adjustments made in the Japanese table of organization combined with faulty planning actually rendered them for the first and likely the last time vulnerable to an aggressive counteroffensive by MacArthur's forces. The Japanese unit shifts had left them significantly weaker than at any time in their Philippine campaign. American intelligence and planners simply did not recognize the potential for a well-coordinated strike with what was at that moment in time actually a superior military force and instead dug in for a completely defensive and ultimately fatal strategy. No one will ever know what this lost opportunity might have achieved in altering the overall allied military position.

9 JANUARY 1942: THE BATTLE FOR BATAAN BEGINS

At 3 p.m. on 9 January, the roar of a concentrated artillery barrage against II Corps shook northern Bataan and heralded the opening of the Japanese assault. General Nara ordered his infantry to commence their attack on the presumption that the American and Filipino defenders had been so chewed up in their withdrawal that resistance would be light. It was also assumed that the II Corps line was farther north than it was.

The first Japanese indication of the real situation came with the shock of a vicious counterbarrage from II Corps artillery putting down tons of explosive on the attackers. The earth heaved all along the east road up to four miles back up Route 7, sending the unmistakable message that Bataan's defenders were determined to stand and fight. Only after the fighting started did Nara realize his error in incorrectly locating the position of the II Corps MLR. He had assumed he would encounter II Corps outposts upon opening the attack and based on this had directed his infantry to advance in such a way as to overwhelm the enemy's left flank. Simultaneously, part of his force was to go wide in an encircling movement to take II Corps from its rear. A secondary thrust by a smaller force was to move down the west side against Wainwright's I Corps.

For his attack, Nara had organized his reinforced 65th Brigade and supporting units into three regimental combat teams backed up by a reserve. Against II Corps he directed two regiments with tank and artillery support. To the East, Col. Takeo Imai's 141st Infantry with a supporting battalion of mountain artillery, a battery of antitank guns, and engineer and signal troops were to advance south down the east road as far as the Calaguiman River. The 7th Tank Regiment, which had spearheaded the debacle at Baliuag and Plaridel, was to take position in the rear to be available to support Imai if necessary until bridges were repaired and roadblocks removed on the east road.

Nara's hopes for a quick victory lay in a combat team under Col. Susumu Takechi, which consisted of the experienced 9th Infantry reinforced by an artillery battalion, antitank guns, and service and support troops. Takechi was ordered to overwhelm the western II Corps left flank, take Album, and then send a force to encircle the flank and join up with Imai's 141st Infantry advancing down the east road. Nara directed his reserve, the 142nd Infantry, to take position behind the 9th in order to exploit Takechi's anticipated breakthrough. Additional support was to be a battalion of field artillery coming from Olongapo on Route 7.

Nara sent his third regimental combat team made up of the 122nd Infantry commanded by Col. Yunosuke Watanabe to advance west on Route 7 to Olongapo, then south to Moron to attack I Corps.

They were then to take Bagac and thus secure the west end of the one east–west road across Bataan. Nara did not expect resistance above Bagac. Little did he know that he would encounter the annoying 26th Cavalry, which had recently caused the Japanese so much trouble. Nara was at Dinalupihan when the Japanese big guns opened up at 3 p.m.

9 JANUARY

On the Abucay Line

II Corps' Abucay line extended from Mabatang on Manila Bay to the northeast slopes of Mt. Natib. To the east, in prepared positions, the Scouts of the 57th, guarding the road, hunkered down and waited for the storm. They had a company of 4th Marines next to them. Before them were excellent, level fields of fire. To their left in positions along the Mt. Natib trail and Balantay River, defending the center of the line, was the untested 41st Division (PA). The Balantay River is shallow but had the defensive aspect of flowing through a deep gorge. On the extreme western end of the line lay Gen. Albert M. Jones's badly weakened 51st Division (PA) in position mainly on a raised jungle clearing. Their defenses consisted of little more than scattered foxholes.

The Japanese commenced their attack on schedule. At 3 p.m. on 9 January, Col. Imai's force started down east Route 110 but had hardly begun before they were pounded by murderous fire from II Corps artillery, which had the road interdicted. To the west, Takechi's 9th Infantry reached Album with little difficulty, a probe encountering only a reconnaissance patrol from the 57th Scouts just below Hermosa. The scouts withdrew after a brief firefight. Nara had expected to encounter a II Corps outpost the first day but was under the mistaken optimism that his 141st and 9th Infantries had made such successful advances that the Americans had generally withdrawn and "fled into the jungle without putting up a fight." He still did not know his troops had not come up against the II Corps MLR.

It was the next day, 10 January, when MacArthur made his sole inspection tour of the Bataan lines. During the tour, MacArthur complimented Wainwright's NLF withdrawal and stated that he was going to have Wainwright made a permanent major general of the regular army. When Wainwright asked MacArthur to speak to some of the men for morale's sake and offered to show him his 155mm guns, MacArthur replied, "I don't want to *see* them. I want to *hear* them!" The next time Skinny Wainwright was to see MacArthur was when he saw El Supremo off from Corregidor on his ordered journey via PT boat to Mindanao and plane to Australia. MacArthur assured the officers he encountered that II Corps would soon counterattack; that airfields were being prepared on Mindanao to receive planes to overcome Japanese air superiority; and that the twenty thousand troops on Mindanao would reinforce Bataan for a counteroffensive to retake Manila. It was inspirational and sowed seeds of hope deep in the minds of the defenders of Bataan. MacArthur and Sutherland had a private conference with Wainwright about problems of such things as supply and morale, and Wainwright gave blunt answers. One thing MacArthur and his entourage accomplished was to earn resentment of all, seeing them by their appearance in fresh-pressed khakis in contrast to the stained, ragged, and dirty uniforms of the men on the line. Considerable doubt exists as to the morale value of that visit.

Ironically, the Japanese that very day made their first demand for surrender. A message from General Homma was air-dropped behind American lines telling MacArthur his men, already on half rations, were doomed and the end was near. He said the only question was how long they could resist and, their honor and prestige being already upheld, MacArthur was advised to avoid further bloodshed and save his troops by surrender. He continued, "Failing that, our offensive will be continued with inexorable force." Homma also sent separate, pointedly divisive warnings to the Philippine troops, saying MacArthur was "stupidly wasting their lives."

The Japanese received their reply promptly in the form of an increased volume of artillery fire from II Corps.

Imai, to avoid the heavy bombardment on the east road, split his regiment into two columns. The eastern column was made up of the 2nd Battalion 141st Infantry (less two companies), which went down the east road and struck the 57th Scout outpost line late on the afternoon of the 10th. Hindered by artillery fire, the 2nd Battalion advanced only to the Calaguiman River about eighteen hundred yards below Samat. To the west, the remainder of the 141st Infantry encountered less artillery but more delay by rugged terrain. It reached the 41st Division outpost line sometime during the night of 10–11 January.

The Japanese finally ran into the Abucay MLR on 11 January. The first II Corps unit to come under heavy infantry attack was the 57th Infantry Philippine Scouts under command of Col. George S. Clarke. His 1st Battalion was on the right and the 3rd Battalion on the left, with the 2nd Battalion in reserve. An outpost south of the Calaguiman River, manned by a reinforced company of the reserve battalion, was the first unit to be hit. Advance elements of Colonel Imai's eastern column, the 2nd Battalion/ 141st Infantry made the assault, crossing the Calaguiman about one mile north of the MLR. By 11 p.m. the Japanese reached a sugar cane field on the left of the 3rd Battalion/57th directly in front of Company I. About 150 yards in front of the MLR, this cane field hadn't been cleared, it being presumed that artillery would suffice to block enemy approach through it. That night, the Japanese in the field struck the MLR. They commenced with an artillery and mortar barrage. The sound of bugles came from the Japanese lines. It was soon realized that these routinely sounded calls were signals for Japanese gunners to ready their breaches, swab the barrels, and commence firing. Tree bursts were the most devastating, causing considerable casualties in the Allied lines.

There was an immediate reply by guns of the 24th Field Artillery (PS), but they had hardly begun firing when the Japanese jumped off, accompanied by the blare of bugles in a frenzied banzai attack across the moonlit ground directly in front of Company I. The scouts laid down murderous fire as wave after wave of screaming Japanese flung themselves forward into and onto the barbed wire to the front. Amidst the din were heard cries of "*Tsukkome!*"(Charge!) by officers wildly waving samurai swords. Those in the first wave threw themselves across the wire, literally forming human bridges of dead over which the succeeding waves could cross.

The slaughter was appalling from the combined effects of machine guns, M-1s, and point-blank fire from 75mms. Gun barrels literally became nearly white hot. Despite the brutal losses, the Japanese continued their fanatic attack until Company I, its commander seriously wounded and its exec killed, finally gave ground. To the right, Company K refused its flank but couldn't hold. Colonel Clarke committed a company of his reserve battalion and finally managed to stem the tide. By the morning of 12 January, the action broken off at last, some 200–300 dead Japanese left on the grisly battle ground.

Pfc. Wilburn Snyder later recalled the gruesome assaults. "You can't describe combat. It's like trying to describe the taste of an orange. Once the Japs hit our wire, they stacked up to where you couldn't see the wire. They were piled so high our machine guns didn't have any more field of fire. We killed them with pistols as they came over. It was horrible. They came with these shrill cries. *'Banzai! Banzai!'* The only way you could stop them was to kill them."

That night, Japanese infiltration began in the 3rd Battalion area on the left of the line. The 57th spent nearly all the following day combing out infiltrators one by one and engaging in hand-to-hand combat with them. Cpl. Wayne Lewis, Company D/31st Infantry, later remarked, "Fear is not a problem when you're active in hand-to-hand fighting. It's in the quiet spells in the night that the fear comes." Snipers nesting in huge sausage trees and teak trees were a constant menace. One Philippine Army commander, Capt. Bill Montgomery, fed up with the trouble they were causing, organized a special detachment of shotgun-toting soldiers to clean them out. One by one Japs came tumbling down, bedecked in fine netting laced with leaves and brush. Uncovered, they wore uniforms of poor cotton, brown shirt-sleeves rolled up, short-visored caps with white stars on them, and neck coverings.

Cpl. William Garleb, Company H/31st Infantry, observed, "There's a kind of subliminal fear—not the fear of imminent death which is always there, but that underlying, gnawing tension that makes you so tired, so bone tired that even your hair gets tired."

The wounded coming in to the Abucay field hospital had varied injuries, usually from small-arms fire from the relatively small-bore, high-velocity Japanese .25-caliber weapons and jagged shrapnel wounds from enemy mortars. The wounded were brought in by medics on foot, often who had to cross open meadows to aid stations as far as ten kilometers to the rear where IVs and transfusions were available. Ambulances were few. Doctors and medics in the aid stations were kept frantically busy performing triage, tagging wounds, compressing to stem bleeding, administering oral medications as well as intravenously, bandaging, and fitting slings. Hands constantly bloody, these exhausted, intrepid medical corpsmen got the wounded to rear hospital facilities as fast as humanly possible, mostly on hand-carried litters.

Now a captain, Lloyd "Bus" Mills of the 57th PS had purposely chosen a Moro as his aide for his fierce fighting qualities. It paid big dividends for him in close-quarter fighting in which scouts exhibited a level of savagery in keeping with their long heritage, many being descendants of Chief Lapu Lapu of Abu on Cebu Island who decimated Magellan's company in 1521, becoming the first defenders of the Philippines against a foreign invader, Portugal. After suffering a number of scouts KIA (killed in action), more systematic methods of dealing with infiltrators were devised. Sniper parties made up of riflemen and demolition engineers began to methodically comb the 3rd Battalion area to root out the hidden intruders. By the end of the day, most of the Japanese had been found and killed. One of these sniper party actions resulted in the death of 2nd Lt. Alexander R. Nininger Jr. who, as a result of his single-handedly taking out a concealed enemy machine gun nest, became the first American in WWII to be posthumously awarded the Medal of Honor. (Philippine Scout Sgt. Jose Calugas, Battery B/88th FA Regiment (PS), had received his earlier at Layac Junction.)

All through the day of the 11th, General Nara's forces kept up constant pressure on II Corps' lines, but his units were plagued by confusion, getting lost in jungle areas and losing efficient control of his heavy weapons due to being hampered by terrible terrain. It had by now become clear that the Americans intended to resist far more firmly than had been presumed, but gradually the Japanese began to adjust to the situation. By the 12th, they moved into position to attack and put pressure on all units on the II Corps line with massed attacks, which were continually met by deadly fire from the stubborn II Corps. On the left of the line to the west, the Japanese made their most significant gains on the 12th when they tore a gap in the 51st sector. A reserve battalion regained some of the ground with a counterattack, but the cost was heavy. At the end of the day, it became evident that the Japanese, unsuccessful on the eastern end of the line, were now probing westward.

By nightfall, in the airless, oppressive Philippine heat, the stench of the dead in front of the lines grew overpowering beyond endurance.

Elmer Long of some 4th Marines with the 31st described what then happened. "The Americans and Filipinos had mowed Japs down by the hundreds as they came across the rice paddies and through that tall cane. The smell was Godawful, and then the blowflies came in big clouds on the bodies. Dysentery spread on both sides. Somebody got the bright idea to bring up bulldozers and cover up the dead Japs. This turned out to be a bizarre mistake. They dozed the bodies into mounds and covered them. When the Japs came again and again, they kept using the mounds for cover to get in close. That was the beginning of their breaking through the American and Philippine lines, I think."

The threat on II Corps' eastern end had not ended by any means. The 57th continued to repel the assaults of the 2nd Battalion 141st Infantry trying to break the MLR, but the pressure on both the right and left increased. Still, the Japanese were making unacceptably slow progress in pushing back the II Corps end of the Abucay line, and there was increasing dissatisfaction with Homma at high command levels.

On the I Corps end of the line to the west, there had been four days of relative calm after MacArthur's visit. Wainwright had carefully monitored the reports pouring in from the heavy fighting to the east and was constantly checking his men and seeking to improve their defensive positions. Still, no severe pressure was brought against his end of the line. The tense waiting was almost as wearing as combat itself. On 12 January, he received another inspector, this one Brig. Gen. Richard Marshall, who came over from the I Corps' sector. He was concerned with the staff's complaint about the weak Mt. Natib area gap between the corps, but Wainwright reassured him that he and Sutherland had discussed the matter thoroughly and concluded that the improbability of an attack over the forbidding mountain range did not warrant pulling men off more vulnerable points in the line to reinforce the gap. This would prove an almost disastrous miscalculation in the days to come.

10–11 JANUARY: THE CENTER OF THE ABUCAY–MAUBAN MLR

Japanese progress in other sections had been even less successful than that of 2nd Battalion 141st.

The rest of Imai's force, in front of the 41st Division, had pushed against the outpost line on the night of 10–11 January and had little success. They then moved west looking for a soft spot in the line and by afternoon found themselves facing the 43rd Infantry left of the 41st Division line. Nothing was going as planned. Noting the mountainous gap in the American center, Imai ordered the 9th Infantry under his old, trusted friend Col. Susumo Takechi to advance across the harsh slopes of Mt. Natib to get into position to cut back to the east coast highway, thus encircling the enemy. While Col. Takeo Imai's 141st Infantry started down the coastal Route 110 behind an hour-long artillery barrage, Takechi and his men entered the tangled jungle gloom of the supposedly impassable mountain. Takechi soon became far off his assigned line of advance. Depending solely on dated tourist maps (similar to those used by the Americans through much of the campaign) he and his force were becoming more lost by the minute in their tortuous progress through the dense, mountainous jungles of central Bataan. His men, many of them older troops, were suffering badly from the effort—from thirst, worn-out shoes, and malaria.

Meanwhile, Imai had scarcely gone a hundred yards down the highway when the road in front of him erupted in a thunderous storm from Parker's artillery. The Americans and Filipinos had no inclination to back off from the first Japanese volley. Instead, they cut to pieces the Japanese scattered by their own barrage and in the next forty-eight hours cut Imai's regiment to a third. General Nara had to replace what was left of the shattered force with reserves. In addition, there was no word from Takechi, who should have, by then, reached the bottom of Natib and cut behind the enemy. Night fell and it seemed as if Takechi had been swallowed up by the jungle. Nara's grand plan had come apart, a disaster he reported to Homma or entered into brigade reports or his war diary. He now directed his efforts to reconstructing his lines. He sent Imai's exhausted troops west to plug the hole left by Takechi's disappearance and ordered probes for a weak point in the Abucay line.

On that same day, Philippine president Quezon on Corregidor sent a radiogram to FDR in Washington accusing the U.S. president of failing to keep his pledge to send aid to the Philippines. He pleaded for a commitment of America's full force to be directed against the Japanese. He also voiced his indignation in a note to MacArthur questioning Washington's commitment to the Philippine people. He questioned the justification for allowing his people to keep on shedding blood for a Washington government that did not comprehend the feelings that apparent neglect of Filipino well-being roused in a people sacrificing everything they had for the promise of freedom and independence. Further, he expressed his anger to MacArthur, who himself was frustrated with empty promises from Gen. George Marshall in Washington. MacArthur responded with an inspirational message (which he himself probably did not believe) assuring, "Help is on the way from the United States. Thousands of troops and hundreds of planes are being dispatched. . . . No further retreat is possible. We have more troops in Bataan than the Japanese have thrown against us. Our supplies are ample [a surprise and a laugh to most of the hungry troops on the line on Bataan]; a determined defense will defeat the enemy's attack. . . . If we fight, we will win; if we retreat we will be destroyed."

The Filipinos rather than the Americans were stirred by El Supremo's words, and their inspired determination to prove themselves translated into a desperate counterattack by the 51st (PA) on the morning of 16 January, which in its fervor pushed beyond the units on its flanks and caused a dangerous bulge in the line.

The vulnerable salient was an answer to Colonel Imai's prayers. Not only did he immediately assault the eastern side of the bulge, but that very day Colonel Takechi's orphaned regiment suddenly appeared out of the jungles of Natib and struck the west side of the salient. The battered Filipino advance was shattered by noon and left a two-mile hole in the Abucay line.

That afternoon, Takechi and his bedraggled troops linked up with Imai's forces. Takechi's face was drawn with hunger and fatigue and his uniform was literally in tatters when he reported to General Nara how he and his men had become so hopelessly lost on Mt. Natib. Nara compassionately ordered Takechi to take his men into reserve. Takechi acknowledged with a firm salute and then, without pause for resupply or rest, led his exhausted troops back south again. Fearful and ashamed that he had gotten lost, Takechi was determined to lead his men back over Natib or die in the attempt.

By now, Homma, seeing the progress against II Corps almost floundering, decided to alter his plans and reinforce by some five thousand men the troops he was sending down the west coast against Wainwright. His hope was that the combined pressure against the whole line would finally push the Americans and Philippine Army the rest of the way down to Bataan's southern tip where they could be wiped out once and for all. On 14 January, while his 141st Infantry put its heaviest pressure down on the 43rd Infantry (PA) in the east, forcing the 51st to pull back from the MLR to new positions on the Balantay River, Homma ordered his push in the west under command of Col. Yunosuke Watanabe to begin to move in earnest from Dinalupihan west to Olongapo, then south to Moron and down the coast to Mauban (the western anchor of I Corps' line). The coastal town of Moron was just three miles north of Wainwright's advance west coast outposts and the sector was being continually and thoroughly patrolled by the 26th Cavalry.

Leaving Dinalupihan on 9 January, Watanabe's force went along Route 7 to undefended Olongapo, which had been adjacent to the main U.S. naval base at Subic Bay. Until just a few days before, the submarine tender "Canopus" (called "can o' piss" by its fond crew), several submarines, and several PT boats had been berthed there after escape from destruction at Cavite. These vessels now had been moved to Mariveles. Watanabe's route of march was delayed only by some blown bridges and demolitions planted earlier by engineers. His field artillery was left behind at Dinalupihan until the road and bridges could be repaired. On 12 January, by order of the 14th Army, the 122nd Infantry, using native boats, seized unopposed Grande Island, at the entrance of Subic Bay. In doing so, they captured Fort Wint, dubbed "Little Corregidor," which guarded the entrance to Subic and control of the whole northwest shore of Bataan. The fort had been abandoned by a coast artillery command under Col. Napoleon Boudreau on 24 December, but the evacuation had cost the loss of several thousand rounds of 155mm ammunition and the installation's fixed guns. The Japanese thus obtained a valuable prize at no cost. Fort Wint's guns could have provided a serious threat to any Japanese advance down the west coast. Now it had simply become a valuable enemy supply base. Not until 14 January, however, did Watanabe with his 122nd Infantry begin to advance south along the west coast of Bataan. Part of the force moved down the narrow trail between Olongapo and Moron. The rest embarked in landing craft to where the west coast road began. Watanabe, hoping to avoid an inevitable block if his entire force followed the winding inland trail to Moron, was unfamiliar with the coastline, and poor maps hindered his water-borne elements, which then came ashore about midway to Moron and set out to go the rest of the way on foot. He was headed for serious trouble with the 26th Cavalry.

Wainwright's 26th Cavalry patrols informed him of the enemy moves, and to stop them he sent the entire 1st Infantry plus the 1st Engineer Battalion and two artillery batteries north to Moron. He also relieved Troop G of the 26th, which had been on patrol in that area since the 10th. He replaced it with a combined force of Troops E and F under command of Capt. Johnny Wheeler and G Troop's Lt. Ed Ramsey, who was already familiar with the area from patrolling it. In overall command was 1st Division (PA) CO Brig. Gen. Fidel V. Segundo. First Infantry CO Major McCullom was given tactical control. Twenty-Sixth Cavalry Troops E–F moved toward a date with destiny in the small coastal town of Moron.

General Homma had decided to commit additional troops against I Corps, not to Nara who was leading the assault against the II Corps sector of the Abucay–Mauban line. On 13 January, Homma made the decision to revise his plan of attack because he had correctly concluded that Nara's attack against II Corps was not progressing favorably. To procure additional troops for his revised plan, Homma drew on the 16th Division. He directed the division CO to provide two infantry battalions and as many 75mm and rapid-fire 37mm guns as possible. Finally organized, the force consisted of Headquarters, 16th Infantry Group, the 20th Infantry (less one battalion), an antitank battery, and half of the 33rd Infantry regimental gun battery. This force, led by 16th Infantry group CO Maj. Gen. Naoki Kimura, left Manila for San Fernando on 15 January, and late that night Homma created the Kimura detachment. He placed it directly under control of 14th Army, relieving Nara of further responsibility for operations against I Corps. Kimura was also given command of the units already operating along the west coast, giving him a total force of about five thousand men.

Wainwright now found himself facing a substantial Japanese force advancing down the coast against I Corps' lines. Although the China Sea on the left flank presented an almost unapproachable barrier for the Japanese, their commander, Maj. Gen. Naoki Kimura, found another flaw in the defense. The American lines extended only about halfway up the steep western slopes of Mt. Silanganan some two miles west of Mt. Natib. This prompted Kimura to decide on a plan of attack that had failed for Takechi's force. He ordered Lt. Col. Hiroshi Nakanishi to take seven hundred men with several small mountain artillery guns to make a punishing crossing over the mountain, secretly circle Wainwright's right flank, and then turn directly west. Like Takechi, Nakanishi was hampered by inadequate maps, but his small battalion, unobserved and unopposed, struggled over the mountain, laboriously dragging the small cannons and battling dense jungle the whole way. Nakanishi and his exhausted men finally reached the foot of the mountain and the west road some three miles east of Mauban in the vicinity of kilometer post 167 by dawn of 21 January. There they established a roadblock behind the 1st Division, effectively straddling the only major road capable of bearing heavy equipment, supplies, and ammunition. Though only a small force, Nakanishi's troops posed a dire threat to Wainwright's entire position. First Division CO General Segundo sent three company-sized patrols from the 92nd Infantry reserve to block the trails. They got bogged down in action on the lower slopes of Mt. Silanganan and were prevented from eliminating the threat behind the line. The rest of Wainwright's force, the 26th Cavalry and units of the 71st Division, were already tied up with the defense of the Pilar–Bagac road and could not be pulled away without putting the vital highway in peril.

Meanwhile on the east end of the line at Abucay, Parker's II Corps was disintegrating rapidly. The disintegration of the 51st Infantry on 16 January had unhinged Parker's left flank and left the rest of the line badly exposed. A counterattack by the 57th (PS) and American 31st Infantry troops sent in to plug the breached front were bogged down in dense undergrowth and rugged ravines and couldn't reach defensive objectives. All along their front, the troops were worn thin from continuous fighting by day and constant harassment by night from infiltrators, nonstop, confusing noise diversion from firecrackers, and constant blaring of taunting enemy loudspeakers spewing out a stream of demoralizing propaganda and threats. A counterattack was attempted, but it was piecemeal and failed.

General Sutherland was sent on an inspection tour of the line, and, stunned by what he had seen, returned to Corregidor and promptly urged MacArthur to order an immediate withdrawal south to the Orion–Bagac line. On 24 January, starting at darkness, a general retreat, authorized by MacArthur, was under way. By midnight the route to the rear was clogged with buses filled with Filipino troops in blue fatigues and coconut helmets, exhausted officers in a battered assortment of vehicles, and marching and fleeing troops, all in filthy, ragged uniforms. The withdrawal was chaos. There was no regulation of traffic, nothing to keep units together, just prayers that the Japanese would not bombard or descend on them amidst the disaster.

Already harassed by Japanese air strikes, the withdrawal became a rout when on 25 January the tenacious Colonel Takechi and his ragged, starving men suddenly burst out of nowhere, having done the impossible. They had finally made it over Mt. Natib to chase the enemy. The true danger of the mountainous gap in the Abucay MLR was revealed once and for all.

After arrival on the new defense line, Lt. Henry G. Lee of the Philippine Division felt moved to compose a dismal poem about the withdrawal:

> . . . saved for another day
> Saved for hunger, wounds and heat
> For slow exhaustion and grim retreat
> For wasted hope and sure defeat. . . .

Not only the Americans and Filipinos but also the Japanese were in poor condition to continue. Nara's battered "Summer Brigade" had suffered over two thousand casualties. The survivors were exhausted and in shock from their brutal, initial taste of combat.

The fighting was far from over, however, and the 26th Cavalry was still to play a memorable part in Wainwright's desperate battle for the west coast of Bataan.

21

C Troop's Raid on Tuguegarao Airfield[1]

11 JANUARY 1942

Settlement Mallig No. 1, North Luzon

The orphaned 26th Cavalry C Troop was resting and regrouping, awaiting their next move. After assessment of Lt. Warren Minton's reconnaissance report on the Tuguegarao airfield, Ralph Praeger called an officers' conference to make plans for an imminent attack.

Early the next morning, Praeger moved the whole remainder of his unit to a bivouac area just west of Enrile, almost opposite Tuguegarao. (Sgt. Tomas Quiocho, in his later interviews, noted that there were only seventy-six effectives left, the rest being stricken with malaria, typhoid, and severe blisters.) Lieutenants Minton and Camp arrived at about 4 p.m. and submitted detailed plans for a raid. After another conference, Praeger approved the plans with only a few minor changes. Minton reported that Pvt. Roman V. Aguas of his patrol had breakfasted during the morning with seventeen Japanese fliers who were quartered beside the airfield. There were few planes left, and some were scheduled to leave the next day for Clark in the south. The Japanese officers were very friendly to Aguas, who had brought them a chicken as a "gift to welcome them to the Philippines." They had tweaked his nose and asked him to breakfast, where he had been given pancakes. Aguas had prepared a sketch of the airfield from his freedom of observation. His recon was reinforced by observations from local laborers and men posing as chicken and egg peddlers.

Frank Camp had wasted no time getting busy with fabricating some sixty makeshift grenades out of dynamite and scrap iron bound in bamboo tubes with short fuses attached. He demonstrated the technique of their use to a select group of "grenadiers." The so-called grenades had to be set off by fuse, and since it wasn't really practical to light matches in the darkness of the planned raid on the airfield, it was decided that his grenadiers would each carry a lighted cigar concealed in the palm of a hand to ignite the fuses.

At around 7 p.m., the raiding force left the bivouac area and proceeded to the village of Solano (Cagayan), directly opposite Tuguegarao. There they met up with Sgt. (now Lt.) Bill Bowen, who cockily declared, "Tomorrow we'll lunch in Tuguegarao." He was sorely disappointed when Praeger snapped that this was only to be a raid, not a full-scale attack. Bowen persisted, arguing that there were no more than two thousand Japs in Tuguegarao, that a large number of them were air force ground troops, and that "with a half-track, we could take the whole town from them."

Disturbing to all of Praeger's instincts and predilection for secrecy, some five thousand people gathered around his group in Solano to wish them luck. Midnight masses were said in all the town's churches to bless the attack. Most of the people there regarded C Troop's little force as forerunners of a major American counteroffensive. They were euphoric in their belief that Japan would be defeated in a few weeks.

Neither Bowen's enthusiasm nor the presence of so many people, which dimmed any sensible hope for surprise, deterred Praeger from proceeding with his attack plans. At around 10 p.m. on 12 January, the raiders crossed the Cagayan River in *bancas* (dugouts) previously procured by Lieutenant Minton and reached the outskirts of Tuguegarao about an hour later. Previous reconnaissance showed the field to be L-shaped and about three kilometers long. The location of barracks, hangars, and support buildings had already been determined by Private Aguas's accurate reports. To a man, the raiders had memorized the Tuguegarao layout and were prepared to navigate the entire base blindfolded. This was crucial due to the dark, moonless night prevailing.

Almost miraculously, despite the thousands of local civilians who knew of the impending raid, the enemy was asleep, apparently confident that no Allied forces were within hundreds of miles of Tuguegarao. There was a minimal guard in place with only a few sentinels, thus allowing the raiders to crawl to the edges of the base without detection.

MIDNIGHT, 13 JANUARY 1942

As anticipated, the night of the raid was moonless, cloudy, and pitch black. Praeger's advance scouts crawled into their preplanned positions and waited for the appointed time to initiate the attack. Then, as if with a single mind, they systematically took out the Japanese sentries whose movement patterns had been meticulously observed and noted. Soundlessly, with any gasps or cries cut short by slit throats or blades jabbed into spinal cords, the perimeter was cleared of its meager guard. Word was passed back to the main raiding party, and at about 2 a.m. they quietly moved in on the complacent, sleeping Japanese base. It took the raiders some two hours of searching in the dark to locate the several planes on the field. Praeger then signaled the full assault with a grenade, and all hell broke loose. Suddenly, some alert Japanese sounded an alarm, and the plan of attack was prematurely rushed, causing limited success to the destruction of aircraft. The small detachments under Lieutenant Bowen and 1st Sgt. Tomas Quiocho, which had been intending to destroy the fuel dump, abruptly found themselves under almost point-blank machine gun fire. Fortunately their group hit the ground before anyone was hit. Bowen wasted no time taking out two enemy guns with his homemade grenades.

Now under heavy machine gun fire, the all-out assault began. Daring became the order of the day. The darkness was pierced with flashes from a steady drumroll of Thompson submachine gun and rifle fire, and flames from Lieutenant Camp's homemade grenades and gasoline-filled San Miguel and Coke bottle Molotov cocktails heaved into Japanese barracks and airplane hangars and onto parked Zero-Sen fighters and Aichi dive bombers. Stunned from sleep, hundreds of terrified Japanese groped frantically for lights and weapons. Lights flashed on in buildings only to be promptly shot out by the storm of fire from the raiders. Bewildered, shocked Japanese were cut down by the murderous, direct fusillade of rounds as Praeger's deadly little force plowed relentlessly through the base and, without stopping, back into the hills beyond. Thoroughly panicked, the Japanese survivors were firing their weapons in every direction, succeeding only in killing more of their own people. Enemy fire had been badly organized at best from the outset, their guns being sited in exposed positions and for long-range targeting. Had they been set for short-range firing, the raiders might have suffered considerable losses. One Philippine constabulary soldier crossed the runway alone to singlehandedly eliminate an enemy guard post. Lieutenant Camp with his small patrol inflicted an effective attack on the enemy barracks (mostly old Philippine Army buildings). Another group under Cpl. Andres Montiadora, having accomplished its assignment to deny a critical road junction to the Japanese for thirty minutes, proceeded to the planned assembly point. There he learned that most of the troop was still on the airfield. He returned his patrol to the junction, a march of some four kilometers, and held his position until dawn. It was a characteristic example of 26th Cavalry troopers' courage, initiative, and reliability.

The C Troop raiders and their mixed reinforcements reached the cover of darkness again with not a single casualty and returned to Solano at dawn.

Two men, Lieutenant Bowen and Private Tumanut, got lost in the confusion and were missing but showed up the following day. Bowen had been caught between Japs on the airfield after he had knocked out the enemy machine guns with his makeshift grenades. He was forced to hide in bushes beside the runway until late the next day while the Japanese combed the area. On his return he had to endure sarcastic jibes that he had indeed lunched in Tuguegarao as he'd wanted, except there had been no lunch to eat.

The raiders had left behind some two hundred dead Japanese (this was based on later reports of the number of truckloads of dead from civilians who had observed them); two, possibly three, combat aircraft destroyed (to Praeger's disappointment; he had hoped to destroy more); and the Tuguegarao air base in flames. Despite Praeger's emphasis on secrecy, news of the raid was spread by word of mouth and the "bamboo telegraph" and eventually reached Australia. It would soon lift the hearts of the desperate defenders of Bataan and Corregidor and drive the Japanese command into a frenzy to clear the rugged mountains of North Luzon of an elusive and dangerous enemy.

Two days after the raid, in reprisal, the enraged Japanese murdered an untold number of Filipino civilians in the vicinity around Tuguegarao. In addition to slaughtering innocent persons, they burned down one entire barrio and houses in another. After the Tuguegarao raid, Praeger had established outposts in Solano, Enrile, and Dungao. Local security was established in Tuao, although the Japanese bombed Tuao and the barrio of Tuguegarao on the afternoon after the raid. A woman and four children were killed. Praeger's people soon learned that civilian morale in Cagayen Province, where the Japanese had landed first, was high, contrasting sharply with the relatively low morale in areas the troop had passed through. There, people had been loyal and kind to the Americans and scouts but also were fearful and dispirited. They were openly glad to see the latter leave before their presence drew Japanese wrath upon them. Not only the Lingayen defeats but constant enemy air presence instilled a sense of hopelessness in the people there. They feared Japanese occupation before any help from America or even most of the Philippine defense forces.

At dawn, after the attack, the raiders had reassembled at Solano. Cagayan's governor, Marcelo Adduru, personally greeted them. He was told that while his presence was appreciated, he should not have taken such risk lest there be enemy pursuit. His reaction was, "Well, if you can fight for us, I can at least be on hand to see you are taken care of!" Following that, Praeger and his men were taken to Tuao, the temporary headquarters of the Cagayan government. There, quarters and breakfast awaited them. Praeger's people were quartered in the houses of one Captain Sanchez and Don Colistino Rodriguez, a Spaniard. Senor Rodriguez, during the rest of 1942, placed himself, his home, and his family and servants at the disposal of the Americans and their Filipino allies. Ultimately, he paid the price of having the Japanese burn his home and possessions for the help he had given their enemy. Señor Rodriguez himself finally surrendered to the Japanese only after his wife and children had been seized as hostages.

Señor Rodriguez was Spanish born but had lived in the Philippines for over twenty years. His wife had given him three sons and three lovely daughters. All were warm-hearted, parents and children alike. Nothing was too good for the Americans and their comrades. The boys and the girls, only in their teens, willingly slept on the floor, giving their beds to officers and soldiers and could not be persuaded otherwise. The oldest boy and girl, both nearly twenty, were in Spain when the revolution broke out in the '30s. They had been forced to live in the hills for more than three years until they were able to get to France. They then were repatriated as U.S. nationals on an American destroyer. Their experiences in Spain proved a useful education in survival. Toni, the oldest girl, now insisted that her parents lay in a large store of food, soap, and matches, which she knew from her experience in Spain would soon be unobtainable. The family acquired a large amount of canned goods to that end, but they were so generous that they insisted on sharing their supplies.

Within a few months, their entire stock was exhausted.

Toni was a beautiful girl, in a classic Spanish manner, but there were many who considered that Nanita, who was then only about fifteen, would outshine even Toni. The war seemed not to encroach on them, as these two were vivacious and full of fun. Nanita seemed strangely to be the only person who almost enjoyed being bombed. When a bomb exploded harmlessly, she would shout, "Why, they can't hit a goddam thing!" The troopers admonished her for it, cautioning her that her father would punish her for such swearing, overlooking that she had picked it up from the soldiers. Understandably, Praeger's men all fell hopelessly in love with the two irresistible girls.

On their first night at the Rodriguez's, Nanita announced she hoped the war would not last too long, for she wanted to be married. The men replied almost as one, "But you're only 15!"

"Oh, it is the custom for a Spanish girl to marry at 16," Don Colistino interrupted. "It is a great pity that Toni is not yet married, but," he remarked sadly, "maybe it will come in time."

More than one 26th trooper in the group chased away the reality of that time with dreams of being the one who would capture Toni's eye.

At the time, Señor Rodriguez spent his entire day smoking cigars, about twenty-five during waking hours, and listening to San Francisco broadcasts. A buyer for Tabacalera, a great Spanish-owned Philippine tobacco corporation, he fully disregarded any adverse elements of the news and chose to accept positive, obviously propagandistic portions of the broadcasts as gospel of victories against the Japanese. Everything in the Rodriguez household was openly offered, although there was no toleration for listening to Tokyo broadcasts over his radio. Even though Allied reporting offered no clear picture of what was happening, and Tokyo with its stream of successes could afford more detail, honest reporting was in short supply.

When word of the Rodriguez family's capture by the Japanese reached Praeger's men, there was not a dry eye among them. The thought of the two beautiful, innocent young girls in Japanese hands especially tore their morale to pieces. Oddly enough, the common impression that the Japanese behaved with ferocity toward Filipino civilians is misleading. The occupation in the Philippines was guided by a strict policy of restraint, and the occupiers made a genuine effort to win the friendship and support of the Filipino people. Crimes by Japanese soldiers against civilians were in large part severely punished. In some twenty months in the area of Praeger's operations, only one case of rape against a Filipino woman was heard of. The Japanese offender was beheaded. Still, it was small comfort to those whose memories of the Rodriguez family were so close to their hearts.

C Troop's Lt. Tom Jones (later, Col., USA Ret.) recorded in his memoirs the story of the people of Cagayan Province. "It had a man as its leader, Governor Adduru. He took the capture of his capital in stride, shifting his headquarters to Tuao the day before the Japanese arrived. His provincial government continued its operations with almost maximum efficiency. Though he had lost his two largest cities, he had not lost his province, and he certainly didn't think he'd lost the war.

"He was glad to see us because he wanted someone to do some fighting. He felt keenly the withdrawal of the units which had been training in Cagayan at the beginning of the war for their failure to attempt delay of the Japanese. When the Japanese dealt reprisals for the Tuguegarao raid, he was deeply grieved, for many of those murdered had been life-long friends. Still, he did not regret the raid. 'One has to pay a price to make war,' he observed. 'We here in Cagayan are prepared to pay that price; otherwise I would have asked you not to make the attack.' Adduru did not doubt that he, as leader of the resistance in his area, might be called upon to pay the heaviest price of all."

When news of the Tuguegarao raid and official accounts from now Capt. Warren Minton of C Troop and Major Warner, CO of the 88th Field Artillery, was belatedly forwarded to MacArthur on Corregidor, his response was a message of commendation of the action broadcasted through both shortwave and broadband radio to the beleaguered American and Filipino defenders of the islands. The isolated act of vengeance was received joyfully by all Allied personnel and citizens as the first truly good news since the dark days of Pearl Harbor and Clark Field. The reports read as follows:

KZPG January 1942
Commanding General U.S.A.F.F.E.
Troop "C". Twenty Sixth Cavalry
  Commanded by Capt. R. B. Praeger with First Lieutenants Warren A. Minton and
Thomas S. Jones, also 2nd Lt. De Leon, Philippine Army with ninety two enlisted
men made successful surprise attack on enemy controlled air field at Tuguegarao.—
STOP. Enemy killed first estimated at one hundred ten. Later revised to two hundred
or more. Three combat aircraft destroyed. Enemy scattered estimated at three
hundred.—STOP. Prominent in this attack all officers mentioned plus Tech. Ser-
geant William E. Bowen, Signal Corps USA and Private Francis H. Camp. Just
enlisted. Formerly U.S. Marine Corps.—STOP. All these soldiers deserve Special
Recognition.—STOP We shall Especially try to identify Second Lt. De Leon—STOP.
All officers and men Returned Safely.
  (Signed) WARNER
  Maj. 88th F.A.
  Commanding

The following is an extract of an account of activities of Troop C, 26th Cavalry (PS):

  On this date of January 29, a radio report was received from USAAFE headquarters re-Tuguegarao raid.
  308 RC/JC 8:25 A——KZPT Jan. 29, 1942
  Att: Warner/Major 88th F.A., Commanding
  Warner: Tuguegarao Raid splendid—STOP. Officers and Men Distinguishing
  themselves gallantly hereby cited for D.S.C.

  MacArthur 4141P
  The above was in reply to original report.
  (Signed) Warren A. Minton
  Captain, 26th Cavalry
  A True Copy:
  William S. Gochenour, Jr.
  Captain: Veterinary Corps (Detailed to 26th Cavalry)

In a later letter of commendation from MacArthur dated 20 July 1943, the
Supreme Commander, Pacific stated the following:

  Troop C, 26th Cavalry Soldiers:
    I wish gratefully to acknowledge and commend the unconquerable spirit
  that has kept together your little band and enabled you, in a conquered area,
  to carry on for so long a time combat operations against the enemy. In doing
  this, you have enshrined in glory the guidon of your troop and given an inspir-
  ing, brilliant example for soldiers wherever they may be to follow. To those of
  you who are depressed and ill, I trust merciful Providence will protect and suc-
  cor you and give you new faith, hope and courage in the certainty that your

sacrifice and struggle shall not have been in vain. I commend your officers who survive—Captain Praeger, Lts. Jones, Needham, Minton, Bowen and Furagganan—for the highest qualities of leadership, unswerving devotion, and resourcefulness.

MAC ARTHUR

MacArthur's authorized commendations were confirmed for Capt. Ralph Praeger for the Distinguised Service Cross, all of his junior officers for Silver Stars, and the remainder of the raiding party participants for bronze star awards, regardless of their military status.

Word of the Tuguegarao raid would be the only uplifting war news the Philippine defenders would receive until that of the 18 April 1942 daring feat of Col. Jimmy Doolittle and his unprecedented USN carrier *Hornet* launched raid of Army B-25 medium bombers' attack on Tokyo and the Japanese home islands and the subsequent escape with minor losses into mainland China.

On 15 January, Lieutenant Minton proceeded to Isabela to inspect what was left of the troop and to obtain supplies. He returned on 19 January with a letter from Lt. Col. E. L. Warner requesting that Minton be detached to serve as a staff officer with the regiment being formed in Isabela. The services of the scouts who'd been left in Santiago were also requested as instructors. Praeger approved, and subsequently, Minton and designated scouts were detached to the 14th Infantry (PA). The next day, Minton and the scouts left for Isabela and Lieutenant Bowen departed to make reconnaissance in the Lubuagan area.

The principal concern was shortage of ammunition. Since the area where the troop was now located hadn't been fought over, little could be recovered there. Hours were spent dragging a downed P-40 fighter plane out of the Cagayan River only to discover its .50-caliber machine guns were damaged beyond repair. Lieutenant Camp continued to "manufacture" grenades—they were better than nothing, even though almost as hazardous to their throwers as to their intended targets.

On 25 January, the Solano outpost reported that the Japanese had regarrisoned Tuguegarao. Apparently, the Japs were very nervous. They had sent a Japanese-Filipino woman into Solano to confirm that there were no guerillas there before they went into the town. Once satisfied, they moved in, initially killing one civilian on a horse. They then threatened to shoot anyone on horseback on the grounds that "enemy cavalry" had attacked Tuguegarao. Praeger's forward observers, Pvts. Lee Tullungan and Tamundo Camonayan, had hidden in the underbrush to maintain their outpost. A 26th outpost was manned in Solano until 1944, long after the Japanese had firmly occupied the town. Camonayan was not relieved until July 1942, but Tullungan, although seriously wounded, remained on watch at Solano until 1944 when he was captured and executed by the Japanese. Their out-post not only demonstrated the courage and devotion of the two troopers but also the steadfast loyalty of the Solano civilians, typical of the allied sympathy throughout Cagayan.

INTERIM RAIDS

Withdrawing far enough north and determining that enemy discovery would be difficult, Praeger ordered his communications troopers to go to work. His first sergeant, Tomas Quiocho, himself a trained radio man, set up their hand-cranked generator and shortwave radio. Contact was then made with USAFFE and Australian headquarters in Brisbane. Initial radio contact from the cut-off C Troop in North Luzon was received by an army on-duty communications officer, Lt. Charles Ferguson from Fishers Island, New York.[2] To determine the authenticity of the communications, a string of personal questions was put to Praeger and his second in command, 1st Lt. Tom Jones. Included were such trick questions as "How old are your two children?" to which Praeger replied, "Some other bum must have gotten into my bed while I've been over here, because I don't have any kids." Once his communications were determined genuine and not some kind of crafty Japanese ploy to harvest information, radio contact was as frequent as Praeger could risk. There was an unceasing effort on the part of the infuri-ated Japanese to determine by radio triangulation the location of Praeger and his force. Their efforts were in vain for almost two years until treachery by a turncoat Filipino revealed their location (such traitors were branded by their fellow Filipinos as *macapili*).

Praeger, Tom Jones, and other surviving Troop C personnel and some of their valiant civilian allies, including Lt. Col. Arthur K. "Maxey" Noble, were taken in captivity to the infamous Manila prison compound of Fort Santiago, where the fabled Filipino national hero and patriot poet Jose Rizal had been imprisoned before his death at the hands of the Spanish.

On 21 December 1943, after months of torture and fruitless questioning, the Japanese, concerned about the public notoriety in favor of Ralph Praeger and noted guerilla fighters Cols. Arthur Noble and Martin Moses, both formerly of the 11th Infantry Division PA who had been officers in the large anti-occupation force led by 26th Cavalryman Capt. Edwin Ramsey, ordered their execution. The Japanese took the men in the dead of night to a small Catholic church adjacent to Manila's large Chinese cemetery where the sentences were to be carried out. The Japanese thought they had trans-ferred their prisoners secretly but had been watched the whole time by fur-tive Filipinos, who wasted no time spreading the news of the fate of the admired anti-Japanese fighters. The prisoners were taken into the walled courtyard of the little church, still thought by the Japanese to be out of sight, and all beheaded. The bodies were then taken into the Chinese cemetery where, to maximize use of the limited acreage, their remains were buried in layers, one on top of another. The Japanese buried their victims deep under the layers in hopes the bodies would never be discovered or recovered.

Lts. Tom Jones and Warren Minton were taken instead to Bilibid Prison in southern Manila to be held for their own scheduled execution. Capt. Joe Barker of B Troop, who had gone into the hills with Ed Ramsey and had been fighting as a guerilla for over a year until his capture, was in Bilibid at the same time as Tom Jones. Jones later commented that Joe Barker was "one of the toughest men he had ever known, unendingly withstanding brutal treatment by the Japanese and proving himself an outstanding example of bravery. Horribly battered and beaten, he never stopped constantly encouraging the rest of us to stand fast against 'the miserable little bastards' and not give in an inch to them. Barker never gave in right until the last when the Japanese took him into the prison courtyard and shot him. His bravery is what kept most of us alive right up to the end."

NOTES

1. Accounts about C Troop's actions are for the most part taken from interviews with and memoirs of Col. Thomas Jones (USA Ret.), Lt. Warren Minton's recorded reports, and notes and interviews from Lt. (then 1st Sgt.) Tomas Quiocho (USA Ret.).

2. It is a fitting coincidence that "Charlie" Ferguson is the author's second cousin on his mother's side. Ferguson is a noted nature, wildlife, and sailing artist and retired director of the Museum of American Art in New Britain, Connecticut. He spends much of his time at his birthplace of Fishers Island, New York, in his studio there and his self-built home, "Flounder In," which incorporates a generous amount of driftwood from the island's prolific beaches. His admiration for and memories of his contacts with Praeger remain deep in his heart to this day.

22

Moron: The Last Charge

14 JANUARY 1942

I Corps Sector on West Coast of Bataan

On 12 January, after rest, reorganization of the regiment, and re-shoeing of the horses was to the satisfaction of Pierce, Vance, and Chandler, the 26th Cavalry commenced regular patrolling of the western flank sector of Wainwright's I Corps defensive line. Troops of the regiment conducted constant patrols of the west coast road and along the shoreline, both on the lookout for Japanese incursions and to get fully familiarized with the entire sector and its trails and terrain. The regiment was now acting under command of Brig. Gen. Fidel V. Segundo with 1st Infantry CO Major McCullom directing tactical control.

On 14 January, Col. Yunosuke Watanabe, following the orders of 14th Army CO Akira Nara, began his advance south from Olongapo toward Moron with elements of the 122nd Infantry, amounting to some eight hundred troops. About three hundred of these Watanabe led down the jungle trails overland toward Moron (referred to as Morong on many maps). Approximately another five hundred of his force were embarked in small landing boats to approach Moron's beachfront from the sea. Wainwright had already dispatched a battalion of the 1st Infantry to Moron when he first got word that the Japanese had taken Olongapo on the 11th. When the Japanese did not advance farther south, he withdrew the battalion two days later and put it in reserve. To cover Moron, Wainwright left G Troop/26th (commanded by Capt. John W. Fowler), which had been patrolling the area around the small coastal town since the 11th and knew the lay of the land around there.

Colonel Watanabe's progress was slow and hesitant, handicapped by poor maps and unfamiliarity with the coastline. The seaborne troops became hopelessly lost and put ashore between Olongapo and the town of Moron. After conferring with them, Watanabe re-embarked about half their number back to sea to circle around to Moron. Watanabe soon found that his landborne approach to Moron was interdicted north of the town by the Batalan River, about thirty to forty yards wide but deep and steeply banked on both sides, forming a challenging barrier to infantry on foot. The river ran west all the way to a creek, branching abruptly south off it through a burri reed swamp for a few hundred feet before reaching the beach and emptying into the sea. A small wooden footbridge crossed over the creek to a narrow trail through heavy underbrush to the shore.

Wainwright got word of the movements of Watanabe's forward elements toward Moron and, to counter them, he ordered the whole of the 1st Infantry plus the 1st Engineer Battalion and two battalions of artillery to the village. In command were General Segundo and Major McCullom. Wainwright sent a composite of E and F Troops from the 26th Cavalry, under command of Capt. John Z. Wheeler, to relieve G Troop, which had been on nonstop patrol there for about six days. First Lt. Edwin Ramsey of G Troop remained behind with E–F because of his familiarity with the ground. This contingent of cavalry would be the first American force to clash with the Japanese at Moron. Segundo got his units into position at Moron, but then late on the 14th, he pulled his troops back from the town, presumably to find better fields of fire. An irate Wainwright arrived on the scene and laced into Segundo, ordering him to get his people back to take position just south of the Batalan River.

16 JANUARY 1942

Taking his attention off Segundo, Wainwright saw Wheeler and Ramsey mounted nearby. The general ordered Ramsey to immediately take the advance guard back into Moron. Wheeler answered, requesting respectfully, "Sir, Lieutenant Ramsey has been here on long reconnaissance and only volunteered to stay behind because he knows the terrain better than I do. Couldn't I possibly send someone else to lead the advance party?"

Wainwright replied abruptly, "Never mind that, Wheeler. Ramsey, move out, now!"

Wheeler and Ramsey returned to the troop. On the way back, Johnny Wheeler apologized, saying, "Ed, tired as you are, I'm really sorry to see you get stuck with leading this action, but there isn't much I can do about it since Skinny gave the word. Hell, you heard him."

Wheeler then ordered E–F Troop to mount up and move off in the order of march with Ramsey's 1st Platoon to the front as point. Wheeler followed next with 2nd Platoon under command of an exceptional Filipino Scout,

Lt. Eliseo V. Mallari, a slightly built but resilient reserve officer who had formerly been sergeant major of the 26th's 2nd Squadron. The 3rd Platoon brought up the rear of the column led by Sergeant Masangcay. They moved in a northwesterly direction following the two-lane, dirt and gravel Bagac–Moron Road, which runs about one kilometer in from and parallel to the China Sea. Rutted and filled with potholes, the road had been mainly a route for carabao carts, ponies, and horses. This was the dry season, and a layer of powdery gray dust covered everyone and everything, filling eyes, noses, and mouths with choking grit. Most of the men wore the World War I style helmets, but many stubbornly stuck to wearing floppy-brimmed fatigue hats. Unanimous among all American and Philippine troops was a dislike of the helmets because of their intense, often painful discomfort caused by the rough liners, especially in Philippine heat.

Ramsey, mounted on his prized mount Bryn Awryn, which he had brought with him from the states, had formed his lead platoon into a staggered column straddling the road with intent to present a more difficult target for whatever they might encounter. He directed Cpl. Jacinto Gonzales, nineteen-year-old Pfc. Pedro Euperio, and two other troopers to ride point. They rode about three miles before coming upon the eastern-most borders of Moron. There, the route split into four or five trails passing for streets running west to the left from the main road through a thick wood of palm trees and light vegetation. The main road ended at a rickety wooden bridge over the river.

Ramsey signaled a column left on what appeared to be the center trail or main street. He then had the platoon deploy into a line of squads and move in the direction of what looked like the village center. Going into the edge of town, Ramsey had the troop turn off the primary line of march and began to disperse around the buildings. He then ordered his men to draw and "raise pistols" as they split along three trails and began to disperse around the buildings. The village was little more than a collection of thatch-roofed nipa huts with sawali walls (woven strips of bamboo forming siding) mounted on wooden pole stilts reaching about six feet above the ground. Beneath most were bamboo fences for pigs and chickens. Most were gone now, the majority plundered by hungry, foraging soldiers. In the town center was a very old, stucco and mud block-walled Catholic church standing in a thick grove of coconut palms. Ramsey's platoon was still in the lead with Wheeler and the rest of the troop following.

To their direct front, about a hundred yards ahead, was the Batalan River. Unknown to the cavalrymen just yet was that a small advance patrol of Japanese had made their way across the Batalan and were probing through the village between the church and the river. As the 26th point neared the village center, Corporal Gonzales and three troopers with him saw infantry in what looked like dark mustard-colored army fatigue uniforms stalking in column through the village between the church and the creek. Some had already passed through and had started moving south. Suddenly both sides saw one another, and there was a sudden crackling of small-arms fire and automatic weapons. Gonzales and his point turned and galloped back toward Ramsey and the bulk of the platoon. The young Private Euperio was badly shot up. When he rode up to Ramsey, blood was spurting from three bullet holes in his left shoulder down in a line across his chest like some kind of gory Sam Browne belt. He had another hole in his left arm, and Ramsey thought the nineteen-year-old was a goner. Euperio's reins were draped across his wounded arm, and his pistol was still firmly gripped in his right hand.

Ramsey ordered the young scout to the rear and reported to Wheeler what was happening in the town; then he was to take cover with help from Private Gonzalez until he could be evacuated to an aid station.

Quickly reading the situation, Ramsey raised his right arm high and signaled his men into a "line of foragers" (all horses and men in line with their leader). He then shouted the order "CHARGE!" and the entire platoon as one plunged forward at a dead run through the shocked and now terrified Japanese column. Every trooper was rapid firing and heaving grenades from almost prone positions in their saddles, killing and wounding a large number of the Japanese and scattering the rest into the palms. They were faced with a solid wall of twelve-hundred-pound horses coming at them full tilt, ridden by shooting riders yelling like legendary banshees, and the combined effect on the stupefied Japanese soldiers was total. Some simply got run down by the charging horses; some fled into the swamp; others sprinted through the village into the heavy underbrush on the far side. A panicked few hastily scrambled up into the nipa huts in an effort to get out of sight. The remainder closest to the river turned and splashed back into the dense jungle cover on the north side where they finally turned and began returning fire.

When the onslaught reached the coastal creek, Ramsey shouted orders to dismount and fight on foot. Men snatched rifles from their scabbards as they swung to the ground and then slapped horses on their quarters chasing them to the rear. Loose horses, some that had lost wounded riders and others that bolted from dismounting troopers, were still milling around in the midst of the fighting, adding to the chaos.

Ramsey, armed now with his favorite weapon in a fight, a Thompson submachine gun, was frantically deploying his troopers while at the same time firing. He deployed one of his squads, including two machine guns, along the river to counterfire from the jungle on the far side to the north. He led the rest from hut to hut hunting down snipers who had found hiding places and were starting to take a toll of the troopers. Most often, the cavalrymen simply ripped the huts to pieces with rifle and automatic weapons fire. Grenades against such flimsy structures in close quarters were considered more of a hazard to the throwers than to the snipers.

> The advance party under Wheeler reached the part of the line established as point following the charge. His Troop clerk Corporal Felipe Fernandez observed Private Euperio, gunner for the point, dismounted and manning a light machine gun although wounded and bleeding. (This was the same trooper who had reported earlier to Ramsey while severely wounded.) Wheeler ordered the Fernandez's part of a detachment to clear snipers from the houses. The dismounted rushed the nipa huts firing with pistols and tommy guns. Grenades were still a risk to the throwers as well as their targets.

Even though badly outnumbered, the ferocity of the 26th troopers' daring charge had decimated the advance elements of Watanabe's force; but at this point, the main body of Japanese had come up to the north shore of the river and were putting down a withering hail of rifle, machine gun, and mortar fire into the village of Moron now held by the cavalry. Ramsey's troopers were now in a vicious crossfire both from the shore and from across the river.

At this point, Wheeler and Mallari, alerted both by the firing and by Private Euperio's message from Ramsey, brought the remainder of Troops E–F into the village and joined the fight. Lt. Eliseo Mallari got his people on the scene in time to see fleeing Japanese still struggling through the water of the river to get to the north side. "I got my platoon dismounted, and we joined the men on the river line under heavy Jap fire from the other side. The Japs still crossing through the water were sitting ducks, but the fire from the Japs in the jungle on the north side was murder. Ramsey's charge had a heavy psychological effect on the Japs, and now our dismounted troopers were putting out very disciplined fire. The value of the constant training of the regiment was really evident, and we were holding the enemy again to a standstill."

Sergeant Masangcay got the third platoon positioned to counter the Japanese trying again to move back toward the town from the shore and the coastal swamp. The 26th troopers stopped them cold.

Wheeler dispersed his men in the town to help Ramsey's platoon clear the place of the Japanese who had stayed behind and had begun to snipe from the nipa huts. All during this time, the *thunk thunk!* of Japanese mortars could be heard as their fire began to fall heavily on the area. The noise was deafening, and the situation had become chaotic from the constant Japanese crossfire coming both from the jungle north of the river and in from the shore where the Japanese had regrouped and were trying to press their advance again.

Ramsey ducked between some coconut trees close to the church where a loose horse stood with a dismounted trooper next to it. A Japanese mortar round landed with a stunning *cruummp!* only about six feet in front of Ramsey. The loose horse reared on its hindquarters with a pitiful scream and slowly collapsed down on its haunches, weaving almost gracefully as would an outsized ballet dancer. It was dead when it settled to the ground, but the trooper, also wounded, was still fighting. Ramsey later commented that it was a heartrending image so vividly imprinted on his mind that he could still see it clearly. Nearby, Private Rebera was hit by a sniper as he dismounted. Corporal Abad was struggling to regroup his squad when Private Sibalon came up carrying Rebera and leading his horse. Rebera, however, was beyond help and died a few minutes later. Abad shouted at some of his men to get the horses to cover.

Ramsey's luck held for him. His only wound from the frightfully close call was a small shrapnel sliver in the fleshy part of his left knee. He was so charged up with adrenaline from the action that he didn't realize he was hit until Wheeler came up to him and said, "Ed, you've got blood on your left leg in case you don't know it."

Ramsey made a quick check of the puncture in his knee and then looked over at Wheeler.

"Look who's talking, Johnny. What the hell's that leaking out of your boot?"

Wheeler's foot was soaked with blood running from a bullet wound that had gone right through his boot but luckily had not hit the bone in his leg. Both men were a mess, covered with a mix of dust and blood. Their mouths were now so dehydrated from nerves that their tongues were literally stuck to the roofs of their mouths. Ramsey recalls with dry humor that he was embarrassed to find that the crotch of his britches was wet but not with sweat. "Now I finally knew the real meaning of the expression 'getting the piss scared out of you.' The worst times always came before a fight started. Once the shooting started, I was too busy to worry about it, and the fear itself became a kind of anesthetic."

While fighting on foot, Ramsey encountered Private Euperio still again in the shadow of the church. He looked over his shoulder to see the young trooper standing behind him, "weaving like a drunken sailor from shock, weakness and loss of blood." Ramsey never forgot his words. "Sir, I cannot go back—I am still on guard." Then he collapsed. He had reported to Wheeler but instead of joining the wounded, returned to find Ramsey. The latter moved the boy over and laid him down against the church. He remained there until the battle was over and he was finally taken to hospital. One of Ramsey's first administrative actions after returning to the rear was to cite Euperio for the Distinguished Service Cross, the award given for extraordinary heroism in battle second only to the Medal of Honor. For a time it seemed that the boy's award might become posthumous, but he survived his wounds and received his medal after the final liberation of the Philippines in 1945.

At the height of the Moron fight, Ramsey spotted an American officer apparently cowering against the church about twenty yards from him. Not knowing or caring who he was, Ramsey cursed him roundly and yelled at him, "You yellow sonuvabitch; get the hell over here and fight." Unbeknownst to Ramsey, it was Wainwright's own chief of staff, there to observe and not even supposed to be that close to the action. Later, Ramsey found out that Johnny Wheeler thought he was yelling at him and "went nuts taking all kinds of chances to prove it wasn't so!" Oddly enough, later, Wainwright's observer, who had been so vehemently cursed by Ramsey, cited the latter for the Silver Star. Ramsey chuckles to this day that he suspects it was the first time any soldier got a medal for cussing out a superior officer. However, that Silver Star negated a Distinguished Service Cross recommended for Ramsey by Wheeler, but being given a second Silver Star partially compensated for it. John Wheeler, himself, was cited for a well-deserved Distinguished Service Cross but, sadly, never received it. He died two years later as a POW on one of the "Japan-Go" Hell ships sunk by American planes whose pilots didn't know the *marus* were transporting American prisoners to Japan to prevent their liberation.

The crossfire became hellish. The continuous sound of mortars accompanied the persistent rattle of small arms as the high arching shells thundered into the little town. A constant storm of bullets "filled the air like a swarm of mad bees," recalled Ramsey later. The small .065-caliber, high-velocity rounds from Japanese small arms made a peculiar *pic-boom* sound that no one who ever heard could forget. But, once again, the 26th held its ground. The Japanese were neither able to cross the river again nor advance in from the beach.

It was not until late in the afternoon that E–F Troop succeeded in clearing Moron of the much superior Japanese force. The exhausted cavalrymen were relieved by the 1st Infantry and ordered withdrawn, their terrible but historic ordeal finally ended. So it was that the last mounted charge in history by an organized, regular unit of the U.S. Horse Cavalry took place on 16 January 1942.

Almost miraculously, in spite of the terrible ferocity of the fight at Moron, the only 26th Cavalry casualties that day were two dead (Troopers Lopez and Mallaris), six wounded, and several horses lost. The Japanese, on the other hand, suffered scores of dead and wounded. Three of their wounded were captured, a terrible disgrace for men deeply imbued with the grim philosophy and stern discipline of Bushido. One of the wounded Japanese prisoners lay beside two of his dead comrades near the Moron church. They had been downed by the wild charge of the 26th. The man kept motioning to Wheeler, who was trying to give him water from his own canteen, to kill him instead with his bayonet. Ramsey and Wheeler thought him pitiful in his terrified shame. That prisoner, along with two other enemy wounded, were put on stretchers and sent to the rear, guarded by a Philippine infantry noncom with orders to get them back unharmed for interrogation. None of them survived to be questioned. Filipino anger was running deep from the blood of that day.

Despite this, Jonathan Wainwright, the old cavalryman, had good reason that day to be proud of the unhesitant initiative and dauntless courage of the Horsemen of Bataan, who immortalized the traditions of the horse cavalry right down to its historic final charge.

23

The Last Dismounting of a U.S. Horse Regiment

17 JANUARY 1942

Having been relieved after their epic fight at Moron by the 1st Infantry (PA), the badly worn survivors of the combined E–F Troop returned to the Mauban bivouac area. Following their historic last cavalry charge they were missing some twenty-five horses. Maj. Lee Vance immediately dispatched 1st Lt. Clifford Hardwicke to take a detail to return to Moron to recover a number of horses that had been left behind, including Johnny Wheeler's personal horse Michael, a handsome dark chestnut thoroughbred that had been broken on arrival at Stotsenburg by the able E Troop Sgt. Felipe Fernandez. The Troop E–F withdrawal south from Moron had been made cross-country through ground near the beach. The main road had come under heavy enemy sniper and mortar fire from across the river, and a number of horses that had been tied in that area during the fight had to be left behind.

In the scramble, Ramsey had lost his bedroll, and one of his G Troop fellow officers, a good-hearted Texan, Lt. Cliff Hardwicke, offered to share his. While the jungle days are hot and steamy, the nights tend to be cold and damp. Ramsey, exhausted and dehydrated from the trauma of the Moron fight, had his leg bandaged by a medic, changed his breeches, and drank a great deal of water. After eating sparsely, he literally collapsed into sleep on Hardwicke's blanket. He awoke late the next morning to learn that Hardwicke had taken a detachment back into Moron to recover the horses left behind. The group found the picketed horses near the river still under the care of three 26th E Troopers with Sergeant Belhara. As they started out on their return, Cliff Hardwicke was shot in the head by a sniper, dying

308

instantly. The death of the well-liked officer was a stunning loss to his fellows in the 26th, especially Ed Ramsey. He felt terrible guilt that it had not been he who had returned for the horses, and he sought solace with the regimental chaplain. Somehow, Hardwicke's death heightened in Ramsey a sense that all the men on Bataan were feeling: one of betrayal and abandonment by their country. Fighting for weeks on end with the forlorn hope of some kind of relief was wearing thin the strength of their morale, despite the repeated assurances issued from MacArthur's headquarters on Corregidor.

The regiment stayed put in their Mauban positions for several days waiting for an expected assault from the main Japanese force behind the advance force encountered in Moron. The waiting took its toll on everyone, especially Ed Ramsey. He began to experience severe general weakness and saw that his skin was turning yellow. There was no doubt that it was jaundice. He was sent to No. 2 field hospital near Mariveles, the town on the southern tip of Bataan. It was a charnel house sheltered in a ramshackle arrangement of tents and makeshift shelters of miscellaneous materials located beneath a protective canopy of enormous lauan trees. Ed recalls that he "could hear the place before I saw it." There was a steady din of screams and cries from men suffering from every kind of wound imaginable. As he neared, he was greeted with the sight of row upon row of beat-up metal bedsteads with mosquito netting hung over them and scores of hammocks for those without a cot. One could almost see a cloud of stench that arose from this dismal gathering. *Ghastly* is a weak term for what lay here. Doctors and nurses, army and some valiant civilian volunteers, were doing heroic and tireless work to save men and their torn bodies. Gangrene and tropical infection were rampant in these conditions, and the battle against them was incessant. Short of disinfectants and anti-infection medicines, doctors drew a leaf from the books of ancient Roman surgeons. They did open-reduction incisions on gangrenous wounds and planted colonies of maggots onto the exposed raw flesh. Primitive as this sounds, the results were remarkable. Maggots, which feed only on dead flesh, did a yeoman's job of cleansing the affected areas, and many a Bataan survivor today can thankfully display scars rather than amputated limbs.

Back at Mauban, the waiting went on. Discipline served to interrupt the tension. Colonel Vance saw to it that ample attention was spent primarily regrouping and re-arming Troop E–F and general regimental maintenance and care of animals. Colonel Vance noted one incident of interest in his war diary. A dogfight between an American P-40 and several Japanese Zeros took place above Bagac. Army Air Force First Lieutenant Anderson's P-40 was shot down, and the fortunate pilot was rescued by 26th Cavalrymen after a harrowing bailout. Cut off from any hope of returning to aerial duty,

Anderson was issued a rifle, ammunition, and a pack and became an infantryman from then on.

19 FEBRUARY 1942

After the return of the horses from Moron, realizing that Bataan's dense jungle terrain made fluid mounted cavalry impractical and with the overall ration situation fast declining seriously, General Wainwright found himself forced to make an agonizing decision. The 26th Cavalry had to be dismounted and the horses and mules sent south to paddocks at Agloloma near Mariveles, where they would be taken as needed by the quartermasters to be slaughtered and butchered for food at the nearby abattoir established by the corps of veterinarians who inspected and approved all meats obtained. It was a terrible and pitiful order, but all knew that without forage, the already near starving animals would soon die, regardless.

The preparations for evacuation of the animals was a heartrending scene. Tough, seasoned troopers wept openly as they hugged the necks of their horses and bid their final good-byes to the valiant animals that had carried them so faithfully and bravely throughout the long, bloody ordeal since the war had begun. Sgt. Felipe Fernandez of E Troop openly wept as he clung to the neck of his beloved Dyang Dyang. Accompanied by veterinarian Capt. Clayton E. Michelson and the veterinary truck, Supply Sgt. Juan Dalipe was put in charge of the dozen or so troopers who drew the sad duty of escorting the animals south. There was a choke in his voice as he ordered the forlorn group of 251 horses and 48 pack mules to assemble and move off for their final journey into history. Later, it would be a fitting tribute to the mutual loyalty of men and their animal comrades that, near starvation as they were like the rest of the Bataan defenders, 26th troopers refused to eat any portion of horse meat offered, making do instead with any other meat available, such as carabao, monkey, fowl, snake, or even rodents to sustain them.

General Wainwright sent along the fateful instruction that the first horse to be killed was to be none other than his own beloved survivor, Joseph Conrad. Veterinarian Michelson accompanied the animals to Agaloma corral. Actual slaughtering began on 20 January 1942. On that note, the full significance fell on Wainwright of the impact of this tragic order. Not only did it signal the death of 26th Cavalry as the last combat operational horse-mounted regiment, but this was the ultimate symbol of the finish of America's horse cavalry as an integral fighting force.

Johnny Wheeler soon also developed jaundice and was sent to join Ed Ramsey in No. 2 field hospital. When he found Ramsey, Johnny gave him the tragic news of the fate of the 26th Cavalry horses. It hit Ed hard, but all he could say was, "I guess it was inevitable. The poor devils were nothing but skin and bone." In an attempt to lighten the air a little, Wheeler told Ed, "I thought you should know that they put you in for the Silver Star."

"Who?" asked Ramsey in dismay.

Wheeler smiled and replied, "You remember that officer you called a yellow son of a bitch in front of the church at Moron? Well, that just happened to be Wainwright's chief of staff. He wasn't shirking. He'd just come up to report on the action. Well, he's the one who recommended you."

Ramsey shook his head and chuckled at the irony. "Well, I guess that makes me the first soldier who ever got a medal for cussing out a staff officer."

"Oh, and by the way," Wheeler added, "but I damned near got shot because of you. When you yelled at that guy, I thought you were yelling to *me* that *I* was yellow. I got so damned mad I ran all over the place trying to get myself shot at just to prove you wrong." He laughed then. "Now look who's yellow!"

Upon being examined by the doctors, Wheeler's wounds from Moron were judged severe enough that he was immediately evacuated to No. 1 field hospital, which had been transferred south from Limay to the outskirts just north of Mariveles on the southern tip of Bataan. Nurse Capt. Ann Wertz was assigned to his care, but when Juanita Redmond heard Wheeler was there, she was at his bedside every opportunity she could get. The warmth between them was a healing force for both their spirits.

When Johnny was finally able to get out of bed and walk about, he and Juanita found private places in the forest at the base of Mt. Mariveles and found something rare in each other's company despite the war and horror around them. But such things were too good to last, and finally the day came when Wheeler was judged fit to return to duty. Few words were spoken, but when the lovely Carolina girl watched the gentle young lieutenant turn to get in the jeep returning him to the crucible, her heart sank into depths only one with such feelings could ever know.

On his return after a bumpy ride from the hospital, Wheeler arrived to find that events were taking a hard turn. The Japanese, after Moron, were now hard pressing their attack on the I Corps lines. To make matters worse for Wainwright, Lt. Hiroshi Nakanishi's force of seven hundred men, after their grueling trek across the mountains and supported by their several small mountain artillery guns, had succeeded in turning southwest and getting around Wainwright's right flank. By late 20 December, they were now in position about one mile behind Skinny's main line and had established a dangerous block across the only west coast route to the south and were in the process of cutting both communications and the supply route to the I Corps front line. It was a trap that called for immediate counteraction. Wainwright had Pierce and Vance alert the motor squadron to commence patrolling the Pila–Bagac Road to counter enemy detachments reported working south from their Abucay positions. On 20 January the Japanese were seen taking up positions behind the 1st Division (PA) at kilometer post 164 on the west coast road, and Vance ordered the 26th Motor Squadron under 1st Lt. Donald H. Wills to move south to engage them. It soon became evident that an effective assault on the enemy roadblock was going to require more force than the one 26th squadron.

Early on 21 January Wainwright, accompanied by Tom Dooley and Tex Carroll, undertook a tour of his front. At the 1st Division CP he found to his shock that the enemy had worked their way behind the American lines across the Moron Road. The Division officers warned him that he was at risk going any farther south because of enemy observation and snipers. The general would have none of that and proceeded to organize a makeshift platoon of anyone who could leave the CP with him. Taking up a rifle, he was able to collect a mix of about twenty men, including a few Filipino soldiers, a navy commander, some beached sailors, and the pilot, Lieutenant Anderson, who'd been rescued just days before by the 26th. Wainwright led his patched platoon as far as the roadblock where he found a platoon of Filipino soldiers already in a firefight.

Wainwright took charge of the situation, and the small, combined force undertook a two-hour assault. It was vicious fighting on steep terrain and in a dense tangle of jungle trees potted with deep gorges offering ideal concealment for Japanese snipers who could pick their shots mere yards from their targets. Wainwright was exposing himself dangerously while directing the action, and after a near miss, Tex Carroll yanked him down, cursing. A moment later, two Filipinos, who had been next to the general, were hit, one being killed and the other wounded. It was fast becoming clear that a considerably larger force was going to be needed to dislodge this dangerous roadblock. Heading north to gather reinforcements, Wainwright was able to muster some units of the 91st Division, the 26th Cavalry, and one battalion of the 194th Tanks. He put John Rodman, the 92nd Infantry Regiment CO, in command and ordered an attack in force at dawn of the 22nd.

Meanwhile, the front line of I Corps was on the verge of cracking from pressure to its north. It was a terrible situation. If they broke and attempted to withdraw south, they would be blocked cold by the Japanese roadblock at their rear. Wainwright turned back to his southward assault force, which had not yet been able to dislodge the enemy positions. The 194th tanks had been stopped by a combination of Japanese antitank guns and mines laid in the night. All day the storm of the attack was without letup, but the tenacious Japanese took everything thrown at them. I Corps was still between a hammer and an anvil and weakening.

The 192nd tanks were having no easy time of it themselves. When the attack led by Colonel Lilly jumped off for the attack on the area of Anyasan and Silaim points, the 192nd was in the thick of it. Company C (less one platoon at Quinauan), consisting of nine tanks, had been sent forward from sector headquarters. Colonel Lilly placed them between the two rivers, the only area at all suitable for tank operations. Hemmed in to a narrow trail by dense jungle, the tanks were forced to move forward in column and essentially could only be used as mobile pillboxes. At the outset, tank infantry coordination was poor, the foot soldiers being directed to stay 100–200 yards behind the armor. With their limited close-range fields of fire in column formation, the tanks were highly vulnerable to enemy mine and grenade attack. It is no surprise that the first day the armor was used, the results were far less than positive. In at least one case, the result was tragic. The Japanese, unhampered by the scouts who were following well behind the tanks, managed to disable one tank, set it on fire, and then fill it with dirt. The hapless crew was first cremated, then buried. Following this incident, riflemen were instructed to work closely with the armor, four infantrymen assigned to each tank. When the Japanese dropped down in their foxholes to let the tanks pass over them, they were picked off by foot soldiers before they could rise again to their feet.

The greatest danger to the tanks came from mines. Some of these were already planted in the trail. However, the most deadly attack came from Japanese who would dash from cover, fix a magnetic mine to the tank, and then dash for the trees. Another tactic was to attach a mine to a string and drag it across the trail in front of an oncoming tank. Had it not been for the scout infantry, the tanks would not have lasted long in the Anyasan–Silaim fight, which dragged on until 26 February. The allies were holding on tenaciously.

At his wit's end, Wainwright told his officers that all bets were off. Either the line facing north held until the route south was broken open, or I Corps was a cornered, trapped rat. He picked up a stick and scratched a ragged line in the dirt. "This is as far as you can let them go. There is no option. Now dig in your toes and stop the bastards here and now!"

He essentially delivered the same message to his dogged southern assault force. "You have no choice! You've got to break them—now!"

Then, as if Wainwright's desperation was not already at a boiling point, he received the absurd order from USAFFE HQ to withdraw. That day, Dick Sutherland had come over to Bataan from The Rock directed to make an assessment of the American position across the peninsula. Not comprehending Wainwright's critical situation and seeing that the enemy had crossed the mountains and split the two corps, threatening to surround them, he made the snap advice to MacArthur that Parker's Mauban–Abucay line must be abandoned and that Wainwright must pull I Corps south to Bagac thus forming a new MLR from Bagac east to Orion. The great strategy simply overlooked the facts on the ground.

24

The Beginning of the End of the Defense of Bataan: The Battle of the Points Begins

22 JANUARY 1942

A Japanese scheme to land behind American lines, similar to a maneuver being successfully employed by General Yamashita in Malaysia, originated with General Homma. When General Kimura, commanding the force driving down Bataan's west coast road against Wainwright's I Corps informed Homma of unexpected resistance on the east coast and what had become a stalemate on the west coast, he pointed out the potential advantages of landings to the enemy's rear. Landing barges had already been ordered from Lingayan to Olongapo positioned to strike. Kimura with his detachment of some five thousand men, including most of the 20th and 122nd Infantries, had advanced down the west coast and established a line firmly on the west road behind Wainwright's main line of defense and, therefore, to the rear of the 26 Cavalry's positions. They were now well positioned to reach Bagac, from where he could move east to take II Corps from the rear. Kimura anticipated no difficulty in his drive on Bagac, but to protect his right flank once moving east along the Pilar–Bagac road, he saw need to block enemy reaction south of Bagac. Kimura saw wisdom in Homma's suggestion to send part of his force by water from Moron to Caibobo Point five miles below Bagac. He assigned Colonel Tsunechiro's 2nd Battalion 20th Infantry, then in reserve, to make the landing. A combination of lack of time for preparations, poor maps, and the deceptive configuration of Bataan's heavily indented shoreline made it difficult even in daylight to distinguish one shore point from another. At night, it was virtually impossible.

As soon as they embarked, the Japanese found themselves in trouble. Treacherous tides and rough waters took a toll on the troops crowded in the small barges. Then all hell broke loose with the unexpected arrival on the scene of USN Lt. John D. Bulkley's PT Boat 34, on a routine patrol mission. The 34 boat sank one barge and, unaware of more, continued on its way. An hour or so later, Bulkley encountered another landing craft and sank it. The Americans managed to capture two Japanese prisoners along with a dispatch case revealing much of the Japanese plan to attack Bataan from the coast in the rear of American defense lines. By now, the Japanese landing flotilla had completely lost its bearings and, to make matters worse, it had split into two groups. None reached the destination at Caibobo Point. One group, about a third of the battalion, made shore at Longoska-wayan Point, some ten miles southeast of their objective. The remainder of the force, a hodge-podge of platoons, companies, and sections, landed some seven miles up the coast at Quinauan Point. While the Japanese enjoyed tactical surprise at both places, they labored under complete, although temporary, confusion.

In the meantime, the 26th Cavalry was ordered to counter Japanese pressure south on kilometer 164 south from Moron. The regiment was now operating entirely on foot, the horses having been sent on this day to the quartermaster's pastures at Agaloma due to lack of forage and difficulty in maneuvering in the terrain of the 26th's defensive area. They were reinforced by a motor squadron attached to 1st Regiment Division (PA) on the Pilar–Bagac Road and joined by elements of 1st Division (PA) south of kilometer 164 on the Moron road. The 1st Division force was ordered to attack but was stopped cold by antitank mines. The motor squadron pressed on to kilometer 168, but the remainder of division elements failed to follow, and the motor squadron was forced back to its former position. In the action, a highly regarded 26th officer, 1st Lt. Ethan R. Cunningham of HQ Troop, was killed by sniper fire with a direct hit to his head. Wainwright's notes pointed out that the 26th Cavalry's mobile communications equipment on its scout cars had become I Corps primary source of contact with his various units during this period. Tireless, round-the-clock effort was all that kept any semblance of liaison between NLF units active. The 26th continued to be a mainstay of Wainwright's command.

On 23 January the 26th Cavalry in their defensive positions experienced a rout of 1st Division (PA) streaming down the beach in what could only be called a mob, guns and small arms mostly discarded, in total disarray. Japanese landings had put them in a state of panic. Remnants of the 91st Division (PA) took up positions astride the Moron road as best they could, but the I Corps MLR was crumbling. By the 24th of January with the 1st Division (PA) gone in rout, Wainwright ordered I Corps retirement to main battle positions along the Pilar–Bagac road. The 26th Cavalry along with the 2nd Battalion Philippine constabulary were assigned to cover the withdrawal while the 91st executed its pull back. Another significant change also took place on the 24th. Col. Clinton Pierce, the bulldog commander of the 26th since before the Japanese invasion, was promoted to brigadier general by Wainwright with MacArthur's approval and transferred out of the 26th to Wainwright's staff for the defense of Bataan. It was a loss felt sorely by the men of the 26th, who had been so ably led through so much by Pierce, who had experienced the dangers and rigors of the frightful campaign shoulder to shoulder with his men since 8 December. Pierce, in turn, never let the condition and disposition of the 26th stray far from his attention even when his staff position with the NLF command demanded his focus on the overall defensive concerns on Bataan.

At that time, the remainder of the 26th Cavalry, now under command of Maj. Lee Vance, took up positions on high ground three kilometers north of Bagac covering the enemy advance from Moron. Dismounted patrols were active on trails northeast of scout car positions on the Pilar–Bagac road. The Japanese were active in attacks but broke off around 2:30 p.m. The 26th slowly withdrew and by 8 p.m. took up positions on Trail 9 near junctions 7/9 after a hard march. By the 26th of January, they managed to stabilize their lines. Troop G was sent to HQ I Corps as guard. The rest of the regiment was rested and reorganized. On that day, the regiment received news of Troop C's successful attack on enemy Tuguegaraou airfield in Cagayan Valley. The news was a great uplift to the morale of all. It also indicated the continuing welfare of the long-lost C Troop. MacArthur lauded the action and made recommendations for high and well-deserved decorations for C Troop's participants in the raid.

Since the fight at Moron, Col. Clint Pierce and (now) Lt. Col. Lee Vance had never let up on a rigorous routine of training and conditioning of the regiment in jungle warfare tactics and movement. They were up against a tough, seasoned enemy with long experience in this style of combat. The training paid off as the 26th, now on foot and facing constant maneuvering in the thick forests and jungle terrain of Bataan, fought almost daily to counter Japanese incursions and infiltration on Bataan's maze of trails in the defensive combat zone. Twenty-sixth Cavalry casualties on the trails were all too numerous for the small regiment, and the men were beginning to show the effects of constant patrolling and sharply reduced rations. Wainwright's lines continued to hold more firmly than MacArthur's staff comprehended from Corregidor.

Daily now, Colonel Vance ordered aggressive 26th officers' and NCOs' patrolling of front lines, beach areas, and trails to cover all possible enemy approaches. There had been numerous reports that a Japanese landing at Agaloma Point had been reinforced. The 26th was put on sharp alert, and the 1st Battalion 45th Infantry Scouts was dispatched to the area. Japanese landings in force began at Longoskawayan Point jutting out from the west coast only three thousand yards west of Mariveles harbor. Four hundred yards long and some seven hundred yards wide, the point skirts a narrow coast with hundred-foot rocky cliffs covered with tall hardwood trees and thick jungle. Visibility from the ground is severely limited, and the landing endangered Mariveles, the critical entry point for Bataan only two thousand yards away. Naval commander Bridget had posted a twenty-four-hour lookout on the high ground overlooking the point and promised General Selleck to commit his now land based naval battalion into the area in case of Japanese incursion.

The series of fights known as the Battle of the Points gradually became a relentless denial to the Japanese of beachheads on the outreaching southern Bataan promontories by both NLF mixed forces inland and persistent and effective action by the navy's PT boats (whose plywood craft with no hull armor and plywood gun turrets earned their gutsy crews the dubious nickname of "The Expendables"). Japanese landing barges and attempts to get troops ashore were either smashed in the water or were murderously repelled on the shores. Their end run was, to all purposes, a total failure, but not without ill-afforded losses by the stubborn defenders.

General Homma's orders on 25 January, two days after the disastrous landings at Longoskawayan and Quinauan Points, were issued still with his intent to outflank I Corps from the sea. He believed the amphibious attack to be sufficient to overcome I Corps without the full weight of his 14th Army behind it. Thinking of the assault on Quinauan Point, the only one Homma's staff had knowledge of, Lt. Gen. Susumu Morioka, commanding the 16th Division (scattered at this time), decided to reinforce Lt. Col. Nariyoshi Tsunehiro's 2nd Battalion there. Morioka, immediate senior of Maj. Gen. Mitsuo Kimura (whose detachment had been so effective against Wainwright's Mauaban line) shared with him the belief that a landing in force at Quinauan would bear positive results in both relieving the Japanese force there—the 2nd Battalion, 20th Infantry, who were trapped, in sore need of supplies, and "fighting a heroic battle against a superior enemy"—and striking a hard blow against I Corps. The assignment fell to a company of the 1st Battalion 20th Infantry, which was ordered to embark from Olongapo loaded with supplies and ammunition and sail to Quinauan. The small force set sail from Subic Bay on the night of 26 January, but once again, poor seamanship and bad navigation plagued the Japanese operation. This resulted in their landing some two thousand yards short of their objective, running aground on a beach between the Anyasan and Silaim Rivers, which was part of a sector defended by the 1st Battalion, 1st Philippine constabulary.

The terrain where the hapless Japanese landed was dense jungle and thick underbrush reaching down to the shoreline. It was an area where a maze of rivers and streams added to the confusion of the identity of the shore points and totally bewildered the forces on both sides. The density of the jungle precluded or at least limited any use of mortars and artillery. The job of defending it would fall to the rifleman. The lost new enemy landing force, numbering about two hundred men, came ashore at about 3 a.m. of the 27th and met only light resistance from the constabulary troops, who were quick to flee at the first sight of the approaching Japanese, and the entire constabulary battalion was soon scattered. At dawn, hearing of the landing and the ineffective defense, Gen. Clint Pierce quickly ordered airmen, now infantry, of the grounded 17th Pursuit Squadron to meet the attack. The airmen moved out shortly after dawn and found breakfast still hot and waiting at the abandoned constabulary command post. The airmen ate the breakfast and moved out for the coast, some of them still asking how to operate their rifles.

At MacArthur's headquarters there was mounting concern over the new landing, presuming it was the point of a major Japanese offensive that would present a serious threat to the west road and the danger of cutting off I Corps route south. USAFFE staff simply did not know the confused state of the enemy.

On the morning of the 28th, the airmen, now joined by reorganized constabulary, attacked. Their advance carried almost to the coast of Anyasan Bay, and the Japanese scattered into the jungles in dangerous confusion, many of them infiltrating into I Corps interior lines and trails. At nightfall there were signs indicating the Japanese would launch a full counterattack. The constabulary elected to withdraw, leaving the 17th Pursuit men to go it alone. Concern at I Corps headquarters heightened with fear that the Japanese landing force, whose exact size and disbursement were still unknown, might break out from their beachhead, creating havoc behind I Corps main lines and cut the west road. The 26th was put on high alert.

Prompted by these concerns, Philippine Scouts of the 2nd Battalion 45th Infantry under Capt. Arthur C. Biedenstein were ordered to save the situation. Gen. Clint Pierce put Biedenstein in command of the operation and reinforced him with troops of the 1st Constabulary and 1st Battalion PA. These units had just been brought from the fight at Quinauan Point to clear out enemy infiltrators threatening the west road and I Corps communications lines. He also assigned Company A 57th Infantry (PS) and Troop A of the 26th Cavalry to thoroughly patrol the endangered rear areas and trails. Thus the Philippine Scouts continued to be a vital factor in Wainwright's defenses.

Also on 28 January Colonel Vance ordered increased patrolling and reconnoitering led by NCOs and officers of the front lines and beach positions. Trails leading to and from them were also thoroughly scouted on the lookout for Japanese from the Agaloma landings. On the 28th, a Japanese dive bomber was shot down by 37mm AA fire adjacent to the 26th positions. Vance saw fit to move the regiment's bivouac east about one kilometer on Trail 9 for both safety and sanitary reasons. Once there, reports came in that enemy snipers were active on Trail 9 around kilometers 137–138, and on orders from I Corps, he sent a platoon from Troop A in an attempt to find them. "Sniper teams" were usually armed with shotguns, which were most effective in blasting the hidden riflemen out of the thick foliage of the teak and sausage trees, which seemed to be the locations of choice for snipers. Action on Trail 9 was steadily increasing as enemy troops infiltrated in from the points landings, and sniping was an ever increasing threat. It gradually became difficult to discern Japanese bodies from the huge sausage growths.

The next day, the 29th, in another air action, the regiment got word that American planes had succeeded in bombing Japanese-held Nichols Field in Manila. The attack was carried out by dauntless American pilots flying their few remaining, patched-up Curtiss P-40 fighters from hidden jungle airfields on Bataan, armed with one-hundred- and five-hundred-pound antipersonnel and explosive bombs released from jury-rigged bomb racks. This infuriated the Japanese who were convinced they commanded complete control of the skies, but it was great tonic for the weary American and Filipino defenders. The 26th Cavalry celebrated by adding an extra portion to its meager supper rations.

In reality, Wainwright still commanded a force strong enough to hold off the Japanese, now far more depleted in strength by casualties and disease than estimated by MacArthur's intelligence sources, and even capable of mounting a counterattack. However, USAFFE's continual policy of withdrawal and retreat undermined this, and the longer American and Filipino forces were made to withstand unrelenting attack, the more their physical condition as a fighting force deteriorated from the depletion of food and medicine. Ammunition was plentiful and morale was relatively high, but these too were waning fast in the face of an air of defeated spirit. (On the Japanese side, from their entrance on to Bataan, Homma's 65th Brigade alone of sixty-five hundred men had, by 15 February, lost four thousand killed and wounded, and many of those who remained were sick, on half rations, and short of critical supplies and rations.) Still, the Japanese attack went on without abating.

Now, the crucial final stages of the Battle of Bataan really began.

THE BATTLES OF THE POCKETS AND TRAILS

As I and II Corps continued to dig in and hold a series of fixed NLF defensive lines, the Japanese attackers increased a fluid style of offense with flanking maneuvers and infiltration through allied lines, causing "pockets" of aggressive incursion, all of which had to be cleaned out and eliminated by Americans and Filipinos. An additional few of these pockets consisted of the remnants of Japanese who had managed to get inland from the earlier landings, causing some overlapping of the points and pocket battles.

It was in the course of these fights to eliminate the pockets and hold the trails open that the 26th Cavalry officers and troopers, now fighting on foot, engaged in some of their bloodiest fights in the thick jungles of Bataan. During the daylight hours, Japanese movement was relatively quiet, but after dark they became increasingly aggressive. The action became an unrelenting cat and mouse game, with every tree and thicket a potential death threat. On 27 January word came that the Japanese landing at Aga-loma had been reinforced. The 26th was put on high alert, but again the 1st Battalion 45th Infantry (PS) was dispatched by I Corps to clean up the threat.

Meanwhile, by the morning of the 26th, most of USAFFE's force was in place along its reserve position, its final defense line on Bataan. This new line extended from Orion in the east, west to Bagac along a course generally parallel to and just south of the Pilar–Bagac Road, crossing it roughly in the center. Mt. Natib, which had caused the separation of I and II Corps, was now left behind and for the first time, the USAFFE troops were able to form an unbroken line across Bataan and establish firm contact between the two corps. The tightening of defenses was also made possible because the with-drawal had reduced the area in USAFFE's hands by almost 50 percent. Wainwright had depended heavily on the thinly stretched 26th Cavalry to cover the withdrawal on the west coast from the Mauban line. Now they were being called on heavily to cover the interior trails, especially around Mt. Samat, almost dead center on Bataan. It was going to be a bloody and costly job for the 26th as the closing battles for Bataan took shape.

(The following entries are from Maj. Lee Vance's diary, hidden and kept throughout his later captivity.)

27 January

Started officers and NCOs' patrols along front lines and beach positions cover-ing all possible approaches and trails. Heard that enemy landing at Agaloma had been reinforced. Regiment was alerted but 1st Bn. 45th Inf. was dis-patched.

28 January

Enemy plane shot down by 37mm anti-aircraft. Moved the regiment's bivouac 1 km. east on trail for sanitary reasons. Report of enemy snipers at Km. 138–

139. One platoon from Troop A dispatched to investigate, but results were negative.

29 January

Got report that our planes bombed Nichols Field in Manila. I Corps reported snipers at Km. 200. Dispatched Motor Squadron to investigate. Unable to locate any snipers.

29–30 January

Continued reconnaissance, training in jungle warfare and conditioning of men for marching dismounted. Taking toll on them.

31 January

No change

1 February

Captain Forest Richards relieved as C.O. HQ Troop and sent to HQ 11th Div. as liaison. Capt. John Fowler assigned to replace him as C.O. HQ Troop.

2 February

Regiment ordered moved to beach north of Caibobo Point to counter reported landing there. Arrived at 12 noon. No landing evident yet of enemy landing in that area. Captain (H.S.) Farris relieved Major Blanning at I Corp HQ. Blanning assigned to command 2nd Squadron. Constant night patrols to beach positions maintained. Report last 4 P40's from Cabcaben attacked Jap landing force at Quinauan Pt. with good results. Bombed and strafed enemy.

Major Blanning's return to the regiment was a welcome event to all. Not only was he held in high regard and deeply respect by all in the regiment, he seemed to possess an uncanny level of foresight and a cool assessment of a combat situation even before a firefight fully developed. Many a 26th trooper had his life to thank for Jim Blanning's instinct in a fight. Blanning's spirit never dimmed, right to the final surrender of Bataan. Blanning, like many of his comrades in the 26th, opted to go into the hills and join up with die-hards and guerillas and keep fighting when given the choice by his superiors. He was captured by the Japanese as the result of information from a *macapili* Filipino turncoat and imprisoned at the infamous Fort Santiago, where he endured weeks of brutal interrogation. After months of imprisonment he was put into one of the ill-fated drafts of prisoners being transported to Japan—both to prevent them from liberation by invading

Allied forces and in an attempt to prevent American submarines from sinking Japanese transports. Unable to survive the unspeakable conditions in the ship's prison holds, Blanning died in an air attack on the death ship *Brazil Maru*.

At the hotly contested battle to take over the "pockets," Japanese General Morioka dug in doggedly at the "Upper Pocket" to secure and protect his hard-gained reprovisions and supplies and to stabilize the gains of his forces. In this area soon developed a vicious fight, which became a key factor to win the struggle for the Upper and Big Pockets. Soon a brutal clash developed. On 2 February, General Brougher with his 1st Division pressed hard to execute an armored supported offensive in the thick jungle of the area. For this he used a platoon, four tanks, from Company A, 192nd Battalion. This armor was closely supported on the ground by a platoon from the tough 45th Infantry Philippine Scouts. This force pushed hard, running a gauntlet along Trail 7, losing only one tank but making little gain. The next day's assault brought similar gains but also the costly loss of another tank. In that day's fight, Lt. Willibald C. Bianchi, who had volunteered from another unit to command the 45th Infantry troops supporting the armor, took charge of the supporting platoon sent out to destroy two enemy machine gun positions holding up the American progress. Leading part of the platoon forward, Bianchi was wounded in his left hand. Waiving off first aid assistance, he continued on, firing his pistol and knocking out one of the machine guns with grenades. The tank nearest him, unable to sufficiently lower the muzzle of its 37mm gun, had been having trouble eliminating the machine gun on the other side. Bianchi, now with two more bullets in his chest, scrambled to the top of the tank and there put fire from its antiaircraft gun into the remaining enemy position until the impact of still a third round fired from close range knocked him off the turret. He survived to be evacuated to hospital, where he was awarded the Congressional Medal of Honor. A month later, he was back in action with his unit.

(The following continues from Major Vance's diary.)

3 February

Established bivouac on an old logging road. While there an enemy pocket was discovered in rear of 11th Div. positions. The regiment was alerted and ordered to junction of Trails 8 and 9. These orders were cancelled and continued concentration on the Aglaloma situation in close contact with 57th Inf. PS. Scout cars constantly patrolled west road for snipers with special orders to search Aglaloma road for groups of snipers said to have broken through our lines. Night patrols particularly dangerous.

4–5 February

1st Lt. Leisenring with a platoon of Troop A ordered to relieve scout cars on Aglaloma road and scour ridge to left at dawn. 1st Lt. Domenick G. Troglia (recently transferred back to regiment from MP duty) killed by unexploded bomb planted on side of West road by Japanese. Leisenring and patrol returned at Midnight. Reported no enemy found but unsettling news that patrol had discovered a 300 yd. gap in our line.

Rice ration cut. Rice ration increased back to 7 ounces. New food reserves released. 71st Inf. P.A. troops captured enemy soldier swimming from Aglaloma area. In proceess of being interrogated.

6–7 February

More trouble. Enemy break thru on left of 11th Div. Regiment alerted but no orders to move. Battery of 155 artillery moves to within 100 yards of 26th bivouac. 11:00 a.m. ordered to move to junction of Trails to support our troops in heavy fighting in Tuol River pocket. Made daylight move (no night activity) to junction of Trails 9 and 17 as more suitable for purpose.

On 8 February, four days after General Marshall's conference with General MacArthur in Australia, the War Department received a message from Manuel Quezon. In it, Quezon proposed that the United States immediately grant the Philippines its full independence; that the islands be neutralized; that American and Japanese forces be withdrawn by mutual consent; and that the Philippine Army be disbanded. This alarming message, although granting independence was fully intended, was received with highly mixed feelings in Washington.

8–9 February

Our troopers and 45th Inf. holding their own at Tuol. Regt. pulled back and returned to recon patrols and training. Effect of short rations beginning to show in physical condition of officers and men.

Shortage of rations causing real trouble with concentration and reflexes. Capt. Gochenour turned over a Bren Gun Carrier on West Road. Killed one enlisted man and injured another and Gochenour.

10–14 February

Little change. Training and patrols. Officers and men becoming more familiar with front lines and beach positions. 45th Inf. still making good progress in Tuol "pocket" fight. Troops changed weekly at I Corps Guard.

15–16 February

Troop A en route to I Corps Hq. Encountered enemy patrol. One killed, one captured, one escaped. 2/16—Regiment awakened at dawn by small arms fire in our vicinity. About 80 enemy; evidently part of those that had escaped through our lines in South Bataan fighting. Had struck north to regain their own lines and encountered rear echelon of the 91st Div. 12 killed, one wounded. Our regt. turned out and scoured woods in our area. Picked up 2 enemy wounded but remainder escaped in thick jungle to the northwest.

Wounded prisoners said they were part of a group of about 80 that had landed in the south and escaped from our troops in that area. At about 4:p.m. orders came from I Corps to clean out group of enemy in rear of 91st Div. Second Squadron (less Troop G) was dispatched on this mission. Enemy found located just at dusk in river bed on Trail 41. Our force plans to attack at dawn.

17 February

At dawn found enemy had slipped out. 2nd Sq. sent out patrols. Troop "E-F" under Capt. Wrinkle located part of enemy force in front of a Battalion of 71st Inf. P.A. but in rear of our front line wire. Wrinkle sends message to Major Blanning who moved to reinforce Wrinkle's force. On the way Maj. Blanning encountered main part of enemy force. Joined Capt. Wrinkle's force and drives Japanese out of their positions. Capt. Wrinkle killed by rifle fire in final assault. Ridge came under shelling by enemy artillery and our detachment withdrew to our bivouac area with mission accomplished. Moderate losses including Capt. Wrinkle, a good officer.

18, 25, 26 February

Continued patrolling, reconnaissance and training. Troop A starts second week of I Corps Guard. No further change except news Lt. Whitehead had joined our forces at Iloilo. Feb. 26: Sasain Ridge and Bobo Points bombed. Casualties light.

27–28 February

More patrolling and recon.

MARCH 1942

March 1942 would prove a time of terrible attrition, bloody losses, suffering, and exhaustion for both sides of the conflict.

Wainwright's defense area now comprised about two hundred square miles in which he had some ninety thousand men compressed in his line. Before the withdrawal, Mt. Natib had dominated the defensive line, which ran east–west from Abucay and Mauban connected by the Pilar–Bagac road, which straddled Bataan. Now a new mountain range, the Mariveles, loomed over the defenders. Except for just a narrow strip of coastal plain, the entire region of southern Bataan was rugged and mountainous, blanketed by jungle, forest, and almost impenetrable undergrowth. At that time of year, daytime temperatures averaged around 95 degrees, to which even the shade of the thick forest canopy gave little relief. This was the dry season with no rainstorms to offer any relief; men found that even minimum physical exertion left them soaked with sweat and suffering from parching thirst.

The now exhausted Japanese were no better off. General Nara noted that "the heat was so extreme that the men had great difficulty with the simplest of movements." When the sun set on the horizon, temperatures dropped dramatically, and all who had sweltered in broiling daytime heat now shivered with cold under their army blankets and extra clothing.

The new southern Bataan defense line was dominated by the 1,920-foot-high Mt. Samat, situated four miles from the east coast and just south of the Pilar–Bagac road. Its slopes were a thick tangle of towering hardwood trees, dense creepers, and almost impenetrable thorny vines. It was a thoroughly uninviting place to wage war, but the mountain offered an important, clear view of the entire battle area below, therefore making it a place of extreme tactical and strategic value, which both sides wanted badly. A high price in lives would be paid by both sides in vicious, close-quarter fighting on its slopes for the military advantages offered. North of Samat, extending to the Pilar–Bagac road, the terrain was similar to the Samat slopes. North beyond that, the area, now held by the Japanese, was mostly low and swampy. East from Samat lay a plateau with sugarcane fields and a thicket-covered plain along the coast. From the high ground in the center ran several large rivers and many small streams (some of them dry at this time of year). The banks of these water courses provided steep, forested natural barriers causing great difficulties for the advancing Japanese and affording natural defense positions for the defenders. To the west in I Corps operations area, there were no plains or cane fields. The terrain was steeply sloped down from the Mariveles Mountains almost to the sea. The jungle and undergrowth were probably denser than anywhere on Bataan, and notably less suitable for military operations and maneuver. This is what the 26th was forced to cope with in its operations.

When withdrawing to their new defense line, the Americans and Filipinos gave up their command of vital Pilar–Bagac road, the central belt across Bataan. But they had taken steps to deny the Japanese free use of the route by choosing strategic positions from which they could bring enemy movement on the road under fire. They also extended their MLR across the road in Bataan's center. They then hacked out a four-mile detour extending from Orion to the main road and thus extended II Corps' eastern end along the new branch road rather than along the original main route for vehicular traffic. Any other troop movement behind the MLR had to be made on rough footpath and pack trails. Seldom did anyone travel without a sharp machete.

The new defense line differed significantly from the former Abucay–Mauban line. Units were now smaller, and there was a growing shortage of trained combat commanders and new difficulties in communications between units. In light of this, troops on the MLR were directed now by sector commanders in direct contact with corps HQs. While changing unit designations to a great degree, command of sectors rather than smaller individual units simplified overall control of operations by corps. In the line, General Parker's II Corps was responsible for an area extending from Orion on the east coast westward for about fifteen thousand yards. The new organization now had the corps composed of four sectors designated A through D and included the Philippine Division's 31st Infantry on the east flank; to its left two thousand yards was held by the Provisional Air Corps Regiment, made up of some fourteen hundred airmen now converted to infantry and commanded by Col. Irvin E. Doane, an able veteran of the 31st Infantry. The next in line, under command of Gen. Clifford Bluemel, was manned by his 31st Infantry (PA) and remnants of the 51st Division (PA), which was formed into a regimental combat team. These units held a line of some forty-five hundred yards. The remaining six thousand yards of II Corps sector lay at the foot of Mt. Samat and extended to the Pantingan River. This section of II Corps was under Brig. General Maxon S. Lough, commander of the Philippine Division. He was responsible for the 21st and 41st Divisions (PA) and Lloyd Mills's distinguished 57th Infantry Philippine Scouts.

Emplacement of II Corps artillery was based largely with the consciousness of the value of holding the commanding heights of Mt. Samat and its observation advantages for gunners. Emplacements were hacked out on the slopes and around the base of the mountain. Lough's guns consisted of sixteen 75mm cannon and eight 2.95-inch pack howitzers from the 41st Field Artillery (PA). Along the line east of the mountain on the high ground to support the other sectors were artillery components of the 21st, 31st, and 51st Divisions (PA). These emplacements included some forty 75mm cannons and two scout battalions with 75mms and 2.95s.

On beach defense, the constabulary units were supported by some dozen naval guns. The corps artillery included the 86th Field Artillery Battalion (PS) with 155mm guns emplaced near Limay and the 301st Field Artillery (PA).

To the east, General Wainwright's I Corps, divided into right and left sectors, had to make do with much less heavy gunnery. He had one scout battalion (less one battery) of 75mm guns. Brig. Gen. Albert Jones had for his left sector of the I Corps line guns of the 91st Field Artillery and some elements of the 71st Division, which had lost most of its heavy weapons at Mauban. On the right sector was the artillery of the 11th Division and one battery of scouts artillery. Only a piecemeal few heavy guns had been

assigned originally for beach defense, but after the Japanese assault landings on the points, Clint Pierce managed to convince staff to provide Wainwright with two 155mm howitzers for that end of the sector. The I Corps
line extended for some thirteen thousand yards from the Patingan River
westward toward the South China Sea. Intersecting the two I Corps sectors
was Trail 7 winding north to south. The sector on the right joining II Corps
area had a front of some five thousand yards, including Trail 7, and was
held by the 11th Division (PA) and attached elements of the 2nd Philippine
Constabulary. General Brougher commanded both the 11th Division and
the whole right sector. Gen. Albert M. Jones, who had led the South Luzon
into Bataan, was in command of the left sector between Trail 7 and the sea.
The eastern segment of his sector was held by the 45th Infantry Philippine
Scouts, a unit that had already distinguished itself on both Luzon and
Bataan. The western part of his sector was held by the 91st Division (PA)
under Brig. Gen. Luther Stevens. Wainwright, along with Parker, was
assigned responsibility for the beach defenses in his area of operations. For
his corps reserve, Wainwright had his steadfast 26th Cavalry, which had so
effectively covered the withdrawal south from the Mauban Line. Up to now,
USAFFE G-3 had thought it prudent to hold the Philippine Division regiments in reserve. This order was now reversed, leaving the defense line with
no reserve at all. General Sutherland believed the corps commanders
needed all the forces that could be mustered to hold the new line, so the
Philippine units were assigned to critical points along the line with the
approval of USAFFE. When Japanese landings at Longoskawayan and
Quinauan Points struck, the potential danger convinced USAFFE to reverse
its thinking once more, and a reserve was reestablished to counter the
threat. The job fell to the Philippine Division, which included one American and two scout regiments. The problem, however, was that this would
leave dangerous gaps in the carefully organized new corps line.

The disposition and makeup of the new USAFFE Bataan defense line has
been described for the purpose of giving a clearer picture of the context in
which the 26th Cavalry was now operating. While the regiment was still
Wainwright's mainstay on the China Sea coastal area, its scouting operations and forays into the pockets and Samat areas were frequent and costly.
The 26th scout cars were often called on to support other units in their constant struggle to clear out Japanese in pockets behind the corps line and to
keep Samat a stronghold for the USAFFE MLR. The 26th was stretched thin
and gradually became exhausted with non-stop fighting and patrolling in
the whole eastern sector of the line. Increasingly short rations, disease, and
fatigue were taking their toll on the troopers, now on foot, but the indomitable spirit of the regiment kept serving as an effective and invaluable force
for Wainwright to count on when trouble arose.

The month of March 1942 was destined to be a time of bloody ferocity for the American and Filipino forces. The Japanese, however, would pay a terrible toll in death and suffering for their relentless advances and their tactical blunders in the Points and Pockets fights. The Japanese soldier, too, was ragged, hungry, and ravished with tropical diseases, but the hopes of victory served to fortify him for the series of devastating offensive pushes he would execute in the month to come.

By mid- to late February, Homma's ambitious offensive operations against I Corps were floundering and Morioka was in full withdrawal from the Pockets. MacArthur was feeling high confidence that the main of the enemy, the 14th Army, had been halted and forced back enough to discount any immediate threat of attack.

Homma, however, was still confident enough to put into effect his plans to tighten his blockade of all of the southern coast of Manila Bay to prevent Filipinos from sending food and supplies to Corregidor and Bataan. Japanese 105mm and 150mm artillery stationed earlier in the same area was ordered to intensify bombardment of the fortified islands at the entrance to the bay.

On 22 February, President Roosevelt issued the fateful and devastating order to Douglas MacArthur to leave Corregidor and proceed to Australia, where he was to organize massive American countermeasures in the South Pacific. MacArthur received the order with intense trepidation, mainly fearing that his departure would have a major, debilitating effect on the morale of his defense forces still battling to keep their foothold in the Philippines. He initially voiced his refusal to obey the order and vowed to resign his commission and fight alongside his men if necessary. He was persuaded otherwise by superiors and staff who pointed out that his value in retaking the Philippines would be put to far better use organizing sufficient strike forces from Australia. Prior to his departure, he assigned command of all Allied forces in the Philippines to General Wainwright. His farewells were difficult for him to make, for MacArthur, despite any mistakes or shortcomings, was genuinely loyal to the Philippine people and loved the country deeply. The news was received with mixed reactions by his army. Many, mostly American troops, hailed MacArthur's leaving with derision, resentful nicknames such as "Dugout Doug" (referring to the general's rare ventures outside of the tunnels of Fortress Corregidor), and songs and poems, the most prominent of these being the "Battling Bastards of Bataan—No papa no mama no Uncle Sam." The overriding sentiment was one of abandonment.

On the other extreme was the undying faith and loyalty of the Filipinos. MacArthur's famous "I shall return" speech broadcast from Australia was embraced by the main of the Philippine people as gospel, and their tenacious resistance to the Japanese occupation despite brutality and reprisals for hostile acts against the Japanese bore convincing testimony to their feelings of undying faith and hope that MacArthur would eventually prove to be their savior.

On an extremely dark evening of 12 March, General MacArthur, along with a party of twenty-one persons (including his brave and enduring wife, Jean; his young son, Arthur; the child's Chinese governess, Ah Cheu; his personal staff; a remainder of staff officers of the army, navy, and air force; plus president of the Philippines, Manuel Quezon), gathered on the pier on the Manila side of Corregidor and began boarding four PT boats. On hand for a personal good-bye was General Wainwright. MacArthur and his family departed for the perilous trip on a PT commanded by Lt. John D. Bulkeley. The small PT boats—"The Expendables"—of primarily plywood construction, known for their daring attacks on large enemy warships, were also called "Plywood Dreams" because of their light construction. Nevertheless, they gave more than they got in their daring attacks and sorties. Nevertheless, the voyage to Mindanao was a hazardous one that included running a gamut of Japanese warships and weaving through minefields. On the 14th MacArthur's group reached Mindanao, where they were met by Brig. Gen. William F. Sharp, commander of the Visayan-Mindanao force. They proceeded to Del Monte airfield and then to Australia via B-17 after MacArthur's firm insistence that his party be provided with the absolutely best flight equipment and crews. This cautionary instruction arose from several crash incidents recently of B-17s in the Philippines from mechanical problems and/or crew error, of which MacArthur was well aware. He emphasized the importance of this group of passengers to the war effort in the Pacific.

On 4 March, prior to his departure, MacArthur began to formulate a plan to utilize the forces he was leaving behind. The Visayan-Mindanao force under General Sharp was split and the islands in the Visayas transferred under command of Brig. Gen. Bradford G. Chynoweth. Sharp continued in command of the Mindanao force, the only island south of Luzon on which a significant Japanese force had landed. Sharp was instructed to utilize his entire force to defend Mindanao, the location from which MacArthur held on to his intent to counterattack the Japanese in force. He also intended to make changes in the command structure on Bataan.

MacArthur's plans were a closely guarded top secret held until 10 March when General Wainwright was informed of it officially by Sutherland. As put to Wainwright, the changes did not yet include appointment of another supreme commander of forces in the Philippines. MacArthur himself intended to continue his control from Australia through his G-4, Colonel Beebe, who was given a star and appointed deputy chief of staff of USAFFE. The command was to be divided into four groups. The chief of these would be the force on Bataan and those holding out in the mountains of Luzon. This command was to be known as the Luzon Force under the command of General Wainwright. Wainwright, in turn, chose Gen. Albert Jones (who had shown exceptional command skill in guiding the South Luzon Force through its withdrawal into Bataan and in dealing successfully with the pocket fights) to be given Wainwright's old command of I Corps. Sutherland decreed that these arrangements would become effective upon MacArthur's departure. Wainwright was then taken to meet with MacArthur. After outlining the new table of organization, the General vowed his determination to "come back as soon as I can with as much as I can." MacArthur then urged Wainwright to defend Bataan in the greatest depth possible. "You're an old cavalryman, Jonathan, and your training and conditioning has been along thin, light, quick hitting lines. The defense of Bataan must be as deep as you can make it." He then continued, "Make sure to hit them with everything you have with your artillery. That is the strongest arm you have." Before the gaunt old cavalryman turned to depart for Bataan, MacArthur promised him a third star "if you're still on Bataan."

"I'll be on Bataan," Wainwright pledged, "if I'm still alive."

It was a promise that fate and circumstances would not allow Skinny Wainwright to keep. One last instruction left by MacArthur was to Col. Joseph Moore, commander of the Corregidor fortress. "Your principal function for you and your staff would be to do everything possible to get supplies to Bataan and Corregidor." He continued, "You will set aside enough food to last 20,000 men until June 1942. If Bataan falls, the Philippine Division will be brought to Corregidor for its final stand." MacArthur's final instructions were that Moore was to hold Corregidor until his return. If that proved not possible, Moore was to make certain that all armament and strategic supplies were to be destroyed so that they could not be used against an American effort to recapture the Philippines.

On his arrival in Australia, MacArthur was met with a grim reality. The Allied force in Australia was in no condition whatsoever to attempt a counterattack on the Philippines. American ground forces available consisted mainly of rear echelon and communications troops and what was in reality a skeleton force of green, barely trained infantry and armor. The air force had more planes under repair than it did ones fit for combat. The Australian army was completely preoccupied organizing defense lines in preparation for imminent Japanese invasion. MacArthur's assurances of relief and his "I shall return" speech were dismally hollow words for the desperate defenders of the Philippines. The plight of the individual soldier on Bataan was little affected by MacArthur's grand new plans and command changes. He was preoccupied with the endless search for food, and his frontline battle was against rampant disease so endlessly nurtured by exposure in the tropical environment. The horror of relentless Japanese bombardments and assaults drove his despair to unimaginable depths. And, of course, psychological assaults from friend and foe alike added anger and disillusionment to it all. The Japanese hammered him with constant messages that he was both abandoned and forgotten by his country and his loved ones. Hollow Allied messages and unfounded assurances of relief and rescue gave birth to an angry, cynical verse that became the hymn of Bataan's foxholes:

> We're the battling bastards of Bataan;
> No mama, no papa, no Uncle Sam;
> No aunts, no uncles, no cousins, no nieces;
> No pills, no planes, no artillery pieces,
> And nobody gives a damn.
> Nobody gives a damn.
> —Frank Hewlett, 1942[1]

Meanwhile General Homma was facing hard realities of his own. Ironically headquartered and living in General MacArthur's grand, former apartments in the Manila Hotel (Homma was intrigued by the array of books in Mac-Arthur's extensive library), the Japanese commander was agonizing over how to continue his offensive to capture Bataan once and for all. Faced with his disasters of the points and pockets and with large segments of his forces either encircled or cut off, Homma reluctantly came to the conclusion that to continue with his present defensive might well lead to a military disaster.

On 8 February, he held a heated meeting of the 14th Army staff at San Fernando. The discussion developed into two critical points of view. First, Col. Motoo Nakayama, senior operations officer of Homma's staff, held that the offensive should continue to be pushed aggressively, arguing vigorously that the main assault be made along Bataan's east coast and be closely controlled by the 14th Army. Lt. Gen. Masami Maeda, Homma's chief of staff, strongly opposed, speaking for those who felt offensive operations on Bataan should be broken off and that a blockade should be put in place while the rest of the Philippines were securely occupied. In the time this was done, the Americans and Filipinos would collapse from starvation and disease, and victory would be achieved at little cost.

Homma, hard pressed and acutely aware of his waning timetable to conquer the Philippines, listened carefully to both strategies and then came to a reluctant decision. Not relishing the loss of face, he agreed to break off action and withdraw his troops to more secure positions. He did not agree, however, to wait for famine to force victory for him—time was his enemy now. He decided to make the demeaning request to Imperial General Headquarters in Tokyo for reinforcements, which would enable him to launch a decisive offensive to capture Bataan. He would rest and reorganize the remainder of his force and tighten the blockade on the peninsula. His offensive orders forced a prolonging of the fights for the points and pockets and necessitated Generals Morioka and Nara to fight withdrawal actions to disentangle themselves from the trapped and difficult situations they had gotten themselves into and establish defensive positions from which they could prepare another offensive. A series of diversionary actions and air raids were used to cover Homma's withdrawal, but the evidence of a pullback was too strong to cover up. General MacArthur felt compelled to write, "The enemy has definitely recoiled. He has refused his flank in front of my right six to ten kilometers and in other sectors by varying distances. . . . His attitude is so passive as to discount any immediate threat of attack."

Homma tightened the blockade. Col. Tatsunosuke Suzuki's 33rd Infantry occupied all of Luzon south of Manila and was then given the 16th Reconaissance Regiment to guard the southern coast of Manila Bay to prevent shipment of food and supplies to Corregidor and Bataan. At the same time, bombardment of the latter and the fortified islands in the bay was intensified using 105mms and 155mms already stationed in that area.

Information, both scuttlebutt and real, including interrogation of enemy prisoners, indicated Japanese negative shifts in their operations and was greeted with a heightening of morale among the American and Filipino defenders and even a spirit of eagerness to take the offensive and pursue the apparently weakened enemy. Some patrols actually even advanced back to the initial Allied main lines of resistance on Bataan. Many major frontline Allied officers urged a counteroffensive, but this course of action was refused by corps headquarters and met outright rejection by MacArthur's staff. While the situation on Bataan was never more favorable, a counteroffensive would only mean having to make another fighting retreat in the face of newly reinforced and refreshed enemy forces. MacArthur's mission was to buy time.

Nevertheless, General Homma was enduring unacceptable loss of face at home. In the overall Japanese war plan, he had been allotted fifty days for his conquest of the Philippines. It was now already at an embarrassing excess of one hundred. With a dirge of brutal successes in Southeast Asia, troops were being sent to Homma from Singapore, the Netherlands East Indies, and Hong Kong to bolster Homma and get his timetable back on track. There were ominous murmurings from Imperial General Headquarters in Tokyo that Homma should be sacked from his command in the Philippines. The series of disastrous delaying actions performed by the 26th Cavalry with support from the Provisional Tanks accounted for at least nine days of delaying Homma's timetable, critical because this bought time that kept the gate to Bataan open for MacArthur to get the bulk of his Luzon defense force on to the peninsula. The roles of the 26th and the Provisional Tanks were prominently mentioned in reports to the emperor in explanations of why the campaign had been going badly. (These reports were conspicuous in evidence presented at postwar hearings of Japanese conduct of the war. Homma testified to the Allied Military Tribunal, which sentenced him to death, that his assessment of the situation was so disheartened that he thought American and Filipino troops could have walked to Manila "without encountering much resistance on our part.") So dispirited was Homma, by both the military situation on the ground and the stain on his name and reputation from his detractors on the Imperial General Staff, that it was widely rumored at one point that he was seriously considering committing seppukku, but his strength of character and his bulldog determination to achieve his mission overcame this consideration; and he set about reorganizing his forces and restructuring his plans for renewed offensive.

(The following continues from Major Vance's diary.)

15–16 March

General Wainwright visited our positions and stayed for mess. He looks as skeletal as the rest of us. All we could offer was our usual four ounces of rice, but the cook had somewhere uncovered a small can of corn, a delicacy which he presented to the General with a flourish.

It was reported by Maj. Achille C. ("Archie") Tisdelle, a 26th Cavalry officer detached as Gen. Edward King's aide, that the last of 250 cavalry horses and 48 mules had been eaten. The 26th troopers, though near starvation themselves, did not participate in consumption.

6–14 March

Still in Sasain Ridge positions. Training and extensive patrolling continued despite frequent shelling and bombing. Japs trying to knock out our artillery. Bivouac here like one continuous earthquake. Little sleep and less food. Received report that Maj. General Wainwright has become Luzon Force Commanding General. 26th Cav. has been detailed Luzon Force main reserve and has been ordered to relocate our H.Q. to Caibobo Point.

16–31 March

Army Reserve duty at Caibobo Point. More training and reconnaisanse on beach positions continued. Constant shelling and bombing with no let up. Luck held. No casualties.

1–2 April

Still at Caibobo. More of same. A general lull has fallen over battle lines. Wainwright mused out loud to his staff, "the Japs are either tired of chasing us or something is up."

NOTE

1. Frank West Hewlett (c. 1913–7 July 1983) was an American journalist and war correspondent during World War II. He was the Manila bureau chief for United Press at the outbreak of war and was the last reporter to leave Corregidor before it fell to the Japanese.

25

The Final Chapter for Bataan

APRIL 1942

Something was most definitely up. Both sides were hard at work licking their wounds and laboring on preparations to cope with what was now imminent offensive action on both sides. It was a matter of which side readied itself first and best. On the American and Filipino side, troops seized every opportunity for rest, resupplying, and regrouping and deploying its forces.

The total strength of Luzon Force units was 79,500. Three-fourths of this were regular Philippine Army troops. The remainder comprised 8,000 Philippine Scouts and 12,500 Americans. With the exception of a few detachments operating in the mountains of Luzon, all of Gen. Edward King's force was crowded into the southern tip of Bataan. In an area of less than two hundred square miles were positioned I and II Corps, force reserve, Service Command, two coast artillery/antiaircraft regiments, the Provisional Tank Group, two battalions of 75mm cannons (self-propelled), plus engineer and signal troops. This sector of Bataan was so densely crowded that General King's staff concluded that Japanese aircraft "could bomb or strafe practically any point or location in the packed Allied operations theatre and hit something of military value." Added to this chaotic mob were some 6,000 civilian employees of Luzon Force and some 20,000 Filipino displaced refugees to be fed and sheltered. It was, in short, a logistical nightmare.

The organization and deployment of the defense forces on Bataan in the closing days of March were much the same as they had been during the preceding two months. The MLR still extended across the peninsula behind the Pilar–Bagac road from Orion on the east end to Bagac on the west, a distance of thirteen miles. The east half of the line was held by Gen. George

M. Parker's II Corps. The west half was defended by Maj. Gen. Albert M. Jones's I Corps, which included the Philippine Division (PA). The dividing line between the two corps roughly bisected the southernmost part of Bataan and extended southward along the Pantingan River, upward across the Mariveles heights and downward to Mariveles Bay by way of the Pantingan. This was the bottom end of the peninsula, the end of the line.

The dismounted 26th Cavalry was serving as a mobile reserve for Parker's western I Corps total force of 32,600 men. Two other Philippine Scout units, who had distinguished themselves in the past months—the 88th Field Artillery and the 45th Infantry—were also serving with I Corps. The 57th Infantry (PS) and the remainder of the Provisional Tank Group were serving in the motley collection of units serving as General King's Luzon Force reserve, which included engineer units pulled off work on defense positions.

During the February lull over Bataan, all on both sides sensed a coming major offensive. For most of March, General Homma oversaw an all-out effort to bolster his forces by intense training and organization of a steady stream of reinforcements, which came to him from points all over the expanding map of Japanese conquests. He was determined now to break the stubborn American-Filipino defense lines and made elaborate plans for what he was determined would be his final assault to capture Bataan. What the defenders, on the other hand, needed most to strengthen their ability to continue resistance was food and medicine. Ammunition was plentiful, but the strength of the troops was fast deteriorating. Homma's plans were timed to fall on them full force at the end of March when their strength and combat efficiency would be at their lowest, and his hopes were for a final attack. The congested, cumbersome positions of the defenders, which made for great difficulty to effectively maneuver and make maximum use of their resources, were all in Homma's favor. The Japanese forces, on the other hand, had plenty of room to maneuver and freedom to choose when and where to strike.

The 26th remained intact, still being counted on by their beloved General Wainwright to act as a mobile reserve, ready to move at a moment's notice to support I Corps to the west or II Corps on the east, all of this expected to be done on a food ration now amounting (when available) to that for one half day at most. Army Gen. Clifford Bluemel begged for the plentiful stores of food on Corregidor to be unlocked to share with the men on Bataan. His pleas went unheeded, however, since Bataan's starving defenders would probably never have received the requested food anyway. The magnitude of unpredicted Filipino civilian migration in to Bataan literally ensured starvation for the troops. As for Corregidor, the reality was actually grim. Food stores for a hundred thousand people for thirty days was exhausted. In all, rations had been halved three times, yet the Filipino troopers of the 26th used every ounce of their native instincts and know-how to grub anything and everything, short of dirt itself, to sustain themselves to the final end. It was no wonder, then, that their officers were proud of them almost to the point of worship. Never once was there a 26th trooper ever accused of lack of complete devotion to duty.

On 15 March, a form, censored note was distributed to all of the defenders who could be reached. It would be the last mail of any kind to be received by families and loved ones of the main majority of American troops for years. It was sent out by submarine from Corregidor to families and newspapers all over the United States, supposedly as a morale booster to the folks back home. The text of the letter was written under the dateline, "Things are not too bad . . ." and followed by general false assurances that life on Bataan was not that bad and their health and the war were generally going ok. It would be the last news of any kind the Americans back home would hear for a long time, until fragments of the real story leaked out in bits and pieces from Americans who had escaped capture (or from it) and got word to Australia, either in person by escapees such as 26th Capt. (later Maj.) Arthur K. Whitehead and Air Force Capt. William Dyess (both of whom made epic treks to Australia), by Filipino guerilla radio, or hand-smuggled messages. The home front at first received the horrifying accounts of the ordeals of Americans and Filipinos in their valiant but hopeless defense of the Philippines and the brutalities of Japanese captivity with disbelief, then with burning outrage against the Japanese and all things Japanese.

The following continues from Maj. Lee Vance's diary.

15 March 1942

Maj. General Wainwright becomes Luzon Force Commander upon Mac-Arthur's departure. 26th Cav. detailed to Luzon Force Reserve and bivouac moved to Bobo Point. Expected to be ready to cover rear of both I & II Corps in emergency.

15–31 March

Army and 26th Cav. Reserve forces at Bobo Point. Training and recon of all beach positions. Shelling and bombing frequent and heavy but fortunately only light casualties.
With the end of March, Homma put his all-out push into gear to end the Bataan struggle.

1–3 April

Much the same until 3rd. Reports of heavy attack on left of II Corps. 26th moved to junction of Trails 8 & 7 and prepared to counter attack on right of I Corps in case left flank of II Corps gives way. Move made by bus at dusk.

4–5 April

4/3 Good Friday and 4/5 Easter Sunday—26th new bivouac near Samat shelled heavily. Shock effect severe but men held up. Some wounded. Hospitals were shelled also.—Major Fleeger in command of rear detail consisting of Troop Band a section of scout cars on Trail 8 on Pantingan River to keep in contact with 45th Inf.(PS) in their attack up Trail 29. April 5 much the same. Becoming more difficult to keep contact with 45th Inf. (P.S.). Situation now extremely vague. Heavy action in Mt. Samat area.

6 April

3:30 pm. Regiment ordered to move at dusk by bus via Mariveles to junction of Trails 2–10 as Luzon Force reserve. Mt. Samat positions have completely given way.

Although General Homma had not received nearly the full complement of the reinforcements he had requested, his situation was nevertheless considerably improved. Heavy artillery had arrived as well as two army air force heavy bombardment regiments numbering some sixty bombers and several additional naval squadrons, all adding fearsome firepower to support Homma's all-out push to end the battle of Bataan once and for all.

Summarizing the situation and the forces at hand, he prepared his battle plan. He observed that the center of I Corps' defense line was anchored by the heights of Mt. Samat, which afforded the defenders clear observation of Japanese movements and high ground on which the Americans had positioned the bulk of their artillery on the slopes of Samat. Homma saw clearly that he must take the mountain if he was to realize his plan to have his forces make an all-out push southeast toward Limay circling the mountains and then driving west towards Mariveles. Thus the stage was set for Mt. Samat to prove one of the most vicious, bloody close-quarter battles of the war, and the 26th Cavalry would be in the thick of it.

Satisfied that his plans were as complete as possible, Homma briefed his top commanders and on March 30 issued orders to make preparations for the attack. He was determined to give the defenders as little time as possible to harden their lines and ordered the advance to commence as immediately as possible. The assault on Samat was to be made by the recently arrived elements of the 4th Division commanded by Lt. Gen. Kenzo Kitano and supported by Lt. Gen. Akira Nara's 65th Brigade advancing from their positions on both sides of the Pantingan River. Meanwhile, a detachment of some four thousand troops of the 21st Division under Major Gen. Kameichiro Nagano would cover the eastern flank of the attack with a feint movement. Simultaneously the 16th Division under Lt. Gen. Sasumo Morioka would feint on the I Corps front. The ground assaults would be preceded by massive air bombardment and then, just before jump-off,

Japanese artillery would deliver a withering barrage on the entire defensive line. The 1st Artillery HQ under Maj. Gen. Kineo Kitajima, a known authority on Imperial Japanese Army artillery, joined Homma's assault force. They had some 190 artillery pieces, which included bigger guns like 150mm cannons and the relatively rare Type 96 240mm field howitzer with Bataan being the latter's only known campaign use. The attack was scheduled to commence on 3 April at 3 p.m.

Oddly, in a belated gesture of consideration, Homma attempted one last appeal to General Wainwright, who he was aware had succeeded MacArthur. Notes beseeching Wainwright to accept the reality of an "honorable defeat and thus spare his men needless bloodshed" were stuffed in ribbon-bedecked beer cans and dropped from aircraft. Wainwright ignored the offer out of hand. Strengthening his decisiveness was a report that a Filipino patrol had found as early as 24 March documents on a dead Japanese officer outlining orders for a reconnaissance in force on Mt. Samat preliminary to a later all-out assault. Wainwright's reaction was immediate. He ordered all defensive preparations doubled in the area pending a heavy attack. What he had far too few of were antiaircraft guns. On 2 April Japanese aircraft commenced concentrated, heavy bombardment of the entire defensive line with particular attention to Mt. Samat. With almost no ground fire to worry them, Japanese pilots bombed and strafed at will. The incessant pounding of heavy explosives for two days had a hellish, numbing effect on the Americans and Filipinos huddled helplessly in trenches and dugouts. No man felt he could dig deeply enough. The devastating bombardment was compared by many to the massive barrages of World War I. Slowly, the shaken defenders, many in or near shell shock, pulled their frail selves together and manned their posts for the storm to come.

What Homma determined to be his final offensive to conquer Bataan once and for all was scheduled to commence on Friday, 3 April—Good Friday, the day of the Crucifixion for the largely Christian defenders (which was to be a cruel irony). For the Japanese, however, the day had another auspicious reason to represent a national, religious holiday. This day marked the anniversary of the death of the revered, legendary Emperor Jimmu, said to be the first ruler to occupy the Japanese imperial throne. At home in Japan, the day was celebrated with much ceremony and feasting. On Bataan, however, the holiday was marked with a mocking cacophony of bugles preceding a thundering barrage beginning at 9 a.m. with a complete array of some 150 heavy guns, howitzers, and mortars combined, all firing for effect in what was without a doubt the heaviest, single bombardment of the campaign. The day was hot and dry, and the observers on Samat, unable to direct any counter battery fire, watched helplessly as the mass of enemy artillery prepared to obliterate them. At the same time, Maj. Gen. Kizi Mikami's Japanese Air Force 22nd Air Brigade came overhead to unload some sixty tons of ordnance over the whole defensive front and, in addition, strafed at will. Nothing was spared. Most of the elaborately constructed defense positions were pounded into so much tangled rubble, communications were all but eliminated, and fires spread everywhere, even including hospitals in the rear where defenseless wounded were mauled to pieces.

General Homma and his staff now had high hopes they could compound the completion of their Philippine campaign with celebration of another Japanese holiday, that of Emperor Hirohito's birthday on 29 April. The defenders of Corregidor would dash that optimistic hope with a stubborn defense of "The Rock" by holding out until 6 May, and the last of the 26th Cavalry would be there. It would be a costly humiliation to Homma.

But the defense of Bataan was fast being butchered.

The aerial bombardment and artillery barrage lasted well into the afternoon when the Japanese infantry and tank assault jumped off. The Japanese had concentrated most of their artillery first on the narrow front on the extreme left of II Corps. The thinnest stretched part of the American line was held by Americans under Brig. Gen. Maxon Lough, and this was hit first by the overwhelming assault. This was part of Homma's plan to feint attention from Mt. Samat. In front of the base of Mt. Samat the line was being held by Philippine Army and Constabulary troops, on the right (east) the 21st Division under Gen. Mateo Capinpin and the extreme left by Brig. Gen. Vincente Lim's 41st. Behind the center, the 26th Cavalry was still being held dangerously positioned as reserve. Both divisions were roughly spread parallel to the Pilar–Bagac road bisecting Bataan just south of the Tiawir-Talisay River. By now, General Wainwright's entire Bataan force consisted of roughly seventy-seven thousand Filipino and American soldiers, of which medical reports indicated only twenty-seven thousand were considered "combat effective" and of which only about seven thousand were considered "healthy." Men were actually being pulled, literally staggering, out of hospitals in an attempt to reinforce the line. On their desperate trek north to the line at night many passed through a sugarcane field, emerging chewing on a short stalk, which provided deceiving quick rushes of energy but inevitably ended up gracing the eaters with "Queen Isabella's syndrome" —rampant diarrhea from the raw sugar. This was the ragged reality of what faced the Japanese juggernaut. But sheer courage drove them to try to stand their ground.

At about 3:00 in the afternoon, the Japanese shifted their bombardment south. Then Lt. Gen. Nara's 65th Tank Brigade supported by Maj. Gen. Kureo Taniguchi's Right Wing force moved out to the assault against the 2nd Philippine Constabulary holding the Patingan River to reach I Corp's main line. Meeting less resistance than expected, the attackers continued on southward along Trail 29. Taniguchi's force to the left, led by tanks of the

7th Tank Regiment, advanced across the Tiawir-Talisay River, overwhelming the weakened resistance by Philippine Army defenders who had only two 37mm antitank guns emplaced to oppose the crossing, but these had already been put out of action earlier by bombardment. After feeble resistance, the overwhelmed Filipinos, weakened by hunger and shock, retreated. The lack of opposition met by Nara's main effort was largely because, dazed and demoralized from five hours of artillery barrage and ferocious strafing by fighter aircraft, choked and blinded by smoke and dust, and literally burned out of their positions by searing brush fires all along the line, the Filipinos, not from lack of courage, had simply fled south blindly in disorganized, unruly mobs. One officer who tried to order his men to stand their ground "was dumbly stared at simply" as they continued to the rear. The 41st had ceased to be an effective military force before the combined Japanese tank infantry had even really begun to roll. The ease and speed of the advance moved the usually cautious Homma to abandon all restraint and order his force to go ahead and take Mt. Samat on 4 April. II Corps commander General Parker, aware of the collapse of the 41st and that the danger to the whole line was now immediate, was forced to release his only reserves in an attempt to plug the gaping breaches that had been driven into his line. A blind man could see that Mt. Samat was the main target. II Corps was in ragged shape, and if I Corps couldn't hold, the Japanese had a clear path to the mountain stronghold, such as it was.

In the meantime, the 26th Cavalry Regiment was still mainly acting as guard for I Corp's line. The men were becoming daily weaker from hunger. Even so, Vance kept busy making sure that replacements were familiar with their weapons—testing, cleaning, and firing them. When the 3 April shelling began, all the cavalrymen could do was hunker down and wait out the incoming shells and bombs. Some men had blood running from their noses and ears from the concussion of close blasts. As the day wore on, reports came in about the collapse of the 41st and the tenuous condition of II Corps. Vance moved the regiment to the junction of Trails 8 and 7 in preparation for a counterattack to protect the right flank of I Corps, should II Corps give way completely. The regiment was transported at dusk by bus to the new and far more dangerous positions.

Fighting raged up and down the lines all night and the 26th came under heavy shelling. Maj. Harry Fleeger was ordered to take Troop B and a section of scout cars on to Trail 8 on the Pantingan River in an effort to keep contact with the 45th Inf. (Philippine Scouts) who were attempting an attack up Trail 29 to block the enemy advance on I Corps' flank. In the ferocity of the fighting the situation became increasingly confused. Contact with the 45th became, as Vance recorded it, "difficult and extremely vague"—putting it tersely.

The Japanese push on April 4, the Saturday of Holy Week, was devastatingly ahead of schedule. General Nara's force flanked the remaining defenders in his sector on the way to Samat and at the same time Col. Haruji Morita's 4th Division, entering action for the first time and of which Homma had expected little, pushed forward rapidly with few casualties. Next, an armored assault gained final control of the vital Pilar–Bagac Road. The 21st Philippine Division withdrew in disarray with nowhere to go but Samat and south. That same day Colonel Morita's reinforced 8th Infantry (less one battalion), also seeing action for the first time, broke the Philippine lines at another point, thus, at roughly 10 p.m. the entire American-Filipino main line of resistance had been overwhelmed.

To take Mt. Samat, Homma had planned to regroup his 4th Division's two columns as soon as the northern foothills of the mountain had been seized, thus shifting the strength of that force from the right sector to the left, then attacking in force along the eastern slopes down Trail 4. Simultaneously, his 65th Brigade would continue driving west of Mt. Samat toward Mariveles (this would lead to an inevitable clash with the 26th Cavalry in its coming movement south). At the same time, the 16th Division and the Nagano detachment made ready to join the assault on the Limay line. Yet, because of the rapid gains of Saturday, Homma's schedule was some twenty-four hours ahead of time to assault Mt. Samat.

5 APRIL 1942—EASTER SUNDAY

On Sunday morning, despite the impending violence, Americans and Filipinos on Mt. Samat gathered under the gracious shelter of Bataan's jungle and were holding Easter Sunday services when they were irreverently interrupted by an unholy renewal of Japanese bombardment. (Japanese bombardment actually commenced at dawn.) Chaplains hurriedly invoked divine guidance and added a plea for "deliverance from the power of the enemy" as men hurriedly went to their fighting positions.

By late morning, fighting on Mt. Samat was total mayhem. Hand-to-hand fighting was vicious and costly as the fight swung back and forth. The American and Filipino defenders desperately fought to hold their last Bataan stronghold despite their pitiful condition, causing Homma to later observe that this was the "fiercest fighting his soldiers had in the second phase of the battle for Bataan." This was certainly no walkover for the Japanese as they were getting accustomed to. The Americans and Filipinos mustered themselves and "fought like samurai demons," remembered Japanese staff members out of respect, but their numbers and debilitated state ultimately proved the deciding factor. The defensive gun positions were flanked and had to be abandoned. General Capinpin had become separated from his staff and was captured. The brave resistance ultimately and necessarily became a rout. A number of troopers from the 26th Cavalry who were acting as reserve liaison to the Mt. Samat command got involved in the close quarter brawl, fighting with all they had, including bayonets and machetes. Several got back to the regiment with bayonet wounds, but none were killed on the bloody mountain.

Late in the day of the 5th, Colonel Vance made an entry in his journal stating, "Difficult to keep contact with the 4th [an understatement]. The situation is extremely vague." The truth was that the 26th was mired in a mass of chaos. On 6 April, Vance wrote, "Regiment ordered to move out at dusk by bus south toward Mariveles to junction of Trails 2–10 as Luzon Force Reserve. Mt. Samat position has completely given way [this movement would put the 26th directly in the path of Homma's 65th Brigade advance]."

Major Chandler (26th G-3) put it this way in his amazingly complete journal later uncovered at Cabanatuan:

Reports of breakthrough on the left of II Corps. Gen. Parker threw in all his reserves, and one by one, Northern Luzon Force released all of its reserves to Parker who promptly committed those also in his attempt to halt the penetration and stabilize his front. Despite these efforts, the situation continued to worsen and on 6 April Maj. General Edward King, now commanding the Luzon Force, released his last reserve—the 26th Cavalry.

We were to move to the Junction of Trails 2 and 10 just east of Limay to await orders. But just as we were pulling [out] of our assembly area at junctions 8 and 9 just south of Samat we received word that Gen. Parker's center had completely folded and that our direct route by Trail 8 was now threatened. We would have to use the much longer route by way of Mariveles and the East Road [Highway 110 on map], once again by bus. Col. Vance and I went ahead by Scout Car to Luzon Force HQ just northeast of Mariveles in search of information. Arriving just before midnight, we found that Brig. Gen. Arnold Funk, the Chief of Staff, and the G-2 and G-3 knew little more than we did due to an almost complete breakdown of front line communications. It appeared that the brunt of the most recent Japanese thrust had fallen in Sector C near Mt. Samat. Gen. Clifford Bluemel was somewhere in that vicinity with the last reserves, the 31st Infantry(US), a battalion of the 57th Inf.(PS) and elements of the 14th Engineers(PS). Just where was the question! Trail 8 had been cut and units of the 45th Inf.(PS), which had been counterattacking north down the Pantingan River were now cut off from II Corps. We were to continue our march, try to find Bluemel and see what we could do. Though no one put it into words, it was apparent that the defense of Bataan was now in desperate straits.

So began the last of our long series of delaying actions, one which was to see the final break-up of the 26th Cavalry (PS).

[This was not true as Major Chandler was unaware that an entire machine gun platoon under Sgt. Felipe Fernandez would escape capture and make their way to Corregidor to fight on with the 4th Marines on beach defense until Corregidor was finally taken by the Japanese.]

Arriving at the junction of Trails 2 and 10 well before dawn, we could not find friendly troops anywhere in the vicinity. We had time to feed breakfast, such as it was, before daylight when we moved north along Trail 2 in approach formation. About four kilometers north of Trail 10 all vehicular movement was stopped dead by either bomb or shell craters in the trail. Col. Vance decided to set up a temporary defense line on nearby high ground while I went forward on foot to try to contact Gen. Bluemel. About a km. farther on I found him, accompanied only by two Filipino staff officers. The general was on foot and carrying a rifle. He was moving slowly and reluctantly southward, head turning frequently over his shoulder as he listened to the sound of firing to the north. He had lost all contact with his units when their counterattack failed and the withdrawal started. He told me they should be along soon, having to move through the underbrush on each side of the trail. He appeared to cheer up noticeably when told that the 26th Cavalry was now added to his decimated command.

After two desperate days of nonstop bombardment, II Corps virtually collapsed and began streaming southward in a confused retreat toward Limay, Limao, and Mariveles. This breech of the line forced I Corps to bend back to protect its now naked right flank. Reports of penetrations all along the line came in a frantic wave. On 6 April, Wainwright threw the 26th Cavalry and whatever remaining reserves he had forward in a futile attempt to counterattack. No sooner had the move started than word came through that the Japanese had broken through on the right and all roads to 2nd Corps had been cut.

Col. Edwin Ramsey recalls: "The whole center had collapsed and the eastern flank was in danger of being turned. Wainwright ordered us to circle back around the foot hills of Mt. Mariveles and then cut across country northeastward to the coastal town of Limay. It was an index of how desperate the situation was becoming, for Limay was nearly ten miles south of Orion, once the eastern anchor of our line.

"We loaded on to buses and trucks and threaded our way along the trails that traced the Mariveles jungles to the coast. The coastal road was littered with evidence of our army's retreat. Equipment had been blasted and abandoned, and troops were pulling sullenly back toward Mariveles at the bottom of Bataan. We had no air force left, and the skies were crisscrossed with Japanese planes. At every clearing they sliced down at us, bombing and strafing with lethal efficiency. When we reached Limay early on the morning of 7 April, we were directed to a bivouac near the ruins of a hacienda; but no sooner had we dropped down for a few hours of sleep than the Zeros spotted us and we had to scatter back into the jungle."

The following is from Maj. Lee Vance's diary.

7 April

The regiment arrived at Jct. Trails 2–10 sometime before dawn. Just got under cover before enemy air activity began again. Cover very poor. Fed men meagre rations. 26th Cav. assigned to II Corps by Luzon Force HQ at 11a.m. Were directed by II Corps to report to Exec Officer Brig. Gen. Bluemel somewhere in this vicinity. Sent Major Chandler, our S-2-3 forward with a command car to locate Gen. Bluemel. Regt. to follow under me. Chandler found him 2 km. north on Trail 2. Gen. Bluemel had a small detachment of 31st Inf. (US) in front of him and was accompanied by 2 Filipino staff officers, all on foot. Other detachments of the 31st were drifting back on our left flank, very tired and exhausted after a failed counterattack. The 57th Inf. (PS) under the intrepid Maj. Lloyd Mills were still engaged with the enemy further west on Trail 10. The 14th Engineers had moved in just prior to the 26th Cavalry and bivouaced just south of us on Trail 2. These organizations came under Gen. Bluemel's command. He directed that the withdrawal South would be continued and ordered the 26th Cav. to take over the defense of Trail 2 and cover the movement of the other troops along that trail. 2nd Squadron took up positions on a hill about 1 1/2 km. just north of Trail 10 and 1st Squadron north of but closer to Trail 10. Regimental trains, Bren Gun Carriers and Machine Gun Troop ordered to take cover at Rodriguez Park on east road and await instructions. Busses sent south on east road to report to M.T.O. (motor transport). 2nd Squadron withdrew through 1st Squadron. Enemy bombed and shelled area at junction of Trails 2 & 10 as 2nd Squadron made its withdrawal through 1st Sq. and motor transportation of 14th Engineers moving south. All offered good targets for the enemy. 26th Cav. ammunition truck struck by bomb near river crossing south of the Trail 1–2 junction. Bedlam, great confusion.

Col. Ramsey continues: "Our orders were to report to Gen. Bluemel of the 31st Division, which was now reeling under continued Japanese attacks. Where the general himself was, however, was by now unclear. At 7 a.m. we started out in the direction of his headquarters, somewhere between Limay and Orion. On the dry coastal trail our convoy raised a dust cloud that sifted up over the trees, pinpointing our movements. The Zeros swooped to it instinctively. They dived and strafed for hours, bullets decapitating trees and ripping up the jungle canopy with a sound not unlike the dull rent of soggy bedsheets. At last our ammunition truck was hit, spewing fire and shards hundreds of feet into the air. The explosion sent us all headlong for cover, and it was some time before we were able to clear the road to continue."

Vance:

2nd Sq. took position on high ground south of the San Vincente River. 1st Sq. withdrew from positions north of junction 2–10. Troop A came along in good order, but Tr. B lost its way and was not to be located until 8 April at Little

Baguio. The regiment (less detachments) reorganized in position south of the river and held there until dark.

General Bluemel at a hastily held staff meeting on the 26th's regimental staff car (he had lost his HQ and staff in the previous day's fighting) had designated the 26th 2nd Squadron to go forward to delay the Japanese advance as long as possible to buy time for the withdrawal south of the remaining elements of the 31st Division, the 45th and 57th Infantry (PS). One more time, the 26th was thrown into a delaying role. It did not take long for things to get hot. The cavalrymen opened up a fierce volume of fire to force the Japanese to scatter and deploy. After the defense held for ten, fifteen, and finally thirty minutes, the Japanese recovered and began to turn the flank of the 26th, who grudgingly pulled back a few kilometers and dug in to hold again.

Here is another excerpt from the diary of Maj. William Chandler:

6–8 April

On reaching Colonel Vance's position on the high ground north of Trail 10 it was decided to move back slowly along Trails 2 and 20, delaying the enemy advance as much as possible, thus forming a rallying point for Bluemel's other units as they moved southward. Once again, and this time finally, the regiment fell into its well-practiced role of delaying force. Units of the 31st Inf. (U.S.) now began appearing through the trees and were directed to an assembly area south of the Momolo River. Messages were sent to the 57th (PS) to the north to the same effect. Small Japanese forces appeared hard on the heels of the 31st and the 26th was soon outflanked. They began an orderly withdrawal by successive positions to the Momolo, allowing Bluemel's other units maximum time to re-assemble and reorganize. As Major Jim Blanning's 1st Squadron [Blanning had recently rejoined the 26th from detached duty as I Corps HQ Commandant] passed the intersection of Trails 2 and 10, he and the tail of the Motorized unit just ahead were hit with a storm of interdiction fire from Japanese artillery. They had caught up and we, as usual, had no supporting artillery for counter-battery fire. This was by far the worst we had ever encountered and casualties were heavy in men and materiel. We lost two more scout cars and several ammo trucks we could ill spare. These interdiction fires were to continue with telling effect at intervals for the next two days as Jap batteries were able to catch up to us. Those who were able took to the brush on each side of the trail and moved on through difficult terrain. Some elements, including all of Troop A were unable to join until the next day.

However, enemy artillery was far from the only peril the 26th had to endure for several terrible days.

From 7 April, Colonel Ramsey again: "Here the trail we had followed mounted an escarpment and intersected another along the top of the bluff.

The drop was sheer, falling several hundred feet to a river. Atop the bluff the trail crossed a clearing some hundred yards wide and deep in dust. As soon as we set foot on it Zeros of the Japanese 16th Light Bombardment Regiment honed in on the dust cloud, and in a moment the whole bluff was heaving with explosions.

"There was nothing we could do. Hundreds of men were crowded into the clearing, helpless under the bombs. Some fled for the jungle while those of us closest to the bluff had no choice but to dive over the edge. It was terrifying. Dozens of us hung there, grasping at vines and shrubs, flattened against the cliff face as plane after plane roared in bombing and strafing. The concussions were endless, convulsing the ground, blasting our ears and raining down on us debris of equipment and flesh.

"At one point I pulled myself up to the lip and peered over. Through the flailing earth and smoke I saw several soldiers make a dash for cover. Just as they did, a 500-pound bomb dropped among them. The whole group was hurtled into the air and I watched sickly as the mucous bulk of one man's body was smeared against a tree. I was horrified and shaken by shell-shock. It seemed that it would go on forever, this brutish killing and maiming, and there was nothing anyone could do to stop it. I fought mad impulses to let go and fall from the cliff or heave myself over the edge and run screaming across the open ground.

"The attack lasted for five hours, until dusk put a silence to it. When at last the ground stopped pounding, I unclenched myself and crawled up over the edge. The carnage was horrible. Most of our staff and rear guard had been wiped out, men and vehicles ground into the earth or flung among the trees."

Dazed, wounded men stumbled about everywhere, moaning pitifully or screaming curses in vain at an enemy who could not hear them. Some had limbs literally torn off; others groped at gaping wounds that revealed splintered bones or hideously florid sacks of organs. One man sat with his back against a tree, eyes fixed stupidly at the open hole that had been his stomach, now leaking out coils of intestines over his thighs.

Ramsey weakly called out to his remaining men to assemble, his voice almost eerily loud in the sudden silence in the absence of bombs. Slowly, the survivors pulled themselves up over the lip of the cliff and formed up to continue down the blasted trail.

"What about them?" asked one trooper pointing at the helpless wounded.

"There's nothing we can do," said Ramsey abruptly. "We've got to get the rest of us under cover—now!" But mixed feelings of pity and shame surged in him as he heard the pitiful cries and moaning grow dimmer. Only his anger could serve to fight down his feelings.

That night, a weary General Bluemel gathered the shattered remnants of the 26th and had them deploy along a ridge farther to the rear. Once more, the hapless cavalrymen were called upon to hold and delay until the rest of his command, what was left of them, could regroup. Not having slept for over two days nor eaten in three, the troopers struggled to dig and build cover against plane and artillery attacks they all knew would come with first light.

From 8 April, Colonel Ramsey again: "When the storm came, it was as terrifying as the day before.

"The bombardment lasted well into the afternoon and finally ceased to clear the way for advancing Japanese infantry. From their shallow dugouts and from behind fallen logs, the cavalrymen watched as dozens of small figures crawled and felt their way cautiously up the ridge over bomb shattered ground. Short as the lull was, it did offer some small respite. Food, meager as it was, was brought up to the line—one tin of salmon for every five men. Even as the precious food was precisely divided and savored, the Japanese continued their steady movement ever closer to finish off what was left of the defenders."

And this from the continuing diary of Major Vance:

8 April

Rear guard reached Alangan river position about 7:45 a.m. Entire command exhausted. Position occupied as follows from left to right: 14th Engineers—26th Cavalry (gap of about 600 yards)—31st Inf.(U.S.) (gap unknown)—57th Inf.(PS) (gap unknown)—Col. Irwin with miscellaneous Philippine Army units on east road, and Co. "G" 57th Inf.(PS) in reserve on Trail 20. Some tel. communication along line but no other. Enemy air activity heavy, especially on right. Col. Irwin's command broke at about 3 p.m. Enemy tanks appeared in front of 26th Cav. at 4:30 p.m. Road blocked but enemy infantry appeared and fighting becomes heavy. Our casualties heavy. Major Chandler wounded. Gen. Bluemel orders withdrawal at dark. Troop "G" misled by report of enemy tanks on trail to rear and leaves trail on right. In darkness gets separated from Regiment. Regt. continues march south on Trail 20 with remainder of Bluemel's force and reached Lamao River at midnight.

The following is from Chandler's diary:

7–8 April

By this time General Bluemel and Colonel Vance had met with the COs of the 31st and the 57th and with Lt. Col. Freddy Saint, commanding the supporting battalion of the 14th Engineers (PS) at the assembly point on the Momolo. In the absence of orders from II Corps Bluemel decided to withdraw to the line of the Alangan River, a somewhat more defensible position, breaking contact with the enemy in the darkness if possible in order to provide time to organize a stronger line and assemble more troops. Bluemel had, in effect, adopted the

26th's regimental staff as his own and directed all subsequent operations through us. At least we were still organized and there. Accordingly, at nightfall the march was resumed with the 26th covering the movement as usual.

The Alangan River position, though naturally stronger than previous ones, was not held as long as we had hoped because when we arrived there at daybreak 7 April, we found that the 31st and 57th, supposedly preceding us, had lost the route in the darkness due to the confusion of unmarked trails in the area. Though they had reached the Alangan River, they had done so far to our right, and so far as communications or mutual support were concerned, they might as well have been on the moon. A thousand yard cap of heavy jungle and rough terrain stretched from our right to the 31st's left, a gap which took a foot patrol over an hour to cross. The 3rd Battalion of the 57th was somewhere in front of the 31st, both equally inaccessible to us. The regiment was all in place, however, and the battalion of the 14th Engineers had stayed with us. Early on the morning of 8 April Major Joe Ganahl joined us with one of his 75mm self-propelled gun batteries and during the day G Company of the 57th, which had been separated from the battalion during the night, joined us and was held in reserve by General Bluemel. Unfortunately but not unexpectedly, the 75s were ordered to the East Road and moved out just before the Japs hit our line, which they did in mid-afternoon.

Due to our reinforcements and the natural strength of our position on the high ground around south of the river we were able to repulse the first Japanese attack, even though it was supported by tank and artillery fire from the opposite bank. By night fall, however, the Japs had found the gap on our right and we were receiving small arms fire from our flank and rear. One round caught me in the chest as Colonel Trapnell and I were comparing notes after inspecting the line. Fortunately, I am a small man and Trapnell, an ex-Army half back, was not. He picked me off the ground, threw me over his shoulder and carried me back to the CP where a wandering 57th Infantry weapons carrier was found to take me back to Hospital No. 1 on the East Road.

During the previous days, both Wainwright and King had sought desperately to find some way to stem the Japanese advance. While Bluemel was struggling to form a line at the Mamala River, King decided to concentrate "everything possible" there. Since all his reserves as well as the reserves of both corps were already committed, he took a desperate chance that the Japanese would not attempt to land behind the lines and ordered Generals Jones and Parker to withdraw their Philippine units, the 1st and 4th Constabulary Regiments, and throw them into the line being formed. General Bluemel, who was now literally the only general officer in the front line, tried to form a line of sorts along the Mamala River. General Parker directed 26th Cavalry commander Col. Lee Vance to report to Bluemel, and subsequently he ordered Vance to place the badly decimated 26th once again into a holding position. Bluemel spent the late afternoon of 7 April positioning his ragged forces along the south bank of the Mamala River. In addition to the cavalry regiment, he now had remnants of the 31st and 57th Infantry and the 14th and 803rd Engineers. None of the men had eaten more than a meager breakfast, and most had not had anything at all since the morning of the 6th. He had few vehicles and virtually no heavy weapons. As for the bulk of American armor, after vicious resistance it had either been destroyed or blown itself up during and shortly after the battle for Mt. Samat. The outlook for holding off any determined Japanese attack was slim to none.

Around dusk, artillery fire started coming in followed by Japanese troops observed slowly working their way forward, firing sporadically as they crawled and snaked through the undergrowth. Forward elements of Col. Haruji Morita's 4th Division had reached the north bank of the Mamala, followed by the Nagano detachment, which was still just north of Trail 46. Actually the Japanese had not yet crossed the river, but they now held the commanding high ground on the bluffs along the north bank, rendering Bluemel's positions wholly untenable. Hoping desperately to prepare a stronger line and to feed and rest his troops, Bluemel ordered a withdrawal to the Alangan River, some four thousand yards to the south. The plan called for breaking off enemy contact, pulling back under the cover of darkness and in new positions by dawn of 8 April. There he hoped for time to brace for a fresh enemy attack. His plan was approved by Corps HQ. General King decided to "place everything possible" on the new Alangan River line. All of his reserves were now committed, leading him to order Jones and Parker to pull their troops off beach defense and throw them into the main line now forming, thus taking the desperate chance that the Japanese would not attempt to land behind the lines and cut off the whole force. General King then sent word by his chief of staff, Brig. Gen. Arnold J. Funk, to Wainwright that the situation on Bataan had now become critical.

Wainwright's reaction was a forlornly hopeful plan to retrieve the situation by launching a counterattack eastward from I Corps along the general line of Trail 8. His purpose was to attempt to tie in I Corps with the troops along the Mamala and again establish an unbroken line across the peninsula. But he was not yet aware that the Mamala line was already being withdrawn and that II Corps had deteriorated to the point that even if such an attack succeeded, there would be no line for I Corps to tie into. On his only current information, Wainwright ordered the attack to jump off at 4 p.m. on 7 April. The 11th Division (PA) would make the assault.

On receiving the order, Jones sent his G-3, Col. James Collier, to confer with General Jones. It was concluded that such an attack would be literally impossible. The men of the 11th Division were too weak to cross Patingan Gorge even unopposed, much less struggle to take any heavy equipment or artillery with them. Next, it would take at least eighteen hours just to get the division repositioned out of their present line and ready to attack. After intense telephone conversations among the commanders, Wainwright decided to leave the decision to General King. Considering Jones's estimates, King cancelled the order to attack. He instead chose to order Jones to withdraw in four phases to the line of the Binuangan River, roughly five miles south of the present main line of resistance. This move would leave I Corps' right flank exposed on the slopes of Mt. Mariveles and reduce the already thinly defended beach line to almost a skeleton force.

That night, a discouraged Wainwright could only report withdrawals in his communiqué to Washington:

> Continued heavy enemy pressure, constant bombing, strafing and shelling of front line units forced all elements of the right half of our line in Bataan to fall back. A new defensive position is forming on the high ground south of the Alangan. . . . The left half of our line, due to an exposed flank, withdrew on orders and is taking up a defense position south of the Binuangan River. Fighting intense. Casualties heavy on both sides.

From the Japanese standpoint, matters had gone beyond expectations. What Homma had expected his offensive to gain in a month was all but finished by the night of 7 April. II Corps had been forced to withdraw from its main line of resistance and the Americans and Filipinos had been forced out of their main defensive positions on the Mamala River. Cost to the Japanese had been relatively light. The assault spearhead 4th Division had lost 150 men killed and 250 wounded, and their rapid advance had taken some 1,000 prisoners and a considerable number of small-caliber weapons. General Nara's 65th Brigade lost but 77 dead and 152 wounded while taking over 100 prisoners and considerable enemy equipment. The Nagano detachment had taken no casualties at all.

Homma had planned to pause his advance at the Mamala River, but now satisfied that the Americans and Filipinos were in full retreat he decided to push on without haste to Cabcaben on the southeast tip of Bataan and strike for Mt. Limay and the heights of Mariveles. After moving his headquarters south behind Nagano's 4th Division to Cabcaben, he would prepare for his final strike to Mariveles itself. As before, his attacks would have coordinated heavy support from the 14th Army Artillery and the 22nd Air Brigade. With satisfaction, Homma was now able to order his artillery commanders to open fire on Corregidor once in range of the island stronghold.

8–9 APRIL 1942: ARMAGEDDON ON BATAAN

On 8 April the 26th Cavalry (300 men) was still with General Bluemel's mixed force including remnants of the 31st Infantry (US; 160 men), 57th

Infantry (PS; 500 men; Lt. Lloyd Mills was still with them), what was left of the 803rd Engineer Battalion (US) and the 14th Engineer Battalion (PS; about 400 men). This mixed group of some 1,360 men, considerably less in number since the Mamala River line, was ordered to hold the west half of the line from Trail 20 about twenty-five hundred yards to where the Alangan and Paalungan Rivers joined. On the right side of the line, a force of about 1,200 men under Col. John W. Irwin made up of 31st Infantry (PA) and constabulary troops taken from beach defense was to hold the eastern part of the line and block the east road. There was supposed to be artillery support provided by the still intact 21st Field Artillery (PA), a Provisional Field Artillery Brigade (formed from three battalions of Scouts), several fixed naval guns, and the last three 155mm guns of the 301st Field Artillery (PA) under Col. Alexander Quintard.

This ambitious plan began to fall apart almost as it started. The day began in general chaos. In the confusion of the withdrawal, units went off course in the thick undergrowth and settled in positions well away from those assigned. The American 31st and the Scout 57th Infantry got mixed up and had to trade back positions. The 803rd Engineers did not occupy its position at all but continued south after it crossed the river. Only the 14th Engineers and the 26th Cavalry managed to go into their assigned positions. The engineers settled in on the left straddling Trail 20 while the cavalrymen fell in to their right (east). From there east, things went generally haywire with large gaps in the line. Between the 26th Cavalry and the 31st Infantry (US) was an open space of over a thousand yards. East of the 31st was another hole in the line, and the 57th Infantry (PS) had both its flanks exposed. The unplanned withdrawal of the 803rd Engineers south of the river made the tie-in between Bluemel a virtual impossibility. Chaos reigned.

Actually, the units on the line were so decimated in numbers that in all reality their designations were made meaningless. All of the men were half starved and exhausted. Wrote one officer, "We were all so tired that the only way to stay awake was to remain standing. As soon as a man sat or laid down he would go to sleep." After five days under intense air and artillery bombardment, one had to doubt if the men cared anything much about what happened.

The Alangan "line" was crumbling fast before the Japanese infantry even attacked. Constant heavy air bombardment lasting all morning took a terrible toll, not just in casualties but the already splintered psychological will and capability to fight. Japanese observation planes pinpointed allied troops hastily preparing fighting positions, and at about 11 a.m. fighters and light bombers swooped in low for the kill, strafing and dropping incendiary bombs, especially heavily in the areas held by the 31st Infantry (US) and the 57th Scouts. The fire bombs ignited the thick, dry cogon grass and bamboo thickets, causing the infantrymen to concentrate on fighting fires to avoid being burned alive in their positions. At about the same time Col. Irwin's force along the east coast road came under similar attack. Repeatedly Filipino troops of the 31st (PA) who were digging foxholes when the planes came in fled for cover and had to be rounded up to return to the line. With each attack the number of men returning to the line, some forced to do so at pistol point, were fewer. The constabulary troops east of the 31st also bolted. By around 3 in the afternoon, the rout left Colonel Irwin's sector of the line completely deserted.

For trained regular army units such as the core of the Bataan defense force to be driven into such muddled, confused situations was bad enough, but for the under-trained, ill-equipped, understrength, and starving units of the Philippine Army, this had to be a state of total chaos and despair. They were now in the last stages of exhaustion and disintegration despite their proven courage and spirit.

The Japanese planes continued their deadly work all along the Alangan line, and the trails were crowded with dazed, weakened men, many of them wounded, making a turkey shoot for enemy pilots. The ditches beside the trails and clearings were littered with dead and wounded. It was nothing less than a holocaust. Those who held fast in the line, mostly Philippine Scouts, cavalrymen, and American troops, endured the bone-shattering impact of explosives while huddled in foxholes and trenches literally clawing at the ground to get deeper in the questionable safety of the earth.

At around 2:00 that afternoon, advance patrols of Japanese infantry reached the Alangan River appearing first in front of the 57th Scouts. Soon enemy infantry found the badly exposed right flank and began to filter to the rear of the scouts. At about the same time other groups of Japanese hit the 31st Americans, now reduced to less than company strength in numbers. At around 5 p.m., completely outflanked, the Americans and the 57th had no choice but to fall back. But the 26th Cavalry and the 14th Engineers took the main brunt of the Japanese assault that afternoon by a force consisting of the 8th Infantry and the 7th Tank Regiment. Amazingly, enemy tanks advancing along Trail 20 were stopped in their tracks by a block that the scout engineers had constructed from disabled cannon. The tanks, unable to maneuver on the narrow trail, were held at bay by small-arms fire, which drove the crewmen inside their hatches. With no infantry support, the tanks became little more than stationary pillboxes. But even their 47mm main guns and their machine guns could not budge the roadblock. It became a classic Mexican standoff as the scouts, though they had the tanks completely at their mercy, had no antitank weapons to finish them off.

East of the roadblock, the 26th Cavalry came under attack from the 8th Infantry, whose advanced points had forced the 31st (US) and the 57th

(PS) to pull back. The cavalrymen were in severe danger from their badly exposed, hastily refused right flank where the Japanese worked their way around and threatened to take the 26th from the rear.

For the afternoon of 8 April, Col. Edwin Ramsey noted: "Suddenly there was a report of enemy behind us and tanks moving up the coastal road. Within an hour they were lobbing shells at us from both our right and rear. Again we were pinned down, unable to move or respond. Under the fire our engineers managed to build a roadblock out of some crippled cannon which halted the tanks on our flank. The Japanese then deployed infantry to try to get behind us, and another firefight erupted. As the penetration of Japanese forces [under Col. Haruji Morita, whose 8th Infantry had executed the successful flanking attacks on Bluemel's beleaguered force] widened the gap in the 26th line, Vance ordered the right flank to be refused sharply. The movement proved to have little effect, and it soon was evident that the regiment would again have to withdraw. We were now surrounded on three sides, but we managed to hold until midafternoon when Major Jim Blanning, our squadron commander, received orders for us to withdraw.

"There was only one escape: a narrow jungle track carving south and west toward Mariveles. As we filed down it, shoving abandoned trucks and half-tracks across the path to stall the Japanese, we came upon a cache of food, hundreds of cans of salmon. Major Blanning ordered us to stuff our pockets and move on. A few kilometers farther on we found Captain Joe Barker, who had gone ahead to scout, working his way back toward us. The trail ahead, he told us, had been cut by the Japanese. Blanning ordered us into the jungle. For the next six hours we hacked a path through undergrowth so thick that one man could not see another. Platoons became separated, then squads. After midnight we reached a ridge and worked our way down to the river below where we bivouacked. By now only the remnants of Troop G and one platoon of E/F Troop were left, altogether about sixty men. We were surrounded, cut off, and lost. We were not so much soldiers now as fugitives, seeking lines that we doubted existed, trying to rejoin a fight that we suspected was already over."

Here is Maj. William Chandler's diary entry from 8 April:

> As the Jap penetration forces built up in the gap, we refused our right flank sharply, but it soon became evident that the regiment would again have to withdraw. General Bluemel, still with no word from II Corps, decided to pull back, to the Lamao River and try again, a movement which was executed in reasonably good order under the cover of darkness. Jim Blanning and G Troop, who were at the tail of the column, became separated somewhere to the right of the trail in the dark, but we also picked up elements of the 31st (US) which had also been outflanked.

The officers and troops on the line were enduring on all levels the agonies of a steadily collapsing situation. Frantic communications and hopeless schemes to retrieve the situation and stabilize the mere shadow of a defense were received with a mix of overtures and demands for immediate and unconditional capitulation from the Japanese to Wainwright and King of all Allied forces in the entire Philippines to "prevent further, needless bloodshed." At the same time, from MacArthur's headquarters in Australia came a bizarre order (which could only have arisen from imaginary maps and total logistics disinformation) to implement and execute an impossible plan ("when the situation became desperate . . .") to carry out the following:

1. A feint by I Corps in the form of an "ostentatious" artillery preparation.
2. A "sudden surprise attack" by II Corps toward the Dinalupihan–Olongapo road at the base of the peninsula, made with full tank strength and "maximum artillery concentration."
3. Seizure of Olongapo by simultaneous action of both corps, I Corps taking the enemy in reverse by an attack from the west, along the Dinalupihan–Olongapo road.

"If successful," elaborated MacArthur, "the supplies seized at this base might well rectify the situation. This would permit operation in central Luzon where food supplies could be obtained and where Bataan and the northern approaches to Corregidor could be protected." Even if the attack did not succeed, many of the men would be able to escape Bataan and continue to fight as guerillas. (Force report of operations states that the 26th Cavalry [PS] actually did go into line as ordered, but other records do not confirm this view. Colonel Vance states that the orders were not received and even if they had they could not have been executed.)

Being the professional soldier he was, Wainwright knew full well before he even passed on his superior's orders that MacArthur had asked the impossible of his army on Bataan. At the same time, however, he communicated to Washington the state of affairs, that both corps had been forced to withdraw because of losses and the utter weakness of troops who had had to subsist one-half to one-third rations, sometimes less, for so long. He indicated that even the best of his regiments "were capable of only a short advance before they would collapse from complete exhaustion." In his message of reply to MacArthur's order, he had warned in clear language that the end was near for Bataan. The tactical situation, he explained, was fast deteriorating and the men were so weakened by hunger and disease that their power of resistance was nonexistent.

"It is with deep regret," he had replied to MacArthur, "that I am forced to report that the troops on Bataan are fast folding up." Receiving no change in orders, a distraught Wainwright had no recourse other than to direct General King to launch the attack toward Olongapo. King's Luzon Force HQ received the incredible order during the height of confusion and chaos brought on by the disintegration of II Corps. The general feeling was that MacArthur and his staff had lost all touch with reality. Food for the defenders of Bataan was down to one last half ration, then nothing. Ammunition and supply depot commanders were under standing orders to begin destroying all equipment and supplies, and chemical warfare personnel were already dumping all military chemicals in Manila Bay. At the little seaport of Mariveles southernmost on Bataan, demolition work had already begun. In spite of all this, General King contacted I Corps commander General Jones and explained the orders to go on the attack immediately. Incredulous, Jones replied that his corps was in the midst of withdrawal to the Binuangan River at that very moment and that the physical condition of his troops made any such attack impossible in any form. King accepted Jones's evaluation and with it all responsibility of refusing to transmit an order to Jones that he knew could not be executed. Furthermore, he did not inform Wainwright of the decision.

As the final fateful hours of Bataan wore on, no word of initiation of an attack reached Corregidor. Wainwright had his chief of staff, Brig. Gen. Lewis C. Beebe, contact General Jones directly and ask if he had received the order to attack. When Jones replied that he had not received such an order, Beebe told him he would receive instructions to attack shortly. General King learned of Beebe's call shortly afterward, and at 3 a.m. on 9 April, he telephoned USFIP at Corregidor to ask if I Corps had been removed from his command. Though Beebe took the call, Wainwright assured King he was still Luzon Force Commander and in charge of all the forces on Bataan. There was no further discussion of the attack order, but Wainwright appeared to still believe an effort would be made to carry it out. This telephone call was the last conversation with King, who already had sent two emissaries forward with a white flag to meet the Japanese field commander. He had already concluded that there was no alternative but surrender. A growing combination of collapses had influenced King's judgment, but it was General Bluemel's inability to hold the Alangan River and the grueling night march to Lamao with his thirteen hundred scouts, including the 26th Cavalry, that had been the final deciding factors in King's decision to throw in the towel.

SURRENDER OF BATAAN

When General Wainwright finally and reluctantly made the 3 a.m. call to King to order the Olongapo attack, King had already reached the conclusion that he had no alternative but to surrender. The disintegration of II

Corps and the flood of routed, retreating troops at the mercy of combined Japanese ground and air forces was bad enough. There was also free enemy passage to the south, where some twelve thousand wounded and diseased patients lay helpless in hospital and already in the reach of enemy light artillery positions. Added to this was total loss of contact by headquarters, with virtually all front-line units and thus any semblance of control over defensive action except through runners and half-tracks. In short, the defense of Bataan had ceased to exist. Even if there had been some order and with sufficient weapons, three months of malaria, malnutrition, and intestinal disease had rendered the men totally incapable of mounting any form of reasonable resistance.

General Wainwright was fully aware of the dismal extent of the situation on Bataan and in communiqués to both MacArthur and Marshall in Washington he minced no words on the gravity of the impending doom for the Bataan garrison. MacArthur finally broke his thin air of confidence to Washington with an alert warning to the chief of staff stating, "I regard the situation as extremely critical and feel you should anticipate the possibility of disaster there very shortly." By the time this message reached Washington, silence had fallen on Bataan. If the situation was seen as bleak to MacArthur and Marshall, it was seen as pitch black to King and Wainwright. To press home his point, on the 7th King sent his chief of staff, Gen. Arnold J. Funk, to personally inform Wainwright that the fall of Bataan was imminent and that he might have to surrender. Funk's face when telling Wainwright of the condition of the troops and the collapse of the line was described as "a map of the hopelessness of Bataan." While he never directly stated to Wainwright King's thought that he must surrender, Funk left the USFIP commander with the impression that there would be a request made for consent to capitulate. Though Wainwright was in full sympathy with King's feelings for the tragic plight of the men on Bataan, his noncommittal answer to Funk was dictated by a chilling set of orders from MacArthur on his desk absolutely prohibiting surrender under any conditions. When Wainwright had written ten days earlier saying that if supplies did not reach the troops on Bataan, they would be starved into submission, MacArthur had flatly denied him authority to surrender and coldly directed "if food fail" to prepare and execute an attack on the enemy. To Chief of Staff Marshall he had written that he was "utterly opposed, under any circumstances or conditions to the ultimate capitulation of this command. . . . If it is to be destroyed it should be upon the actual field of battle taking full toll from the enemy."

Wainwright's hands were further tied in his reply to Funk with a 9 February "no surrender" message from President Roosevelt himself, who had, at the time, given MacArthur authorization to propose to Quezon to neutralize the Philippines. On assuming command from MacArthur, Wainwright had been given a copy of Roosevelt's letter and to the president he had promised "to keep our flag flying as long as an American soldier or an ounce of food and round of ammunition remain." Bound by these documents, Wainwright had no recourse but to tell Funk on 7 April that Bataan must not surrender under any circumstance and that General King must counterattack with the objective to regain the MLR from Bagac to Orion. "I had no direct discussion with King which might in any way have led him to believe that capitulation was contemplated or authorized." Funk left Wainwright's office literally with tears in his eyes. Both he and Wainwright knew full well what the outcome would be and that the hapless General King would be made the foil in the events to come. Wainwright, on the other hand, knew full well he had to take the brunt of disobeying Mac-Arthur's orders to him or stand by and watch the wholesale slaughter of all on Bataan.

After a weighty, unforgettable conference with his two staff officers, King reviewed the tactical situation carefully, considering every possible line of action. It always came back to the same problem. Would the Japanese reach the high ground north of Mariveles from which they could dominate the southern tip of Bataan as well as Corregidor as rapidly if the Northern Luzon Force opposed them as they would if there advance was unopposed? King and his staff finally concluded the Japanese would reach Mariveles by the evening of 9 April no matter what course were taken. With no relief in sight and no possible way to delay the enemy advance, King resignedly decided to open negotiations with the Japanese for the end of hostilities on Bataan with full knowledge that he was acting contrary to orders.

The first task was to establish contact with the Japanese and reach agreement on the terms of surrender. Two men, both bachelors, Col. E. C. Williams and Maj. Marshall H. Hurt, volunteered to go forward under a flag of truce to request an interview between King and the Japanese field commander. Their departure was timed so as to arrive at the front lines at daylight, just as the destruction of equipment was being completed. In the event that the Japanese commander refused to meet King, Williams carried a letter of instructions outlining a discussion of terms by himself. In it, the most urgent concession sought was that Luzon Force be allowed to control movement of its troops to prison camps. Specific points were outlined for discussion in this regard.

1. The large number of sick and wounded in the two general hospitals, particularly No. 1 field hospital, are dangerously exposed to areas where artillery projectiles may be expected to fall if hostilities continue.
2. The fact that our forces are extremely disorganized and that it will be quite difficult to assemble them. This organization of our own forces

necessary prior to their being delivered as prisoners of war will take some time and can be accomplished by my own staff and under my direction.

3. The physical condition of the command due to long siege, during which they have been on short rations, will make it very difficult to move a great distance on foot.

4. Request consideration for the vast number of civilians now present in Bataan, most of whom have simply drifted in and whom we have had to feed and care for. These people are in no way connected with American or Filipino forces, and their presence on Bataan during hostilities is simply coincidental.

While Williams and Hurt were making preparations to leave on their truce mission at about 3:30 a.m. on the 9th, King and his staff made every possible effort to warn all unit commanders of the decision to surrender. At that time destruction of equipment was already under way. Depot and warehouse commanders had already been alerted on the afternoon of the 8th to prepare for demolitions and received orders to begin at about midnight.

In an eerie event at 9:30 p.m., as if nature had conspired to add to the man-made upheaval, an earthquake of considerable magnitude shook Bataan "like a leaf." About an hour later, the navy commenced destroying its installations at Mariveles, including scuttling ships. A fitting climax came with a tremendous explosion of the venerable old submarine tender *Canopus* (known affectionately by all as the "can-o-piss"), which had the only ice cream maker in the Philippines and aboard which the dogged nurses from the hospitals could relax and have impromptu parties with officers and men from various nearby units.

The display of navy pyrotechnics was soon followed by the demolition of huge stocks of heavy explosive shells and arms ammunition stored by the army. The dumps went up in a tremendous roar of exploding ammo and cooked-off bullets whizzing everywhere. No one in the crowded nearby No. 1 hospital, the Luzon and II Corps headquarters, and other various buildings was injured, although everyone in the surrounding vicinity was forced to dive for cover. Never had there been a 4th of July fireworks display to equal it.

Major Chandler's diary continued:

During the night of the 8th, Gen. Bluemel finally got a message from II Corps but hardly what he was prepared to hear. Although not wholly unexpected, the news came as a jolt. Maj. General Edward P. King, Jr., through negotiation, and without direct orders from Wainwright, had decided to seek the best terms under the circumstances and surrender Bataan the next day!

The message went on to instruct Bluemel, whose force had now almost reached the Lamao River, to hold his line only until daylight when a car carrying a white flag would go through the lines on the east road; there was to be no firing after it passed. The news was a blow, but in view of the disastrously muddled situation and the condition of the remnants of the allied forces, it was the only realistic conclusion, however painfully obvious. The battle of Bataan had become generally a rout of sick, starving, exhausted men. General Bluemel was determined to get his battered force as far as possible out of the path of any attacking Japanese units who might not have heard of the surrender—or care. Accordingly, the march was resumed at first daylight of 9 April with the 1st Squadron leading.

At the close of 8 April, the situation everywhere along the front was obscure. Troops jammed all the roads, and with communications all but nonexistent, even front-line commanders did not know where their units were at any given time. In the final hours of resistance, General King had desperately tried to establish a defense on high ground just north of Cabcaben with the last of his reserves and heavy weapons. Instead he ordered Col. Charles Sage (who King put in command of the last of his artillery) to destroy all antiaircraft weapons except those that could be used by infantry. While this was going on, Bluemel's battered force was nearing the Lamao River. The retreat from the Alangan had been a torturous one, but the 26th Cavalry—still intact as a unit—had been assigned by Bluemel to cover the withdrawal, and for one last time the 26th was in a delaying role.

Shortly before 9 p.m. on 8 April the regiment's advance guard ran into a wasp nest Japanese force, and the 1st Squadron, led by Captain H. S. Farris, soon was engaged in a vicious firefight. The cavalrymen fortunately took no casualties and fell back into their rear guard assignment. It was not until 9:30 that Bluemel and the last of the 26th Cavalry covering force got to Lamao. Bluemel directed his regimental commanders to alert all of their own officers immediately of the truce. A few units were slow to get the word and narrowly escaped disaster the next morning.

Chandler's diary went on:

> At Lamo, Bluemel reluctantly sent out his own white flag in hope the Japanese had heard of the surrender. Apparently they had for ours was accepted. While Bluemel's main column moved forward . . . individuals and small groups of men slipped off and darted into the jungle right and left. One of those who slipped away was the 26th Regimental Color Sergeant Basco with the colors. . . . Unfortunately, he did not survive the war and definitive facts as to the colors' whereabouts are not available. At least they were never exhibited as spoils of war by the Japanese.

The diary of Colonel Ramsey said:

> Dawn of April 9, 1942 broke silent. It was a weird though welcome calm after the calamitous noise of the night before, the first morning since the attacks

began that daylight did not bring artillery and bombing. Major Blanning ordered me to take a squad downriver to scout for a trail, but we had not gone far through the jungle before we heard the tread of troops. The Japanese were crossing the river not a hundred meters beyond, masses of infantry and vehicles pushing south toward the town of Mariveles.

There was simply no place left to go. We knew now that the Japanese were behind, in front and to our left. The bank on the far side of the river was too steep to climb, and so our only choice was to wade up stream in search of a trail leading up Mt. Mariveles. From its slopes we might at least be able to observe the countryside and determine whether there was any escape.

Lieutenant Ramsey and his companion, Capt. Joseph R. Barker, decided prison camp was not for them, made good their escape in uniforms ragged and filthy from weeks of fighting and marching, and went on to protracted years of guerilla fighting against the Japanese occupation of the Philippines.

Meanwhile, King's surrender emissaries Williams and Hurt reached the front line with the aid of various rides against beaten, bedraggled traffic of retreating men until they found Lt. Col. Joseph Ganahl with a few surviving tanks and two 75mm guns (SPM) and a few troops. At around 5:30, Ganahl and his men withdrew, leaving Williams, Hurt, and a driver alone. At first light they drove a jeep slowly forward into Japanese-held territory. Shortly afterward, some thirty or so "screaming" Japanese with bayonets flashing rushed at them. Waving a white flag improvised from a bedsheet, the two disconcerted men dismounted from the jeep with raised hands. The Japanese wore olive green uniforms topped by forage caps with flaps down over their shoulders. They appeared enraged. For a time it looked like their end, but fortunately a Japanese officer intervened, and by signs and waving the message in the officer's face Williams was able to make himself understood. The officer made motions for the two Americans to follow. Relieved, they mounted a jeep and drove on, passing American prisoners with wrists tied behind them and Japanese soldiers readying for the day. After a three-mile ride, their jeep was halted and they were taken to meet General Nagano, whose detachment was moving down the east road. An interpreter read Williams's letter of instructions, and following a brief discussion, Nagano agreed to meet General King at the Experimental Farm Station near Lamao, close to the front lines. Hurt was sent back to bring General King, and Williams was held at Japanese headquarters. Escorted by Japanese tanks to the front lines, Major Hurt returned down the east road passing a devastation of burning trucks, blown-up tanks, and broken guns, reaching Luzon Force HQ at 9 a.m. It took General King (in his last clean uniform) only minutes to depart accompanied by his aides Maj. Achille ("Arch") C. Tisdale (formerly of the 26th Cavalry) and Maj. Wade Cothran and his operations officer Col. James Collier. The three-mile trip in two jeeps was a harrowing one as, despite white flags on the vehicles, they were strafed and bombed once, and had to get off road while a Japanese ground machine gunner warned off the plane. King's clean uniform was now almost as disheveled as the one he left behind. He remarked that he felt like an unkempt General Lee going to meet Grant at Appomattox and "would rather die a thousand deaths than this."

On arrival, they were courteously greeted and escorted to the front of a house where General Nagano was seated with Colonel Williams. It was now 11 a.m., the wild three miles having taken two hours. General Nagano explained through an interpreter that he had notified General Homma that an American general was seeking a meeting to discuss terms for cessation of hostilities. Shortly thereafter, a shiny Cadillac drew up in front of the building where the envoys were waiting. Col. Mootoo Nakayama, 14th Army senior operations officer, stepped out accompanied by an interpreter. General King rose to greet him but was snubbed as Nakayama took a seat at the head of the table. King sat back down, his hands forward and in front of him. "I never saw him look more like a soldier," wrote Tisdale later, "than in this hour of defeat." To this writer Tisdale said sadly, "They tried to humiliate my general, but he wouldn't let them."

Nakayama had come to the meeting with no specific instructions for accepting surrender or the terms under which a surrender would be acceptable. It would seem that Homma had no thought of a negotiated settlement. He believed that King was simply a representative from General Wainwright and had sent Nakayama to represent him since he refused to meet with any person of lesser rank.

The talk got off to a sour start when Nakayama, staring straight at King, curtly asked, "You are General Wainwright, no?" When King identified himself, Nakayama asked where Wainwright was and why he had not come. King replied that he did not speak for all Allied forces in the Philippines but for his command alone. King was then told that Homma would not accept any surrender without Wainwright. Again King emphasized that he represented only the forces on Bataan and that he could not get Wainwright there. The Japanese kept pressing King to clarify his relationship to Wainwright in order to avoid having to accept a piecemeal surrender of Wainwright's forces.

General King finally persuaded Nakayama to at least review his terms. He explained insistently that his forces were no longer fighting units and that he was seeking a condition that would prevent further bloodshed. He asked for an armistice and a halt to air bombardment at once. Nakayama rejected both requests with the explanation that pilots already had missions until noon that could not be stopped. King then made the request that his troops be permitted to march out under their own officers and that the sick, wounded, and exhausted men be taken out in vehicles saved for this specific purpose. He promised to deliver the men to any place and at any time designated by General Homma. King repeatedly asked for assurances that

American and Filipino troops be treated as prisoners of war under the provisions of the Geneva Convention.

Nakayama stared at the ceiling and turned a deaf ear to King's proposals. The only basis on which cessation of hostilities would be considered would be one that included the surrender of all forces in the Philippines. "It is absolutely impossible for me," he told King flatly, "to consider limited negotiations in any area. If your forces on Bataan wish to surrender, they will have to do so by unit—voluntarily and unconditionally." He then demanded King's saber, to which King replied that he had left it in Manila at the war's outbreak. Reluctantly, Nakayama accepted a pistol instead of the saber, a gesture followed suit by the other American officers. The group then officially passed into captivity.

While these dismal proceedings were going on, a malignant presence, dispatched by the General Staff in Tokyo to check up on Homma and the delays in his progress, was busily agitating to all who would listen that all American captives (not prisoners) should be summarily executed as rapidly and in any manner practical as well as all Philippine regular army officers and particularly Philippine Scouts. These horrendous proposals were being circulated by none other than the mad, maverick colonel Masanobu Tsuji, his authority wrapped in the fourteen-petal chrysanthemum of imperial princes and a sake cup from Hirohito with the sixteen-petal chrysanthemum, reserved for the emperor himself. Homma despised the man and spread the word among his commanders to ignore his ravings. A number of them did not, and the cost to helpless men would be great.

In actuality, General King's provision that sick and wounded prisoners be transported by vehicles was honored by Homma. The snag was that there just were not enough vehicles to handle the pitiful volume of men who qualified for such mercy. Homma was simply overwhelmed by the numbers of military prisoners and civilians that had fallen under his control.

Nevertheless, no effort was made by either side to make the surrender a matter of record with a signed agreement. King believed then and later that even though he had not secured a signed statement any of his terms, he had formally surrendered his entire force to Homma's representative. The Japanese interpretation did not grant anything of the sort. As Nakayama explained later, "The surrender . . . was accomplished by the voluntary and unconditional surrender of each individual or each unit." Thus the negotiations for general cessation of hostilities failed. King's surrender was therefore interpreted not as a general surrender of an organized military force but instead the surrender of single individuals to the Japanese commander in their area, General Nagano. King, his two aides, and Colonel Williams were kept in custody as a guarantee that there would be no further resistance. Though not informed as such, these men were in fact now hostages, not prisoners of war.

Colonel Collier and Major Hurt accompanied by a Japanese officer were sent back to King's headquarters to pass on to General Funk the news of the surrender. On the way, they were to inform all troops along the road and adjoining trails to move to the east road, stack arms, and wait for further instructions. Final orders for the disposition of all troops would be forthcoming from Homma himself, but in the meantime, by agreement with Nagano, any Japanese forces along the east coast were to advance only as far as Cabcaben airfield.

For all practical purposes the Battle of Bataan was ended—the fighting was over.

The men who had survived the brutal ordeal could feel justly proud of what they had done. For three torturous months they had held Homma's forces at bay at a high cost and upset timetable to the Japanese, only to be ultimately overwhelmed by starvation and disease. No replenishment of supplies, food, or medicine, no hope of relief or reinforcement—they were truly the abandoned bastards of Bataan.

Their desperate saga reached a heartrending climax with the horrors and atrocities of a sixty-five-mile "death march" from Mariveles north to the rail head at San Fernando, where they were packed in metal, 120-degree-heat boxcars for transport farther north to Camp O'Donnell. En route on the march, the men were denied food and water, robbed of all personal possessions, clubbed, beaten, shot, bayoneted, in some cases buried alive, and held in brutally hot areas without even primitive sanitary conditions, the only water to drink from caribou wallows—and then at the risk of being bayonetted. This was the reward for valiant men who had fought with courage and loyalty: the awful, ongoing horror of being abandoned men.

THE FINAL HOURS FOR THE 26TH

Bluemel had about a thousand men with him at Lamao. The only intact unit left was the 26th Cavalry, which, despite confusion, chaos, and heavy fighting had kept its integrity. Major Blanning made the decision to move the decimated regiment some distance away from the main force and off the trail to the north. There he encountered two military policemen who told him of the main surrender, a report confirmed several times over by other escapees and hill tribesmen. Not under direct pressure and not having received direct orders to surrender, Blanning offered his men a choice: he would lead them to the east road to find a Japanese unit to accept their surrender, or they could take to the hills and make their own way. Out of the 800 men who rode out from Fort Stotsenburg, 250 men of the 26th remained. Most of them chose the jungle rather than go into captivity.

One of these was Sgt. Felipe Fernandez, in charge of the Troop B Machine Gun Platoon, an assignment given him by the venerable 1st Sergeant Bulawan. He had eight machine guns under his control in all, and he took all of them and their crews and made their way south to Mariveles. On the way there was much discussion about whether the jungle was the best choice and a chance to join Thorpe's guerillas (well known), but after Fernandez conferred with Sergeant Viray and Corporal Miguel, they decided that too many of the men were too green for jungle life and elected to find a boat for Corregidor.

When they got to Mariveles, the town was a madhouse. Everything that would float was being commandeered to get to Corregidor. Nurses had been evacuated first. Then he heard a commotion and a group of soldiers shouting, "Cebu! Cebu!" Fernandez recalls, "I sent Private Manliclic to find out what the excitement was. On his return I found out that a battery of antiaircraft with the code name 'Cebu' was to board a barge bound for Corregidor. I assembled my men and told them we were not going to surrender but all of us were going to jump onto the Cebu barge at gunpoint if necessary. But the 'Cebu' soldiers opened C rations and shared their food with us. The sight was touching, and I was not hungry anymore.

"We arrived at Corregidor just before noon, and before we debarked twelve Jap planes started strafing and bombing us. We jumped off the barge and waded to shore. We took cover in every depression until the all-clear sounded. A military police lieutenant took us to Lt. Col. Dalao, the provost marshal who processed us, and assigned us to HQ Company 4th Infantry Marines. We were assigned to the platoon of Lieutenant Anderson under direct supervision of Sergeant Tigh. 'What unit y'all from?' he asked me. I straightened up and replied '26th Cavalry, Sir!' 'Well, by God, you're in the Marine Corps now and we sure can use you guys!'"

And so Sergeant Fernandez finished out his war on deadly beach defense for the last days of Corregidor, survived, and ended up a prisoner of the Japanese anyway. He and most of his men survived the war.

Meanwhile, Blanning's men, including Blanning himself, elected to trust the jungle rather than the Japanese. Sadly, Blanning was later captured, and after a brutal time in the infamous Cabanatuan prison camp was put in a draft of prisoners being transferred to Japan. Blanning died on the notorious prison transport *Brazil Maru*, hit by our own navy dive bombers.

Here is Chandler's final diary entry:

With the dispersion of Blanning's force the last organized unit passed into history.

So died the 26th Cavalry (PS) a loyal, gallant regiment, without previous combat history, which gave its utmost when called upon, gave without question or complaint until it was completely expended. It has combat history now, in the best traditions of both countries for which it fought. Its own traditions are fast disappearing though, because neither nation has recognized, by giving its name some still active unit the part played by the 26th in those desperate days of 1942.

I also know that the regiment still lives in the memories of those who served with it in the long, happy days before Pearl Harbor and particularly in the hearts of those few of us still living who fought in its last battles.

On the final page of Maj. Lee Vance's 26th Cavalry battle diary, he wrote:

9 April 1942

Surrendered to superior enemy force.

These truly were the last of America's fighting horse soldiers, and perhaps there is no unit that carries its name and unit designation, for the brave troopers on Fiddler's Green have taken them in for themselves.

Ramsey's diary continued:

All quiet morning of April 9—Decision to Escape—Regiment stays intact to end—Blanning & Vance giving choice to 26th men to surrender or take to hills. . . .

Back at the now deserted Fort Stotsenburg, a gentle breeze whispered through the uncut, once immaculately groomed grass of the parade ground polo field, murmuring ghostly sounds and voices of better times, when the only sounds of combat were the smack of wooden mallets on bamboo balls and the only shouts were the encouraging voices of players.

Your ball, Trip! Take the shot!

Cheers from the troopers and families on the sidelines give way to soft winds whistling through the acacia trees along the rows of empty quarters on officer's row, carrying the warm breeze upward toward Mt. Pinatubo—an era now passed into history.

Epilogue

Horror and ordeal for the hapless defenders of Bataan (and later Corregidor) did not by any means end with capitulation to the Japanese. On Bataan, Homma and his staff encountered almost twice as many captives as his reports had estimated. A massive transport and movement problem was facing the Japanese. In actuality, Homma, eager to eliminate the final stronghold of Corregidor, had only cursory information on the size of the surrender. Besides, the military prisoners and refugee civilians were a hindrance that had to be cleared out of the way of his operations. He and his staff found themselves with over sixty-seven thousand (some fifty-eight thousand Filipino and roughly nine thousand American) starved, sick, and debilitated military prisoners on Bataan (with the exception of about two thousand defenders who escaped to Corregidor for a grueling couple of months' respite before their own capitulation) and over thirty-eight thousand equally weakened civilian noncombatants caught up in the battle. The prisoners and refugees had to be moved north to get them out of the way of Homma's final assault, but there was simply not enough mechanized transport to move the masses of wounded and sick, let alone the weakened remainder of troops.

And so the components of the infamous Bataan Death March came together. Pitifully few prisoners were fortunate enough to make the trek sixty-five miles north to the San Fernando railhead (where they would all, walking or not, be stuffed into stifling, brutally hot metal freight cars for the one-hour trip in 110-degree heat for transfer to the Philippine Army Camp O'Donnell—where thousands more would die). The less lucky prisoners were forced to make the trip north on foot. The American hospitals in the south of Bataan were not evacuated (one of Col. Masanobu Tsuji's suggestions so that they would interfere with Allied shelling from Corregi-

367

dor). These wounded prisoners were either executed outright or hauled in trucks to Camp O'Donnell, where most died anyway.

On the death march, which lasted ten days, 7,000–10,000 Filipinos died or were openly murdered on the route. At the beginning of capture there were rare instances of kindness by Japanese officers and English-speaking soldiers, such as sharing of food and cigarettes and allowing personal possessions to be kept. This was fast followed by unrelenting brutality, theft of every necessity, and even knocking men's teeth out for gold fillings. The common Japanese soldier had also suffered in the Battle for Bataan and had nothing but disgust and hatred for his "captives." Colonel Tsuji had issued clandestine orders to Japanese officers to summarily execute all American "captives" (Nippon did not recognize these people as POWs) but for some fortunate troops, Tsuji's order was not carried out. That did not lessen the brutality, however. Philippine Scouts, when discovered, were singled out for particularly savage treatment by the Japanese, who had suffered so many casualties from the scouts' superb soldiering. They were subjected to torture, then summary execution, mostly beheading by the hundreds. Many of these men were descendants of the original defenders of the Philippines against Portugal. As for the Americans, the exact number who died or were killed is not known but is estimated at between six hundred and seven hundred men—hundreds more would die in boxcars or at the infamous Camp O'Donnell death camp, where Filipino and American POWs were divided in two huge compounds. Fifteen hundred Americans and 22,500–25,000 Filipinos perished there from disease and starvation. The brutality that prisoners suffered on the march almost defies description (I refer my readers to a number of books in the bibliography of this book written by survivors and containing eyewitness accounts by survivors).

At the outset of war, the 26th Cavalry strength consisted of 54 officers and 784 enlisted troopers. By Colonel Vance's count that strength had dwindled to roughly 300 men, the losses counting dead and missing. Although technically the 26th Cavalry Regiment ceased to exist at the Bataan surrender, two of its units remained intact. The 26th Cavalry's orphaned Troop C, under command of the intrepid Capt. Ralph Praeger and his second in command, Lt. Tom Jones (now a retired full colonel living in Florida), had made their way steadily into the deepest regions of Luzon's northern mountains. After their sensational raid on the Japanese airfield at Tuguegarao, Praeger and his troop plus a collection of lost Philippine soldiers, miners, and civilian volunteers trudged northward in some of the Philippines' most rugged mountain country. They shifted locations constantly, trying all the while to make radio contact with friendly forces (which, as previously mentioned, they did; they contacted by radio army intelligence officer Charles Ferguson in Darwin, Australia, their only contact for months to come). At one point, the group came upon a mountain *negrito* (a Filipino native of small stature) and let it be known they wished to speak to the chief or head man. A tiny, wizened old man came up to them in a tattered blue jacket. He expressed that he was amazed these were Americans because the last American soldiers he had encountered wore blue coats with yellow markings.

For some two more years, constantly shifting camps to avoid detection, Praeger and his men made hit-and-run raids on Japanese patrols, convoys, whatever was a ready target, and kept radio contact with Darwin. Their luck ran out in May of 1943 when their location was betrayed by a Filipino *macapili* (turncoat) and Praeger, Jones, and some of their men were trapped and captured by the Japanese.

They were taken to the Santiago fortress prison where they were interrogated and tortured mercilessly along with other guerilla member leaders. These included U.S. Army Cols. Arthur K. "Maxey" Noble and Charles M. Moses, who had had frequent contact with Ramsey's guerrilla units and had participated in numerous raids on the Japanese until capture. The 26th Cavalry captain, Joe Barker, also captured, was taken to Bilibid Prison in southern Manila where he was also tortured extensively but gave no information whatsoever before finally being taken out in the courtyard of the prison and beheaded. "He was the toughest sonuvabitch I ever knew," said his prison mate Col. Tom Jones. Jones was rescued by liberation forces a mere hour before his execution was to be carried out and survived to write an extensive account of C Troop's exploits.

The captured leaders at Santiago were hardly as fortunate. Feeling that these men were too important as figureheads to the guerilla movement, the Japanese planned a secretive disposal of Praeger, Noble, and Moses. In the middle of one night in May 1943, the men were taken quietly to the Chinese cemetery in northern Manila for execution. (Unbeknownst to the Japanese, Filipinos were secretly watching their every move but were helpless to aid the prisoners.) The men were first taken into the walled courtyard of a small Catholic chapel adjacent to the cemetery, where they were beheaded. The bodies were then taken to the cemetery, which was ideal for concealing the bodies because the Chinese buried their dead one on top of the other to save space. Other than the cemetery itself, the resting places of Praeger, Moses, and Noble are not known.

The second intact unit that remained an effective fighting force was Troop B Machine Gun Platoon, which had evaded capture and connived to make its way from Mariveles to Corregidor. As for the holdout of Corregidor until May 1942, the Japanese paid a high price to overcome the stubborn resistance of its defenders. Most of the fighting was done by the men, mostly marines and Filipinos on "beach defense" and men in Corregidor's big gun emplacements. The tunnels were jammed with wounded, nurses, medical personnel, and numerous persons with no real reason to be in the shelter of the mountain and nicknamed "tunnel rats" by the men outside doing the fighting.

Upon landing on Corregidor, Fernandez and his men and guns were assigned by Provost Marshall Colonel Dalao to HQ Company 4th Marines, where they were further assigned to the platoon led by a Lieutenant Anderson. Fernandez was then informed that his platoon was to be deployed with the marines' beach defense with only foxholes in the open for shelter. Fernandez, now under command of Marine Staff Sergeant Tigh, had eighteen men left when the Japanese assaults began. Between the Jap artillery shelling, aerial strafing, and the amphibious assaults, the "beach defenses" became a nightmare of whizzing lead, shrapnel, and death. The few Japanese who survived the thorough annihilation of their initial landing attempts to get ashore went to work as snipers. Fernandez and his men soon found themselves busy rooting out and killing these hidden riflemen, but he lost several of his troopers doing so, including his own second in command, Sergeant Tatlonhari.

Fernandez, in his final opportunity to address the last of his men, told them to feel tall, for they were the last of their nationals, the last of the 26th Cavalry, being seen by Americans as fighting for the last small toehold of their homeland still fighting for their freedom. All intensely religious men, they prayed together and separately in the face of what was coming. It was not long before the constant assaults took their toll and Fernandez saw most of his men dead or wounded on the line. Only one gun was still firing, manned by Pfc. Manuel Fernandez, as he struggled to get the wounded to Malinga Tunnel and the remainder of his men to a fairly sheltered position near the tunnel. Sergeant Tigh informed him that the Japanese had broken through at Hawker point. Fernandez shifted his men and his one gun to face them. As he was crawling over to tell his men that he was withdrawing the rest of the wounded and to prepare for a retrograde movement, Fernandez was hit in the neck by shrapnel. "I started to bleed profusely," he recalled, "and then everything was dark. I felt someone carrying me and then all my senses were gone and knew nothing of what happened after that."

Later, when he came to in a concentration camp, he learned that Tech Sergeant Viray—wounded earlier and evacuated to Malinta Tunnel and given first aid—tried to rejoin his platoon but found them already gone to a new fighting position. He found the others at daybreak in time to see Fernandez hit. He grabbed a couple of medics and told them to take care of his people. Thus Fernandez and the other seriously wounded were saved. Then Viray gathered what was left of the platoon and brought them to the southern end of Malinta Tunnel where everybody was assembling in preparation for surrender. After the surrender, all prisoners were herded to the

92nd Artillery garage for concentration. Viray held the unit intact and organized details to gather all the food they could find.

The following day Viray sent Manliclic to the hospital to tell Fernandez and the others all that happened and that the platoon survivors were at the 92nd garage waiting. Although weak from loss of blood, Fernandez got off his cot and went with him to join the others. On the way, he spotted Lt. Robert Carusso from E Troop of the 26th who was with a detail collecting the dead. Fernandez attempted to stop and talk to him but was hustled on as the Japanese forbade conversation between Filipinos and Amerians. Fernandez recalls, "To the best of my recollection the last fighting remnants of the 26th were Carusso, T/Sgt. Viray, Cpl. Miguel, Pfc. Banaga, Pvt. Estrada, Pvt. Quevedo [from the Philippine Air Force], Pvt. Manliclic, Pvt. Lopez, Pvt, Nieves and I."

The ordeal for the men of Corregidor was far from over, however. Most were kept on the Manila shoreside beach for about five days, some for a week or more, deprived of food and water and made to collect all abandoned weapons, ammunition, equipment, and bodies and pile them on the beach. Large barges then came in from Manila and collected the prisoners for transport to the mainland. They were held in the harbor area for several days until all were assembled. Then in a gesture to show their disgrace to the Filipino people of Manila, they were prodded with bayonets and pushed in their own "death march" up Dewey Boulevard and then northward toward Cabanatuan and other permanent concentration camps. There, hundreds of the American survivors of Bataan and Corregidor would die or be shipped to Japan for hard labor in coal mines or just to forestall their liberation at some point. The latter process was dubbed "Japan Go" by their captors, and it was on these *maru* transport ships that a number of 26th Cavalry survivors died. One of these was the handsome, gentlemanly Capt. John Z. Wheeler, who lost his life in the hold of the infamous death ship *Oryoku Maru*, under attack from American planes, when a steel beam under which he had crawled for cover fell on him.

Within the brutal death camps, some 2,650 Americans died at Camp O'Donnell in April and May of 1942, more than twice the number of deaths of Americans on the Death March, and at the time of liberation, a recorded 2,656 Americans were buried in the Cabanatuan cemetery.

As for the Filipino POWs, the death toll was far higher. They were treated literally as animals to slaughter by their ruthless captors. In addition to those who died on the march, another 22,500–25,000 perished at O'Donnell. For some unknown reason, the majority of the Filipino POWs who survived were released by the Japanese, who reserved death mainly for scouts and Filipino officers. The main number of those released went to the hills and organized as guerrilla forces against the occupation.

A complete roster of the 26th Cavalry Regiment members and their fates in the war and in the years following is found below. The list is compiled by individual veterans and the Philippine Scout Heritage Society. Every effort was made to leave no man out.

Also following is a complete table of organization of MacArthur's Philippine forces and an account of casualties by unit.

There are also separate accounts of the Philippine campaign timeline, the Japanese hell ships, and other points of interest.

—Raymond G. Woolfe Jr.

ROSTER OF OFFICERS OF THE 26TH CAVALRY REGIMENT AS OF 8 DECEMBER 1941

Commanding

Col. Clinton A. Pierce, Commanding
Maj. Lee C. Vance, Executive Officer
Maj. Harry J. Fleeger, S-l (Deceased aboard Japanese hell ship)
Maj. William E Chandler, S-2–3 (POW liberated)
Capt. Walter J. Buboltz, S-4 (Died as POW)
1st Lt. Ward (Detached to Philippine Army, returned to 26th at Tayug)

Headquarters and Service Troop

Capt. Forest C. Richards (Killed in action; KIA)
1st Lt. John A. George (KIA Damortis)
1st Lt. Ethan R. Cunningham (KIA)
1st Lt. Carol I. Cahoon (KIA)
1st Lt. William P. Leisenring (Killed on hell ship)
1st Lt. Donald H. Wills, Reg. Motor Officer (POW escaped)
1st Lt. Russell Bowers (KIA Binalonan)

Machine Gun Troop

Capt. Jack A. Ford
1st Lt. Paul H. Allen (KIA Damortis)
1st Lt. Dominick G. Troglia (KIA)

1st Squadron 26th Cavalry Regiment Philippine Scouts

Maj. Robert W. Ketchum (KIA 24 December 1941 Binalonan)
Capt. Houston Farris

Troop A

Capt. Leland W. Cramer (Died as POW on hell ship 26 February 1945)
1st Lt. Fred B. Evans
1st Lt. Arthur Whitehead (Separated at Damortis and escaped to Australia)
1st Lt. Stephens D. Chamberlain (Died as POW)

Troop B

Capt. Joseph R. Barker (Refused surrender, served as guerrilla, captured,
  executed at Bilibid Prison, Manila)
1st Lt. Henry D. Mark (KIA Binalonan)
2nd Lt. Clinton C. Seymour

Troop C

Three officers fifty-nine EM detached at Rosario

Capt. Ralph B. Praeger (Captured as guerrilla, executed 1943, buried at
  Manila Chinese cemetery)
1st. Lt. Thomas S. Jones (POW liberated Bilibid)
1st Lt. Warren Minton (POW liberated)

2nd Squadron 26th Cavalry Philippine Scouts

Maj. Thomas J. H. Trapnell, commanding (POW, Death March, liberated in
  Manchuria)
Capt. James C. Blanning (listed as KIA or MIA, date of death 25 January
  1945 according to Philippine Scouts Heritage Society website)

Troop E

Capt. John Zachary Wheeler (POW, killed on hell ship *Oryoku Maru*)
Lt. Robert L. Carusso (Died as POW)

Troop F

Captain Paul H. Wrinkle (KIA Bataan)
1st Lt. George J. Spies (Died on Bataan of "natural causes")
1st Lt. Stephen Graves (KIA, Culis Junction)

Troop G

Capt. John W. Fowler (KIA Bataan)
1st Lt. Clifford Hardwicke (KIA, Bataan)

1st Lt. Edwin Price Ramsey (Refused surrender, guerilla leader, survived war)

ROSTER OF PHILIPPINE SCOUTS

Headquarters, Troops A through C

From Philippine Scout Heritage Society Parts 1 and 2

http://www.philippine-scouts.org/the-scouts/ps-rosters-of-1941-2/26th
  -cavalry-regt-ps-part-1.html
Legend:
+ Listed as Killed in Action (KIA) or Missing in Action (MIA)
* Survived WWII and served in C Troop/Company, 1st Military Police
  Battalion (PS)

Headquarters & Service Troop Roster

Master Sgt. Cornelio Batoon
Master Sgt. Juan Dalipe
Master Sgt. Apriano Masiclat*
Master Sgt. Ramon Purugganan+
1st Sgt. Paul A. Marinas
Tech Sgt. Basilio C. Layoc
Tech Sgt. Victoriano Torio*
Staff Sgt. Matias Gacgacao+
Staff Sgt. Eliseo Mallari
Staff Sgt. Ernesto Tesalla*

Sergeants

Juan Alonzo*
Romulo O. Badua
Protacio Cabiao
Arsenio Cristobal
Domingo de Mesa
Vicente C. Diala
Cesario Domingo+
Melchor Gascon+
Pedro Nacional+
Ernesto Roux
Pablo Segundo
Buenaventura Supina+

Pascual C. Tembrina
Patricio Ubarro
Juan Visperas
Bartolome R. Ysmael

Corporals

Eulaio Arzaga
Amado A. Dela Cruz*
Nicomedes Dela Cruz
Felipe Francisco
Jovito Gubrian
Zacarias Y. Millado +
Antonio Olego
Mamerto R. Palacio +
Amado A. Pascual*
Francisco Ramirez

Privates 1st Class

Salvador A. Abad
Eugenio Abalos
Marcelino R. Advincula
Eliodoro B. Alejandro
Marcelino Almazan +
Andres L. Angeles
Honorio D. Badar
Gabriel Bala +
Alfredo Bandleman
Vicente S. Barcelo
Alejandro Bautista
Simeon L. Bobila +
Jose Bonifacio +
Aquilino E. Bumanlag*
Josue C. Bunda +
Pablo Buyson +
Silverio Cabellon
Isidro Calimlim*
Jose Carino*
Miguel Carino +
Geronimo Carreon*
Honorio C. Celeste
Alberto Daguison +
Agustin Dela Cruz

Geronimo Demate+
Teofisto Dizon+
Rosendo Estal
Jorge Fabia
Marcelino V. Frago
Honorio Galicia+
Bartolome R. Geroka+
Paulo N. Gregorio
Hugo Guarin
Emilio S. Guligado
Mateo G. Hernandez
Marvin R. Hill*
Emigdio Jomillo+
Remegio Kausin
Raymundo Lago*
Arturo N. Leonardo+
Enrique F. Macaraeg*
Agustin Malpaya
Felipe S. Masanque
Juan Miguel
Isidro B. Millado*
Benjamin Morales
Ricardo Q. Nicolas*
Dalmacio Ocampo
Marcelino L. Ordonia
Melecio R. Ovcena*
Lardion B. Pablo*
Leonardo Q. Palanca*
Cresencio R. Parado+
Menandro B. Parazo
Pedro P. Pardilla
Antero Rillera*
Domingo Rivera+
Mariano Rodriguez
Asisclo V. Tabil+
Luis N. Tanos
Narciso C. Ternate+
Sebastian J. Tolenada+
Isabelo S. Torio*
Tomas M. Ulanday*

Troop A Roster

1st Sgt. Nicolas Mendoza+
Staff Sgt. Emilio A. Alcazar

Sergeants

Angel Alcaiao
Dionisio Almonte*
Natalio Benedicto
Urbano Daclan +
Marcelino E. De La Cruz +
Conrado V. Diocson
Agapito Mojo +
Pedro Mopera +

Corporals

Serapio Abad
Teofilo M. Amutan.
Donato Cabardo +
Emilio Cepriano
Crispulo R. Garcia
Primitivo Lacson +
Adriano F. Salangsang
Juan Ysip*

Privates 1st Class

Antonio Aganon +
Anastacio Angaangan
Faustino Anicete
Candido Aquino +
Alejandro Bacud
Fernando Bonifacio +
Clemente E. Briones +
Mauricio Bustos
Marcelino S. Caylao
Palabiano Daniel
Juan Estoya*
Fidel Flores +
Leon Guevara
Crispin Guiala
Bernardo Leandicho*
Alejandro Lomboy
Arcadio Mabanglo
Arcadio Morales
Remigio Pamintuan
Crispulo F. Salangsang +
Marcelino Ventura*

Deogracias Villamayor
Leonardo M. Viray*

Privates

Federico Ambatali
Severino T. Amo
Federico Anicete
Emeterio Antonio +
Francisco V. Balanza
Francisco Bautista*
Inocencio J. Cabrera
Policarpio Cabrera +
Severino Carabbacan
Vicente T. Carreon
Irineo T. Castaneda
Juan Centino +
Eliseo J. Dalipe
Benjamin D. Felicitas
German G. Garcia
Prisco C. Garcia +
Egipto Gonzales +
Fernando Gonzales
Selmo Guevarra
Lazaro Liot
Hilario Lomboy*
Nicolas S. Macayana +
Godofredo Magalued
Avelino C. Manansala
Jose Marquez +
Monico Mercado
Marcos M. Musni
Raymundo Nepal
Fernando Ochoco +
Anastacio B. Pacis +
Policarpio Pascua +
Francisco Pingul
Juan G. Quia
Jose G. Quimel
Elino Ragon
Cosme Reyes +
Ricardo V. Roque +
Crescencio B. Sayajon +

Crisanto A. Solomon
Mamerto V. Suller+
Agaton Torres+
Vicente Velasco
Narcisco C. Viray+

Troop B Roster

1st Sgt. Justiniano A. Bulawan
Staff Sgt. Potenciano G. Aquino*

Sergeants

Concepcion R. Dela
Pedro B. Dolores
Elidoro Estrada
Eugenio Gimenez
Domingo Mallari
Heremias Manalese
Crisologo Racelis+
Santiago M. Valenton*

Corporals

Wencislao Balico
Alfredo Balina
Catalino Bolaza*
Ignacio Caguimbal
Gerardo Garife
Rufino De A. Illo
Viciorino Pepito+
Lorenzo L. Sunga

Privates 1st Class

Terzo Alacar
Roque Alejo
Juan Beduna+
Adriano Bernido
Primitivo Bolcan
Crispin Colisao
Gregorio Danez
Gerardo Delantar+
Martin Domalanta+

Domingo Hidalgo+
Victorio Hulguin*
Epitacio Jubinal+
Artemio Marquez
Hilario F. Mata
Gaudencio Merafuentes
Vicente Nacua+
Anastacio Pautin
Roman O. Ramirez
Dominador A. Rongero*
Crispulo V. Sison
Teodoro Tagao
Charles Thompson
Francisco E. Tomas*

Privates

Abril, Marcelo+
Arriola, Martiniano S.
Balina, Conrado
Banola, Benjamin P.
Barte, Cipriano C.
Bernal, Alfredo+
Bernal, Patricio V.
Bulatao, Federico+
Cacal, Esmeno+
Causapin, Bayani
Celedio, Crisanto R.
Claseto, Ponciano+
Dalipe, Valentin
Danao, Catalino L.
De Guia, Ortanes
De Vera, Leocadio G.*
Espiritu, Samson+
Estavillo, Emetirio+
Estrada, Pedro P.+
Figueroa, Melencio+
Gatan, Arlis L.+
Laroya, Bernardino N.*
Laxamana, Patrocinio
Loquinte, Jose A.
Madriaga, Anacleto P.+
Madrid, Zacarias L.

Malonda, Maximino I.
Manucdoc, Godofredo
Mariano, Alfredo
Masancay, Leonido
Matias, Francisco V.
Pamonag, Sofronio A.
Panganiban, Clicerio
Pasion, Felicisimo +
Raymundo, Agustin
Restauro, Bernardo R.
Rivo, Emilio I.
Roll, Ricardo R. Jr.
Ropadas, Ciriaco C. +
Salvador, Sergio E.
Soria, Juan L.
Tomas, Federico*

Troop C Roster

1st Sgt. Daniel H. Ulanday
Staff Sgt. Clodualdo B. Aquino +
Staff Sgt. Isidro Jamoral +

Sergeants

Balugo, Cecilio A.*
Fajardo, Clodualdo +
Labordo, Maximo
Marquez, Urbano +
Nues, Pablo
Ordonio, Teodoro
Paclebar, Florentio P.
Quiocho, Tomas

Corporals

Ambrocio, Carino +
Briones, Maximo*
Costes, Jose P.
De Ocampo, Quintin +
Games, Atanacio +
Ignacio, Agustin*
Montiadora, Andres

Taguba, Hermojeno
Viray, Candido

Privates 1st Class

Aguas, Roman V.
Alcayro, Vicente
Andrada, Roberto
Angeles, Alfonzo
Aquino, Marcelino +
Cabicen, Agustin
Cala, Florencio
Camaddo, Enrique +
David, Cornelio S. *
De Vera, Antonio +
Dela Calzada, Martin
Dingcong, Eminiano +
Emperial, Arsenio +
Gaduang, Eulogio
Martinez, Blas
Monsanto, Illuminado +
Morta, Pedro
Nuneza, Isidoro +
Pangilinan, Juaquin *
Sevilla, Primitivo B. *
Valdez, Emigdio
Yumang, Leonardo +

Privates

Abagat, Pablo +
Aggasid, Antonio +
Ambrose, Jose G.
Arreola, Florencio A. *
Baldivicio, Mauricio +
Brillo, Bruno
Camonayan, Raymundo M.
Casaba, Pedro R.
Castillo, Alejandro +
Causapin, Benjamin +
Celedon, Doroteo
Dajutoy, Martin +
Domingo, Felix E.
Ducusin, Juan S.

Elias, Eligio +
Embry, Benjamin
Flores, Zacarias
Galam, Fabian A.
Gollaba, Isidro
Gutierrez, Sixto P.*
Labog, Rosendo +
Lacsina, Felino*
Legaspi, Jacinto B.
Lomenario, Macario +
Magat, Macario
Maliari, Godofredo
Mangabat, Alfonso +
Martinez, Anecito
Miguel, Adolfo
Molina, Blas
Nepis, Joaquin
Nieves, Saturnino B.
Ocampo, Constancio
Orfiano, Desiderio +
Palacio, Alfredo R.
Paloma, Quirino*
Peregrino, Amado A.
Perello, Adriano R.
Rilla, Donato G.
Sanez, Arturo
Soriano, Antero +
Tallungan, Leo +
Tugab, Jose
Tumanut, Jose

Troops E through G and Machine Gun Troop

Troop E Roster

1st Sergeant Leon Amigable +
Staff Sgt. Juan Beleno*

Sergeants

Acosta, Rafael
Basco, Damaso K.
Burcelis, Aurelio
De La Pena, Eugenio

Delos Santos, Jose
Masangcay, Manuel +
Oyzon, Proceso
Varela, Juan +

Corporals

Baluyat, Enrique*
Dela Cruz, Jeremias*
Estipona, Federico
Fernandez, Felipe A.
Gualta, Gonzalo
Marmolijo, Florentino
Padilla, Rufino
Ramirez, Antonino
Rozales, Fidel

Privates 1st Class

Abaci, Alejandro
Ballesteros, Mauricio
Balmores, Lorenzo R.
Basa, Isidro
Bautista, Terso*
Bautista, Victoriano
Cabigas, Saturnino
Carino, Jacob
Claseto, Eufrocino +
Gonzales, Jesus
Guianan, Tranquilino
Herrera, Jose R.
Lazo, Alberto
Limon, Graciano
Lopez, Ricardo M.
Magbanua, Selvino
Maionzo, Severino M.
Millano, Pedro
Ordono, Perfecto I.
Ramos, Guillermo
Rimorin, Nemecio
Salangsang, Gregorio
Tamayo, Victorio Q.

Privates

Abarquez, Angel A.
Acedo, Vincente G.
Aloquin, Federico +
Baccay, Germiniano*
Banaga, Manuel D.
Bernal, Bernardo
Bondoc, Alfredo
Cabigas, Alberto +
Canaberal, Felipe B.
Carrera, Anastacio G.*
Castaneda, Delfin
Cataulin, Edgardo F.
Claseto, Norberto C.
Corpuz, Alfonso D.
Cristobal, Quirino B.*
Dano, Alejo D.
De Vera, Agripino
Dumaoal, Marcelino D.
Echavarre, Alfonso
Erne, Miguel
Euperio, Pedro*
Gelacio, Elias G.
Ibanez, Amado*
Laboc, Joaquin P.
Manuntag, Servando
Marzo, Juan +
Medina, Fernando +
Melegrito, Bernardo B.
Mercado, Emilio*
Mercado, Felix
Mitchell, Ritchie +
Pablo, Benito B.*
Paculanan, Leonido +
Palma, Francisco
Palmejar, Gregorio
Rabino, Rodolfo +
Rio, Gregorio
Rivera, Pedro
Rogan, Louis
Sablay, Francisco S. +

Salonga, Dominador
Santa Maria, Jose A.
Sibalon, Nicholàs
Supnet, Federico C.*
Tubig, Emilio*

Troop F Roster

1st Sgt. Juan C. Bilcera
Staff Sgt. Severo Masangcay+

Sergeants

Aplaon, Geronimo
Damazo, Jose
Diccion, Vincente C.
Espinosa, Basilio
Garife, Gaudencio M. +
Landinguin, Venancio +
Sampaga, Nepomocino*
Vargas, Brigido

Corporals

Apilado, Higenio
Aurigui, Serapin*
Bolosan, Simeon E. +
Garbin, Eligio*
Reclosado, Francisco
Romingquet, Bernardo*
Tolentino, Fidel +
Umipig, Pedro A.

Privates 1st Class

Alcobendas, Pedro*
Alonzo, Rodrico
Anastacio, Eustaquio +
Benabese, Eutiquio +
De Leon, Longeno +
de la Cruz, Jacinto*
Dela Cruz, Manuel
Dela Vega, Breccio G.
Diaz, Florencio
Eslava, Juan O. +

Gonzalez, Luis
Guzman, Apolinario
Lao, Benjanin B.
Nool, Zacarias
Regala, Timoteo V.
Restauro, Florentino
Rom, Restituto +
Samzon, Gonzalo P.
Tirante, Alfredo
Velasquez, Felix +
Ventura, Efigeneio C.*
Villas, Eusebio +

Privates

Abarquez, Hilario +
Ancheta, Jose*
Antonio, Joffre C.*
Aquino, Alejandro
Banez, Urbano
Bautista, Funciano*
Cabauatan, Tito +
Cruz, Nicanor M. +
Dacio, Emiliano +
Dayrit, Domingo
De Los Santos, B.
Del Rosario, Eduardo*
Dominguiz, Benito
Domulot, Diomedes
Espino, Jose A.
Evangelista, Reymundo +
Felicitas, Emiliano
Figuracion, Dominador (Dan)
Gamido, Eulogio G. +
Garcia, Andres T.
Gargaritano, Felipe
Gaspar, Anselmo
Gollaba, Eduardo
Gomes, Hermengildo*
Gragasin, Santiago +
Ignacio, Celestino
Lanuza, Salvador
Lapitan, Antonio +

Lucero, Cayetano V.*
Mangosing, Simplicio G. +
Marinas, Agripino C.*
Masela, Arturo N. Jr.
Mataban, Eduardo D.*
Mendoza, Gregorio M.
Noriega, Jesus G.
Pelaez, Antonio L.
Ramos, Felix +
Recomeo, Raymondo
Romero, Eleuterio
Salvador, Jose A.
Simeon, Benjamin Z.
Simon, Narciso
Sonza, Alejandro
Tamoria, Rubin
Tiangsing, Pedro A.*
Urbano, Raymundo

Troop G Roster

1st Sgt. Sabiniano Ibanez
Staff Sgt. Emilio Juntado

Sergeants

Alipio, Amando D. +
Almonte, Julian +
Arangcon, Gregorio
Bitanca, Cosme A.
Figuracion, Juan
Hulguin, German
Joves, Eusebio R.
Sampaga, Clemente
Ybalio, Engracio

Corporals

Agtotobo, Calixto +
Borra, Jose
Corrales, Aproniano M.
Dasalla, Alejo
Farinas, Clemente C.
Luzada, Victoriano*

Mendoza, Pedro
Nemenzo, Fasiano
Porlaris, Estanislao*
Sanpedro, Jose

Privates 1st Class

Acidello, Braulio
Amara, Vidal +
Apilado, Jose
Baldos, Cirilo +
Bitanga, Amador
Cirineo, Guillermo +
Cornel, Antero +
Cosme, Rosendo
Cristobal, Cornelio
Dacanay, Pedro
De Vera, Egmedio
Garcia, Segundo D. +
Lerguna, Gregorio
Loremas, Benito
Medina, Francisco
Orlaris, Simplicio
Ortiz, Zacarias U.
Saveliana, Luciano +
Sinlao, Angelo +
Sotelo, Valentin
Vargas, Feliciano*
Yabut, Patricio
Yumal, Antonino

Privates

Abalos, Reinfredo +
Abril, Crispiniano J.
Aquino, Melecio +
Balmaceda, Leopoldo +
Bauzon, Rodolfo
Belvis, Rogelio D. +
Berras, Ismael
Borongan, Daniel +
Burcelis, Tomas +
Cabardo, Pio
Cabiao, Floresto

Caguioa, Teofilo P.*
Camat, Longabardo +
Carino, Eulalio +
Castro, Fortunato
Cortez, Onofre +
De Leon, Gregorio
De Manzana, Moises +
Dela Cruz, Juan
Domingo, Procopio +
Drilo, Alfredo
Duco, Pedro M.*
Dugay, Juan
Frago, Santiago +
Games, Tranquilino
Gerochi, Jovito A.
Lacierna, Julio
Legaspi, Miguel B. +
Leonin, Ciriaco C. +
Mabanglo, Quinciano +
Macasieb, Ricardo
Mangawang, Bernardo M. +
Nastor, Emeterio M.
Nato, Leovegildo B. +
Nool, Dionisio +
Ojastro, Canuto P. +
Perez, Emeterio +
Remorin, Mariano +
Repunte, Teofilo +
Repunte, Venerando +
Reyes, Maximino R.*
Santos, Crisostomo P.
Tabaquero, Cesareo
Taguinod, Lorenzo +
Terrado, Narciso
Tuana, Jose

Machine Gun Troop Roster

1st Sgt. Gregorio G. Bustos +
Staff Sgt. Doroteo Marayag

Sergeants

Basco, Jose O.
Collado, Castor +

Cruz, Glido N.+
Gundran, Patricio
Gurion, Pedro
Lagamon, Gabriel+
Limjoco, Domingo
Lorenzo, Rufino*
Montemayor, Pedro
Paculanan, Francisco+
Quitoriano, Apolinar
Silva, Jose R.+

Corporals

Abagat, Antonio+
Balmores, Silvino R.
Bardelas, Jesus E.
Bulatao, Pedro*
Corpuz, Jose
Eres, Mateo C.
Gatdula, Mariano
Legayo, Cristobal+
Metchor, Pedro*
Obras, Martin
Ramilo, Eusebio
Ramilo, Ricardo P.
Roqueno, Elias

Privates 1st Class

Belnas, Leopoldo
Cabiging, Fidel*
Cardenas, Eufemio+
Cruz, Florencio*
Cunanan, Roman
De Guzman, Roman+
Dela Cruz, Arsenio*
Domingo, Macario
Elgarico, Apolinario
Felicitas, Gerardo
Funtanilla, Santiago*
Galsim, Pedro A.
Gepalaga, Francisco
Gungap, Luis
Irigon, Mario*

Lomboy, Santos S.*
Manalang, Nicolas
Manangan, Segundo +
Mariano, Antonio C.
Matias, Maximo D.*
Millo, Candido +
Pacis, Roman
Paredes, Emiliano
Polintan, Pedro*
Popoy, Pascual
Samson, Hermelando L.
Selidio, Selvino +
Sonza, Bernabe M.
Toralba, Fermin*
Ysip, Victoriano +

Privates

Allarte, Juan
Bacani, Clemente C.
Baladad, Macario +
Balmorez, Supicio
Bautista, Pablo
Bermuda, Lorenzo T.
Branson, Albert P.
Camarao, Bonifacio C.
Cambronero, Pedro +
Castro, Luciano +
Cayabyab, Marcelo*
Cinense, Bonifacio +
Cortez, Luis
Dalmacio, Pedro
David, Orlando S.
De Grano, Felipe +
De Guzman, Lope +
Dolores, Timoteo S. +
Duplon, Adriano +
Edwards, George Q.
Elcarico, Dionicio
Escandor, Ricardo
Evangelista, Porferio C.
Feir, Benjamin B.
Fernandez, Leon V.*

Florita, Anastacio A.
Gandeza, Anastacio +
Geronimo, Emiliano A.
Gomez, Bonifacio B. +
Gonzales, Francisco
Gurion, Vicente
Hulguin, Demetrio T. +
Israel, Ireneo +
Layug, Felix
Liban, Rufino S. +
Lomboy, Telesforo
Lucero, Mariano V. +
Madarang, Gaspar +
Malonzo, Antonio
Marayac, Abraham A.
Marinas, Jose
Olivares, Rafael P.
Ollero, Juan
Pascual, Aquilino
Punsalan, Amado +
Ramos, Narciso D.
Reyes, Rodegar +
Reyes, Zacarias
Sayan, Emiterio
Soliman, Isaias +
Solis, Francisco
Sonnico, Hermenegildo
Tamayo, Arcadio D.*
Tamondong, Rafael C. +
Tang, Ricardo +
Toralba, Alejandro J.*

Sources

BOOKS

Ancheta, Celedonia A., ed. *The Wainwright Papers*. Quezon City: New Day.

Belote, James H., and William M. Belote. 1967. *Corregidor*. Playboy Press Paperbacks, Internet Library.

Bergamini, David. 1971. *Japan's Imperial Conspiracy*. New York: Morrow.

Blair, Clay Jr. 1977. *Macarthur*. New York: Pocket Books.

Bowen, Robert O. 1953. *The Weight of the Cross*. New York: Bantam Books.

Chesnoff, Richard Z. 1978. *Philippines*. New York: Abrams Books.

Condit, Kenneth W., and Edwin T. Turnbladh. 1989. *Hold High the Torch: A History of the 4th Marines*. Nashville, TN: Battery Press.

Crisp, Major Robert. 2005. *Brazen Chariots*. New York: W. W. Norton.

Falk, Stanley L. 1971. *Liberation of the Philippines*. New York: Ballantine Books.

Grove, Eric 1987. *World War II Tanks*. Longmeadow Press, Open Library, Internet.

Heiferman, Ron. 1971. *Flying Tigers*. New York: Ballantine Books.

Hibbs, Ralph Emerson. 1999. *Tell MacArthur to Wait*. Smithfield, UK: Carlton Press.

Kennedy, Milly Wood. 1971. *Corregidor: Glory, Ghosts, and Gold*. Ann Arbor: University of Michigan.

Knox, Donald. 1981. *Death March: The Survivors of Bataan*. New York: Harcourt Brace Jovanovich.

Mayer, S. L. 1976. *The Japanese War Machine: 1917–1945*. Secaucus, NJ: Chartwell Books.

Mayer, Sydney L. 1973. *MacArthur in Japan*. New York: Ballantine Books.

Morris, Eric. 1982. *Corregidor: The End of the Line*. New York: Stein & Day.

Morton, Louis. 1993. *The Fall of the Philippines*. Washington, DC: Government Printing Office.

Ramsey, Col. Edwin Price. 2005. *Lieutenant Ramsey's War: From Horse Soldier to Guerrilla Commander*. Lincoln, NE: Potomac Books.

Rutherford, Ward. 1971. *The Fall of the Philippines*. New York: Ballantine Books.

Saburo Sakai. 1970. *Zero Fighters*. New York: Ballantine Books.

Schultz, Duane. 1981. *Hero of Bataan: The Story of General Wainwright.* New York: St. Martin's Press.

Spector, Ronald. 1985. *Eagle Against the Sun: The American War with Japan.* New York: Vintage.

Time Life. 1976. *The Rising Sun: World War II.* New York Time Life.

Toland, John. 1961. *But Not In Shame: Six Months After Pearl Harbor.* New York: Random House.

Toland, John. 1970. *The Rising Sun: The Rise and Fall of the Japanese Empire, 1936–1945.* New York: Random House

Truscott, Lucien K., Jr. 1989. *The Twilight of the U.S. Cavalry.* Lawrence: University Press of Kansas.

Turnbull, Stephen. 1985. *The Book of the Samurai.* New York: Smithmark Publishers.

Waldron, Ben D. 1988. *Corregidor, from Paradise to Hell.* Freeman, SD: Pine Hill Press.

War Department Basic Field Manual. 1939. *Animal Transport,* FM. 25.5.

War Department Basic Field Manual. 1941. *Thompson Submachine Gun.*

War Department Field Manual. 1944. *Japanese Tanks and Tank Tactics.*

War Department Field Manual. 1944. *Pack Transportation,* FM. 25.7.

Watson, Helen Orr. 1941. *Top Kick, U.S. Army Horse.* New York: Houghton Mifflin.

Whitehead, Arthur Kendal. 1989. *Odyssey of a Philippine Scout: Fighting Escaping and Evading the Japanese, 1941–1944.* Tucson: Arizona Lithographers.

UNPUBLISHED DOCUMENTS

Col. Tom Jones, Diary, The Story of C Troop.
Col. Lee Vance, Diary of the 26th Cavalry.
Col. William Chandler, Diary of the 26th Cavalry

INTERVIEWS

Col. Thomas G. H. Trapnell
Col. Wiliam Chandler
Col. Thomas Jones
Col. Edwin Ramsey
Col. Lloyd Mills
Col. Arch Tisdale
M/Sgt Justin Bulawam
Col. Eiiseo Mallari
Maj. Gary Anloff
Capt. Major Masiclat
Col. Arthur K. Whitehead
Col. Lee Vance
Capt. William Gochenour (Veterinarian)
Capt. Felipe Fernandez

M/Sgt. Bilgera
Col. John Pugh
Capt. Ed Huntermark
Maj. Elmer Long
Col. Tom Dooley
Capt. R.B. Kausin
Ben Morin (192nd Tanks)

DIARIES ANd PERSONAL PAPERS

Colonel Edwin Ramsey
Sergeant Alexandro Abad
Sergeant Salvador Abad
Lieutenant Gary Anloff, U.S. Army, Carmel, CA
First Sergeant Bulawan
Sergeant Amado A. Dela Cruz
Lieutenant Charles Ferguson, U.S. Army Communications, Australia
Sergeant Felipe Fernandez, Machine Gun Troop, 26th Cavalry
Colonel Ralph Flieger, diary excerpts published in Armor Magazine (formerly U.S.
   Cavalry Journal)
Sergeant Felipe Francisco
Colonel William E. Chandler
William Gochenour
Sergeant Ibenez
Colonel Thomas S. Jones
Sergeant-Major Eliseo Mallari
Ferdinand Marcos, formerly Captain, Philippine Army Artillery
Master Sergeant Cipriano Masiclat
Lieutenant Morin, 192nd Tankers
First Sergeant Tom Quiocho
Colonel C.A. Pierce, Day Reports
Sergeant Miles "Tommy" Thompson U.S. Coastal Artillery
Colonel Archibald Tisdale, Staff Aid to General King on Bataan
Thomas J. H. Trapnell, interviews and diaries
Sergeant Patricio Ubaro
Major Lee C. Vance, Executive Officer, diary
John Vinson, Researcher, AUS Retired
General Weaver, Commanding Officer, 192nd Tankers, Reports
Colonel Whitehead
Colonel Lloyd Wills, AUS Retired
Lieutenant Donald Wills
M. Zerfas
(Also nurses mentioned by name in book)